Exercise Your Faith

Exercise Your Faith

A 21-Day Journey to
Physical and Spiritual Fitness

Rev. Robin Harris Kimbrough

Elizabeth and Adric, Jr.—You were great teachers. You taught me how to exercise my faith.

Be encouraged!

INTRODUCTION

In the course of my adult life, I have long had some interest in exercise and eating right. I went to the gym, but just enough to lessen my guilt for poor eating habits. When going through a divorce, I poured out all my pain and worrying into working out, meditating on the Word, and praying. Preaching became deeper, more powerful— indeed, life-changing. My spiritual and physical life were making progress. I had more energy, made healthier food choices, and could lift from a squat over two hundred pounds. The results became apparent in the form of stronger muscles, tighter glutes, and a winning attitude. My bad marriage, fears, and insecurities had taken me on a journey to physical and spiritual fitness. Exercising and deepening my relationship with God allowed me to take control over myself even though I could not control the circumstances around me. After God moved me beyond this loss, I stopped being so focused. This is just one example of what can happen when we are just interested in something, rather than committed to it.

As always, though, life happened. I had a health challenge, and faced some other painful situations. Although I was exercising, the weight would not come off. Because of my health condition and a lack of discipline with eating, I gained weight. I love food! After a medical procedure solved my health problem, I decided to make some changes. The surgery had taken away the physical bleeding, but I still had a spiritual bleed. Instead of eating and feeling sorry for myself, I turned to exercise because it had helped me get through my divorce and, I believed, surely it would work to get me through this. Something in me said, now or never. My eating program and workouts went to the next level. I began to transform physically, mentally, and spiritually. At first, the weight loss was so important. The scale and I were best friends. Gradually the physical weight loss became less important to me. Instead, I saw myself shedding pounds of *thinking* that were keeping me from being my best self and becoming stronger inwardly as well as outwardly—physically and spiritually fit.

Exercise, for me, had become meditation in motion. Every workout yielded a sense of accomplishment and strengthened my faith. I met the challenge of crazy workouts that seemed impossible to accomplish, this made me realize that the same could happen in my personal and professional life. Learning how to balance my life made me realize that I can do all things through Christ who strengthens me. The truth is we are stronger than any situation that might challenge our faith in God. This understanding helps us to become physically and spiritually fit.

Workout programs can help with physical transformation, but what is needed for complete wellness is a spiritual change. If people were to link their relationship with God to their bodies, they would improve their overall health. We need to be spiritually and physically whole. We are supposed to take care of our physical body in exactly the same sense that God wants us to take care of our spirit. This is a simple concept, but we oftentimes miss it.

Paul metaphorically described the church as the "body of Christ" made up of many members, each serving as a different part of the divine whole. (I Corinthians 12:12-27) He pointed out that one part of the body can have an impact on the entire body. Paul's theological presentation of the body is based upon what he understood about the physical body—if one part of our body suffers, the entire body will suffer, and if we keep every member of our body healthy, the whole body will enjoy health. There are many references in the Bible to the heart, stomach, eyes, feet, mouth, ears, and hands, and how these body parts relate to our spiritual connection with God. Our body was created in the image of God to receive God and reflect his goodness, and when our body operates in this way, we experience spiritual and physical wholeness. The body is the temple of the Holy Ghost. Exposing ourselves to bad things and unhealthy people can make us sick, which is sin against the body. (I Corinthians 6:18). We need God's grace to exercise our faith and move us along the journey to physical and spiritual fitness.

Biblical figures needed strength to accomplish the work of God. God's response to Adam and Eve's disobedience in the Garden of Eden caused them to hide their bodies, and to put their bodies to work in a different way. (Genesis 3) Adam was required to till the ground, while Eve suffered pain in child-bearing. Without an able body and the favor of God over his life, as an old man, Noah would not have been able to build the ark. (Genesis 5:32; 6:13-22). David wrestled a lion and a bear, and would ultimately kill a giant—Goliath—because he was physically and spiritually fit. (I Samuel 17:34-37; 49-51). Jesus's team of twelve disciples could not have walked as much as they did as they preached, healed, learned, and followed the Lord if they did not have strength in their bodies. (Mark 6:7). Being fit physically and spiritually is important to living the abundant life. Maintaining that fitness is a daily exercise of faith.

God will take care of our needs and make us physically and spiritually fit to carry out his will. God provides for us. When the people of Israel fled the Egyptians, they were concerned about their basic needs to eat and to drink. To take care of their thirst, God turned the bitter waters of Marah into sweet waters, and God also promised them good health if they obeyed his commandments. (Exodus 15:22-27) God provided them manna (from heaven) and quail for food. (Exodus 16). Jesus told us not to worry about what to eat, to drink, or to wear: as long as we would first seek the Kingdom of God, these things God would provide. (Matthew 6:25-34). Recognizing that the five thousand people who came to hear him preach were hungry, Jesus fed their hungry spirits with the word, then took five fishes and two loaves of bread and satisfied their stomachs. Miraculously, everyone was satisfied, and there were even leftovers! (Matthew 14:13-21) These miracles demonstrate that we need to take care of both of our physical and spiritual bodies to do God's will.

When we trust God with our body and our dietary needs, we will see positive results. Daniel, Shadrach, Meshach, and Abednego were among those exiled to Babylon. Daniel's heart moved him and those of his three cohorts not to defile themselves with the king's meat and wine. Daniel made this request to the chief of the eunuchs, but the chief hesitated because he thought the prisoners would look worse than the others if they did not eat off the king's menu. Daniel proposed, "Please test your servants for ten days, and let them give us vegetables to eat and water to drink. Then let our appearance be examined before you, and the appearance of the young men who eat the portion of the king's delicacies; and as you see fit, *so* deal with your servants." (Daniel 1:12-13). The chief of the eunuchs agreed, and after the ten days the four men looked better and fatter than those who had eaten the king's food and drink. As a result of their faith, "God gave them knowledge and skill in all literature and wisdom; and Daniel had understanding in all visions and dreams." (Daniel 1:17). Outcomes such as this only happen when we have a fit spirit to make choices that will give strength to our body and mind.

Exercise Your Faith: A 21-Day Journey to Physical and Spiritual Fitness is a tool that will help us become fit. It is a collection of twenty-one meditations that teach self-care through physical and spiritual exercises. The book leads the reader through twenty-one exercises (meditations) to nurture the body and the spirit. These exercises are titled: (1) Journey, (2) Work, (3) Time, (4) Love, (5) Mindset, (6) Focus, (7) Prepare, (8) Weight, (9) Process, (10) Eat, (11) Drink, (12) Breathe, (13) Stretch, (14) Balance, (15) Core,

(16) Strength, (17) Heart, (18) Pain, (19) Repetition, (20) Results, and (21) Rest

. Each one is an exercise of faith. It takes faith to journey toward wholeness.

The information provided here is both scientific and theological. Each meditation begins with a discussion of the physical component of the particular topic, and then provides a theological and biblical exegesis on how the topic relates to our faith. It gives information on how we can exercise our faith to become fit physically and spiritually. There is space at the end of the meditation for reflection and decision-making—what will we do to exercise our faith. As we exercise our faith in God, everything about us improves. We get permission to take care of ourselves, to love ourselves, and to share this love with others. *Exercise Your Faith* will make you strong, fit, and prepared to do God's will. Exercise your faith.

All information provided in this book is for informational purposes only, and should not be relied upon as medical advice. Seek a physician before starting any exercise or weight loss program.

For as we have many members in one body, but all the members do not have the same function, so we, being many, are one body in Christ, and individually members of one another. Having then gifts differing according to the grace that is given to us, let us use them.

Romans 12:4-6

TABLE OF CONTENTS

Journey

Faith is a journey.

We have all heard, "Fitness is a journey, not a destination." The hardest part is getting started. We may join a gym, decide to skip lunch, or enroll in a weight loss program. We may even have unrealistic expectations of what it means to be physically fit. Having six-pack abs, muscular biceps and triceps, or an hour-glass figure may be someone's physical fitness goal, but none of these—nor any one characteristic at all—constitutes true physical wholeness. Physical fitness is a lifestyle; it is a series of healthy choices we make for our body. The journey brings new lessons and victories to encourage us along the way. We find ourselves striving for new insights and becoming our best selves physically and spiritually.

God took the Israelites on a journey to Egypt to escape famine. Years later, they found themselves praying to God for deliverance from Egypt. They prayed for four hundred years before God sent Moses to rescue them. Everything that happened to the Israelites was designed to make them spiritually fit. Life will take us to places like Egypt, where we experience safety and comfort, then suddenly bring on our worst nightmare. This "Egypt" can be a physical place, a relationship, a job, or a way of thinking. If we remain in places that do not give us the opportunity to exercise our faith, we become spiritually unfit. Comfort zones suddenly become uncomfortable— God in his wisdom wants us to go to the land of milk and honey and more often than not our comfort zones will keep us where we are instead.

God made it easy for the Israelites to leave until they were faced with crossing the Red Sea with Pharaoh's army on their tracks.   The Israelites began to complain about going back to Egypt. Sometimes things can become so difficult on the way to the land of milk and honey that we would rather go back to Egypt. This is the true exercise of faith—deciding to tough it out rather than go back to Egypt.   God assured the Israelites, "Do not be afraid, stand firm, and see the deliverance that the LORD will accomplish for you today; for the Egyptians whom you see today you shall never see again." (Exodus 14:13).

God empowered Moses to part the Red Sea, the Israelites walked over on dry land, and Pharaoh's army drowned. When we witness God parting seas in our lives, our faith increases and Egypt no longer calls us back. God may lead us down very different paths, but every step takes us closer to God.   In the words of Dr. Seuss, "Oh, the places you'll go! There is fun to be done! There are points to be scored. There are games to be won. And the magical things you can do with that ball will make you the winning-est winner of all. *Fame!* You'll be famous as famous can be, with the whole wide world watching you win on TV. . . Oh, the places you'll go!" Spiritual fitness is not a destination; it is a journey. Exercise your faith—journey.

Exercise Your Faith Circuit

Warm Up (1 min)

O God provide me with direction and courage to start the journey, and as I meet challenges along the way let me know that you are with me. AMEN.

Workout (8 min)

1. How is God speaking to me?

   _____

   _____

   _____

2. What will I do to become physically and spiritually fit?

   _____

   _____

   _____

3. How will I exercise my faith?

   _____

   _____

   _____

Cool Down (1 min)

   Affirm: God is with me on my journey.

Work

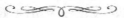

Work for it!

We can wish for change, but until we are willing to put in the work nothing will happen. We must work for what we want. God has given each of us an assignment, and completing it requires work. If we want to make a difference in our life and the lives of others, we cannot be lazy. Our body is always working. The heart is constantly pumping blood; the brain is actively thinking and receiving signals from other areas of the body; our kidneys are diligently cleansing our blood and our tongues producing saliva for digestion. Without all of this work taking place in our body, we could not live.

In just the same way, our faith cannot live unless it is working. "What good is it, my brothers and sisters, if you say you have faith but do not have works? Can faith save you? If a brother or sister is naked and lacks daily food, and one of you says to them, 'Go in peace; keep warm and eat your fill' and yet you do not supply their bodily needs, what is the good of that? So faith by itself, if it has no works, is dead." (James 2:14-17). Each day we must put our faith to work. We can pray for circumstances to change in our life, but if we do not work our faith, nothing will change.

God requires us to step out on faith. We can even say, "I have faith," but that does not mean our faith is alive. A living faith is more than talk; it is action. It's the bark and the bite. Rather than watching suffering, faith does something about it. Faith provides for the naked and the hungry. Weight does not come off by itself. Finances don't take care of themselves. Jobs usually do not come looking for us. All of this requires work. We have to work for it even when we are tired, hurting, and discouraged. This requires faith. Remember that works without faith is also dead.

We may have tried to lose weight, save money, or even find a soul mate. We may have done everything we could do. We ate right, limited our spending, and became vulnerable for someone we cared about, then nothing happened. We did not lose weight. Setbacks required us to spend the money we saved. The person we opened up to disappointed us. Such outcomes can make anyone quit working, but faith requires us to keep moving forward, because eventually, we will lose the weight; we will save the money; God will send someone who loves us as we love them. We will have this opportunity to see our faith come alive if we decide not to quit.

A living faith works through all sorts of challenges, setbacks, rejections, struggles, crises, and disappointments. It does not complain about failure, but looks at it as an opportunity to learn and grow, and try again.   It ignores

the odds, the naysayers, and the fear, and makes an effort

to live out dreams and possibilities. Faith without works is

dead. Exercise your faith—work.

Exercise Your Faith Circuit

Warm Up (1 min)

I open up my heart to you now. Awaken my faith, Lord, give me the energy to take steps that will actualize my faith and the promises you have made over my life. AMEN.

Workout (8 min)

1. How is God speaking to me?

    _____

    _____

    _____

2. What will I do to become physically and spiritually fit?

    _____

    _____

    _____

3. How will I exercise my faith?

    _____

    _____

    _____

Cool Down (1 min)

Affirm: My faith is alive.

Time

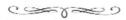

Change will happen in due time.

Spending time wisely can heal wounds and lessen the risk of chronic illnesses. According to the American Heart Association, one hundred and fifty minutes a week of walking, jumping, yard work, jogging, lifting weights, or any other physical activity can reduce the risk of heart disease and stroke. Besides strengthening our heart, these activities over time can lessen the risk of other health issues, including diabetes, obesity, cancer, and depression. Spending time on our spiritual health also has its benefits. The more time we spend with God in prayer, meditation, worship, and other exercises of faith, the more we experience the power of God in our lives. Quality time has the power to change us physically and spiritually.

Upon Moses' death, Joshua took over the leadership of the Israelites. God prepared him with these words: "This book of the law shall not depart out of your mouth; you shall meditate on it day and night, so that you may be careful to act in accordance with all that is written in it. For then you shall make your way prosperous, and then you shall be successful." (Joshua 1:8) Imagine what could happen if we spent one hundred and fifty minutes a week focused on the Lord, meditating and reflecting on his goodness, love, and promises. Our lives would change. Often, we say a quick prayer and move on with the rest of our day. God's words to Joshua give us the solution for prosperity and success—meditate on him day and night.

Time with the Lord will enable us to be more than we ever thought. We can meditate on God day and night if we make wise use of our time. Rather than investing ourselves into things that cannot profit us, we should spend our time nurturing our relationship with the Lord. We have so many responsibilities we forget to seek the Lord first. This causes stress and tightens our muscles. We should relax into knowing that God will take care of us. God as priority in our lives gives us the ability to conquer anything standing in our way of God's promise for our lives, just as it did Joshua. We cannot expect immediate results, but in due time, we will see the outcomes of prosperity and success. Time waits for no one. Let us seize the moment we have and make the most out of our time. Exercise your faith—take the time.

Exercise Your Faith Circuit

Warm Up (1 min)

My God, open up opportunities for me to meditate and reflect on your Word, and my faith will increase, and I will live a successful and prosperous in all areas of my life because of you and for your glory. AMEN.

Workout (8 min)

1. How is God speaking to me?

   _____
   _____
   _____

2. What will I do to become physically and spiritually fit?

   _____
   _____
   _____

3. How will I exercise my faith?

   _____
   _____
   _____

Cool Down (1 min)

   Affirm: I am successful and prosperous.

Love

Loving ourselves unconditionally is a workout.

We can become the fittest person in the world, but unless we completely and unconditionally love ourselves we will not be happy. The key to improving the physical body is to improve the spiritual body. How we feel about ourselves physically is often a reflection of our spiritual state of mind. Sometimes we can be our worse critic and enemy. While others try to be kind and build us up, we may tear ourselves down. As we embrace our faith in God and love for God, we can accept who we are physically and spiritually—the good, bad, and the ugly. We have to learn how to love ourselves inside and out.

According to I Corinthians 13:4-8, "Love is patient; love is kind; love is not envious or boastful or arrogant or rude. It does not insist on its own way; it is not irritable or resentful; it does not rejoice in wrongdoing, but rejoices in the truth. It bears all things, believes all things, hopes all things, endures all things. Love never ends." Love is more than a noun; it is a verb. Love requires action. The beginning of loving ourselves is accepting God's love. God shows us all the time he loves us. In fact, God is love. God is patient, kind, merciful, sincere, and everlasting. As we go through suffering, we may question God's love for us, though in truth it is in these circumstances we experience more of God's love.

Humans often make their love conditional on looks, social status, what the beloved can do for them, or some other requirement. This is not true love. As soon as those temporary qualities disappear, so does the love. We seek real love that accepts us just as we are. God is love, and God's love is real.

We must learn to love ourselves in the same way God loves us—unconditionally. Often we choose to love ourselves based on how we look, the mistakes we have made, other people's opinions, and how we measure up against others. God's love teaches us to treat ourselves with patience, kindness, truth, and mercy. This means taking care of our bodies, making healthy choices about our lives, forgiving ourselves, and accepting ourselves just as we are. It is alright to love and be kind to ourselves. Even on airplanes, the safety rules require passengers to secure their own oxygen masks before taking care of traveling dependents. As we love ourselves, we can love our neighbor in the same manner. Exercise your faith—love.

Exercise Your Faith Circuit

Warm Up (1 min)

Thank you, Lord, for looking beyond my faults and seeing my needs. You show me so much love. Help me to embrace myself in the same manner. As I love myself, I will do the same for my neighbor. AMEN.

Workout (8 min)

1. How is God speaking to me?

   _____

   _____

   _____

2. What will I do to become physically and spiritually fit?

   _____

   _____

   _____

3. How will I exercise my faith?

   _____

   _____

   _____

Cool Down (1 min)

Affirm: I love who I am and who I am becoming.

Mindset

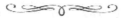

A new mindset produces positive results.

Physical fitness extends to how we take care of our mental health. As we nourish our body, we also nourish our mind. An unhealthy mindset can make us feel insecure, make us fearful, and even make us believe there is no reason to keep on living. The brain is a powerful machine, but it is also fragile and vulnerable to attack. One in five Americans—about 44.8 million people—face mental health issues. Over sixteen million Americans have had at least one depressive episode. There are approximately one million suicides each year in the United States, or one suicide every forty seconds. Loss, abuse, rejection, and other harsh realities can cause trauma, strongly damaging our mindset.

We must embrace our need to take care of and renew our minds daily to live our lives to the fullest. We are not robots. We are humans in need of God's grace to embrace spiritual and professional help to get our thinking on the right track. Our brain needs good nutrition, proper exercise, positive energy, and any other care that will help it to heal and maximize its potential.

Meditation is an important part of mental health and shifting to a healthy mindset. It allows our mind to resist thinking about topics that cause us stress and worry. Meditation helps us focus our energy in a positive direction in the midst of difficult challenges. It releases hormones called endorphins in our brain causing us to feel peaceful and happy. Meditation helps to shift our mindset so that we can accomplish goals and keep our minds healthy.

Paul writes, "Finally, beloved, whatever is true, whatever is honorable, whatever is just, whatever is pure, whatever is pleasing, whatever is commendable, if there is any excellence and if there is anything worthy of praise, meditate on these things." (Phil 4:8)

God cares about our mental health. This is why things that are just, pure, lovely, and of good report and virtue abound all around us. God constantly surrounds us with opportunities to give him the praise. Meditation has the power to give us a new way of thinking about our situation. Instead of having a losing attitude, we progress in confidence. Changing our thoughts about ourselves will change the world around us. Some of us have grown up with certain beliefs, with ideologies about ourselves and the world that have limited our progress. With a new mindset, we can open up new possibilities for our lives.

There was a story about three tiny frogs who were in a tower trying to see who could reach the top of the tower first. The frogs jumped with all their might. Other frogs were yelling from the edge of the tower, "It's way too difficult! They will never make it to the top. The tower is too high!" The first frog eventually collapsed, and the second frog gave up. The third frog made it to the top. The other frogs asked, "How did you do it?" It turned out that the tiny frog was deaf. In this life, to reach the top, we must have the right mindset and tune out discouragement. We have to listen to the one voice telling us we *can* rather than the one saying we can't. That way, like the fortunate deaf frog, we will have the faith to keep trying after others have given up. Exercise your faith—meditate.

Exercise Your Faith Circuit

Warm Up (1 min)

Transform and renew my mind so that I will know your perfect will for my life, Lord. Keep me focused on your goodness, grace, and love for me. AMEN.

Workout (8 min)

1. How is God speaking to me?

   _____

   _____

   _____

2. What will I do to become physically and spiritually fit?

   _____

   _____

   _____

3. How will I exercise my faith?

   _____

   _____

   _____

Cool Down (1 min)

Affirm: My mind is renewed and transformed.

Focus

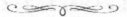

It takes faith to focus.

While we are working on our goals, we must stay focused. Focus means being intentional about our choices, actions, and results. Distractions are all around us, and they all have the ability to disrupt our focus.   Without clear focus, we will find ourselves years later still having unaccomplished goals. Staying on the journey of physical fitness requires focus.   We need discipline, and the ability to make decisions that keep us on task. Eating right, following an exercise regimen, and trusting the sometimes slow process of change require discipline. It takes discipline to resist negative thinking and food cravings. Bad weather, people, excuses, and other temptations can make us give up.   If we keep focused on the reason we started, we will be able to make the necessary choices to accomplish our goals.

God is focused on each of us, and we must keep our focus on God. One evening, Jesus sent the disciples to go ahead of him on a boat to the other side of the Sea of Galilee. While Peter and the other disciples were in the middle of the sea, they noticed someone walking on water. They thought it was a ghost; they were frightened. They could not see clearly who or what they saw out on the water. Jesus urged them not to be afraid, and identified himself. Peter wanted proof: "Lord, if it is you, command me to come to you on the water." (Matthew 14:28) Jesus invited him, and Peter got out of the boat and walked on water. Then, Peter began to pay attention to the wind, instead of Jesus, and he started to drown. He cried out—Lord save me! Jesus pulled Peter out of the water and asked him, "Why do you doubt?"

How many of us have walked on water? Like Peter we often have had the focus, but then we have begun to sink, because we allowed circumstances to make us question our ability to walk on the water. Focusing on "why" instead of "why not" weakens our faith. We start to doubt the possibilities in seemingly impossible situations. Counter doubt with disciplined faith—look to Jesus.

The other disciples wanted to walk on the water, but they were too afraid to test their faith. There is something inside every human being that wants more. There are some who get off the boat to go get it, and there are others who stay on the boat and lose the opportunity to walk on water. It takes faith to respond to the call to be and want more. Peter had that faith, even if he wavered. Let us give ourselves credit for trying even if we start to sink. Pray and

Jesus will correct us—why do you doubt?—and will get us

back on the water. Exercise your faith—walk on water.

Exercise Your Faith Circuit

<u>Warm Up (1 min)</u>

Dear Lord, increase my faith so that I can get off the boat that has kept me from stepping out on the waters, to do the seemingly impossible, and to live the abundant life you have promised me. AMEN.

<u>Workout (8 min)</u>

1. How is God speaking to me?

    _____

    _____

    _____

2. What will I do to become physically and spiritually fit?

    _____

    _____

    _____

3. How will I exercise my faith?

    _____

    _____

    _____

<u>Cool Down (1 min)</u>

Affirm: I will walk on water.

Prepare

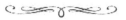

Prepare for God's plan.

Experts suggest those who prepare to exercise are more likely to remain committed to their exercise program. Preparation for exercise usually involves setting aside a particular time to exercise rather than just randomly going to the gym, walking, or engaging in some other activity. Preparing to work out also includes having the proper attire, equipment, and mindset to complete the workout. Besides preparing for the gym, meal preparation is essential to becoming physically fit. Planning meals for the week in portion sizes prevents overeating, and saves time and money. Preparation benefits our overall health as it eliminates stress from disorganization and gives us mental clarity. Unpreparedness gives us an excuse not to do what we have committed ourselves to, and to eat whatever is available, which is usually a candy bar, potato chips, or fast food.

God prepared each of us for a purpose and calling to fulfill his divine plan of salvation. When Mary, the mother of Jesus, received the news she would conceive Jesus, she seemed unprepared. She was a teenager, unmarried, and poor. A baby was the last thing on her mind. Gabriel addressed Mary's fears: "Greetings, favored one! The Lord is with you. . . Do not be afraid, Mary, for you have found favor with God. And now, you will conceive in your womb and bear a son, and you will name him Jesus." (Luke 1: 23;31) Gabriel told Mary that she was prepared for this great responsibility. She had the favor and presence of God.

Like Mary, we may feel afraid and unprepared to perform our divine assignments. We may use our age, financial status, marital status, race, gender, educational background, lack of qualifications, children, and what others think to disqualify ourselves from doing something that could change the world. These excuses often control our decision to ignore and run from God's call in our lives. Instead of doing God's will, we do whatever makes us feel comfortable.

Regardless of what we think or others might say, God has prepared us and made preparations for our journey—on reflection, we can see God's favor and presence in our lives. We must believe God has given us everything we need to respond to his call in words like Mary's when she faced her pregnancy: "Here am I, the servant of the Lord; let it be with me according to your word." (Luke 1:38) Exercise your faith—prepare.

Exercise Your Faith Circuit

Warm Up (1 min)

Thank you Lord for calling me to give birth to purpose and passion. Remind me that you have equipped me with divine favor to answer with a complete—yes, Lord. AMEN.

Workout (8 min)

1. How is God speaking to me?

_____

_____

_____

2. What will I do to become physically and spiritually fit?

_____

_____

_____

3. How will I exercise my faith?

_____

_____

_____

Cool Down (1 min)

Affirm: God's favor has prepared me for my calling.

Weight

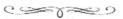

Weight loss requires faith.

Getting rid of excess pounds is not easy. Most of us would like to have an ideal number on the scale. This number, however, can confuse us, make us give up, and even lead us to become unhealthily obsessed with the process. If losing weight is focused on fitness and getting healthy, the number on the scale adjusts accordingly, muscles bulge, fat disappears, and the body energizes. There is no secret about becoming fit. It requires a healthy diet, rest, focus, and hard work. We cannot become fit without something driving us to have the discipline to improve and become healthy.

God is calling us to get fit physically and spiritually, so we can run the race of faith. Paul wrote these words: "Therefore, since we are surrounded by so great a cloud of witnesses, let us also lay aside every weight and the sin that clings so closely, and let us run with perseverance the race that is set before us." (Hebrews 12:1) The cloud of witnesses are those who have run the race of faith and won. We, too, can run the race of faith and win. We must lose any weight that keeps us from crossing the finish line. The weight to which Paul refers is not fatty cells. He is talking about the weight of sin, and *that* weight can feel like a ton. No matter how much we go to the gym or if our BMI (body mass index) is perfect, the weight of sin can still make us feel out of shape. Just as fat clings to our stomach, legs, and back, sin clings to our spiritual body when our flesh wants more than it should have. To get rid of sin requires a mindset to do it, commitment, and good food choices. Most of all, it requires God's grace. Grace makes us fit to run the race of faith. God's grace has the power to speed up our metabolism and burn away those things that weigh us down.

We may gain a little weight back, but grace will remind us of what we did to get the weight off in the first place, and we will continue to make progress. This is the sense in which fitness is not a destination but a journey. Every day, we meet situations and challenges that can put weight on us. For this reason, we must exercise our faith daily. Temptation, discouragement, and negative spirits will try to bend us out of shape, but we will be able to set those weights aside and run the race of faith. Exercise your faith—lose some weight.

Exercise Your Faith Circuit

Warm Up (1 min)

My God, give me the discipline to take care of my physical and spiritual body. Every day, allow me to shed pounds of negative thinking, bad habits, and even people that weigh me down. AMEN.

Workout (8 min)

1. How is God speaking to me?

   _____

   _____

   _____

2. What will I do to become physically and spiritually fit?

   _____

   _____

   _____

3. How will I exercise my faith?

   _____

   _____

   _____

Cool Down (1 min)

Affirm: I can run the race of faith.

Process

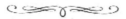

Trust and obey the process.

Physical fitness is a process. We want certain results, but we resist the effort it takes to achieve them. Reaching fitness goals requires exercise, a good diet, and rest. Many times, we suffer with the misconception that we can achieve certain results if we pick and choose what parts of the process we want to follow. We cannot cheat the process—it will eventually let the truth out. For this reason, people start and stop the process, jump from one program to another, and never accomplish their fitness goals. The story of Naaman teaches that the journey to physical and spiritual wholeness is a process, and if we trust in our journey, follow and finish it, we will reap the benefits.

"Naaman, commander of the army of the king of Aram, was a great man and in high favor with his master, because by him the LORD had given victory to Aram. The man, though a mighty warrior, suffered from leprosy." (2 Kings 5:1). Naaman probably thought he would have to live with the leprosy for the rest of his life, but he did not. In his case, leprosy was only part of the process of helping him to grow and exercise his faith. We may face difficulties, seemingly impossible circumstances, and suffer with a condition we think will never go away, but if we are willing to go through the process, we will discover all of it was just the start button getting us to witness God working in our lives.

At first Naaman did not understand the process. He thought the process involved political power, and he sought the king to heal his leprosy. Naaman learned the process required divine intervention, and consulted with the prophet Elisha.

Elisha sent a messenger to instruct Naaman to dip in the Jordan River seven times. Naaman thought this activity was ridiculous. He complained because Elisha did not appear to him in person, and he thought Elisha should have chosen a cleaner river. Then, Naaman's servant explained to him that Elisha had not asked him to do anything difficult. Instead of trying to control the process, Naaman decided to trust it and obey Elisha's instructions. He dipped in the Jordan six times and nothing happened. On the seventh dip, Naaman's skin became like the skin of a baby. Every repetition was part of the process and made him better. The same is true for us.

Many of us would have quit after the first dip with no results. We learn from Naaman that visible results are not always a reliable indicator of progress. What determines how close we are to deliverance is our willingness to obey God completely. If we trust what God has commanded, we will do whatever God says to see the manifestation of God's promise for our lives. Exercise your faith—trust and obey.

Exercise Your Faith Circuit

Warm Up (1 min)

As I hear your voice, give me the wisdom, humility, and faith to obey your direction. Even when I cannot see anything happening, may I have enough trust to know that faith is the substance of things hoped for and the evidence of things not seen. AMEN.

Workout (8 min)

1. How is God speaking to me?

   _____

   _____

   _____

2. What will I do to become physically and spiritually fit?

   _____

   _____

   _____

3. How will I exercise my faith?

   _____

   _____

   _____

Cool Down (1 min)

   Affirm: I will trust and obey the process.

Eat

Feed your spiritual body properly.

We have all heard, "You are what you eat."
Recently, people have become more aware of the risks
associated with eating processed foods, meats, and sugar.
Eating the right mix of proteins, carbohydrates, and fats
help the digestive system to work properly, increases
overall energy and metabolism, and prevents sickness.
Besides watching the kind of food we eat, we also have to
be careful with *how much* food we eat.

Overeating has serious health consequences
including obesity, diabetes, heart disease, and digestive
issues. Binge eaters often overeat because they have lost
control over their eating; they use food as a source of
emotional comfort and an escape to deal with deep hurts.
Eating disorders such as anorexia and bulimia, which may

result from an unhealthy body image, can lead people to eat very little food, vomit their food, use laxatives, or engage in excessive exercise to control their weight and size. Such behaviors often result in depression, digestive problems, and bone diseases. Eating the right amount of food requires education, discipline, and a healthy relationship with food and our body. God created fruits, vegetables, and meat to heal, fuel, and energize our physical body so we can do his will.

God wants us to feed on his Word to nourish our spiritual body. God called Ezekiel in a vision to preach to the Israelites during a very difficult time. God described the Israelites as "rebellious" and "stubborn," telling Ezekiel that his would not be an easy job. God let Ezekiel know he should speak the truth whether the people liked it or not. God said to Ezekiel, "But you, mortal, hear what I say to you; do not be rebellious like that rebellious house;

open your mouth and eat what I give you." (Ezekiel 2:8)

God stretched out a scroll in front of Ezekiel, and told him

to eat the scroll. Then, Ezekiel opened his mouth, and God

gave him the scroll to eat and said to Ezekiel: "Mortal, eat

this scroll that I give you and fill your stomach with it."

He ate it, and it tasted like honey. (Ezekiel 3:3)

Through his act of faith, Ezekiel discovered God's

Word was like honey—sweet, natural, and energizing.

This is true although sometimes God's Word does not

seem palatable. After just one taste of it, however, we

know it is good. God gives us daily bread to deal with

rebellious people and meet challenging situations. God

will not shove his word down our throats. We must choose

to open our mouths, take the scroll, and consume all of it,

just as Ezekiel did, and enjoy the taste of honey we

receive.

Feed the spirit. Feed it with good people, ideas, hope, optimism, dreams, positive words, and other nutrients that give life to the spirit. We can never have too much of God's word. Exercise your faith—eat all of it.

Exercise Your Faith Circuit

Warm Up (1 min)

Bread of Life, feed me until I want no more. Fill my belly with your goodness and love, and I will testify that it is, indeed, good. AMEN.

Workout (8 min)

1. How is God speaking to me?

   _____

   _____

   _____

2. What will I do to become physically and spiritually fit?

   _____

   _____

   _____

3. How will I exercise my faith?

   _____

   _____

   _____

Cool Down (1 min)

Affirm: I will nurture my body and spirit with goodness.

Drink

Living water satisfies all of our thirsts.

Drinking water is essential to the functioning of the body. Although we could live without food for several weeks, we cannot go more than a week without water. Almost two thirds of the human body is water. Water is used to transport nutrients into cells and waste products out of cells. Water helps in reducing certain health problems including kidney stones, urinary infections, colon cancer, and heart attacks. It also stimulates the metabolism, tightens the skin, reduces the appetite, and increases thinking capacity. Dehydration can cause multiple health problems, including dizziness, mood swings, stress, and kidney problems.

All of us have a thirst in our spirit. Jesus's encounter with a Samaritan woman teaches that only a relationship with him can satisfy a thirsty spirit. Jesus, on his way to Galilee, stopped when he met a Samaritan woman at Jacob's well. He found her drawing from the well and asked her for a drink. Surprised that Jesus, a Jew, would ask her—a Samaritan woman—for a drink, she began to question Jesus. Had the Samaritan woman known it was Jesus, she would have realized he was actually extending her an invitation to drink from his well. Jesus made the offer: "If you knew the gift of God and who it is that asks you for a drink, you would have asked him and he would have given you living water. . . Everyone who drinks this water will be thirsty again, but whoever drinks the water I give them will never thirst. Indeed, the water I give them will become in them a spring of water welling up to eternal life." (John 4:10, 13-14) Tired of coming to Jacob's well, the Samaritan woman wanted to know how to get this living water that would never leave a person thirsty.

After she told Jesus that she had five previous husbands and the one she lived with was not her husband, Jesus explained to her the way to draw from the well of living water is through worshipping God in spirit and truth. This new understanding of worship allowed the woman to see Jesus as the Messiah, rather than just a man or prophet. Worship released the living water on the inside of the Samaritan woman. She dropped her water pot and told others about Jesus, and they came to believe because of her testimony.

Worship primes the well of living water. It acknowledges who God is and activates the power of God on our insides. It floods our souls, gives us strength for the journey, and runs over in every area of our lives. Jesus is meeting us at our thirsty places to help us access the living water. It is available to all of us. Once we drink it, we will the drop things that made us thirsty and witness to others the power of worship and knowing Jesus as the Messiah. Exercise your faith—worship and drink from the well of living water.

Exercise Your Faith Circuit

Warm Up (1 min)

Like you did the Samaritan woman, Lord satisfy my thirst for the living water. Prime my spiritual well with true worship filled with your spirit. AMEN.

Workout (8 min)

1. How is God speaking to me?

   _____

   _____

2. What will I do to become physically and spiritually fit?

   _____

   _____

3. How will I exercise my faith?

   _____

   _____

Cool Down (1 min)

Affirm: I am a well of living water.

Breathe

Inhale and exhale through life.

Breathing is necessary for exercise because it enhances the flow of oxygen through the body. It also strengthens the core (the torso), protects the back, helps with form, and relaxes the mind. The proper way to breathe depends on the activity. For example, weight trainers recommend exhaling on the work, or the most difficult part of the exercise, to force oxygen through the body at the most important time. Yoga breathing techniques involve "equal breathing," which means the inhale matches the exhale. This style of breathing relaxes the nervous system, lowers the blood pressure, and reduces stress. Often, when intense exercises increase the heart rate, our response is to hold our breath. This choice restricts the oxygen going to our body, depleting the energy we need to finish the exercise, so we quit. Holding our breath cheats us out of the opportunity to work longer and harder.

Breathing through intense circumstances in our spiritual lives is also important to help us get through our struggles. Circumstances can put pressure on our spiritual body, and we can find ourselves short of breath. Psalm 150 opens with this declaration, "Let everyone that has breath, praise the Lord." Our breath is our praise. Everyone with a living body should praise God. In fact, all of us were created for praise. The psalmist calls on us to praise God with dance, instruments, and song. For us to engage in these praise activities, we must breathe. We breathe because of God, and we cannot take one breath without God. God is the air we breathe. Every inhale and exhale must celebrate the presence and power of God.

Complaining, discouragement, bitterness, depression, and anger are toxins that can make it hard for us to breathe. During these times, we must praise God the most. We must concentrate on every inhale and exhale, increasing the circulation of air in our environment, and watch God begin to shift the atmosphere. Praise will give us strength to last longer, stretch a little further, and get more out of life. God will replenish us, breathe life back into us, and resuscitate our faith. Let us remember to breathe—smell the roses and blow out the candles. Exercise your faith—praise!

Exercise Your Faith Circuit

Warm Up (1 min)

You are the air that I breathe, and every breath that I take. As I take a breath, give me life so that I can breathe life into others, and with every breath, I will give you praise. AMEN.

Workout (8 min)

1. How is God speaking to me?

   _____

   _____

   _____

2. What will I do to become physically and spiritually fit?

   _____

   _____

   _____

3. How will I exercise my faith?

   _____

   _____

   _____

Cool Down (1 min)

Affirm: With every breath, I give God praise.

Stretch

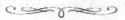

Faith stretches us.

Stretching is often neglected. It is a very important complement to exercise and wellness. Stretching improves flexibility, balance, and range of motion. It also protects the bones and muscles from injury, and if done properly, it does not hurt. Research has shown that a quick stretch during the day can produce needed energy by increasing blood flow to the muscles and brain. To achieve the most benefit from stretching, we must stretch every day; otherwise, the flexibility gained from stretching will go away. What athletic stretching does for our physical body, prayerful stretching will do for our spiritual body.

Stretching our faith gives our spirit the ability to increase its activity in our lives. We become more flexible to meet life's challenges and obey God. Moses struggled

with God's call to free the children of Israel from Egypt.
He explained to God that he had a speech impediment, he
did not know how best to communicate to people about
God, and he had concerns about whether anyone would
listen to him. God stretched Moses. God assured Moses of
his ability to do the job. Moses only needed to stretch his
faith and believe what God said. God promised Moses, "I
know, however, that the king of Egypt will not let you go
unless compelled by a mighty hand. So I will stretch out
my hand and strike Egypt with all my wonders that I will
perform in it, after that he will let you go." (Exodus 3:19-
20) Moses answered the call, and went before Pharaoh on
behalf of the Israelites. Each time God ordered Moses to
approach Pharaoh about freeing the Israelites, Moses
stretched his rod and brought forth a different plague that
would eventually persuade Pharaoh to free the Israelites.
Moses would later stretch his rod to part the Red Sea,

enabling the Israelites to escape Pharaoh's army on dry land.

God's calling on our lives requires us to stretch our faith. It activates God's power in our lives. Our minds, resources, time, and strength become greater than we thought, because God is also stretching with us, just as he promised Moses he would do. God has given us the power to stretch our rods so we can be set free from anything holding us in bondage. We can stretch our way out of a bad relationship, a dead-end job, addiction, depression, and destructive thinking. We can reach beyond our limits and experience the power of God just as Moses did. The more we stretch, the more we will see the lasting results of being flexible and the more we become available to do God's will. Exercise your faith. Stretch.

Exercise Your Faith Circuit

Warm Up (1 min)

Lord, stretch me in every area of my life. Stretch my faith, my thoughts, my resources, and my love for you and for humanity. AMEN.

Workout (8 min)

1. How is God speaking to me?

   _____

   _____

2. What will I do to become physically and spiritually fit?

   _____

   _____

   _____

3. How will I exercise my faith?

   _____

   _____

   _____

Cool Down (1 min)

Affirm: I am flexible to do God's will.

Balance

Balance is required in every area of our lives.

One of the most difficult, but powerful exercise moves balancing. Good balance begins in our core. The stronger our center, the more we are able to balance. We are always balancing even though we do not realize it. The more we practice balancing through exercise, the stronger we become. Good balance reduces injury and lower back problems, promotes good posture, and eases anxiety. Balance exercises include standing on one leg, Tai Chi, Yoga, sitting on a chair without using hands, and exercising with a BOSU ball.

Just as our body needs balance to build strength, so does our spiritual body. Paul wrote, "Not that I am referring to being in need, for I have learned to be content with whatever I have. I know what it is to have little, and I know what it is to have plenty. In any and all circumstances I have learned the secret of being well-fed and of going hungry, of having plenty and of being in need." (Phil. 4:11) Paul had a balanced faith. He learned how to remain steady because his faith and trust in Jesus Christ kept him balanced regardless of what was happening in his life. We should do the same.

Finding contentment only when life is going our way and having a negative attitude in other circumstances throws us off balance. Trusting God for one thing and not for everything shows a lack of balance. Being willing to do certain things but not others can make us unstable. We may put our energy, love, trust, and joy in one place. We may work all the time, and rarely take time out for fun. We may spend all of our time with one relationship and ignore family members, friends, and other responsibilities.

These choices can make life very unbalanced. Eventually, we become burned out, lose focus, and see everything fall apart. God wants us to have contentment in every area of our life.

The stronger our faith, the more we can balance life. Achieving contentment in all circumstances is like learning to ride a bike. At first, we need training wheels to help stabilize the bike until we learn how to ride without them. God provides us with grace to stabilize us as we mature spiritually. Once we grow through grace, God removes the training wheels, and we realize our faith in God has given us the strength to balance life. Our faith enables us to manage struggles, challenges, and disappointments. We learn how to be content in all situations. Along the way, we all wobble and feel like we are going to fall, but grace keeps us from falling. We can do all things through Christ who strengthens us. Exercise your faith—balance.

Exercise Your Faith Circuit

<u>Warm Up (1 min)</u>

Please, Jesus, give me balance in my life. Stabilize me physically and spiritually.   Help me to find contentment in all situations, meeting every challenge with a grateful attitude. AMEN.

<u>Workout (8 min)</u>

1. How is God speaking to me?

      _____

      _____

      _____

2. What will I do to become physically and spiritually fit?

      _____

      _____

      _____

3. How will I exercise my faith?

      _____

      _____

      _____

<u>Cool Down (1 min)</u>

   Affirm: I can do all things through Jesus Christ.

Core

Faith is at the center of our core.

The body's core is often thought of as the abdominal region, but it also encompasses the back of the torso. Our arms and legs stem from the entire core. Having a strong core is essential to physical fitness. There are five benefits of a strong core: (1) helps prevent injuries, (2) protects organs and the central nervous system, (3) prevents back pain, (4) improves posture, and (5) promotes overall wellness. As we strengthen the core, the entire body is strengthened. Walking, jumping jacks, planks, leg lifts, sitting on a stability ball, cycling, Pilates, and PIYO are all exercises that strengthen the core.

Core strength is also important to our spiritual body. The core of the spiritual body is the soul. The soul is the very essence of who we are spiritually. The stronger it is, the more we can count on everything else in our lives to function properly. God strengthens our core. In the book of John, Jesus made seven "I am" statements. He said he was the bread of life; the light of the world; the door of the sheep; the good shepherd; the resurrection and the life; the way and the truth and the life; and the true vine. Jesus is the core of our lives: he is our all in all.

Before his death, Jesus told his disciples: "I am the true vine, and my Father is the vinegrower. He removes every branch in me that bears no fruit. Every branch that bears fruit he prunes to make it bear more fruit. You have already been cleansed by the word that I have spoken to you. Abide in me as I abide in you. Just as the branch cannot bear fruit by itself unless it abides in the vine, neither can you unless you abide in me. I am the vine, you are the branches. Those who abide in me and I in them bear much fruit, because apart from me you can do nothing." (John 15:1-5) God is the vinedresser, and Jesus is the true vine.

We can do nothing apart from God. This is why we must abide in him, and he in us. Think about your body— if your arms and legs were not connected to the core, they could do nothing. In just the same way, our souls are totally dependent on God. Once our spirit unites with God, there is nothing we cannot do or God will not do in our lives. Our relationship with God, at the center of our lives, gives strength to our core. Reading God's Word, listening to what God says, dismissing the negative, forgiving others and oneself, fasting, and praying all strengthen the spiritual core. Our core gives strength to our entire existence. The minute the core gets weak, God's grace will act as a support. Exercise your faith— strengthen the core.

Exercise Your Faith Circuit

Warm Up (1 min)

You are the true vine, and I confess that I can do nothing apart from you. You are the very essence of my existence. Abide in me as I abide in you and give strength to my soul. AMEN.

Workout (8 min)

1. How is God speaking to me?

   _____

   _____

   _____

2. What will I do to become physically and spiritually fit?

   _____

   _____

   _____

3. How will I exercise my faith?

   _____

   _____

   _____

Cool Down (1 min)

   Affirm: I am connected to the True Vine.

Strength

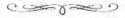

God's grace is the source of our strength.

Strong muscles are not just for bodybuilders or wrestlers--they are necessary for everybody. Most experts agree that the human body has 639 muscles, which are divided into three types: skeletal, cardiac, and smooth. They help us to move, lift things, pump blood, breathe, digest food, prevent diseases, and improve overall well-being. The stronger our muscles, the better they work to improve our health. Weak muscles make the body prone to injury, cause joint problems, and increase the risk of bone diseases. Our muscles do not have to bulge like an athlete's to be strong enough to do their job. We need to exercise and eat a sufficient amount of proteins and other nutrients to ensure our muscles are fit and healthy.

Finally, just as our physical body needs strength, so does our spiritual body.

Samson's encounter with the Philistines and a woman named Delilah taught him that the building blocks of spiritual strength are grace and mercy. Samson was a man of great strength. He had destroyed thousands of the Philistines single-handedly. They hated Samson because of his strength—they could not do anything with him.

The Philistines decided to use another strategy with Samson. They could not discover the source of his strength, but they learned he had a weakness. Samson had poor judgment and lacked self-control. They also knew Samson liked prostitutes and loved a woman named Delilah. They paid Delilah to take advantage of Samson's weakness to find out what made him strong. Every night Delilah tried to get Samson to tell her what made him strong, but he would lie to her. She would report this information to the Philistines, and they tried again and again to capture Sampson, but to no avail. For his part, Samson was not strong enough to see the truth about Delilah and eventually confessed his secret to her: "A razor has never come upon my head; for I have been a Nazirite to God from my mother's womb. If my head were shaved, then my strength would leave me; I would become weak, and be like anyone else." (Judges 16:17) That night, Delilah cut Samson's locks, and the Philistines poked his eyes out and captured him.

At the end of this story, Samson prayed for enough strength to destroy the Philistines, and God gave it to him. Like Samson, we all struggle with some weakness, and the enemy is lurking to use it against us, but we must stay strong. As Samson learned, God's grace is perfected in our weakness. Where we are weak, God makes us strong. Personal struggles reveal God as the source of our strength and our life. God enables us to handle more than we thought possible and gives us super-human powers to win victories over our enemies. The joy of the Lord is our strength. Exercise your faith—get stronger.

Exercise Your Faith Circuit

Warm Up (1 min)

Creator of all things, you are my strength, and you are the strength of my life. Allow me to experience your power in those times when life has weakened me. AMEN.

Workout (8 min)

1. How is God speaking to me?

   _____

   _____

   _____

2. What will I do to become physically and spiritually fit?

   _____

   _____

   _____

3. How will I exercise my faith?

   _____

   _____

   _____

Cool Down (1 min)

Affirm: I am strong.

Heart

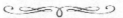

We need to have a strong heart.

The heart keeps us alive. It influences the health of our entire body because it circulates oxygen all through it. This function of the heart is referred to as cardiovascular endurance. If the heart's cardiovascular endurance is weak, the rest of the body will be weak. Low cardiovascular endurance can cause shortness of breath, fatigue, depression, immobility, heart attacks, strokes, and other forms of heart disease. Exercise is essential for heart health. It increases the heart's cardiovascular endurance, releases hormones called endorphins that reduce stress on the heart, and enables the heart to heal itself. Additionally, eating a diet filled with good fats, good carbohydrates, and protein lessens the risk of heart disease. Our human heart determines the health of our physical body. We often talk of the heart as the seat of our emotions and spirits. In this sense, the heart reveals the true nature of our souls.

In response to criticism related to his disciples eating without washing their hands, Jesus responded: "It is what comes out of a person that defiles. For it is from within, from the human heart, that evil intentions come: fornication, theft, murder, adultery, avarice, wickedness, deceit, licentiousness, envy, slander, pride, folly. All these evil things come from within, and they defile a person." (Mark 7:20-23) Jesus's point is that having dirty hands does not make the person bad; the purity of a person's heart reflects true character. A person can have completely sanitized hands, but if the heart is not clean, then the person is not clean. Out of the heart, the mouth speaks. While we listen to others, we also have the opportunity to hear their hearts.

God is concerned with matters of the heart. Hearts get lonely, broken, hardened, and filled with bitterness and hate. A heart filled with jealousy and ungratefulness exposes the person to pride, envy, greed, and slander. A lustful heart can result in all kinds of sexual transgression. Worrying can put stress on our heart and cause us to do things to hurt others and our own body. All of this can put stress on our human heart. We must pray daily—we ask God to create in me a clean heart and renew in me a right spirit. (Psalm 51) God's grace can heal our hearts. It can repair valves, implant pacemakers, and perform a heart transplant instantly.

A healthy heart will give strength to our entire lives. We lessen the risk of having a heart attack over situations we know God will fix. Trusting, obeying, and worshipping God are all practices that help heal our hearts and increase our endurance. The inner chambers of our existence become a sanctuary for the presence of God. Goodness and love will flow from our hearts, and evil will not have the power to enter. Exercise your faith— strengthen your heart.

Exercise Your Faith Circuit

Warm Up (1 min)

I pray as David did, create in me a clean heart and renew in me a right spirit. May my heart become a sanctuary of worship and praise. AMEN.

Workout (8 min)

1. How is God speaking to me?

   _____

   _____

   _____

2. What will I do to become physically and spiritually fit?

   _____

   _____

   _____

3. How will I exercise my faith?

   _____

   _____

   _____

Cool Down (1 min)

Affirm: My heart shall rejoice in the Lord.

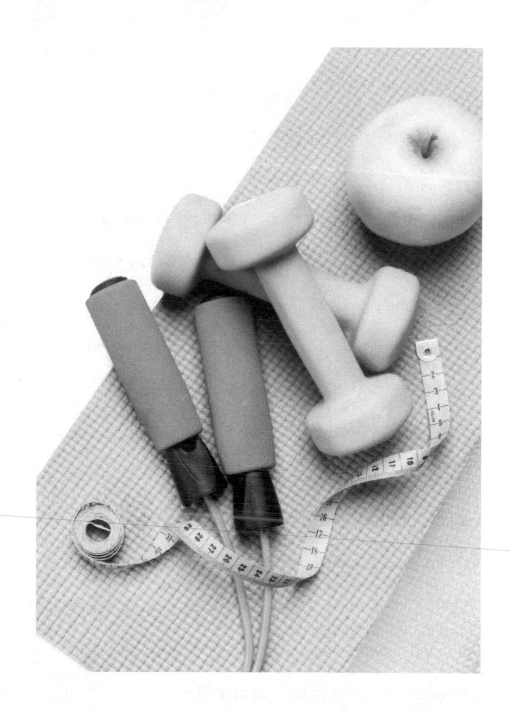

Pain

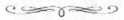

Pain lets us know we are still alive.

Muscle soreness and pain often accompany an intense workout, because the muscles are changing and becoming stronger. When muscles work harder than usual, they tear and rebuild. This pain can start during the workout and last days afterwards. Oftentimes, we give up and allow this discomfort to cheat us out of this transformation. Even though our body wants to quit, our mind has the power to work through the pain. The brain releases two types of hormones during exercise to address the pain. One is called brain-derived neurotrophic factor (BDNF). It produces a sensation of peace and makes us feel good about having worked so hard. Endorphins are also released. These hormones block the feeling of pain, and activate a feeling of euphoria. We have a choice to quit or allow our minds to take over and work harder. The right mindset can make the body work, even when it wants to quit. Those who choose to keep going are the ones who rejoice with a sense of accomplishment and achieve the best results. No pain, no gain.

The bumps and bruises of life keep telling us to quit, but we must keep going. If we work through them, we will transform and get stronger. Right before his crucifixion, Jesus knew his disciples were in a state of crisis because of his imminent death, and he assured them that eventually their hurt would turn to joy: "When a woman is in labor, she has pain, because her hour has come. But when her child is born, she no longer remembers the anguish because of the joy of having brought a human being into the world. So you have pain now; but I will see you again, and your hearts will rejoice, and no one will take your joy from you." (John 16:21-22)

The promise Jesus made to the disciples applies to us. Without an epidural, giving birth is a painful process of the mother breathing and stretching to push out the newborn. The baby makes the mother forget all about the pain. Life's hurts can feel like having a baby, and there is no epidural. Depending on our tolerance for pain, we may be tempted to give up. This is the time we need to breathe and stretch the most, and squeeze the hand of God to get through the pain. With labor comes pain, and through pain can come deliverance. We cannot allow pain to cheat us out of the blessings and miracles God wants to birth in our lives.

Through our tears and disappointments, we have the opportunity to know the power of God's grace to help us endure the pain and to heal from it. God's grace gives us the ability to outlast whatever or whoever hurt us. In those times, we feel that we cannot go on, God's grace gives us what we need to make it through. We make the choice to hurt or to heal. We will keep hurting if we do not have a mindset to forgive, embrace support from others, and have willingness to let it go. Healing happens when we allow our pain to produce worship, deepen our faith, and transform us into someone stronger. We will testify that God's grace heals, and there is gain on the other side of pain. Our euphoria is a rejoicing heart and joy no one can take from us. Exercise your faith—endure the pain.

Exercise Your Faith Circuit

Warm Up (1 min)

It is me, Lord, standing in need of prayer. You know all about my pain, both physically and spiritually, and I know that you are able to heal me and give me the strength to endure. Joy will come in the morning. AMEN.

Workout (8 min)

1. How is God speaking to me?

   _____

   _____

   _____

2. What will I do to become physically and spiritually fit?

   _____

   _____

   _____

3. How will I exercise my faith?

   _____

   _____

   _____

Cool Down (1 min)

   Affirm: I am greater than my pain.

Repetition

Practice makes perfect.

Repetition or, "reps," in fitness lingo is the number

of times a person performs an exercise. The number of

reps in a certain amount of time can determine stamina and

strength. Repetition also increases muscle endurance and

the benefits of exercise. For example, a fitness test for

physical education classes requires the student to perform

a certain number of sit-ups in sixty seconds. As the student

does more sit-ups, the number of reps done in sixty

seconds increases. We cannot expect to benefit from one

Zumba class or lap around the track. If we want lasting

results, we must make exercise a routine activity. The

more reps, the better we become.

Many people think they can survive spiritually off

one church service, one prayer, one fast, or one encounter

with Scripture. The one experience will help, but to grow deeper, we must do it over and over. Peter asked Jesus, "Lord, if another member of the church sins against me, how often should I forgive? As many as seven times?" (Mt. 18:21) This is a good question. Many of us still ask it today. Peter hoped the answer would be, "Up to seven times." Peter is willing to give someone seven acts of forgiveness. This is more than many of us would have considered. Jesus responded, "Not seven times, but, I tell you, seventy-seven times." (Mt. 18:21) Biblical scholars are split on whether the translation means seventy-seven times or 490. This simply underscores the fact that the precise number Jesus gave Peter is irrelevant: we must forgive as often as needed. Jesus illustrated this point in the parable of the unforgiving servant.

After answering Peter's question, Jesus told a story about a servant whose debt was forgiven, but who refused to forgive someone who owed him a debt. The story ended with the servant returning to prison and having his debt reinstated. This is typical human behavior—holding other people accountable for actions we have also committed. The parable illustrates we must forgive as often as we need forgiveness or we will not experience forgiveness in our lives. None of us are perfect. We need practice. Reflecting on our need for forgiveness, and that we have been forgiven, will help us to forgive others over and over. The more we do it, the easier it will become, and we will benefit the most from it.

God never stops forgiving. Every time God does it, we see brand new mercies. God constantly gives us an encore with his grace, love, compassion, and mercies. The more reps of forgiveness and other acts of grace we perform, the better we get and the more results we see in our lives. Exercise your faith—forgive in reps.

Exercise Your Faith Circuit

Warm Up (1 min)

Lord, give me opportunities to show you over and over how much I love you. Remind me that even when I struggle with the reps, each one makes me stronger. Thank you for giving me daily a repeat of your love. AMEN.

Workout (8 min)

1. How is God speaking to me?

    _____
    _____
    _____

2. What will I do to become physically and spiritually fit?

    _____
    _____
    _____

3. How will I exercise my faith?

    _____
    _____
    _____

Cool Down (1 min)

Affirm: With every rep, I am stronger and better.

Results

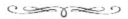

Following the process produces positive results.

We are motivated by results. We do not want to put time and energy into something that does not show anything for our work and effort. This includes a fitness program, a job, a relationship, a project, or anything not meeting our expectations of change and improvement. We have all seen weight program advertisements where people share their success stories about how they looked and felt before and after using the product. We often see ourselves in these ads and buy the product believing we will have the same results.

Our lives should testify to what we looked like before and after we started the journey to spiritual wholeness. We were about to self-destruct, living in fear, insecurity, and satisfaction with mediocrity, but after exercising our faith and living after the spirit, we changed.

Our lives became fruitful and productive. Our testimony

has the power to touch someone and give them the

inspiration to achieve the same results. Paul, in his letter to

the church at Galatia, explains that we can either live by

the flesh or the spirit: "Now the works of the flesh are

obvious: fornication, impurity, licentiousness, idolatry,

sorcery, enmities, strife, jealousy, anger, quarrels,

dissensions, factions, envy, drunkenness, carousing, and

things like these. I am warning you, as I warned you

before: those who do such things will not inherit the

kingdom of God." (Galatians 5:19-21). Living by the flesh

results in no inheritance of the Kingdom of God.

However, those who live by the Spirit bear the fruit of the

Spirit—love, joy, peace, forbearance, kindness, goodness,

faithfulness, gentleness, and self-control. They will have

eternal life. Our lives should witness to the benefits of living by the Spirit.

We need grace to live by the Spirit. As we produce the fruits of the Spirit, there is always the possibility of bearing the bad fruit of the flesh. Grace prunes us by cutting off the branches too weak to bear fruit. These branches are habits, people, attitudes, and other barriers preventing us from living by the Spirit. Although pruning is painful, it is necessary to deal with passions and desires of the flesh. As these branches grow back, they are strong enough to bear good fruit and overcome the power of the flesh. Our lives should witness to what God's grace can do for ourselves and others.

People need to see what we looked like when we were living by the flesh, and how we look now that we are living by the Spirit. They need to see us go through the pruning process and the power of grace to make us better.

As people witness the results of our faith in God, they will want to do the same. What God has done for one, he will do for many. Exercise your faith—live by the Spirit.

Exercise Your Faith Circuit

Warm Up (1 min)

Thank you, Lord, for making me over. Your grace has made me better, stronger, and wiser. It has brought a wonderful change in my life. May my life witness every day to your power and goodness. AMEN.

Workout (8 min)

1. How is God speaking to me?

   _____

   _____

   _____

2. What will I do to become physically and spiritually fit?

   _____

   _____

   _____

3. How will I exercise my faith?

   _____

   _____

   _____

Cool Down (1 min)

Affirm: I live by the Spirit.

Rest

Rest is self-care.

Rest renews and re-energizes us physically and mentally to reach our fitness goals. We have the misconception that taking off from a workout will crush our goals or make people think we are lazy. Relaxation and sleep are the best forms of medicine for a cold, a physical injury, fatigue, and stress. While we rest, the body repairs itself. Lack of sleep can result in a decline of our immune system, in mood swings, and impaired judgement. Instead of feeling guilty, let us give ourselves a break.

Jesus extends an invitation to all of us to find rest for our body and spirit: "Come to me, all you that are weary and are carrying heavy burdens, and I will give you rest. Take my yoke upon you, and learn from me; for I am gentle and humble in heart, and you will find rest for your souls. For my yoke is easy, and my burden is light." (Matthew 11:28-30) The demands of jobs, school, children, spouses, friends, internal struggles, traffic, social clubs, church, and simply living among people can wear us out.

We give energy to so many and we forget about our need to repair and recover. Failing to give our spirit, mind, and body rest can easily make us hit a brick wall. Some of us, although overwhelmed and exhausted, do not even realize we have overdone it and keep going. Others know they have done too much, but guilt prevents them from stopping. Burning the candle at both ends can break us spiritually, emotionally, and physically. We are human. We get tired. We give out. We get overwhelmed. We need a break. God rested after putting in six days of work creating the world. God understands the necessity for rest; He set aside the Sabbath for it.

How many of us have said, "yes" to someone or something at the expense of our body, mind, or soul? We must take care of ourselves. We are not in a good position to take care of others if we do not take care of ourselves. Self-care means setting boundaries with our body, work, and relationships. Jesus' love and grace are like a yoke, a wooden harness used to guide and direct oxen while plowing fields. They guide us and direct us on a path of assurance that everything will be all right. But while other yokes are hard and burdensome. Jesus' yoke is easy and his burdens are light. Jesus invites us daily to exercise self-care—go unto him and rest. Let us let go and let God, and give our spiritual and physical body time to rest. Exercise your faith—rest.

Exercise Your Faith Circuit

Warm Up (1 min)

Thank you, Lord, for being a source of renewal, strength, and rest. Help me to accept your invitation to take on your yoke, especially in those times when the burdens of life become too heavy. AMEN.

Workout (8 min)

1. How is God speaking to me?

   _____

   _____

   _____

2. What will I do to become physically and spiritually fit?

   _____

   _____

   _____

3. How will I exercise my faith?

   _____

   _____

   _____

Cool Down (1 min)

Affirm: I will rest and find peace in the Lord.

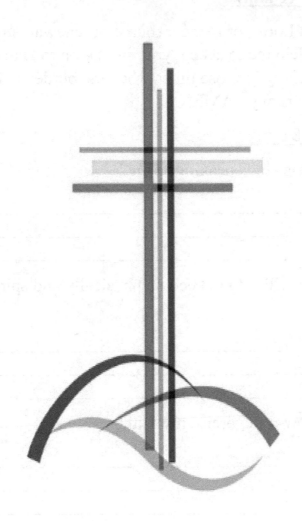

References

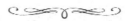

1. "5 Incredible Things That Happen When You Strengthen Your Core." *Best Health Magazine Canada*, 1 July 2017, www.besthealthmag.ca/best-you/fitness/5-reasons-to-strengthen-your-core/.

2. "American Heart Association Recommendations for Physical Activity in Adults." *American Heart Association Recommendations for Physical Activity in Adults*, Feb. 2014, www.heart.org/HEARTORG/HealthyLiving/Physic alActivity/FitnessBasics/American-Heart-Association-Recommendations-for-Physical-Activity-in-Adults_UCM_307976_Article.jsp#.WkpcBDhy59B.

3. April. "Top Benefits of Eating Healthy: Ideas That Go Beyond the Ordinary." *Top Benefits of Eating Healthy | Ideas That Go Beyond the Ordinary*, www.eatinghealthyfoods.org/top-benefits-of-eating-healthy.html.https://www.webmd.com/food-recipes/tc/healthy-eating-overview#1.

4. Avnet, Lily. "13 Mental Health Benefits Of Exercise." *The Huffington Post*, TheHuffingtonPost.com, 27 Mar. 2013,

www.huffingtonpost.com/2013/03/27/mental-health-benefits-exercise_n_2956099.html.

5. "Benefits of Building Muscular Strength." *Med-Health.net*, 18 Sept. 2013, www.med-health.net/Benefits-Of-Muscular-Strength.html.

6. BurnThis.com. "8 Simple Ways to Stay Committed to Your Fitness Routine." *The Huffington Post*, TheHuffingtonPost.com, 9 Sept. 2013, www.huffingtonpost.com/burnthis/fitness-tips_b_3882609.html.

7. George, Shannon. "Cardiovascular & Muscular Endurance." *LIVESTRONG.COM*, Leaf Group, 11 Sept. 2017, www.livestrong.com/article/341360-cardiovascular-muscular-endurance/.

8. "How Many Muscles Does the Human Body Have?" *Innovateus.net*, www.innovateus.net/health/how-many-muscles-does-human-body-have.

9. "How Many People Commit Suicide a Year." *HRFnd*, 10 Apr. 2015, healthresearchfunding.org/many-people-commit-suicide-year/.

10. Klein, Sarah. "Proper Breathing Techniques For Exercise." *The Huffington Post*,

TheHuffingtonPost.com, 16 May 2012,
www.huffingtonpost.com/2012/05/16/breathing-
techniques-exercise_n_1521630.html

11. McGovern, MK. "The Effects of Exercise on the
    Brain." *The Effects of Exercise on the Brain*, 15
    Nov. 2017, 15:15:04,
    serendip.brynmawr.edu/bb/neuro/neuro05/web2/mm
    cgovern.html.

12. "NAMI." *NAMI: National Alliance on Mental
    Illness*, www.nami.org/Learn-More/Mental-Health-
    By-the-Numbers.

13. Nunley, Kim. "Why Do High Repetitions Cause
    Muscle Definition?" *LIVESTRONG.COM*, Leaf
    Group, 11 Sept. 2017,
    www.livestrong.com/article/369432-why-do-high-
    repetitions-cause-muscle-definition/.

14. Shiel, William C. and Stroppler, Melissa Conrad.
    "Pain and Stress: Endorphins: Natural Pain and
    Stress Fighters." *MedicineNet*,
    www.medicinenet.com/script/main/art.asp?articleke
    y=55001.

15. "Stretching Is Not a Warm up! Find out Why."
    Mayo Clinic, Mayo Foundation for Medical
    Education and Research, 21 Feb. 2017,
    www.mayoclinic.org/healthy-lifestyle/fitness/in-
    depth/stretching/art-20047931.

16. "The Effects Of Under-Eating." *National Centre for Eating Disorders*, http://eating-disorders.org.uk/information/the-effects-of-under-eating/.

17. The Healing Power of Sleep." *WebMD*, WebMD, 2015, www.webmd.com/a-to-z-guides/discomfort-15/better-sleep/healing-power-sleep.

18. Vaesa, Janelle. "Why Is Overeating Bad?" *LIVESTRONG.COM*, Leaf Group, 3 Oct. 2017, www.livestrong.com/article/312300-why-is-over-eating-bad/.

19. Watson, Stephanie. "Balance Training." *WebMD*, WebMD, rev. 21 Nov. 2016, www.webmd.com/fitness-exercise/a-z/balance-training.

20. "What Is Dehydration? What Causes It?" *WebMD*, WebMD, rev. 05 May 2017, www.webmd.com/a-to-z-guides/dehydration-adults#1.

21. "What You Need to Know about Exercise and Chronic Disease." *Mayo Clinic*, Mayo Foundation for Medical Education and Research, 20 June 2015, www.mayoclinic.org/healthy-lifestyle/fitness/in-depth/exercise-and-chronic-disease/art-20046049?pg=2.

22. Zelman, Kathleen M. "6 Reasons to Drink Water." *WebMD*, WebMD, rev. 08 May 2008, www.webmd.com/diet/features/6-reasons-to-drink-water#1.

Acknowledgments

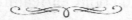

Chestina Mitchell Archibald
Virginia Brennan
Sheila Cooper
April Curry
Naimah Dease
Royce Fentress
Brian Fesler
Bettie J. Harris
Glenda Harris
Norman Harris
Betty Hardy Hines
Major Jefferson
Gloria Johnson
Pam Kellar
Adric Kimbrough, Jr.
Edith Kimbrough
Charles Kimbrough
Blondell Strong Kimbrough
Elizabeth Kimbrough
Ashley McCrary
Rawra Meharri
Kelly Motley
Fatima Mukunde
Chris O'rear
Jonathan Richardson
Cheryl Miles-Stevenson
Ken Turner
Janet Walsh
Meharry Medical College SOD/SOM 2020
Roland Photography

Computer-Assisted
Simulation
of Dynamic Systems
with
Block Diagram Languages

Nicholas M. Karayanakis

Professor
University of North Florida

CRC Press

Boca Raton   Ann Arbor   London   Tokyo

Susan C. Karayanakis was responsible for the page layout and manuscript design executed using Word Perfect® 5.1. The typeface used was CG Times Scalable at 10.7 points before reduction. Formulas were created using MathEdit™ and imported into the document in the TIFF output format. Figures created using Flow Charting™ 3 were converted to WPG files for importation. Finally, TUTSIM™ produced all the simulation outputs which were imported using WP's GRAB feature.

Cover concept by Susan C. Karayanakis.

Library of Congress Cataloging-in-Publication Data

Karayanakis, Nicholas Mark, 1947-
  Computer-assisted simulation of dynamic systems with block diagram
languages / Nicholas M. Karayanakis.
    p.   cm.
  Includes bibliographical references and index.
  ISBN 0-8493-8971-2
  1. Digital computer simulation.   I. Title.
  QA76.9.C65K36   1993
  003'.85'0113513--dc20   93-19596
                                                                            CIP

PREFACE

This book is about the simulation, or mimicking, of dynamic systems using personal computers or workstations. It is also about continuous dynamic simulation (CDSS) languages. These languages are outstanding technical tools for engineers, scientists and mathematicians, because they provide an inexpensive way of turning a digital computer into a simulator of real world phenomena—be they continuous, discrete, or mixed. The term *system dynamics* is another way of referring to Mother Nature and Father Time. We live in a dynamic universe where things are in a state of flux. Their time behavior is important, as evidenced by the fact that almost everybody keeps track of nature's independent variable (time) by using wristwatches and clocks.

Even simple systems can be perplexing. The bounce of a toy ball depends on its weight, its size, the material's coefficient of elasticity, the pertinent aerodynamics and the gravitational constant. Physics and mathematics help us formulate and understand the problem. However, analytical solutions do not provide the big picture, even in a relatively simple system like the bouncing ball. As a result, questions like, "What happens if I take the ball and bounce it on the surface of Pluto?" or "What if I double the elasticity coefficient on a day with 95% humidity?" remain unanswered. Curiosity can be stifled; creativity can drown. Simulation offers virtual reality, an alternative environment. Here, we can perform the bouncing ball experiment under the conditions known to exist on Pluto without going anywhere. We can fly a new aircraft without building it first, and explore ideas and concepts that are conceptually possible but often analytically unsolvable.

The study of systems via dynamic simulators is not new. It goes all the way back to the mechanical differential analyzer of Lord Kelvin in the early 1900s. The roots of modern dynamic simulation are the early analog and analog/hybrid computers. The use of these machines in teaching and research has contributed to the technological advancement of many nations. Today analog and hybrid computers are still going worldwide, although they are gradually being displaced by virtual laboratory software that emulate them. Simulation techniques like those developed in this book can be used in research or as part of an instructional system. Either way, the methodologies shown here afford intensive interaction between human and machine and the uninhibited testing of *what if* ideas.

Block diagram languages, the subject of this book, allow the modelling of systems by function block simulators. First, a model is created by using all we can find out and whatever we suspect about its structure, properties and behavior. Then, the block simulator is created by connecting a number of function blocks. It can be tested for its time response characteristics again and again, each time changing the pertinent parameters and constants. Even signal paths can be readily rearranged until a satisfactory model structure exists. Anasynthetic design processes that yield complete graphic solutions, not just cryptic numbers, are possible. Block diagram languages are accessible to both the practical person and the theorist, to the beginner and the expert alike.

This book is written for anyone who likes to investigate things like control systems, electrical and electronic circuits, algebra, biological population dynamics, differential equations, and a myriad of other things found in life. In many ways it is a modern version of the great books on analog computation, yet it represents the technical and scientific way of the future. Simulation is now a topic of strategic priority in the U.S. and in many places around the world. As the reader soon finds out, it is the answer to scarce resources, to limited expertise, and to exploiting ideas still in a future plane. Our intent has been two fold: first, to produce an interdisciplinary work to serve as a text for courses in dynamic simulation; and second, to provide a reference for workers in engineering, science and mathematics. The book will be of interest to those who always wondered about dynamic simulation, block models, CDSS languages and the like, and how to get started using all that in *their* work. Basically, we are interested in effecting technology transfer to the individual.

Strong effort has been made to use and include a large list of references from the analog/hybrid computer literature. The book is highly visual; the technical detail is presented so that even a nonspecialist can read it. TUTSIM, a readily available and affordable CDSS language, was chosen for all examples. Every example can be easily implemented with other block diagram languages regardless of platform.

As the writing of this work draws to a close, I feel the need to acknowledge those who contributed their thoughts, encouragement, friendship and support. Thanks are due to Walter Reynolds for giving me his confidence early on, his generous assistance and friendship. I thank Prof. Woody W. Everett, Jr. and Mrs. Cheryl A. Fields of the Computers in Education Division of ASEE for their generous research assistance and their cooperation far and above any call of duty. My appreciation goes to Dr. Rodney Hugelman, an old friend and colleague from the U of I years, for inspiring conversations and for being there. The remarkable Greek professors, in particular Prof. Arapatzis, I salute with respect and gratitude for their selfless dedication to training and education.

To Joel Claypool and N'Quavah R. Velazquez of CRC Press I extend my appreciation for making this book possible. Special thanks go to Prof. Donna B. Evans, COEHS Dean at the University of North Florida, for her friendship, kindness and support in these difficult times. I thank my son Mark for helpful comments and assistance with the illustrations. Lastly and foremost, I extend my appreciation to my wife Susan, who in spite of her own busy schedule, became the true architect of this book and its contents.

As this book is the first of its kind, there were no paradigms in the market. The author will be delighted to hear from anyone with better ideas or suggestions toward a better future edition. Finally, we believe that the emphasis in analogies and the coverage of block diagram modelling is unique, because they are written not to impress the author's colleagues, but to satisfy and enlighten the reader. Having written the book he always wanted to own, the author rests his case.

Nicholas M. Karayanakis
Jacksonville, Florida

To the memory of my mother Ναυσικᾱ

TABLE OF CONTENTS

8 The Simulation of Electrical Circuits and Devices—I 195

9 The Simulation of Electrical Circuits and Devices—II

226

A *Appendix: Useful Devices and Experiments*

341

B *Bibliography*

I *Index*

1 THE PROCESS OF CONTINUOUS DYNAMIC SYSTEM SIMULATION

1.1 INTRODUCTION

In the early days of simulation, there were differential analyzers, large analog computers with bulky rack-mounted vacuum tube amplifiers. These were followed by transistorized analog computers which brought dynamic simulation and model building to many disciplines. Analog computers underwent development for a few decades. Various models were produced around the world, ranging from desktop units to large analog/hybrid machines. Paradoxically, this development ceased as analog integrated circuits became more available, more sophisticated, less expensive and easier to use!

The demise of the analog computer can be linked easily to the development of digital continuous dynamic simulation languages. When Selfridge wrote code enabling an IBM 701 to operate as an analog computer in 1955, the early mainframe began competing with the analog machine. The virtual analog computer revolution had begun. From then on, people who understood both analog and digital computers continued to develop simulation languages that turn digital machines into virtual analog computers. Their rationale included the issues of accuracy, ease of programming, and good documentation, Why should we perform integrations with analog circuits subject to drift, saturation, ambient temperature sensitivity, etc., when we can do it with digital accuracy? Today, one might point to the outstanding accuracy of operational amplifier integrated circuits. However, the accuracy of an analog computational element (e.g., an integrator) depends greatly on passive components as well. Accurate resistors and capacitors are still very expensive.

Ease of programming is also a major issue. With the exception of the enthusiast, the analog computer user is easily exasperated with hardware idiosyncracies and with problem preparation requirements. Scaling a problem in time and amplitude is not particularly easy and is mostly art rather than engineering. Then, setting up coefficient potentiometers, reference voltages, initial condition circuits, etc., is a time-consuming activity that requires some electronics background. Continuous simulation languages free the user from those tasks originating from hardware limitations. It is now easier to create and invent through inductive reasoning. Unlike mathematical tools, where things are or are not, inductive thought involves the hypothesizing of analytical relationships between variables. Intuition, speculation and *what if* fantasies are acceptable here.

The advent of the personal computer (pc) with its ever-increasing popularity led to the development of portable simulation languages. One can hardly sustain the image of a big analog machine in the garage, but turning a pc into an analog computer is entirely reasonable and proper. Today pc-based continuous simulation languages are very popular in teaching and research with institutions and individuals worldwide. Block diagram and expression-based continuous simulation languages are inexpensive and easy to use. Although under-estimated and underutilized, they are formidable tools for the workers of many disciplines.

1.2   AN OVERVIEW OF CONTINUOUS SYSTEM SIMULATION LANGUAGES

1.2.1   Introduction

Digital simulation languages can be *discrete*, *continuous* or *combined*. Some well-known languages for discrete event simulation are SIMSCRIPT, GASP, GPSS and SIMULA. There are many discrete simulation languages and the reader is referred to the excellent books by Deo (1983) and Kreutzer (1986) for detailed information on the subject. Also, discrete event simulation is discussed by Kiviat (1967), Dahl (1968), Kay (1972), Fishman (1973) and Bobillier et al. (1976).

Combined simulation languages are useful when the system to be simulated includes interacting discrete and continuous variables. Some well-known combined simulation languages are GASP IV (Pritsker, 1974; Deo, 1983; and Kreutzer, 1984), GASP-PL/1 (Pritsker and Young, 1975) and SLAM (Pritsker and Pegden, 1983). These languages were developed by A. A. B. Pritsker of Pritsker and Associates (West Lafayette, IN). Others are DISCO, developed by K. Helsgaun of Roskilde University (Denmark) (Helsgaun, 1980), CLASS, GSL-A and PROSE (Deo, 1983). Oren (1973 and 1977) and Kreutzer (1986) provide noteworthy reviews of combined simulation languages. Also, excellent information on the design methodology and utility of these languages is found in Cellier (1979a, 1979b).

Continuous simulation languages are the main interest of this book. They were developed as a direct replacement of the analog computer and are often used in verifying the results of analog simulations. Although it first appears to be unnecessary duplicity, analog/hybrid computers and continuous simulation languages work well together, allowing a circuit designer to completely design a real world system on the digital computer, and then to verify its operation on the analog/hybrid machine. Continuous simulation languages can be *block-diagram* or *expression* oriented. TUTSIM is a block diagram language. A discussion of expression-oriented languages is found in Deo (1983). STELLA (Richmond, 1985) is an example of a modern-portable expression-oriented language.

Modern block-diagram languages are very popular in teaching and research. Some are designed for the Macintosh environment like Extend (Imagine That, Inc., 1990), MODEL-IT! (Thompson, 1990), SIMULAB and STELLA (Richmond, 1985). Others, like $MATRIX_X$/PC, SIMNON and TUTSIM operate with MS/PC DOS systems.

1.2.2 An Historical Perspective

The concept of continuous dynamic system simulation, in which a digital machine emulates an analog/hybrid computer, is not new. Over the decades many people devoted their research lives to the development of simulation languages and techniques. In 1955 R. G. Selfridge of the U.S. Naval Ordinance Test Station (Inyokern, CA) published his pioneering work on *Coding a General Purpose Digital Computer to Operate as a Differential Analyzer* (Selfridge, 1955). It is remarkable that Selfridge used machine language and fixed-point arithmetic to develop his simulator on an IBM 701—some years prior to the development of FORTRAN.

Subsequently, the DEPI (Differential Equations Pseudo-code Interpreter) language was developed in 1958 by H. F. Lesh at the Jet Propulsion Laboratory (Pasadena, CA). Lesh also used machine language and employed a fourth-order Runge-Kutta integration algorithm (Lesh, 1958). DEPI was developed further and saw use in the early 60's (Hurley, 1960). In 1958, M. L. Stein, J. Rose and D. B. Parker developed ASTRAL (Analog Schematic Translator to Algebraic Language) at Convair Astronautics. ASTRAL is a compiler that models the analog computer and generates a Fortran program as an intermediate step. The program can be modified prior to compiling and executing. Also ASTRAL provided sorting and centralized integration (Stein et al., 1959; Stein and Rose, 1960).

There were many digital simulators during the 60's and 70's all spun off the early concepts—each featuring one or more unique features and innovations. Some are DYANA (DYnamics ANAlyzer) in 1959, BLODI (BLOck DIagram compiler) in 1961 (Kelley et al., 1961), DYSAC in 1963 (Hurley and Skiles, 1963) and DYNASAR (DYNAmic System AnalyzeR) and PARTNER (Proof of Analog Results Through Numerically Equivalent Routine) in 1962 (Stephenson, 1971). The DAS (Digital Analog Simulator) language was developed by R. A. Gaskil, J. W. Harris and A. L. McKnight at the Martin Company (Orlando, FL) in 1962 (Gaskil, 1963). DAS, based on the Euler integrating algorithm, saw widespread use. It is considered by many to be the most successful early continuous simulation language.

MIDAS (Modified Integration Digital Analog Simulator) was developed in 1963 by R. T. Harnett, H. E. Petersen, F. J. Sansom and L. M. Warshawsky at Wright-Patterson AFB (Dayton, OH). This very successful block-oriented simulation language is a modified DAS with a variable step-size fifth-order predictor-corrector integration algorithm. MIDAS was originally an interpreter (Harnett et al., 1964; Petersen et al., 1964). MIDAS III, a compiler version was written in 1966 (Burgin, 1966). Unlike DAS, MIDAS uses a sorting process to determine the computation steps. Notably, the language was written for the then popular IBM 7090/94, was well documented and was distributed on request free of charge! The MIDAS (MIn/max Delay-Ambiguity Simulator) simulator of Bell Labs (Bierbauer et al., 1991) is not related to the MIDAS described above. The AT&T MIDAS is a system-level simulator used in large integrated circuit designs. The PACTOLUS language was developed in 1964 by R. D. Brennan at IBM (San Jose, CA) for the IBM 1620 machine. It was designed to overcome some of MIDAS's difficulties and served as the foundation of 1130 CSMP (not S/360 CSMP) and DSL/90 (Brennan and Sano, 1964).

MIMIC appeared in 1965 as a successor to MIDAS (Sansom, 1965). It was developed by H. E. Petersen, F. J. Sansom and L. M. Warshawsky at Wright-Patterson AFB. Unlike MIDAS, a pure block-oriented language, MIMIC is an expression language where equations can be entered directly as FORTRAN-like statements. As in the MIDAS case, the language was well-documented (Sansom, 1967) and was distributed free of charge on request. A second, improved version was issued in 1967. MIMIC's variable step size, fourth-order Runge-Kutta integration algorithm improved its performance over MIDAS. MIMIC programs can be directly translated into machine language; it requires less preprocessing due to its limited diagnostics. An extended discussion on MIMIC with many simulation examples appears in Stephenson (1971). An interesting feature of the language is its nonprocedural nature through which a built-in sorting mechanism allows the nonsequential entry of instructions (see also Peterson, 1972).

The DSL/90 (Digital Simulation Language for the 7090 machines) was developed in 1965 by W. M. Lyn and D. G. Wyman of IBM (San Jose, CA). DSL/90 statements are converted into an intermediate language subroutine (FORTRAN IV) and then compiled and executed under one of the four available integration algorithms (Lyn and Wyman, 1965a, 1965b; Lyn and Linebarger, 1966). DSL/90 served as a significant developmental step in IBM's continuous dynamic simulation language development program. The CSMP (Continuous System Modeling Program) was part of IBM's 1965 initiative in developing continuous system simulation languages. The early 1130 CSMP language was built on the PACTOLUS foundation, coded in 1130 FORTRAN IV. An extended version of 1130 CSMP by T. J. Packer (1969) had many noteworthy features and made full use of a 16K core for handling large (300 block) problems. Another variant, the S/360 CSMP, was based on the DSL/90. Both R. D. Brennan and M. Y. Silberberg of IBM are largely responsible for its development and success. Note that S/360 CSMP acts as a preprocessor. A preprocessor translates both the description of a simulation model and the run-time instructions into an intermediate language subroutine (in this case, FORTRAN), which is then compiled and executed (see also Brennan and Silberberg, 1968). CSMP offers a choice of seven integration algorithms and is still in use. An excellent book on CSMP is Speckhart and Green (1976). CSMP III is a later version of the S/360 CSMP. A notable descendent of CSMP is MOBSSL (Merritt and Miller's Own Block Structured Simulation Language), a block-structured simulation language for digital and hybrid computation (Merritt and Miller, 1969). A variant, MOBSSL-UAF, was developed at the University of Southern California in 1969. MOBSSL and MOBSSL-UAF are notable efforts toward the development of a pure block-diagram oriented simulation approach freeing the user from lower-level programming.

CSSL (Continuous System Simulation Language), the outcome of a standardization effort by the Simulation Software Committee of Simulation Councils, Inc. (SCi), was developed in 1967 (SCi Simulation Software Committee, 1967). CSSL is a problem-oriented language for the simulation of continuous dynamic systems that can be modelled by systems of ordinary differential equations. Like DSL/90, GASP IV and FORSIM IV, this is a FORTRAN IV-based language or, according to Stephenson (1971), a superset of FORTRAN IV since all of FORTRAN IV is available to CSSL. Of course, CSSL is a non-procedural language (like MIMIC which served as a foundation for its development). Also, it is quite similar to the S/360 CSMP in orientation and organization (Brennan and Silberberg, 1968). CSSL was designed with extendability in mind and does not have the disadvantages of error control and debugging facilities. An extended discussion of CSSL with many examples appears in Stephenson (1971). The languages ACSL, RSSL, DARE, DARE-P, HYTRAN, and SL/1 are all based on the original CSSL specifications. The CSSL language itself evolved through CSSL-II and -III to the present CSSL-IV. The current version is available on over twenty-five different operating systems. ACSL (Advanced Continuous Simulation Language) is described by Mitchell and Gauthier (1981), Fruhlinger and Aburdene (1986) and Aburdene (1988).

DARE (Differential Analyzer REplacement) was developed as an extension of CSSL. It uses the following integration algorithms: Runge-Kutta Merson, fourth-order Runge-Kutta, third-order Runge-Kutta, two-point Runge-Kutta, Adam's two-point predictor and simple Euler one-point predictor. It also uses the Pope and Gear methods of solving stiff systems. There are many versions of DARE, among them the portable DARE-P language (Aus and Korn, 1971; Lucas and Wait, 1975), DARE/ELEVEN and MICRODARE III (Korn and Wait, 1978; Korn, 1982). The book by Korn and Wait (1978) on digital continuous system simulation is a timely and useful reference in the field. Another language is the EARLY DESIRE (Direct Executing SImulation in REal time), a floating-point equation language for mini- and microcomputers (Korn, 1982).

DYNAMO (DYNAmic MOdels) is a FORTRAN-based simulation language developed in the late 50's by J. W. Forrester of MIT, the noted author of books on systems, industrial, urban and world dynamics (Forrester, 1961, 1968, 1969, 1973). The author is aware of the following versions: DYNAMO, reviewed by Nilsen and Karplus (1974), DYNAMO II (Pugh III, 1976), DYNAMO III (Richardson and Pugh III, 1981) and micro-DYNAMO (Pugh-Roberts Associates, Inc., 1982). It is an expression based or scenario language used widely in economics, management and social science. Dynamic systems are modelled by sets of difference equations. Models are line-oriented and involve initial values, constants, level and rate variables. Although it follows the rigid FORTRAN coding conventions, DYNAMO is conceptually simple and easy to use. Also, in spite of many built-in mathematical and statistical functions, it uses the Euler integration algorithm only, a significant weakness. DYNAMO's application in business and management is discussed by Roberts (1978). A brief description of the language and an example of application is found in Kreutzer's excellent review of simulation programming styles and languages (1986). An interesting comparison with GASP and SIMULA in the context of problem definition is given by Robinson (1972). The book by Roberts et al. (1983) provides a somewhat elementary but wide spectrum of applications. Gray (1984) discusses DYNAMO's nonprocedural nature, its use as a financial planning language, and how it compares with the IFPS language.

The language BEDSOCKS was developed at the University of Bradford, West Yorkshire, England. It is described in the Ph.D. thesis by Brown (1975) and is referenced by Luker (1984). The same author discusses MODELLER (Luker, 1982, 1984) also developed at the University of Bradford. ISIS, a continuous simulation language made for miniframes was developed by J. L. Hay in the mid-70's (Hay, 1978) at the University of Salford, Salford, England. Hay is also the principal author of ISIM (Hay and Crosbie, 1984) and ESL (Crosbie et al., 1985) (see Section 1.2.4). SIMNON was developed by H. Elmqvist at Lund Institute of Technology, Lund, Sweden, in 1972 (Åström, 1983; Elmqvist et al., 1990; Åström and Wittenmark, 1990). It is used in the outstanding textbook on computer-controlled systems by Åström and Wittenmark (1990). In Russia the language NEDIS (NEpreryvno-DIskret-nyje Sistemi or continuous/discrete systems) was developed in Kiev (Glushkov et al., 1975; Kindler, 1978). In Czechoslovakia the combined language CDC SIS (Combined Discrete-Continuous Simulation System) is used (Kinder, 1978). There are many good reviews of simulation languages, like those found in the books by Deo (1983) and Kreutzer (1986), in the book chapters by Kiviat (1971), Krasnow (1969) and Tocher (1979) and in the articles by Clancy and Fineberg (1965), Oren and Zeigler (1979) and Tocher (1965). Of interest are the paper by Korn (1970) and the surveys of continuous simulation languages by Nilsen and Karplus (1974) and Brennan and Linebarger (1964).

1.2.3   About TUTSIM

TUTSIM (Twente University of Technology SIMulation language), the main subject of this work, was developed in The Netherlands and was introduced in the U.S. in 1982. It is very popular in Europe where it is marketed by Meerman Automation, the company of Vim Meerman, one of TUTSIM's original developers.   In North America, TUTSIM Products markets and continuously develops this language. Walter E. Reynolds and Jinner Wolf are responsible for the ongoing development of TUTSIM. An outstanding feature of the language is its user-defined blocks capability. There is a C language option, to include Borland TURBO C and the Microsoft QuickC compilers, and a FORTRAN option (Microsoft FORTRAN version 3.3 or 4.0). TUTSIM's user blocks allow almost unlimited extensibility to the functions and capabilities of TUTSIM (TUTSIM Products, 1991). User blocks can be written to add new functions or for windowing and linking complex code sections. Both the successful textbook on the analysis and design of dynamic systems by Cochin and Plass (1990) and Coughanowr's classic text on process systems analysis and control (1991) use TUTSIM.

1.2.4   About ESL

ESL (European space agency Simulation Language) was created to meet European Space Agency (ESA) specifications. The principal ESL developers were J. L. Hay, J. G. Pearce and R. E. Crosbie (see also Section 1.2.2). The language is currently marketed by ISIM Simulation, a division of Salford University Business Services, Ltd., Salford, England. The University of Salford is where much of the language's development took place.

ESL, a DOS environment language, is available in different versions. It is a sophisticated, general purpose CDSS language with a supporting software environment for the modelling, simulation and analysis of dynamic systems. The core of this environment is the ESL language itself, a modern comprehensive procedural language resembling Ada in style. It features a graphical interface (IMP) which provides the user with a mouse/keyboard-based schematic editor. ESL is a professional-level simulation language including among its numerous features many nonlinear and discontinuous functions. It also has full matrix, vector and array slice support, transfer function notation capability, linearization and steady-state finders. ESL comes with very complete documentation and many worked examples.

1.2.5   About Extend

Created for the Macintosh environment, Extend is an outstanding modelling language with many ususual features. Its creator, Bob Diamond of Imagine That, Inc., of San Jose, CA, wrote Extend in PGM C^{++} to take advantage of the icon environment available to users of Mac Plus, SE or II computers. Given the power of the language, its hardware requirements are minimal (a hard drive). Also, Extend works with the Macintosh operating system 6.0.2 or later. It is MultiFinder and A/UX compatible and supports all common Mac printers and color monitors.

Extend's blocks are held by libraries. There are generic and discrete event libraries. The manufacturing library, an optional toolkit for building factory models, is based on the discrete event library. The generic library has blocks suitable for modelling anything from electronic to financial systems. The discrete library allows the implementation of queuing theory problems to service industry waiting line models. Users may write their own blocks in ModL, a C-like language. Extend comes with excellent documentation on both the program and the ModL language.

1.2.6   About VisSim

A relatively new block diagram simulator, VisSim is a Windows-based CDSS language written in Microsoft C. Its creator is Peter Darnell of Visual Solutions, Inc., of Westford, MA. The VisSim system is a cutting-edge, powerful block diagram language with an outstanding schematic editor and features not found in other block diagram languages. In fact, the power of VisSim is so great that no brief description of the language can do it justice. Essentially it is a user friendly, mathematically robust CDSS language for modelling, simulation, analysis and real-time control. The tactical advantages of VisSim emerge from its creation as pc-based program rather than a conversion from mainframe software. It is available for the Win 3.0+ and UNIX/X platforms. Essentially, VisSim is capable of using 16,300 blocks/model (Win 3.0+ version) and 500 M blocks/model (UNIX/X). Both versions include four fixed and two adaptive integration methods and more than seventy mathematical blocks. Like TUTSIM, users may write their own blocks in C, C^{++}, FORTRAN, Pascal or any language capable of creating a Windows DLL.

In addition to its sound mathematical presence, VisSim offers the advantage of iconical interface, more than other equivalent DOS, UNIX/X or Macintosh block diagram languages. The basic visual cell is excellent; plot blocks can be created at any point within the model for interactive displays of data. Also, virtual instrumentation panels with interactive plots, meter and digital display blocks add significant power toa presentation. The VisSim/ANALYZE add-on enhances the language with linearization (an ABCD state-space matrix generator), transfer function information with roots and poles, root locus and frequency response plotting. The VisSim/RT is a real-time interface that allows the reading and writing of analog and digital real-time data into an application. It allows access to up to thirty-two analog inputs, thirty-two analog outputs and thirty-two digital I/O channels with a long list of supported boards. Another add-on, the VisSim/Neural-Net provides neural network capability. VisSim can read TUTSIM files.

1.3 TIME: The Independent Variable

Any situation involving the numerical solution of differential equations poses questions of numerical treatment errors. The simulation environment can be best understood by considering a differential equation having the general form

$$a_{1,n}\frac{d^n y_1}{dx^n} + a_{1,n-1}\frac{d^{n-1} y_1}{dx^{n-1}} + \cdots + a_{1,1}\frac{dy_1}{dx} = a_{1,0}f_1(x,y_1,y_2,\ldots,y_m)$$

(1)

$$a_{m,n}\frac{d^n y_m}{dx^n} + a_{m,n-1}\frac{d^{n-1} y_m}{dx^{n-1}} + \cdots + a_{m,1}\frac{dy_m}{dx} = a_{m,0}f_m(x,y_1,y_2,\ldots,y_m)$$

(2)

where the parameters $a_{m,n}$ can be constants or functions of either the dependent or the independent variables, or functions of their derivatives. The problem is a *boundary value* problem when y or its derivatives are specified for two variables of x, and an *initial value* problem when known variables of the dependent variable and its derivatives are given for a single value of the independent variable x.

Frequently, dynamic system simulation involves initial value problems. Solving these problems on the digital computer is done by means of some stepwise integration routine. The solution run begins with the known values of y, $[dy/dt]$, $[d^2y/dt^2]$, and so on, at the initial value (or initial condition) $x(0)$. In the next step, y and some of its derivatives are determined in the domain of x at $x = x(0) + \Delta t$, where Δt is the step size. Then y and its derivatives are found at $x = x(0) + 2\Delta t$, and so on throughout the x-range of interest.

Simulating dynamic systems on the digital computer is not an error-free process. First, there are errors inherent to any specific algorithm (see also Section 1.4). Then, there are errors resulting from the discretization (quantization) of the problem variables. The independent variable, usually time, is associated with *truncation* errors. Truncation errors occur when an infinite series is used to represent a function. Naturally, most algorithms are based on such series and during the evaluation of the function the computation can only converge. The function is truncated anytime some of its terms are not evaluated. Step size, duration of the solution and the dynamic nature of the solution determine the final accumulation of truncation errors. *Roundoff* errors involve the dependent variable. They are random and propagate with each delta step. Their accumulation induces a progressive distortion of the results. Roundoff errors occur whenever there is rounding of a digital word prior to its storage in memory. An excellent discussion of the sources of numerical error in microcomputers is in the article by Bushkirk (1979).

A very important criterion in the selection of a continuous dynamic system simulation language is the user's ability to define the simulation step. TUTSIM allows complete user control over this significant parameter. Then the practical question becomes how large (or small) a Δt step should be specified in the context of any given problem. As a cardinal rule, the larger the step interval, the fewer the iterations during a specified solution run and therefore the less the possibility of roundoff error accumulation. On the other hand, the smaller the step size, the higher the number of iterations and the more continuous the solution results. The tradeoff between accuracy and continuity is a user decision. Errors likely to be made by beginning TUTSIM users are due to selecting too large a step (delta time in simulation jargon). Apart from the previous considerations, the solution dynamics factor is of significance here since large delta intervals define iteration steps too large to follow a fast-changing solution, that is, a solution history with large magnitudes of the highest derivative of the dependent variable.

For a Δt on the small side, TUTSIM's roundoff errors are 1 ppm (part per million), a very low number. It is often reasonable to use a delta step that does not exceed one-fourth of the fastest significant time constant of the simulated system. In TUTSIM the user defines *both* the delta step size and the total simulation time, T, and in most cases, a ($T/\Delta t$) ratio of 500 to 5000 may be appropriate. When the fastest significant time constant of a system is unknown, a trial and error procedure can be used to find the largest useful Δt for which there is no change in the results. This is done by doubling or halving the delta time and rerunning the simulation with superimposing screens. If the simulation seems slow an inappropriately large Δt may often be the reason.

Problems with abruptly changing outcomes are special cases to be treated with care, since the simulation outcome is influenced by the magnitude of the derivatives of the dependent variable (e.g, y) during the interval of observation in the x (or t) region of interest. When confronted with abruptly changing solution dynamics, the user may employ either the *Variable Delta Time block* (VDT) or the *GEar delta time step Reduction* (GER) block. Generally speaking, equations with abruptly changing solution dynamics (slow to rapid rates and vice versa) belong to the special category of stiff equations. Their accurate solutions require special techniques (see Enright and Hull, 1976; Wanner, 1977; and Gottwald and

Wanner, 1982). Stiff systems are often found in biology and chemistry and in electrical, electronic and control systems. Although we can use a constant step-size algorithm by choosing a small Δt, it would be counterproductive to maintain a small step throughout the computation. Instead, algorithms that adjust automatically are required here, like those implemented by TUTSIM's VDT and GER blocks (see Gear, 1971; and Shampine and Gear, 1979). In simulation practice, when a preliminary run shows abrupt changes of the solution curve at some known point, the VDT block allows a time-specific reduction of delta time by a user-defined ratio. When and how much the delta time should be changed during the final solution run is determined after the preliminary run.

In the case of unpredictable solution dynamics, the GER block provides for an adaptive delta time step, a most useful and impressive option. This block has a built-in predictor where the next change is anticipated by an amount equal to double the current input step change. It also has a built-in hysteresis that inhibits drifting in and out of a reduced Δt condition. It is best used in conjunction with Euler integrators, since the Adams-Bashford block introduces a small second-order error anytime Δt changes.

1.4   A BRIEF GUIDE TO THE MATHEMATICAL LITERATURE OF NUMERICAL METHODS, DIFFERENTIAL EQUATIONS AND ALGORITHMS

Although the casual TUTSIM user may not be directly involved with mathematics per se, any knowledge of numerical methods, differential equations and algorithms is an asset to anyone involved in dynamic system simulation. One of TUTSIM's outstanding featuures is its extensibility via the user-defined blocks option. User blocks allow the creation of custom USR (history) or USA (nonhistory) blocks and enable the implementation of anything from simple functions to windowing and linking of complex code sections. Therefore, new mathematical functions, displays and input/output (I/O) devices may be built-in and addressed during simulations. User blocks can be written in C, an option supporting both the Borland TURBO C and the Microsoft QuickC compilers, and in FORTRAN (Microsoft FORTRAN Version 3.3 or 4.0). Unlike some other block-oriented continuous simulation languages, TUTSIM's extensibility is real and unlimited. However, both programming and mathematical skills are required to use it. It is in this spirit we offer the following review of mathematical resources.

In numerical methods, there are several very readable textbooks also suitable for self-study. The notable works by Al-Khafaji and Tooley (1986), Chapra and Canale (1988) and Hostetter et al. (1991) are highly recommended for review and reference. Professor Gene H. Hostetter, who passed away on July 30, 1988, was a most prolific author with many outstanding contributions to the fields of electronics, controls and mathematics. The book by Johnson and Riess (1982) is a classic in numerical analysis. Salvadori and Baron's book (1961) covers related engineering topics.

Also recommended are some fine numerical methods books with computer orientation, like that of Chapra and Canale (1985) and a classic in this category written by Constantinides (1987). Its chemical engineering orientation does not detract at all from the book's great value to the nonspecialist. In their somewhat historical but still useful book, James et al. (1977) apply numerical methods in conjunction with FORTRAN and CSMP. Nakamura's book (1991) is modern and useful to anyone linking numerical methods with software. Forsythe et al. (1977) and Shoup (1979) both discuss computer methods in applied numerical computation, while Shoup's book offers a practical engineering orientation. An excellent contemporary work on the application of numerical methods in computer-assisted simulation and modelling is that by Mastascusa (1988). Also Alberth's book in precise numerical analysis (1988) is written from a digital computation perspective. Although not an introductory text, it is recommended here to anyone serious in this field. Related issues in digital computer simulation of engineering systems are found in Chu (1969), Ord-Smith and Stephenson (1975), Shah (1976) and Stephenson (1971).

Algorithm books are numerous and many of them are classics of lasting value like the books by Aho et al. (1976), Arden and Astill (1970), Cheney and Kincaid (1980), Conte and De Boor (1968), Purdom and Brown (1985) and Sedgewick (1983). Arden and Astill's book (1970) is recommended here as the first purchase. The works by Acton (1970) and Dahlquist and Björck (1974) are also of interest. Gonnet (1984) writes about algorithms and data structures, while Knuth (1973a, 1973b and 1981) in his three-volume series on the art of computer programming, discusses algorithms in depth. Knuth's books are considered classics and necessary reading in the field.

The topics of ordinary and partial differential equations (dfq's) are of great interest to anyone engaged in simulation. A very useful and reader-friendly book is that by Spiegel (1981) where both ordinary and partial dfq's are introduced. The excellent book by Trahanas (1989) provides a rare in-depth view of ordinary dfq's. Published by the University Press of Crete (Iraklion, Crete), it is perhaps one of the finest books currently available on the topic. Also, the work by Jordan and Smith (1987) is a classic on nonlinear ordinary dfq's and must be read by anyone exploring nonlinear system dynamics. The articles by Gill (1951), Carr (1958) and Collatz (1951) are of great historical interest. Henrici (1962) writes on the discrete variable methods in ordinary dfq's. Lapidus and Schlesser (1976) deal with numerical methods for differential equations. Gear (1971) discusses numerical initial-value problems in ordinary dfq's. Numerical integration techniques are also discussed by Nordsieck (1962), Traub (1964) and Davis and Rabinowitz (1975). Numerical integration methods within the context of digital simulation are investigated and reviewed by Nigro (1969) and Martens (1969). The Runge-Kutta integration techniques are addressed by Butcher et al. (1979) and Fehlberg (1968). An excellent treatise on the computational methods of boundary value problems is by Na (1979). The numerical solution of partial dfq's is discussed by Lapidus and George (1982) within the context of science and engineering. A little-known but excellent book on the subject is by Duffy (1986). Vichnevetsky's classical two-volume work on partial dfq's (1981 and 1982) covers initial-value problems, elliptical equations and the finite element method. Vemuri and Karplus (1981) examine partial dfq's in the context of the digital computer.

There are, of course, hundreds of good books in the areas of numerical methods, computer algorithms and differential equations. Also thousands of valuable papers can be found in specialized journals and in conference proceedings. The materials listed here are what the author uses and not an exhaustive or even exclusive listing. The intended purpose is to assist readers of different levels of mathematical knowledge and expertise in upgrading to a more functional level.

1.5 ABOUT INTEGRATOR BLOCKS

The integrator has been the most important computational element in dynamic system simulation since the first days of the differential analyzer (the early analog computer). Integration algorithms and their characteristics can be found in the numerical methods references of Section 1.4. In this section our goal is two-fold: first, to bridge analog computer and digital continuous simulation techniques and second, to point out little known operational details of integrators and integration.

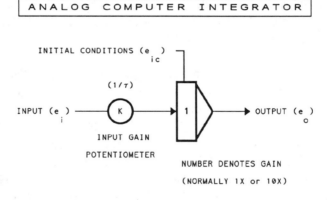

Figure 1.5.1   Classical analog computer integrator.

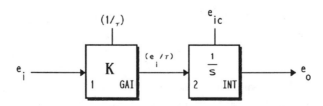

Figure 1.5.2   Block diagram representation of the classic integrator.

The classical analog computer integrator of Figure 1.5.1 consists of the actual integrator unit and an input potentiometer. It is represented by the TUTSIM setup of Figure 1.5.2. The coefficient $K = (1/\tau)$ is the *gain constant* of the integrator. The gain constant provides *time scaling* by means of an adjustable input gain. The gain constant equals *the reciprocal of the time constant τ* and has units of s^{-1}. The concept of integrator gain (K) has been used since the early simulation days to specify the reciprocal time constant of an integrator. Also, e_{ic} is the initial condition value (Figures 1.5.1 and 1.5.2). In analog computation, the output e_0 is scaled for amplitude and time so that the result

$$e_0(t) \;=\; \frac{1}{\tau} \int_{t_0}^{t} e_i(t)\,dt \;+\; e_{ic} \tag{1}$$

does not exceed the physical limitations of the hardware. Although TUTSIM does not require the tedious and time-consuming amplitude and time scaling demanded by the analog computer, there are circumstances where scaling is useful. Requirements for specific time constants within a problem and the simulation of real-life devices and their limitations are cases in point. These concepts are discussed here in terms of the τ-integrator of Figure 1.5.3 (see also Ricci, 1972). We close this paragraph with a comment on the integral notation as it appears in this book. It was originated by the author's brother, Dimitrios, an outstanding mathematician. He pointed out the Byzantine detail of the author's using the same symbol, t, to denote both the variable and the limits of the integration. We hope, however, that the readers will not mind this intentional (and very common) abuse of notation.

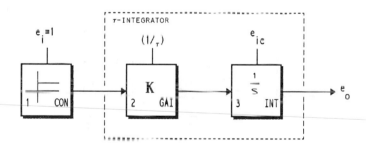

Figure 1.5.3   A tau-integrator simulator.

It is important to note the effect of τ, *where $K = (1/\tau)$ times the input results in τ times the output.* We also notice that if $\tau = 1$, then $K = 1$, resulting in a unity (45°) integration slope. Readers should investigate show the time responses of the τ-integrator for a unit input supplied by the CON block of Figure 1.5.3 and different K and e_{ic} values.

Normally, initial conditions to TUTSIM integrators are specified as parameters. In fact, this is a nice feature absent from analog computers, not a limitation. Hardwiring initial conditions (or just conditions) to an integrator is also possible in TUTSIM programming for all six integrators. As per Equation (1), we can implement the integrator-summer combination of Figure 1.5.4 where

$$e_0 = \int_{t_0}^{t} e_i \, dt + \left(e_{ic_1} + e_{ic_2} \right) \tag{2}$$

It follows that in TUTSIM, initial conditions to an integrator can be introduced either as a *parameter entry*, through an additional *wire path* or *both*.

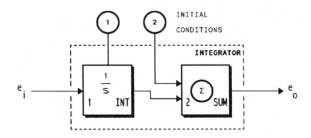

Figure 1.5.4   Integrator with wired initial conditions.

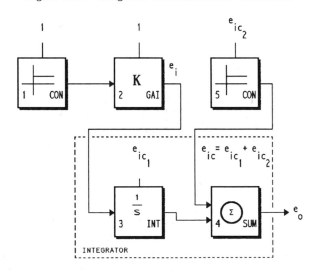

Figure 1.5.5   Experimental integrator accepting both parametric and wired conditions.

The ability to 'wire up' integrator conditions opens wide horizons for the TUTSIM user. Of course, when we speak of 'initial conditions' we refer to a setup existing at the onset of a problem's solution run ($t = 0$). However, initial condition signals are often contingent upon the occurrence of some other even which may or may not happen. Then a parameter-type initial condition entry is not useful and a wired setup is desirable. The experimental integrator of Figure 1.5.5 is useful in testing the concepts presented in this section. Further, basic applications are discussed in the next two sections.

1.6   TUTSIM AS A VERIFICATION TOOL FOR TIME AND AMPLITUDE SCALING IN ANALOG/HYBRID CIRCUIT DESIGN

Time and amplitude scaling is a necessary and important step in preparing a problem for solution with analog and hybrid computers. TUTSIM requires neither time nor amplitude scaling of problem equations, a significant advantage over hardware simulation methods. However, TUTSIM is useful in verifying the proper amplitude or time scaling of machine equations used in circuit design or any other hardware implementation of a mathematical concept.

Time scaling implies that an integrator integrates with respect to some *machine time* T_m rather than *problem time* t, so that if

$$e_i(t) \;=\; \frac{dx}{dt} \tag{1}$$

then

$$e_0(t) \;=\; xT_m \tag{2}$$

Then, a constant b may be designated so that

$$b \;=\; \frac{T_m}{t} \;\rightarrow\; t \;=\; \frac{T_m}{b} \tag{3}$$

and therefore

$$\frac{dx}{dt} \;=\; \frac{dx}{d\left(\dfrac{T_m}{b}\right)} \;\rightarrow\; \left(\frac{1}{b}\right)\frac{dx}{dt} \;=\; \frac{dx}{dT_m} \tag{4}$$

The concept is actually an application of the τ-integrator. Here, the time constant is b, where $(1/b)$ times the input results in b times the output. If $b = 1$, then $(1/b) = 1$, $T_m = t$ and the slope of the integration is unity. If $b < 1$, say $b = 0.25$, it is $(1/b) = 4$ and $T_m = 0.25t$ as per Equation (3). If $b > 1$, say if $b = 2$, it is $(1/b) = 0.5$ and $T_m = 2t$.

The idealized operational integrator provides a basic scaling example of hardware. It is

$$e_0 = -\frac{1}{\tau} \int_{t_0}^{T_m} d T_m + V_c \tag{5}$$

where $V_c = e_{ic}$, the initial condition voltage supplied by the charged capacitor and $\tau = RC$. The minus sign is due to the inverting operational amplifier. From Equation (3) it is

$$T_m = bt \tag{6}$$

so that

$$e_0 = -\frac{1}{\tau} \int_{t_0}^{bt} e_i d(bt) + V_c \tag{7}$$

or

$$e_0 = \frac{b}{\tau} \int_{t_0}^{bt} e_i dt + V_c \tag{8}$$

It is clear that one unit of problem time (say 1 s) corresponds to b units (s) of machine time. Therefore, problem time is changed by changing the gain from $K = (1/\tau)$ to $K/b = b/\tau$. The three integrators of Figure 1.6.1 have the respective settings of $\tau = 1, 0.1$ and 10 or $K = 1$, 10 and 0.1. Readers should plot their outputs $e_0(1)$, $e_0(2)$ and $e_0(3)$ (use 0-10 on both scales) and visualize the effect of initial conditions by first letting $e_{ic}(1) = e_{ic}(2) = e_{ic}(3) = 0$ and then $e_{ic}(1) = e_{ic}(2) = e_{ic}(3) = 5$.

The traces $e_0(2)$ and $e_0(3)$ of Figure 1.6.1 can be interpreted either as *amplitude scaling for the same time scale* or as *time scaling for the same amplitude*. This becomes apparent by choosing an $H = 0, 0, 100$ ($\Delta t = 0.01, 100$) for trace $e_0(3)$ (SCALE.sim) and then by setting an $H = 0, 0, 1$ ($\Delta t = 0.01, 1$) for trace $e_0(2)$. There are many approaches to amplitude and time scaling of simulation problems. Once necessary in implementing analog simulations, scaling techniques are still useful in circuit design.

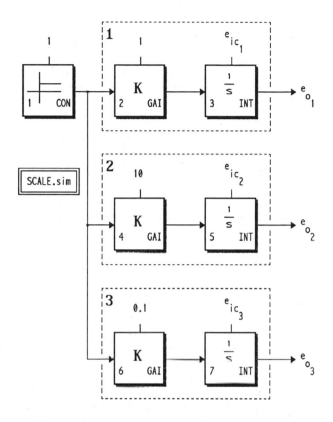

Figure 1.6.1   Amplitude and time scaling demonstrator.

1.7   REPETITIVE OPERATION (REPOP) COMPUTING

Repetitive operation or REPOP is a feature of hybrid computers, where the computer is automatically switched between the RESET (or initial condition) mode and the COMPUTE mode. Repetitive operation enables the user to obtain multiple solutions to a problem while varying some dependent variable. Although many users are unaware of this useful feature, block diagram languages are well suited for implementing REPOP solution schemes. It goes without saying that this type of computing is regarded by many as a thing of the past. George Hannauer's classic *Basics of Parallel Hybrid Computers* (1968) and other books of its kind are of interest here. Unfortunately, most are long out of print and exist as second-hand bookstore materials at best.

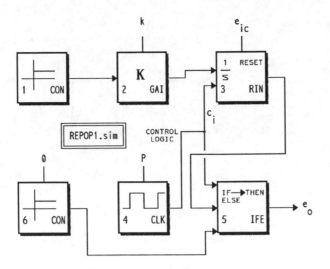

Figure 1.7.1 Basic REPOP setup.

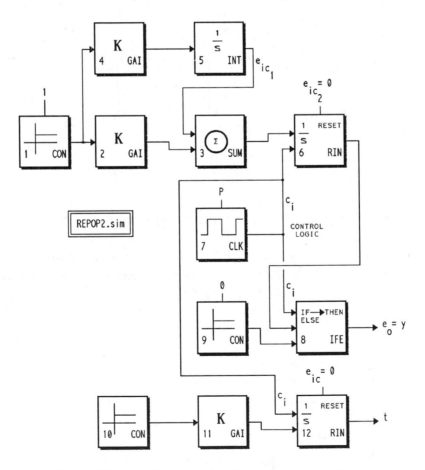

Figure 1.7.2 Repetitive operation with continuously varying e_{ic}.

The following simple examples are used to illustrate the concept, and the reader is prompted to experiment and invent. Operating in the REPOP mode demands a reference clock signal. The first example of Figure 1.7.1 (REPOP1.sim) is a basic one, where control logic governs the operational cycle of a resetting integrator (RIN) and a logic-controlled relay, the IFE block. The reader should investigate the relationship between system timing (system here refers to the particular block setup) and solution output by running this simulation.

The second example of Figure 1.7.2 (REPOP2.sim) demonstrates a resetting integrator (RIN) having an output that depends on a problem variable, an initial condition signal that increases linearly with time (the output of INT #5 block). A delta time of 0.01 and a total simulation time of 100 were chosen, with a clock period of 10. The resulting ten iterations demonstrate the effect of a linearly increasing dependent variable, e_{ic}, on the RIN output. The group of repetitive solutions are shown in Figure 1.7.3 as they occur in time (TUTSIM's zero block). In order to compare these solutions, it is best that a time datum exists, being a common starting point for all repetitive runs. This is easily achieved by generating a time sweep as shown in Figure 1.7.2, where another RIN block is used as a resetting time generator. The control logic of CLK (block #7) governs the operating cycle of RIN (#6), IFE (#8) and RIN (#12), as shown in Figure 1.7.4.

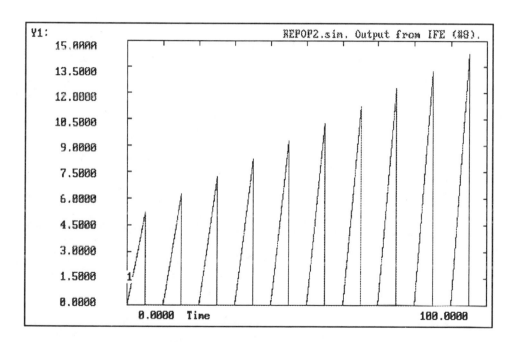

Figure 1.7.3 Results of REPOP2.sim with e_0 from the IFE block.

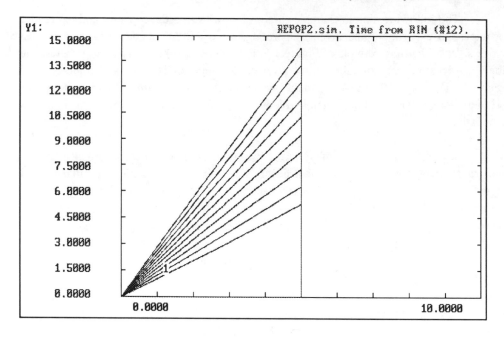

Figure 1.7.4 Results of REPOP2.sim with block #12 as the time generator.

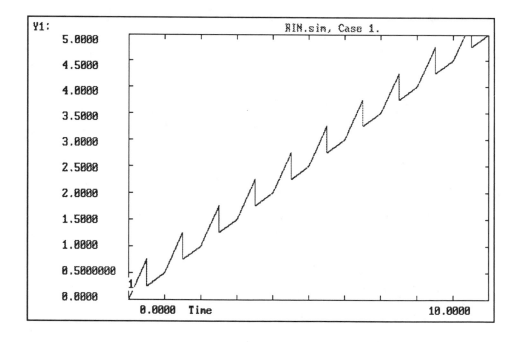

Figure 1.7.5   Results of RIN.sim.

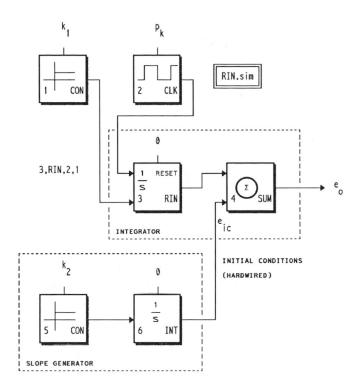

Figure 1.7.6 REPOP setup with wired e_{ic}.

The REPOP principles of operation discussed here may be extended to complex problems where more than one dependent variable must be varied. It is not a substitute for TUTSIM's multirun (MR) function, because this convenient feature can be used without structuring a block diagram for REPOP operation. Often simulating a hybrid computer is a functional step backwards, especially if repetitive operation can be achieved by using the features of a specific language. As a case in point, consider the use of the MR command on a CON block that controls signal path gains via multiplier blocks

If necessary, the initial conditions of the RIN block can be introduced via a signal path rather than by parameter entry. The results of Figure 1.7.5 are generated by letting the CON (block #5) = 0.5, CON (block #1) = 1 and CLK = 1 in the REPOP setup of Figure 1.7.6 (RIN.sim). Here blocks #3 and 4 form a resetting generator with hardwired initial conditions (see also Section 1.5) supplied by a slope generator formed by blocks #5 and #6.

1.8   INTEGRATION WITH RESPECT TO A DEPENDENT VARIABLE (GENERALIZED INTEGRATION)

The mathematical relationship

$$\int_{t_1}^{t_2} \left(x\, \frac{dx}{dt} \right) dt \; = \; \int_{y_1}^{y_2} x\, dy \tag{1}$$

implies that an integrator block may perform integration with respect to some dependent variable y other than time, if its input is multiplied by the derivative of y as shown in Figure 1.8.1 (GI.sim). Known as generalized integration, it is a process that opens many new avenues to signal processing and simulation. The electronic generalized integrator is the modern counterpart of the very old mechanical Kelvin disc integrator (Bekey, 1959). Paul and Gatland (1967), Ahmad (1976) and Bekey (1959) describe several types of generalized integrator devices.

Amazingly enough, the mechanical differential analyzer of Lord Kelvin (Sir William Thomson, 1824-1907) referenced in the *Proceedings of the Royal Society* (Thomson, 1876a and 1876b) could perform an integration with respect to a dependent variable (see also Bush, 1931). Its descendent, the ball-and-disc integrator (Martinez, 1957; Doebelin, 1990), was used extensively during World War II in mechanical computing while flight simulator manufacturers used the device in the sixties. When electronic differential analyzers displaced mechanical computing units, one could no longer integrate a variable with respect to any other, thus limiting analog computation to a certain class of time-varying problems. This, of course, influenced the problem solving methodology. Many early (and valuable) simulation techniques were lost in time. The moral of the story is that old technical literature can still

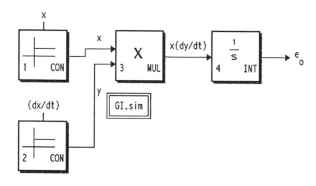

Figure 1.8.1   The generalized integrator.

be useful. Generating analytic functions of dependent variables is best done with generalized integrators. Examples appear in the works by Amble (1956), Paul and Gatland (1967) and Paul and Ahmad (1970a, 1970b, and 1970c) among others.

The following examples show a few representative applications of the generalized integrator. First, the exponential function

$$y = A e^x \tag{2}$$

is considered, where

$$\frac{dy}{dx} = A \exp(x) = y \tag{3}$$

and therefore

$$y = \int_{x_1}^{x_2} y \, dx \tag{4}$$

In the above equation, the initial condition for y is

$$e_{ic}(y) = A \tag{5}$$

The TUTSIM simulation (EXPG1.sim) is shown in Figure 1.8.2. An alternative implementation of the exponential function 2 with the EXP block is shown in Figure 1.8.3 (EXPO.sim). Readers should plot the results and compare the two methods by superimposing the solution curves (there is no difference in the performance of the two simulators).

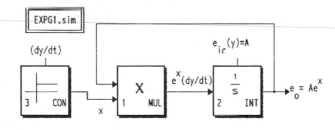

Figure 1.8.2   Exponential function generation with a generalized integrator.

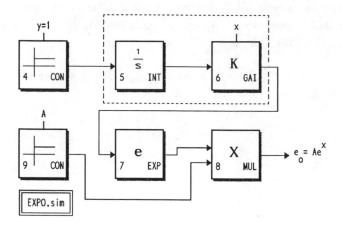

Figure 1.8.3   Alternate implementation of the exponential function.

The second example demonstrates the generation of the sin x and cos x functions, where x is a function of time according to the equation

$$\frac{d^2y}{dx^2} + y = 0 \tag{6}$$

with initial conditions y = A and [dy/dx] = 0 at x = 0. The solution to Equation (6) is

$$y = A \sin x \tag{7}$$

$$\frac{dy}{dx} = A \cos x \tag{8}$$

The TUTSIM blocks SIN and COS are also included in the implementation of Figure 1.8.4 (SING.sim) for validation and comparison purposes. The traces overlap as one.

The function

$$y = \tan x \tag{9}$$

is simulated by the block diagram of Figure 1.8.5 (TANG.sim). In this case, since

$$\frac{dy}{dx} = \sec^2 x = 1 + \tan^2 x \tag{10}$$

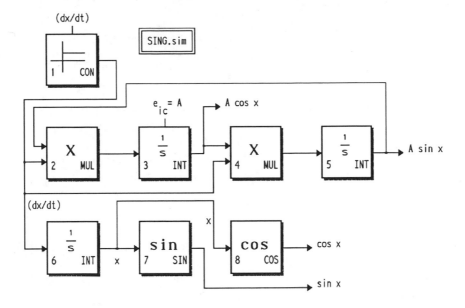

Figure 1.8.4   Sine and cosine generation with generalized integrators.

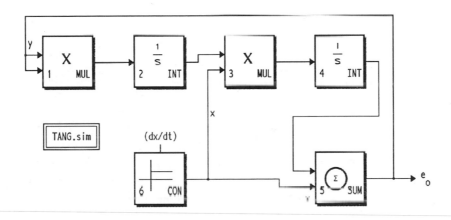

Figure 1.8.5   Generation of the function tan x with generatlized integrators.

We set tan x = y and rewrite

$$\frac{dy}{dx} = 1 + y^2 \qquad (11)$$

Integration of Equation (11) yields

$$y = x + \int y^2 \, dx \tag{12}$$

or, for simulation purposes

$$y = x + \int \left(2 \int y \, dy\right) dx \tag{13}$$

The mechanization of Equation (13) implies a positive feedback loop (Figure 1.8.5) that exhibits sensitivity to large values of x.

In the case of the function

$$y = \log x \tag{14}$$

it is

$$dx = x \, dy \tag{15}$$

or

$$x = \int x \, dy \tag{16}$$

or

$$y = x + y - \int y \, dy \tag{17}$$

or

$$y = x + e_0 = x + \int (1 - x) \, dy \tag{18}$$

where e_0 is the output of the generalized integrator so that

$$e_0 \; = \; \int \; y \, d \, (1 \, - \, x) \tag{19}$$

The TUTSIM simulator (LOGG.sim) is shown in Figure 1.8.6.

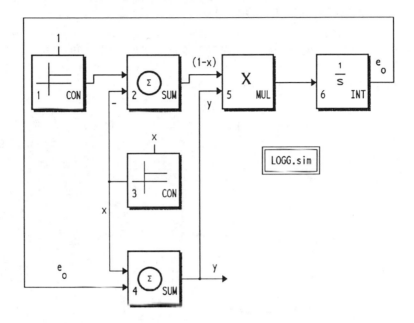

Figure 1.8.6   Generation of the log x function with a generalized integrator.

2 BLOCK DIAGRAMS AND TRANSFER FUNCTIONS: A REVIEW

2.1 INTRODUCTION: BLOCKS, TRANSFER FUNCTIONS AND BLOCK DIAGRAMS

A block like that of Figure 2.1.1 has three properties; it has an *input* (e_i), an *output* (e_0) and a *transfer function* (TF). The transfer function describes what the block does by relating input and output according to the equation

$$TF = A \frac{e_0}{e_i} \qquad (1)$$

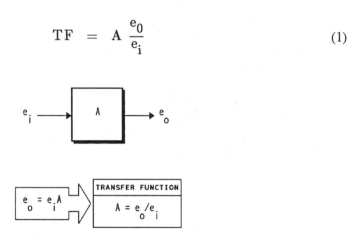

Figure 2.1.1 Expressing the transfer function of a block.

If the block is seen as a system element or as a component, its transfer function is the ratio of output to input of that element or component. *The transfer function serves to define a block's operation.* In more formal terms, the block of Figure 2.1.1 is a two-port system having a single input (excitation) and a single output (response). A single block may reflect a simple mathematical operation, some nonlinear characteristic or a complex system.

Most physical systems can be represented by a *block diagram*, a group of properly interconnected blocks. Each interconnected block represents and describes a portion of the system. Therefore the entire structure has the character and response of the system being represented. In dynamic simulation, the block diagram is a most significant primary tool. Block diagrams may emerge through inspection and intuition, mathematical equations,

28

transfer functions or any combination of the above. Their manipulation adheres to a mathematical system of rules often known as block diagram algebra. Albeit most systems books devote a few pages to this significant topic, *block diagram algebra is clearly a branch of mathematics*. We believe it merits more attention than is currently given. What follows is a review of an important and deceptively simple topic. It is intended to provide the reader with the basics required to read this book, a set of quick and practical instructions. The deviations from the canonical form found in most control system texts is intentional.

2.2   OPEN- AND CLOSED-LOOP SYSTEMS

The single block system of Figure 2.1.1 is an open-loop system, i.e, one without feedback. The closed-loop system of Figure 2.2.1 involves an element B situated in the feedback loop. Block A is situated in the forward loop. The system equations are

$$e_0 = e\,A \tag{1}$$

$$e = e_i - e_0\,B \tag{2}$$

where e is defined as the system error. Substitution yields

$$e_0\left(1 + A\,B\right) = e_i\,A \;\rightarrow\; \frac{e_0}{e_i} = \frac{A}{1 + A\,B} \tag{3}$$

which is the transfer function of the system. We can therefore portray the closed-loop system as an open-loop one having a single block representing the transfer function of the original system (Figure 2.2.1). This approach may be used to shrink large block diagrams. As an example, consider $A = 1/s$ and $B = k$ where $s = d/dt$ and k denotes a constant. Then transfer function (3) becomes $e_0/e_i = 1/(s + k)$. Also, if $A = k$ and $B = 1/s$, it is $e_0/e_i = ks/(s + k)$. If $A = B = 1/s$, the transfer function takes the form $e_0/e_i = s/(s^2 + 1)$.

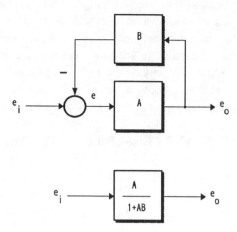

Figure 2.2.1   An elementary closed-loop system.

2.3   THE RULES OF BLOCK DIAGRAM ALGEBRA

2.3.1 About Summing Junctions

A summing junction or summing point is often denoted by the circle symbol of Figure 2.3.1.1. Its equivalency to the mathematical summer is self-explanatory. The following rules are important here:

- Cascaded (serially connected) summing junctions may be combined as shown in the progression of Figure 2.3.1.2.

- Summing junctions may be moved ahead or behind blocks (Figure 2.3.1.3).

The second rule can be applied in many different ways, as shown in Figures 2.3.1.4, 2.3.1.5 and 2.3.1.6.

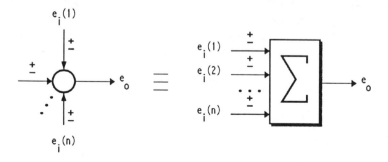

Figure 2.3.1.1   Defining the summing junction.

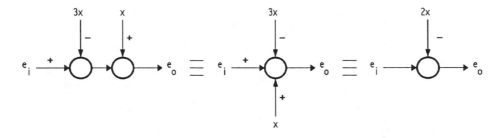

Figure 2.3.1.2   Combining summing junctions.

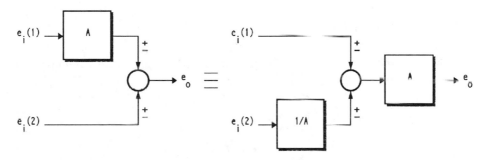

Figure 2.3.1.3   Moving a summing junction.

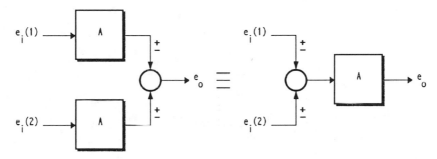

Figure 2.3.1.4   Working with summing junctions—— (a).

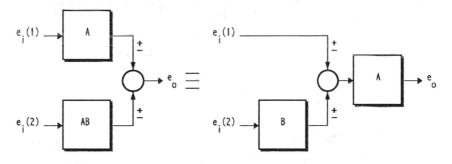

Figure 2.3.1.5   Working with summing junctions——(b).

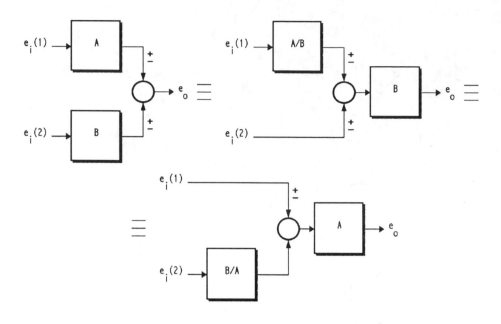

Figure 2.3.1.6   Working with summing junctions——(c).

2.3.2 The Pickoff or Tie Point

The first thing to know here is that pickoff points are NOT summing points. However their use follows the same rules as summing junctions, as shown in Figures 2.3.2.1 and 2.3.2.2. In Figure 2.3.2.1 it is $e_0 = e_i A$ for all outputs. Also, it is $e_0 = A e_i$ or $e_i = (1/A) e_0$ for the right side of Figure 2.3.2.2.

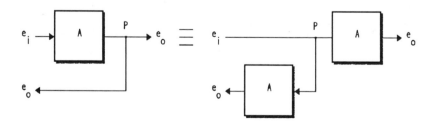

Figure 2.3.2.1   Moving a pickoff point——(a).

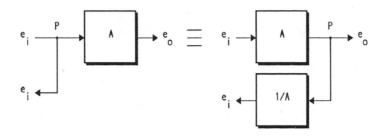

Figure 2.3.2.2   Moving a pickoff point——(b).

2.3.3 Cascaded (Series) and Parallel Blocks

The block diagram of Figure 2.3.3.1 consists of n number of cascaded blocks. The transfer function of the system is

$$\frac{e_0}{e_i} = A_1 A_2 \ \cdots \ A_n \tag{1}$$

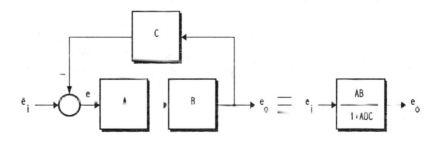

Figure 2.3.3.1   Cascaded blocks.

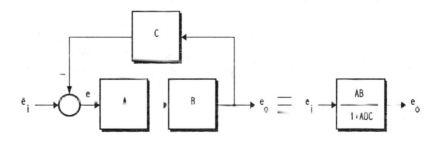

Figure 2.3.3.2   Cascaded blocks in a closed-loop system.

The closed-loop system of Figure 2.3.3.2 has two cascaded blocks, A and B, in the forward path. We apply the rules of Section 2.2 (Figure 2.2.1) and that of Equation (1) (Figure 2.3.3.1) and conclude that the overall transfer function of the system is

$$\frac{e_0}{e_i} = \frac{A\,B}{1 + A\,B\,C} \tag{2}$$

In the case of the parallel blocks of Figure 2.3.3.3, it is

$$\frac{e_0}{e_i} = A_1 \pm A_2 \pm \dots \pm A_n \tag{3}$$

Parallel branches should *not* be construed as feedback loops.

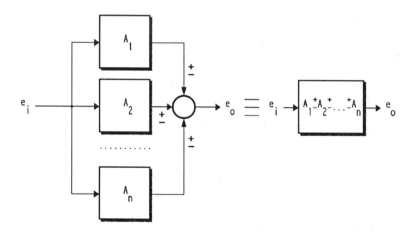

Figure 2.3.3.3   Parallel blocks.

2.3.4 More on Closed-Loop Systems

A very important property of any line path is that a unity gain block may be assumed to exist in that path, as shown in Figure 2.3.4.1. Let us then take a look at the closed-loop systems of Figures 2.3.4.2 and 2.3.4.3. In the first case, we assume a unity-gain block in the forward path, so that we write (see Section 2.2)

$$e = e_i - e_o B \tag{1}$$

$$e_0 = e \tag{2}$$

From the above system we conclude that

$$\frac{e_0}{e_i} = \frac{1}{1 + B} \tag{3}$$

$e_i \longrightarrow e_o \; \equiv \; e_i \longrightarrow \boxed{1} \longrightarrow e_o$

Figure 2.3.4.1   The implied unity block.

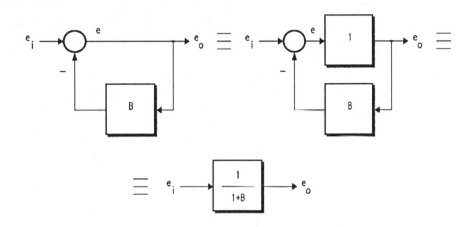

Figure 2.3.4.2   A forward path with a unity block.

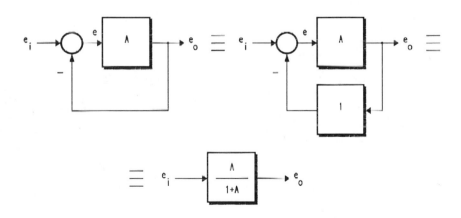

Figure 2.3.4.3   A feedback path with a unity block.

The cardinal point here is the assumption of the unity-gain block (Figure 2.3.4.2) without which the problem could *not* be solved. The block diagram of Figure 2.3.4.3 presents a similar case. In this unity feedback system there exists a unity-gain block in the feedback path, which is often omitted for simplicity but which is *always implied*.

2.3.5 Generalized Examples

Often beginning efforts to formulate a block diagram result in awkward representations. Then the block structure must be reconfigured and drawn to a new format. This format is chosen to make more sense; it is more synoptic or offers more insight into the dynamic architecture of a system.

The generalized closed-loop system of Figure 2.3.5.1 represents the essential form of most linear control systems. Figure 2.3.5.2 shows a system with two feedback terms B and C and their respective inner and outer feedback loops. The cascaded summing junctions can be eliminated as shown. The third diagram is a better logical choice, since the feedback terms are consolidated in the feedback path where they belong. It goes without saying that alternate representations of the same model portray different philosophies. They even dictate different procedures in creating model structures and hardware implementations. Block manipulation skills are important to anyone dealing with dynamic system modelling and simulation.

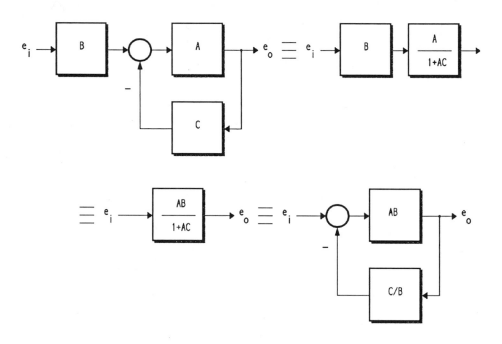

Figure 2.3.5.1   A generalized closed-loop system.

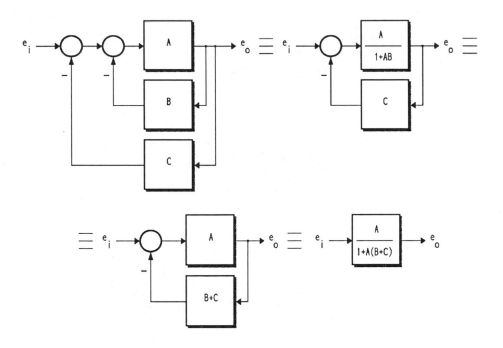

Figure 2.3.5.2   System with two feedback loops.

2.3.6 Feedforward and Combined Systems

The block diagram of Figure 2.3.6.1 is a simple feedforward system where A is parallel with unity. Its transfer function is

$$\frac{e_0}{e_i} = 1 + A \tag{1}$$

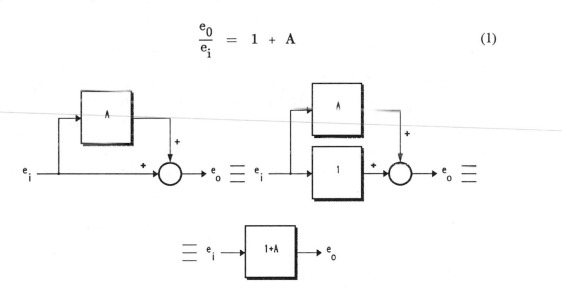

Figure 2.3.6.1   An elementary feedforward system.

The system of Figure 2.3.6.2 consists of a feedforward system in series with a feedback system. Note that in the case where $A = 1/B$, this system constitutes a *zero error system* because $e_0/e_i = 1$. The case of Figures 2.3.6.3 and 2.3.6.4 show examples of combined systems. Most people have trouble solving the latter.

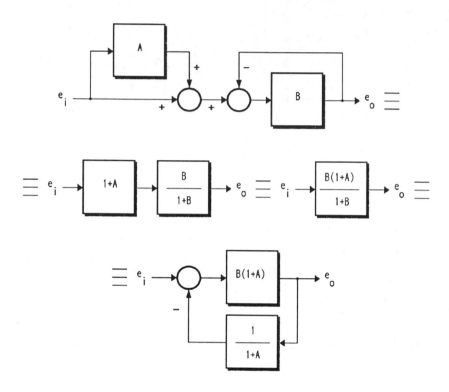

Figure 2.3.6.2   A series feedforward-feedback combination.

We cannot overemphasize that there are many ways and individual styles by which one can approach a block diagram problem. The example of Figure 2.3.6.3 involves the incorporation of the two summing junctions into one (see Figure 2.3.1.2). Then, we recognize that the left side of the diagram includes two parallel blocks, block A and an implied unity gain block (see Figure 2.3.4.1). The right side includes a negative feedback arrangement with block B in the forward path and an implied unity gain block in the feedback.

The example of Figure 2.3.6.4 is not workable until we move block B outside the inner forward path, thus allowing the creation of a single summing junction. The block moving operation for a feedback loop is outlined in reverse in Figure 2.3.5.1. However, the block diagram of Figure 2.3.6.4 presents a complex situation, because block B is not only part of the left side parallel structure, but also affects the negative feedback loop of the right side. The first manipulation is the most difficult and the rest follow the generalized pattern of Figure 2.3.6.3.

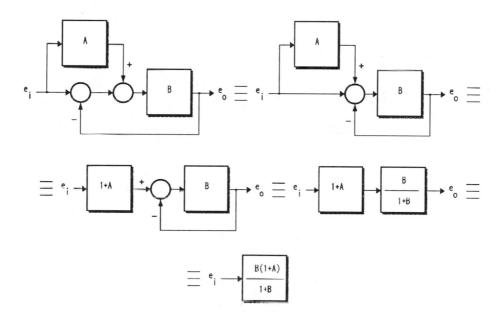

Figure 2.3.6.3   A combined system example.

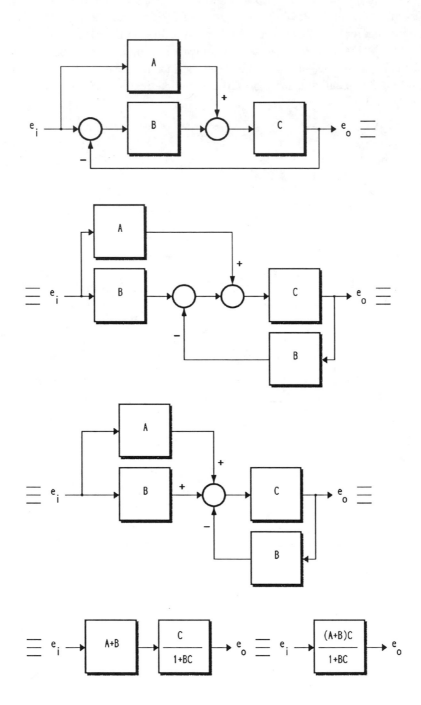

Figure 2.3.6.4   A more complicated combined system.

THE SIMULATION OF
WAVEFORMS AND FUNCTIONS

3.1   INTRODUCTION

Linear and nonlinear oscillator systems are fundamental to nature and consequently are found in every scientific and engineering discipline. Many great books and interesting articles exist on anything from biological oscillators to mechanical vibration. Once we take the signal processing point of view, where an oscillator is expressly designed to output useful waveforms and specialized signals, the subject becomes vast.

The oscillator topic is separated into two parts. Section 3 deals with signals, while the Section 4 examines pendulum devices. The purpose of these collections is two-fold: first to demonstrate the creation of block diagram simulators from existing theory, and second to show typical CDSS language implementations and their outcomes. Readers should bear in mind that in spite of its somewhat elaborate and didactic approach, this book is not a physics text.

3.2   THE HARMONIC OSCILLATOR

A harmonic oscillator, also called a quadrature, sine-cosine or sinusoidal generator, is a two-phase sinusoidal waveform generator of the basic form shown in Figure 3.2.1. It has many applications in circuit design and is a principal building block in analog computation and simulation. Understanding its operation provides insight about oscillatory systems and a viable approach to the introduction of active filter mechanisms.

Figure 3.2.1 shows the electronic analog of a friction-free pendulum, i.e., the block diagram realization of the second-order differential equation

$$\frac{d^2x}{dt^2} + x = 0 \tag{1}$$

Figure 3.2.2 shows the mechanization of the equation

$$\frac{d^2x}{dt^2} + \omega^2 x = 0 \tag{2}$$

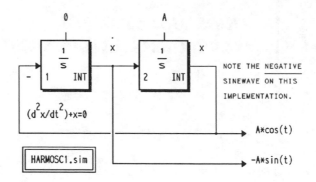

Figure 3.2.1   The basic harmonic oscillator form (ω = 1).

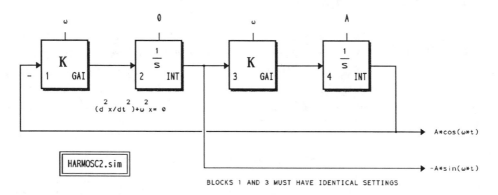

Figure 3.2.2   Harmonic oscillator simulator accepting ω parameters.

that has the solution

$$x(t) \;=\; A \cos \omega t \;+\; B \sin \omega t \qquad\qquad (3)$$

where A and B are arbitrary constants and $\omega = 2\pi f$. In the block diagram of Figure 3.2.2, the two gain blocks are virtual potentiometers. As such they control the frequency of the output waveforms and must have *identical* settings where for all practical purposes $1 > \omega > 0$. Once ω exceeds unity, they act as virtual amplifiers.

The useful operating modes of the circuit are governed by the initial conditions e_{ic} or e_0 applied to the integrators. These are startup signals. The integrator with the applied (nonzero) initial condition outputs the cosine waveform. The explanation for this comes from trigonometry, as only the cosine has nonzero initial conditions. Regardless of the output frequency, the amplitude of each block will remain at the e_{ic} level.

The signals within the harmonic oscillator loop are understood by considering the following trigonometric properties:

$$\int \omega \sin(\omega t)\, dt \;=\; \int \sin(\omega t)\, d(\omega t) \;=\; -\cos(\omega t) \tag{4}$$

$$\int \omega \cos(\omega t)\, dt \;=\; \int \cos(\omega t)\, d(\omega t) \;=\; \sin(\omega t) \tag{5}$$

where the constant ω is introduced to facilitate the integration.

The oscillator can also by synthesized by means of the successive differentiation technique, a powerful analytical tool in analog simulation. It entails the differentiation of an original function until there is a direct correspondence between function and derivative, (i.e., a governing differential equation). We begin by considering the sinusoidal function

$$y \;=\; \sin(\omega t) \tag{6}$$

and its first derivative

$$\frac{dy}{dt} \;=\; \omega_0 \cos(\omega t) \tag{7}$$

or

$$\cos(\omega t) \;=\; \frac{1}{\omega_0}\, \frac{dy}{dt} \tag{8}$$

The second derivation of Equation (6) is

$$\frac{d^2 y}{dt^2} \;=\; -\,\omega_0^2 \sin(\omega t) \tag{9}$$

or

$$\sin(\omega t) \;=\; -\,\frac{1}{\omega_0^2}\, \frac{d^2 y}{dt^2} \tag{10}$$

We recall that

$$\frac{d}{dt} \sin (\omega t) = \omega \cos (\omega t) \tag{11}$$

$$\frac{d}{dt} \cos (\omega t) = - \omega \sin (\omega t) \tag{12}$$

Plotting the outputs of blocks #2 and #4 of Figure 3.2.2 shows that the simulator outputs a *negative* cosine. A multi-trace phase portrait can be created with TUTSIM's MR (multi-run) command. This useful TUTSIM feature allows the observation of a system's response to a controlled stepwise change of some parameter.

The performance of real (as opposed to idealized) harmonic oscillator circuits is subject to physical constraints. In most operational amplifier circuits, external error compensation is the only realistic way of dealing with component imperfection. Good compensation techniques allow the usage of inexpensive components. These techniques are based on the creating and using of subordinate feedback loops, each contributing to the explicit regulation of a system variable and maybe the implicit regulation of others. In that regard, the harmonic oscillator is a fascinating platform for learning and experimenting with feedback. Real systems are still governed by Equation (2), although their nonideal solutions incorporate the error term, e^{-at}, so that

$$x(t) = k e^{-at} \cos \omega_0 t + k e^{-at} \sin \omega_0 t \tag{13}$$

where

$$a = \varsigma \omega_0 \tag{14}$$

$$\omega^2 = \omega_0^2 (1 - \varsigma^2) \tag{15}$$

$$\omega^2 \approx \omega_0^2 \tag{16}$$

Equation (13) reflects a realistic picture of the system and the contributions of the real operational amplifier with its nonideal open-loop amplitude characteristics (Karayanakis and Jones, 1987). Assuming that C_0 and R_0 are the respective capacitive and resistive feedback elements and ϕ_0 is the phase of the system's open-loop transfer function $x(j\omega)$ at ω_0, the value of a can be approximated by the equation

$$a \approx \frac{1}{C_0 R_0} + \omega_0 \phi_0 \tag{17}$$

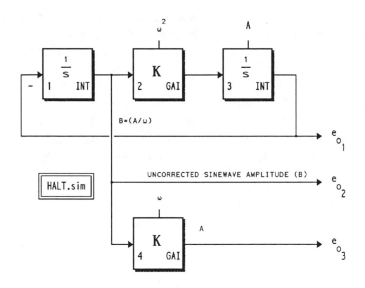

Figure 3.2.3   Alternate harmonic oscillator simulation.

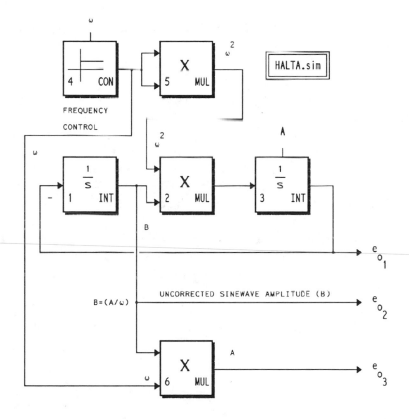

Figure 3.2.4   An automatic correction mechanism for the the HALT.sim setup.

and depends on ω_0 and on the components associated with the time constant of the system. *The amplitude of the oscillation varies with time and is a function of a.* Given small ω_0 values, a is positive and the oscillation amplitude decreases. In the case of large ω_0 values, a is negative and the amplitude increases. Ideally, the harmonic oscillator is a marginally stable system, having its poles situated on the $j\omega$-axis of the complex plane. However, nonideal operational amplifier characteristics and unaccountable phase shifts imply that the poles are permanently situated on the imaginary axis <u>only in theory</u>. Equation (13) suggests that the roots are (r+ = a ± j $\sqrt{\omega^2}$ or r- = - a ± j $\sqrt{\omega^2}$), that is, the poles may drift on either half of the s-plane (Chatterjee and Chatterjee, 1967; Phaor et al., 1974; Rust, 1973; Saraswat and Saha, 1982; Wong, 1978).

Finally, Equation (2) suggests the alternate simulation of Figure 3.2.3. In order to have the same constants for both outputs, a GAI block is used to restore the sine amplitude. This is necessary because in this case it is

$$B = \frac{A}{\omega} \tag{18}$$

An automatic correction mechanism is suggested in Figure 3.2.4

3.3   SIGNAL-CONTROLLED FREQUENCY GENERATOR

The conventional harmonic oscillator can be modified to output sine and cosine waveforms having signal-controlled frequency. The two added multipliers (Figure 3.3.1) control the loop gain by multiplying the output of each integrator with a control signal e_c. The operating frequency of the generator is $f_0 = e_c (1/2\pi\tau)$, where $1/\tau = 1/RC$ is the gain constant of the integrators. The output frequency f_0 is directly proportional to control signal magnitude. Figure 3.3.2 shows both sine and cosine outputs for a ramp control signal. The ramp is generated by an integrator (block #7) and its slope depends on the value of the constant (block #8). This signal generator exhibits instability for certain ranges of e_c and $(1/\tau)$ values and should be used in simulations with caution (Kaplan, 1980).

Another frequency generator of interest is described by Filanovsky (1989). It features independent control of frequency and amplitude, as shown in Figure 3.3.3. The frequency control mechanism is similar to the first oscillator, while the amplitude error term is generated by squaring both sine and cosine outputs, summing them, subtracting the amplitude-setting signal and then using the output to control the strength of a secondary feedback loop. The frequency output for a ramp control input is identical to that of VCFG1.sim.

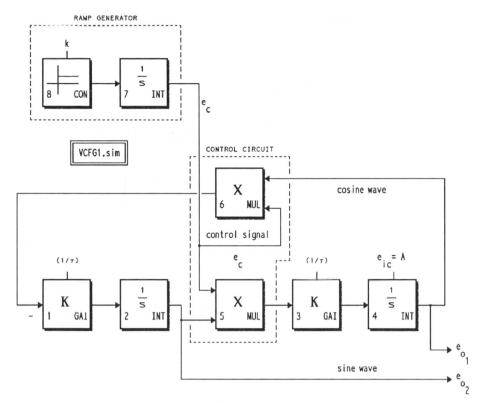

Figure 3.3.1   *A signal-controlled frequency generator.*

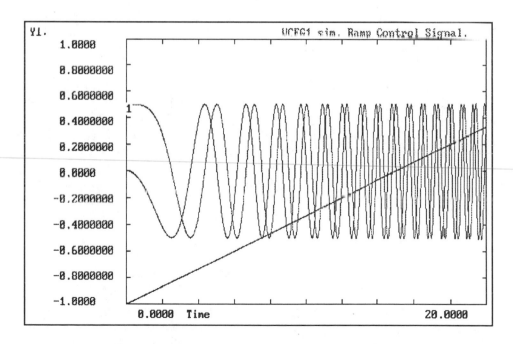

Figure 3.3.2   *VCFG1.sim response to a ramp control input.*

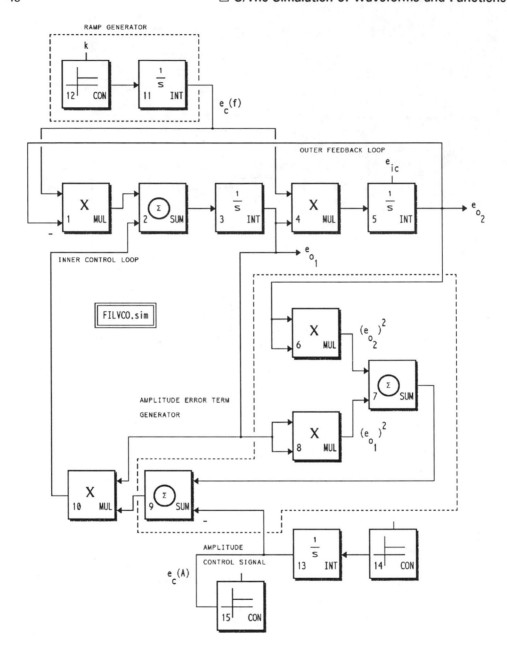

Figure 3.3.3   The Filanovsky frequency generator.

3.4   A TWO-PHASE TRIANGLE OSCILLATOR

A novel use of the SGN (SiGN of inputs) block is made by the oscillator of Figure 3.4.1. This is the TUTSIM implementation of a waveform generator by Pimentel (1978). It outputs two triangular waveforms having a 90° phase difference. Unlike the

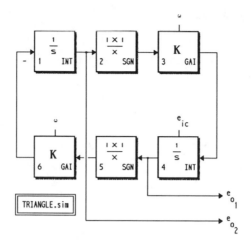

Figure 3.4.1   The Pimentel waveform generator.

harmonic oscillator, this circuit is stable for $\omega > 1$. The block diagram implements the system

$$\frac{dx_1}{dt} = \omega \, \text{sgn} \left(x_2 \right) \tag{1}$$

$$\frac{dx_2}{dt} = - \omega \, \text{sgn} \left(x_1 \right) \tag{2}$$

This is a useful function generator that can be signal controlled by using multipliers in a fashion similar to the VCFGEN1.sim circuit. The plotting of the output waveform and the phase portrait are left for the reader.

3.5   FREQUENCY DOUBLING

The frequency of a sinusoidal signal can be doubled by using a multiplier. Given a common mode signal

$$e_i = e_x = e_y = \sin 2\pi ft \tag{1}$$

the multiplier's output is

$$e_0 = e_x e_y = \left(\sin 2\pi ft \right)^2 \tag{2}$$

From trigonometry, we recall the identities

$$\sin^2 a \ = \ \frac{1}{2} \ (- \cos 2a \ + \ 1) \tag{3}$$

and

$$\cos^2 a \ = \ \frac{1}{2} \ (\cos 2a \ + \ 1) \tag{4}$$

Therefore, it is

$$\left(\sin 2\pi ft\right)^2 \ = \ \frac{1}{2} \ - \ \frac{\cos 2\pi \left(2f\right)t}{2} \tag{5}$$

and

$$\left(\cos 2\pi ft\right)^2 \ = \ \frac{1}{2} \ + \ \frac{\cos 2\pi \left(2f\right)t}{2} \tag{6}$$

We conclude that the circuit's output contains both a dc component and a cosine wave with a frequency of 2f. For a sine input the cosine wave output is negative. This relationship is valid for any input frequency.

As a numerical example, let us assume

$$e_i \ = \ e_y \ = \ e_x \ = \ 10 \sin 2\pi \, 20 t \tag{7}$$

The typical multiplier integrated circuit has the transfer function

$$e_0 \ = \ \frac{e_x e_y}{10} \tag{8}$$

or in this case

$$e_0 \ = \ \frac{e_i^2}{10} \tag{9}$$

By substitution, we get

$$e_0 \ = \ \frac{\left(10 \sin 2\pi \, 20t\right)^2}{10} \tag{10}$$

or

$$e_0 = 10 \left[\frac{1}{2} - \frac{\cos 2\pi 40\, t}{2} \right] \tag{11}$$

or

$$e_0 = 5 - 5 \cos \pi 40\, t \tag{12}$$

Therefore the output consists of both a dc term of 5 volts and a negative cosine wave of 40 Hz with a 5V peak (+10V, 0V). The block diagram of Figure 3.5.1 shows the mechanization of this problem for a cosine input (FDOUBLE.sim). Readers should obtain the results for a sine input also. A time scale of 1 unit = 1 E seconds and a range choice of 0.0 - 6.0 will show all forty cycles. The dc component can be easily removed as shown in Figure 3.5.2.

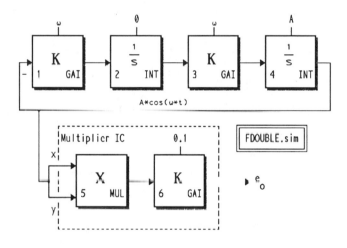

Figure 3.5.1   A multiplier-based frequency doubler.

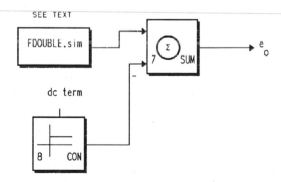

Figure 3.5.2   Removing the dc term from FDOUBLE.sim.

3.6   HARMONICS

Harmonics and signals containing harmonics are often useful in system testing. The frequency doubling circuit described in Section 3.5 can be used with a signal that contains a controlled second-harmonic distortion, where

$$e_0 = A \sin \omega t + kA \cos \omega t = A(\sin \omega + k \cos 2 \omega t) \qquad (1)$$

The ratio of the second harmonic to the fundamental is controlled by a gain block (k), as shown by Williams (1975). Figure 3.6.1 shows an implementation of the concept. We begin with the frequency doubler (see FDOUBLE.sim) and the values used in the previous section. *The dc term is removed* and the signals [A sin (ωt)] and [kA cos (2ωt)] are summed. (THARMON.sim).

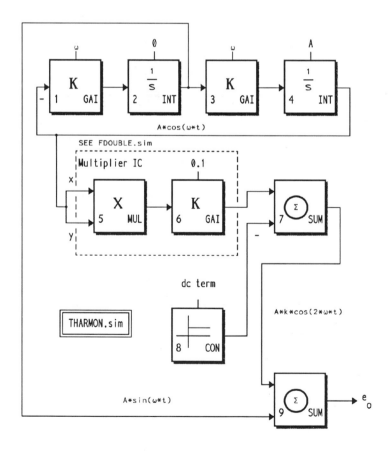

Figure 3.6.1   The harmonics generator THARMON.sim.

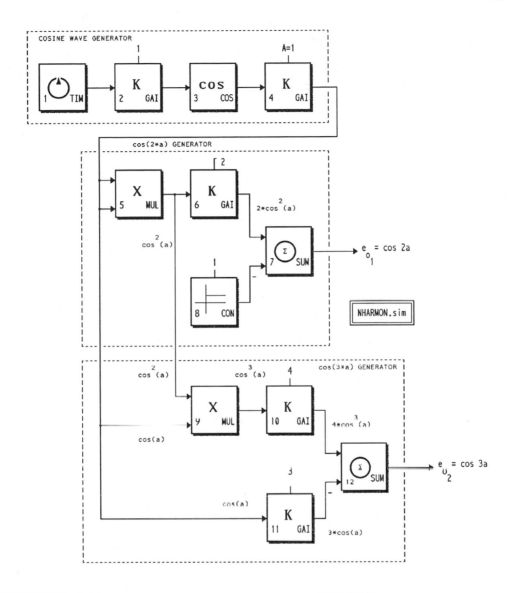

Figure 3.6.2   The harmonics generator NHARMON.sim.

A different approach to harmonic generation begins again with the well known trigonometric equation

$$\cos^2 a \;=\; \frac{1}{2}\left(\cos 2a \,+\, 1\right) \;\rightarrow\; \cos 2a \;=\; 2\cos^2 a \,-\, 1 \qquad (2)$$

It is also

$$\cos 3a \;=\; 4\cos^3 a \,-\, 3\cos a \qquad (3)$$

and so on. The block diagram of Figure 3.6.2 simulates both Equations (1) and (2). The cos 3a output is shown in Figure 3.6.3.

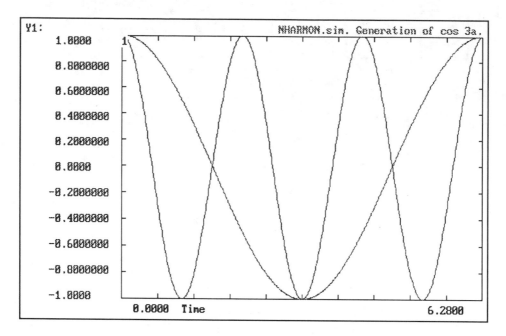

Figure 3.6.3   The cos 3a waveform from NHARMON.sim.

3.7   SIMULATING THE PHENOMENON OF BEATS

The phenomenon of beats is a purely geometrical one, where two wave signals interfere by superposition. There are many versions of the beats, like that of the Wilberforce pendulum (Section 4.4). There are transient beats that occur when a harmonic oscillator is excited with a sinusoidal forcing function. Another version involves the interaction between initial transient and steady-state motion of a harmonic oscillator. Although beats occur in certain coupled dynamic systems where there is transfer of energy back and forth between components, the phenomenon is *not* usually associated with coupling.

Beats occur in systems of similar machines vibrating at near equal frequency as in the case of propeller-driven twin-engine airplanes. Anytime the engines are 'out of synch', propeller-generated sound waves first reinforce and then cancel each other. In music, beats occur when two similar but mistuned instruments are playing tones at slightly different frequencies. Audiophiles refer to this as waxing and waning. In electronics, the principle is used to implement some modulation schemes.

The case of summing two sinusoidal signals of near equal frequency is of interest here. The simulator of Figure 3.7.1 (BEAT.sim) consists of two harmonic oscillators where the frequency controls differ slightly. There is a continuously varying phase relationship between the two signals which, when summed (Figure 3.7.2), combine to form an amplitude-modulated sine wave that first appears strong and then weak. Distinct beat envelopes are formed as the two signals first *enhance* and then *cancel* each other. Given two pure sinusoidal signals

$$x_1(t) = A \cos \omega_1 t \tag{1}$$

$$x_2(t) = B \cos \omega_2 t \tag{2}$$

so that

$$\omega_1 = \omega_0 + \omega \tag{3}$$

$$\omega_2 = \omega_0 - \omega \tag{4}$$

where ω_0 is the *average* frequency and the *difference* frequency is 2ω, the output of the SUM (#9) block is

$$x(t) = A \cos \left[\left(\omega_0 + \omega \right) t + \phi_1 \right] + B \cos \left[\left(\omega_0 - \omega \right) t + \phi_2 \right] \tag{5}$$

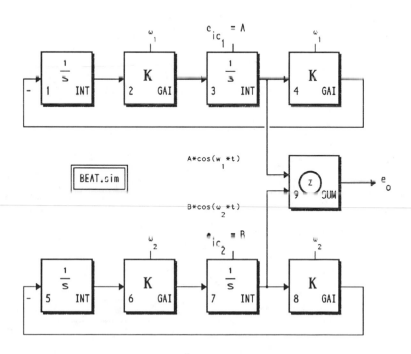

Figure 3.7.1   Simulation of the beats.   Block #9 sums two cosinusoidal signals.

Both amplitudes A and B are established by the initial conditions

$$e_{ic_1} = A \qquad (6)$$

$$e_{ic_2} = B \qquad (7)$$

of integrators #3 and #7, as shown in Figure 3.7.1. The phases of the two signals are ϕ_1 and ϕ_2, respectively. We set

$$e_{ic_1} = e_{ic_2} = C \qquad (8)$$

and write ϕ_1 and ϕ_2 in terms of an average phase ϕ_0 and a differential phase ϕ as follows:

$$\phi_1 = \phi_0 + \phi \qquad (9)$$

$$\phi_2 = \phi_0 - \phi \qquad (10)$$

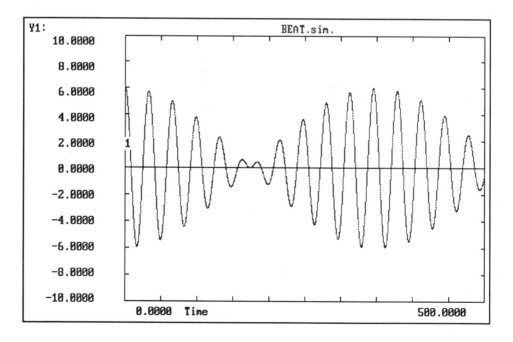

Figure 3.7.2   The amplitude modulated output of BEAT.sim.

from the above, it is

$$\phi_0 = \frac{1}{2}(\phi_1 + \phi_2) \tag{11}$$

$$\phi = \frac{1}{2}(\phi_1 - \phi_2) \tag{12}$$

Then x(t) of Equation (5) can be expressed as a complex phasor:

$$\begin{aligned}
x(t) &= C\mathrm{Re}\left\{ e^{j\left[(\omega_0 + \omega)\,t + \phi_0 + \phi\right]} + e^{j\left[(\omega_0 - \omega)\,t + \phi_0 - \phi\right]} \right\} \\
&= 2\,C\cos\left(\omega_0 t + \phi_0\right)\cos\left(\omega t + \phi\right)
\end{aligned} \tag{13}$$

The equation above describes an *amplitude modulation* process in which a low frequency signal with *modulation* frequency $\omega = \omega_b$ (rad/s) modulates a high frequency signal with *carrier* frequency ω_0 (rad/s). The frequency of modulation is also known as the *beat* frequency ω_b. For further discussion the reader is referred to Abramson (1971), Crawford (1968), Driver (1978) and French (1971).

3.8   THE HARMONICALLY-DRIVEN HARMONIC OSCILLATOR

This oscillator system consists of a driving oscillator and a driven one. The driven oscillator has no initial conditions on the integrators. There are many variations of driven harmonic systems. Here we consider the well-known series LRC circuit equation

$$L\frac{d^2q}{dt^2} + R\frac{dq}{dt} + \frac{q}{C} = E\cos\omega t \tag{1}$$

(the LRC circuit is discussed in detail in Section 8.2.3 and another case of the driver LRC circuit is presented in Section 7.2.3 as an example of the Mathieu equation). E is the amplitude of the driving signal and q is the capacitor charge, representing the problem's solution. It is

$$\omega_0^2 = \frac{1}{LC} \tag{2}$$

and

$$Q = \omega_0\frac{L}{R} \tag{3}$$

Substituting in Equation (1) gives

$$\frac{d^2q}{dt^2} = -\left(\frac{\omega_0}{Q}\right)\frac{dq}{dt} - \omega_0^2 q + \left(\frac{E}{L}\right)\cos \omega t \qquad (4)$$

where ω and ω_0 are the radian frequencies of the driver and the driven oscillator, respectively. This format is used by Wylen and Schwarz (1973) to demonstrate the driven-series LRC circuit on a desktop analog computer. These authors emphasize that simulation reveals the transient response during startup, something that cannot be observed readily in traditional lab sessions. The simulator of Figure 3.8.1 (DHARM.sim) allows us to observe that the higher the Q of the driven circuit, the longer the duration of the transient. We also see that the maximum amplitude during the transient interval is larger than the steady-state amplitude. Readers should investigate responses when $\omega_0 = 0.5$ with $Q = 1 \rightarrow (\omega_0/Q) = 0.5$ and $Q = 10 \rightarrow \omega_0/Q) = 0.05$, respectively.

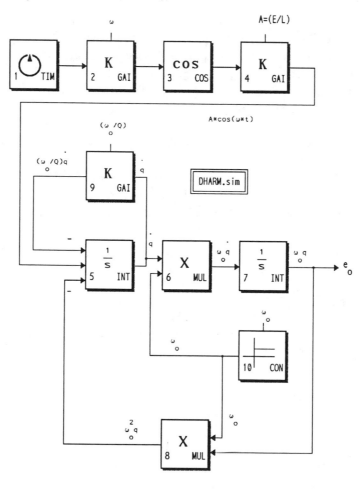

Figure 3.8.1   The harmonically-driven harmonic oscillator.

3.9 SYNTHESIZING RANDOM DISTURBANCE SIGNALS

Summing the outputs of harmonic oscillators having frequencies slightly changed from those required for harmonic spacing allows the generation of essentially random waveforms. These signals closely resemble band-limited white noise with a sharp cutoff at either end. Generally speaking, for n inputs, it is

$$A_j(t) = k \sum_{i=1}^{n} A_j \sin(\omega_j t + \phi_j) \tag{1}$$

where k is an overall gain, A_j is the peak amplitude of the jth input, ω_j is the frequency of the jth input and ϕ_j is the initial phase of the jth input signal.

In the case where *equal* amplitude sine waves are summed and the ω values are slightly *altered* from pure harmonic spacing (this is important as it ensures random phasing among inputs), the distribution of the output is a random signal with inherently *symmetric* statistical distribution. Then it *closely* resembles a Gaussian probability distribution as the number of input sine waves increases. Many purists consider this a pseudorandom signal, since it will eventually repeat itself in the distant future. However for n = 10, the signal will be expected to repeat itself in about 5000 years; we will let the reader be the judge as to its deterministic nature. Over the years this technique has been used by workers in man-machine systems, like Jex and Cromwell (1962), Kuehnel (1962), Sadoff and Dolkas (1966), Newell and Pietrzak (1968) and Greif et al. (1972), to name a few.

Summing the outputs of several *harmonic oscillators* allows the experimenter *control* over the total composition of the disturbance function. It allows the establishment of *specific* phase relationships between frequency components, and the generation of *specific* frequency content. Figure 3.9.1 shows a random disturbance signal generator with five inputs, or

$$A_5(t) = k + A_1 \sin \omega_1 t + A_2 \sin \omega_2 t + A_3 \sin \omega_3 t + A_4 \sin \omega_4 t \tag{2}$$

The equation simulated is

$$A_5(t) = 0.4 + 0.6 \sin 7t + 1.1 \sin 5t + 2.3 \sin 2t + 3.4 \sin(1.2t) \tag{3}$$

and the generator's output is shown in Figure 3.9.2. Note that constant k is a dc component that determines the signal riding level.

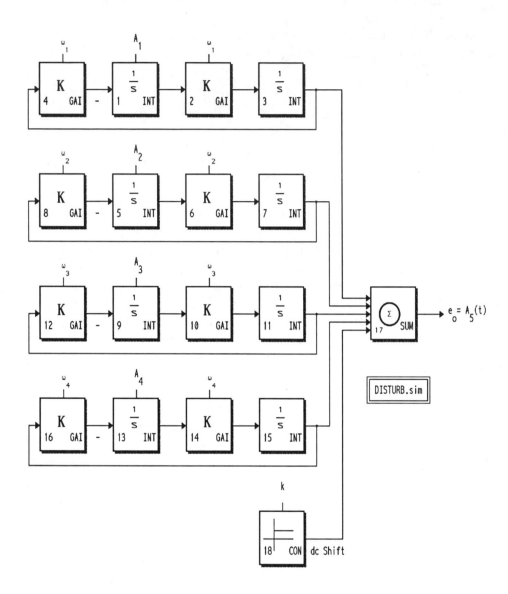

Figure 3.9.1   A disturbance generator with five inputs.

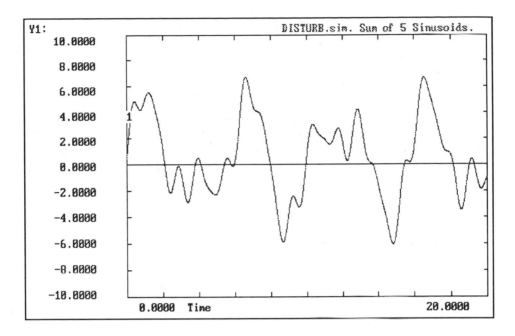

Figure 3.9.2   DISTURB.sim output as per Equation (2).

3.10   THE TAYLOR SERIES APPROXIMATION SINE-SHAPER CIRCUIT

Any real and continuous function f(x) having defined derivatives may be expressed as a polynomial expansion about some reference point. In the case of the sine function considered here, the Taylor series expansion about the zero reference point follows the generalized format

$$\sin(x) \approx \frac{\sum_{n=0}^{\infty} (-1)^n x^{(2n+1)}}{(2n+1)!} \tag{1}$$

A working form of this equation, known as the MacLaurin series, is

$$\sin(x) \approx x - \frac{x^3}{3!} + \frac{x^5}{5!} - \frac{x^7}{7!} + \ldots \tag{2}$$

Equation (2) shows that sin (x) can be approximated from another function involving a linearly increasing value of x, as in the case of the triangle waveform. A useful approximation of the sine function can be made with only the first two terms of the series, where

$$\sin(x) \approx y = x - \frac{x^3}{6} \qquad (3)$$

The above equation is simulated by the block diagram of Figure 3.10.1. The integrator (#2) supplies a linear slope [dx/dt]. A multiplier (#3) is used to form x^2 and a second multiplier (#4) forms x^3. The gain block (#5) has a setting $(1 \div 0.6) \simeq 0.1667$ and forms the term $(x^3/6)$. The summer (#6) outputs the approximate sin (x). Block #7 is the SINe function used here as a benchmark. An error display is made by using a summer (#8). Note that some people may prefer to use the integrator rather than the zero block as a time generator.

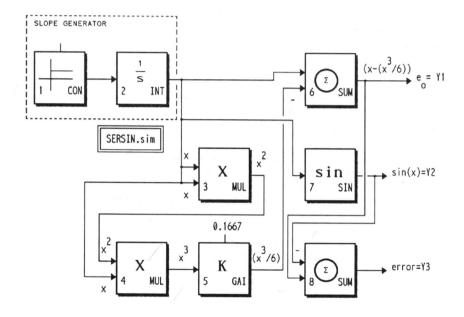

Figure 3.10.1   Taylor series simulator of sin(x) for the first two terms.

The results of Figure 3.10.2 show the limited range of the two-term approximation. Clearly when the series is broken off after the second term, there is only a small region of accuracy. This is in keeping with the fact that the Taylor series provide great precision *only* near the point of expansion and that the error (see Figure 3.10.2) increases significantly for more distant points. Often orthogonal expansions and the Chebyshev polynomial set in particular are preferred.

An alternative solution is to limit the argument values to $(-\pi/2) \le x \le (+\pi/2)$. Then the approximation is

$$\sin(x) \approx y = 0.9825\,x - 0.1402\,x^3 \qquad (4)$$

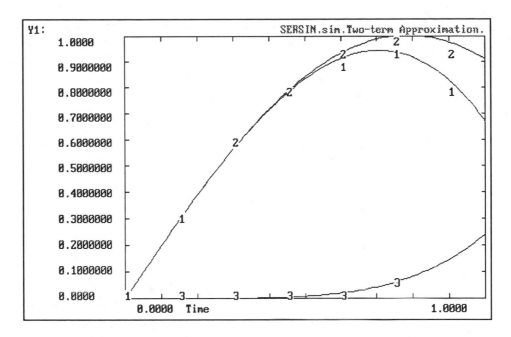

Figure 3.10.2.   Results of the two-term approximation and error display.

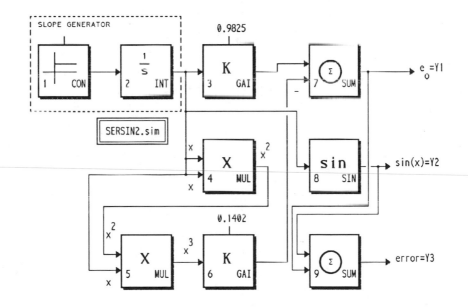

Figure 3.10.3   Alternate simulation of sin (x).

Figure 3.10.3 shows the simulator (see also Sheingold, 1976; and Wong and Ott, 1976). The examples shown here are presented as an enticement for further experimentation with polynomial expansion with polynomial approximation of functions. Nonlinear and function circuits are best designed here *first*, where the dynamic simulator verifies the concept and shows a benchmark performance in the sense of the mathematical block diagram (see also Section 6.3).

3.11   THE GENERATION OF COSINUSOIDAL FREQUENCY MULTIPLES WITH CHEBYSEV POLYNOMIALS

There are many polynomial expansions useful in signal processing, like that of the Taylor series known for its great precision near the center or point of expansion (see Section 3.10). However, the Taylor series do *not* represent functions well at the distant points as the error increases significantly in proportion to a power.

For practical reasons, it is often preferable to use expansions that remain fairly accurate over a larger region than that of the Taylor series. Then the use of *orthogonal* functions allows trading off some of the high precision of the Taylor series near the center of the interval for greater precision over the larger region. One orthogonal function of interest is the Chebysev polynomial set.

This polynomial is among the most popular of orthogonal functions. Its properties make it useful in practice and it requires relatively few terms for precision results. The set of functions cos $(n\theta)$ is an orthogonal set over the interval $0 \leq x \leq \pi$. By integration we have

$$\int_{0}^{\pi} \cos{(m\,\theta)} \cos{(n\,\theta)}\,d\,\theta \tag{1}$$

The integral yields

$$\begin{array}{lll} 0 & \text{if} & m \neq n \\ \pi/2 & \text{if} & m = n \neq 0 \\ \pi & \text{if} & m = n = 0 \end{array}$$

Let

$$\theta \;=\; \arccos{(x)} \tag{2}$$

so that the set of orthogonal functions is redefined as

$$T_n(x) \;=\; \cos\left[n\,\mathrm{arccos}\,(x)\right] \tag{3}$$

that is, the Chebyshev polynomial set.

Since Equation (3) is not useful in practical computation, $T_n(x)$ is expressed in powers of x based on the three-term relation

$$T_{n+1}(x) \;-\; 2\,x\,T_n(x) \;+\; T_{n-1}(x) \;=\; 0 \tag{4}$$

In Equation (4), $T_{2n}(x)$ is an even function and $T_{2n+1}(x)$ is an odd function and the equation coefficients do not depend on n. It is:

$$
\begin{aligned}
T_0(x) &= 1 \\
T_1(x) &= x \\
T_2(x) &= 2x^2 - 1 \\
T_3(x) &= 4x^3 - 3x \\
T_4(x) &= 8x^4 - 8x^2 + 1 \\
T_5(x) &= 16x^5 - 20x^3 - 5x
\end{aligned}
$$

or

$$
\begin{aligned}
1 &= T_0 \\
x &= T_1 \\
x^2 &= 1/2\,(T_0 + T_2) \\
x^3 &= 1/4\,(3T_1 + T_3) \\
x^4 &= (3T_0 + 4T_2 + T_4)/8 \\
x^5 &= (10T_1 + 5T_3 + T_5)/16
\end{aligned}
$$

Note that Equation (4) appears in trigonometry texts as the popular equation

$$\cos\left[(n+1)\,\theta\right] \;+\; \cos\left[(n-1)\,\theta\right] \;=\; 2\cos(\theta)\cos(n\,\theta) \tag{5}$$

Now by letting $\theta = x$ Equation (3) becomes

$$T_n(x) \;=\; \cos n\theta \;=\; \cos(n\,\mathrm{arccos}\,x) \tag{6}$$

This equation describes the trigonometric Chebysev polynomial set of order $n = 1,2,3,\ldots$. It is

$$
\begin{aligned}
\cos 2\theta &= 2\cos^2\theta - 1 \\
\cos 3\theta &= 4\cos^3\theta - 3\cos\theta \\
\cos 4\theta &= 8\cos^4\theta - 8\cos^2\theta - 1 \\
\cos 5\theta &= 16\cos^5\theta - 20\cos^3\theta + 5\cos\theta
\end{aligned}
$$

It has been shown (Osowski, 1980) that the odd and even higher-order Chebysev functions can be expressed by using only odd or even lower-order polynomials. For odd polynomials it is

$$T_1(x) = x$$
$$T_3(x) = (4x^2 - 1)T_1 - 2x$$
$$T_5(x) = (4x^2 - 1)T_3 - 4x^2 T_1 + 2x$$
$$T_7(x) = (4x^2 - 1)T_5 - 4x^2 T_3 + 4x^2 T_1 - 2x$$

or in general

$$T_{2n-1}(x) = (4x^2 - 1)T_{2n-3} - \sum_{k=n-2}^{1} (\pm 4x^2 T_{2k-1}) \pm 2x$$

(7)

for $n = 2,3, \ldots$.

For even polynomials it is

$$T_2(x) = 2x^2 - 1$$
$$T_4(x) = (4x^2 - 1)T_2 - 2x^2$$
$$T_6(x) = (4x^2 - 1)T_4 - 4x^2 T_2 + 2x^2$$
$$T_8(x) = (4x^2 - 1)T_6 - 4x^2 T_4 + 4x^2 T_2 - 2x^2$$

or in general

$$T_{2n} = (4x^2 - 1)T_{2n-2} - \sum_{k=n-2}^{1} (\pm 4x^2 T_{2k}) \pm 2x^2 \qquad (8)$$

for $n = 2,3, \ldots$.

Equations (7) and (8) are useful in signal processing as they can be mechanized to generate the higher harmonics of the even and odd orders with a minimal amount of analog multipliers and summing operational amplifiers as shown by Sheingold (1974). The general procedures in approximating and synthesizing linear networks are described by Vlach (1969). Barker and Reilly (1976) and Osowski (1980) have demonstrated the electronic generation of frequency multiples. Application circuits are shown in Wong and Ott (1976), along with a recursive formula for the approximation of complex functions with the Chebysev polynomial (written in Fortran IV).

Electronic devices based on the mechanization of the Chebysev function are extremely useful in education. They link mathematics and electronics and help bridge abstraction with reality. Consider as a case in point Equation (5). It hardly relates to the real world as it is, but when mechanized it becomes an experimental device of value that has a useful physical output.

Unfortunately, designing and implementing electronic circuits of this nature transcend feasibility in the university setting. Their implementation calls for expensive electronic components like linear multiplier integrated circuits or multifunction converters. Using inexpensive multiplier integrated circuits requires the trimming and balancing circuits normally associated with such devices. All this contributes to a complex and time-consuming breadboarding task. Circuits based on the Chebysev polynomial set (CHEBEV.sim) are ideally suited for implementation with block diagram languages. Figures 3.11.1 and 3.11.3 (CHEBOD.sim) show the implementation of cos 2θ and cos 3θ, respectively, and the results are shown in Figures 3.11.2 and 3.11.4.

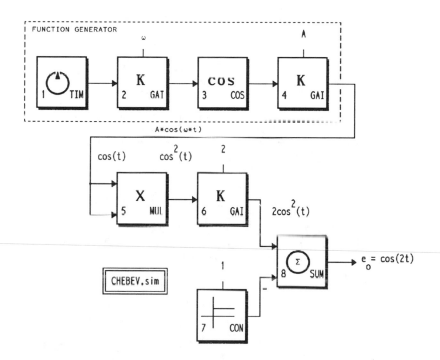

Figure 3.11.1   Chebysev polynomial implementation of cos 2θ.

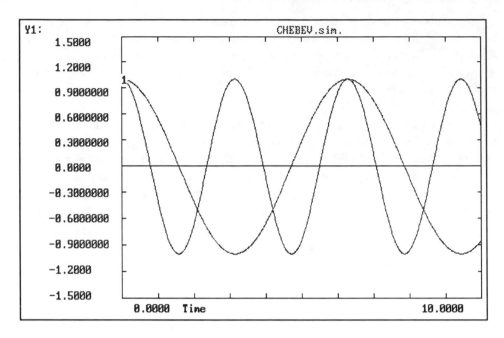

Figure 3.11.2   CHEBEV.sim output.

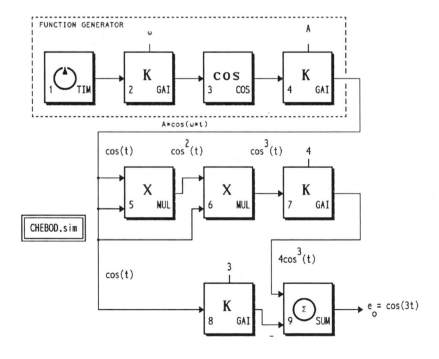

Figure 3.11.3 Chebysev polynomial implementation of cos 3θ.

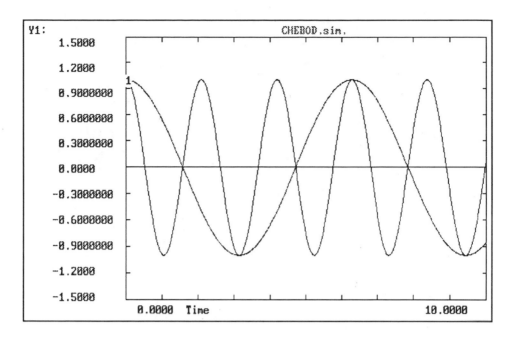

Figure 3.11.4   CHEBOD.sim output.

3.12   THE HARMONIC OSCILLATOR WITH SLIDING FRICTION

The differential equation

$$\frac{d^2x}{dt^2} = -\omega^2 x \pm \mu g \tag{1}$$

represents a harmonic oscillator with sliding friction, as in the case of a mass between springs sliding on a horizontal surface. The analytical solution of Equation (1) is discussed by Lapidus (1970) and an analog computer simulation is described by Wylen and Schwarz (1973). Here we use the IFE block (IF condition input 1, Else input 2) to perform the *polarity-sensitive comparator* function required due to the constant friction term ($\pm \mu g$). The block diagram is shown in Figure 3.12.1 (HOSF.sim) where the IFE block has inputs $i_1 = i_2 = \mu g$ and provides the integrator with an input (μg) having a sign that changes with the changing sign of the velocity [dx/dt]. (For an interesting discussion of this topic, see Barrat and Strobel, 1981.) Readers should investigate the simulation outputs for different friction levels. An excellent paper on the harmonic oscillator with sliding and viscous function is by Ricchiuto and Tozzi (1982).

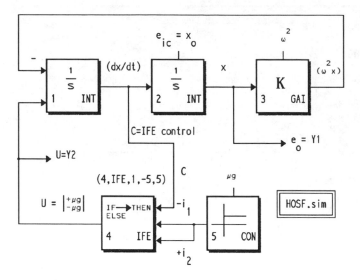

Figure 3.12.1   Harmonic oscillator with sliding friction.

3.13   A PURELY CONSERVATIVE HARMONIC OSCILLATOR WITH NONLINEAR TERMS

A quadrature oscillator can be designed to yield precisely stabilized sine waves by adding nonlinear terms to the purely conservative harmonic oscillator system

$$\frac{dx}{dt} = \omega y$$

$$\frac{dy}{dt} = -\omega x \tag{1}$$

so that

$$\frac{dx}{dt} = \omega y + \epsilon\left[1 - \mu\left(x^2 + y^2\right)\right]x$$

$$\frac{dy}{dt} = -\omega x + \epsilon\left[1 - \mu\left(x^2 + y^2\right)\right]y \tag{2}$$

where ϵ and μ are positive constants. Readers should plot the sine and cosine waveforms generated by the circuit of Figure 3.13.1 (QUAD1.sim), one of the many variants found in the technical literature (Kaplan, 1980 and 1982).

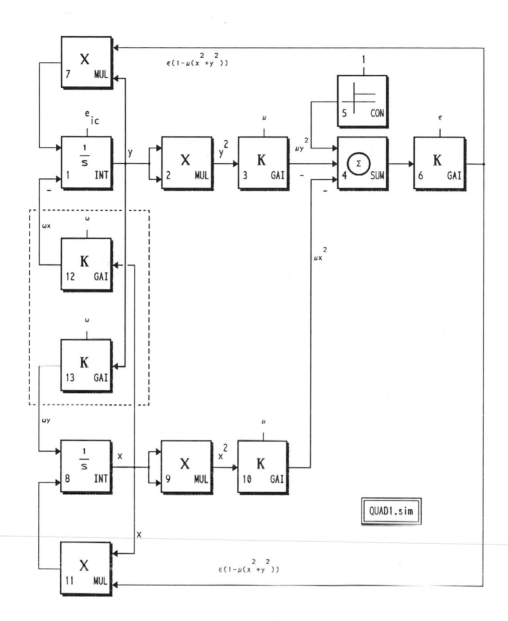

Figure 3.13.1   A purely conservative harmonic oscillator with nonlinear terms.

3.14   THE KAPLAN-RADPARVAR VOLTAGE-CONTROLLED OSCILLATOR

It has been suggested that the previous harmonic oscillator (QUAD1.sim, Section 3.13) be used as a quickly responding VCO (Kaplan and Radparvar, 1982). In the block diagram of Figure 3.14.1 (KAPLAN.sim), multiplier blocks provide the means to a signal-controlled gain and a triangle wave generator is used as the ω source.

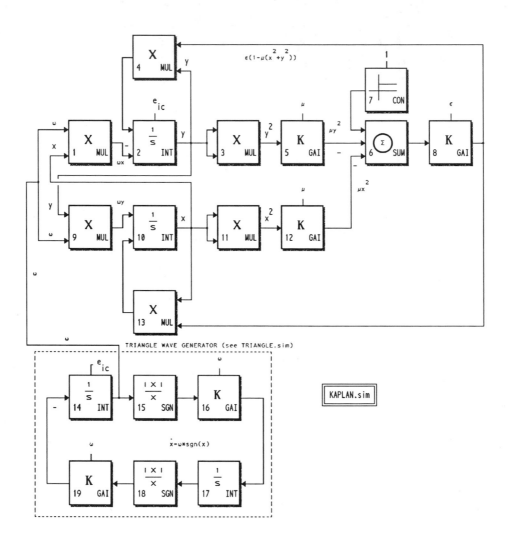

Figure 3.14.1   The Kaplan-Radparvar VCO.

The startup of the VCO and its response characteristics for an arbitrary setup are demonstrated by plotting the output (for good visual results, use a vertical scale of $\pm$ 0.1 and a horizontal time scale of 0 - 60). Its excellent response and stability renders this VCO useful in many simulation projects. In the original paper, Kaplan and Radparvar (1982) show a design variation for a self-phase modulated oscillator capable of producing any waveform as specified by a function block so that $\omega = f(x,y)$.

3.15   WALSH FUNCTIONS

Orthogonal functions and their applications are well known in signal processing. Periodic signals can be described by sets of orthogonal functions based on classical orthogonal polynomials like those of Legendre, Chebyshev, Laguerre and Hermite (Crowder and McCuskey, 1964; Lynn, 1983).

Walsh functions are a set of two-valued orthogonal functions, i.e., binary pulses with nominal values of $+1$ and -1. They form a complete set of orthogonal functions over some unit interval of definition. Langton (1987) provides an excellent introduction to Walsh functions and the mathematical property of orthogonality. Like Fourier synthesis where sine and cosine waveforms can be used in appropriate combinations to synthesize any complex repetitive waveform, Walsh functions employ sets of rectangular pulses to do the same (Jacoby, 1977). Signal representation in terms of the Walsh series is analogous to function representation by Fourier series. Just as we have discrete and fast Fourier transforms (Rabiner and Rader, 1972), we define discrete and fast Walsh transforms (Walmsley, 1974). The tactical advantage of the Walsh functions rests in that any Walsh transform matrix is composed by positive or negative ones, thus requiring only the operations of addition and subtraction.

The earliest work on Walsh functions was published by Walsh in 1923, following an earlier article on orthogonal functions by Rademacher (1922). In 1929 the Rademacher function was shown to be a subset of the Walsh system by Kaczmarz. There are several types of Walsh functions, to include the various Walsh-Kaczmarz, Walsh-Paley, Hadamard, Walsh-Harmuth and Rademacher functions, as explained in the excellent paper by Tzafestas et al. (1976). Essentially Walsh functions afford the replacement of sinusoidal functions for binary functions that can be easily generated with simple digital hardware in many signal analysis and synthesis tasks as shown by Walmsley (1974), Tzafestas et al. (1976) and the excellent introductory paper by Jacoby (1977). Walsh functions have extraordinary properties that easily appeal to those engaged in both analog and digital signal processing, as they are ubiquitous in terms of application. The reader is referred to the works by Lackey and Meltzer (1971), Lackey (1972), Ackeroyd (1973) and Bramhall (1973), and the books by Harmuth (1972) and Beauchamp (1975). Examples of applications are shown by Roth (1970), Corrington (1973), Zagajewski and Moll (1978), Temell and Linkens (1978) and Beer (1981). There are many (hundreds) of reference works on Walsh functions and the interested reader should begin with the published bibliographies by Ackeroyd (1973) and Bramhall (1972 and 1973).

TUTSIM is ideal for work with Walsh functions. In Figure 3.15.1 we show some Walsh waveforms and their sinusoidal equivalents, generated by the simple program of Figure 3.15.2 (WALTEST.sim). The Walsh pulses are easily created by using the SGN block. The reader is referred to the tables published by Walmsley (1974) and Jacoby (1977) of both the sine Walsh functions (SAL) and cosine Walsh functions (CAL). The file WALSH1.sim shows an interesting example of waveform synthesis by Walsh functions proposed by Langton (1987). Here, we implement the equation

$$F(\theta) = 8\,\mathrm{Wal}(0,\theta) + 4\,\mathrm{Wal}(1,\theta) + 2\,\mathrm{Wal}(3,\theta) + 4\,\mathrm{Wal}(7,\theta)$$

(1)

as shown in the block diagram of Figure 3.15.3, resulting in the synthesis of the ramp function of Figure 3.15.4. The constituent waveforms are shown on a common baseline for comparison in Figure 3.15.5.

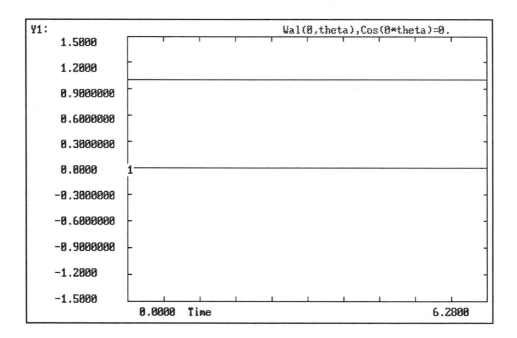

*Figure 3.15.1 (a) Functions Wal (0,θ) and cos (0*θ) = 0.*

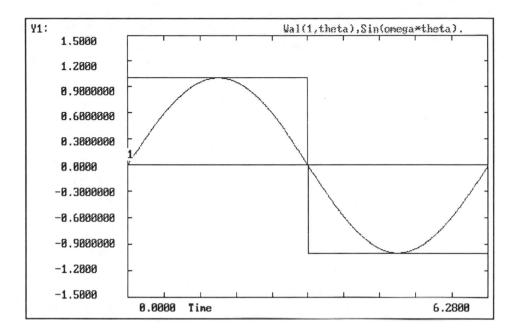

Figure 3.15.1 (b)   Functions Wal (1,θ) and sin ω θ.

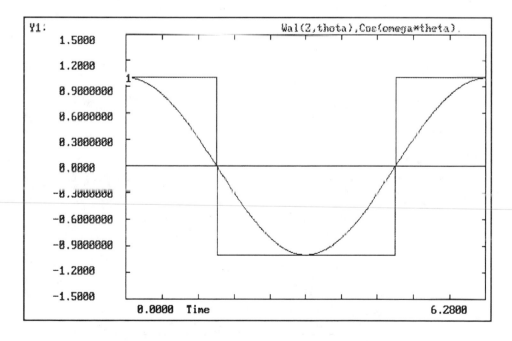

Figure 3.15.1 (c)   Functions Wal (2,θ) and cos ω θ.

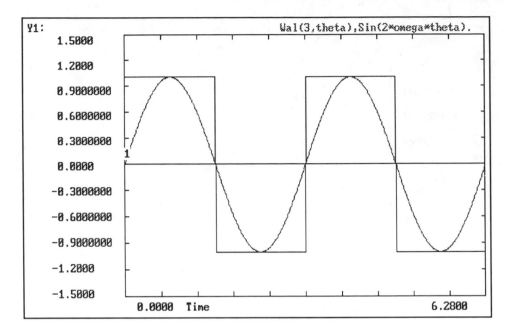

Figure 3.15.1 (d)   Functions Wal (3,θ) and sin 2 ω θ.

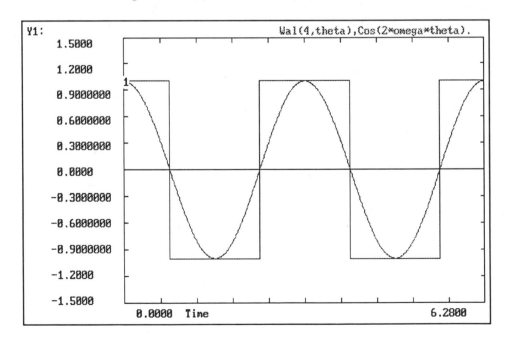

Figure 3.15.1 (e)   Functions Wal (4,θ) and cos 2 ω θ.

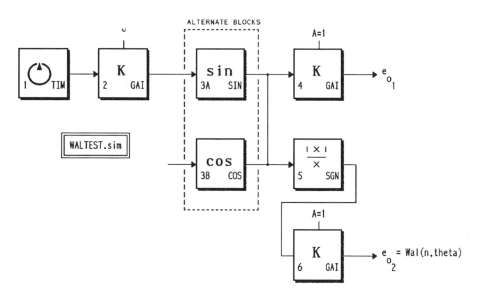

Figure 3.15.2 The Wal (n,θ) generator.

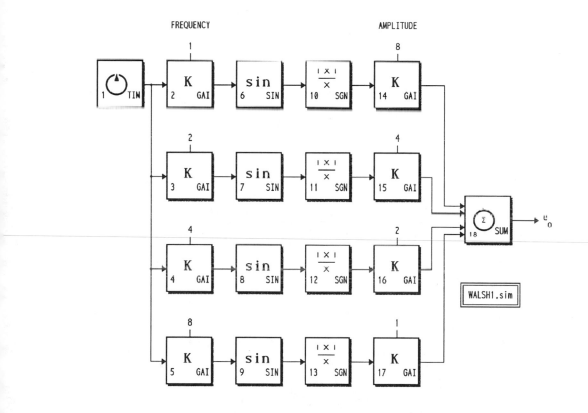

Figure 3.15.3 The Walsh ramp function generator.

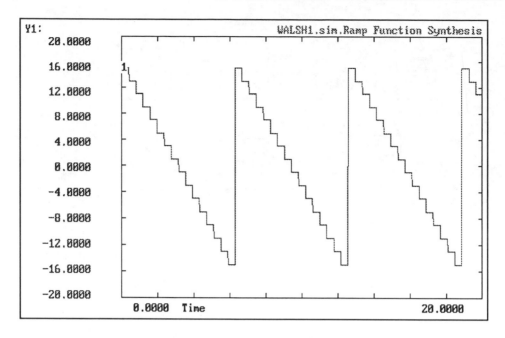

Figure 3.15.4   Ramp function output of the WALSH1.sim generator.

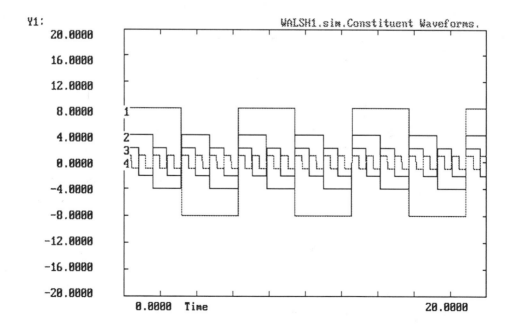

Figure 3.15.5   The constituent waveforms of WALSH1.sim.

3.16   THE PHASE-SHIFT OSCILLATOR

The oscillator is built by applying negative feedback around a network with three coincident poles as shown in Figure 3.16.1. A gain block is used to simulate an operational amplifier with frequency-independent gain. It is combined with three blocks in series, each representing the transfer function $1/(\tau s + 1)$ as shown in Figure 3.16.2. In the simulator of Figure 3.16.3 (PSHIFT.sim), a CON block provides the startup signal. In reality the oscillator has no input and a hardwired operational amplifier network like that of Figure 3.16.4 will likely be self-starting because of the noise generated by the integrated circuits themselves. This is the simplest hardware implementation of the system (see also Irvine, 1981). Roberge (1975) discusses the circuit's stability in conjunction with the Routh test, suggesting that the oscillator can only be analyzed by considering the characteristic equation

$$1 - \left(- K \, \frac{1}{\left(\tau s + 1\right)^3} \right) = 1 + \frac{K}{\left(\tau s + 1\right)^3} \tag{1}$$

because it is not possible to use the e_0/e_i transfer function poles in stability analysis. Readers may wish to plot the output waveforms for a gain $K = 8$ with a $\tau = 2 \to (1/\tau) = 0.5$ setting for the gain blocks #2, #4 and #6. This is a great experimental network.

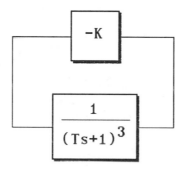

Figure 3.16.1   *The phase-shift oscillator in block diagram form.*

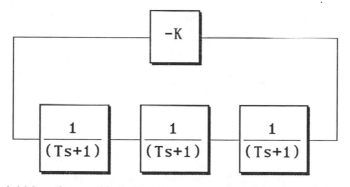

Figure 3.16.2.   *Alternate block diagram representation of the phase-shift oscillator.*

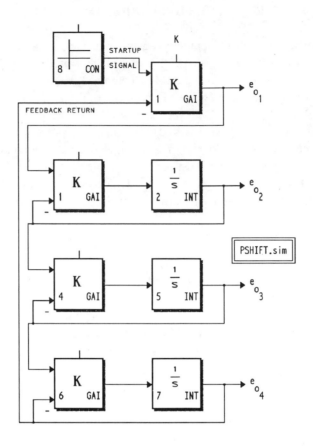

Figure 3.16.3   The simulator of the phase-shift oscillator.

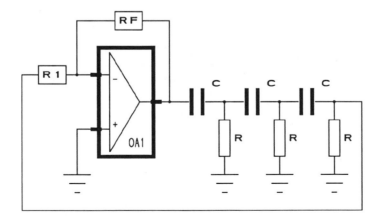

Figure 3.16.4   Hardware realization of the phase-shift oscillator.

4 PENDULUM SIMULATIONS

4.1 INTRODUCTION AND A FEW WORDS ON THE FREE FRICTIONLESS PENDULUM

The study of pendulum devices, where we deal with mechanical rather than electrical and biological oscillators and oscillatory systems, is of great importance in both physics and mechanical engineering. Pendulum mechanisms are introduced in most high-school and college physics courses giving students their first exposure to oscillatory dynamics.

Although pendulum devices are characteristically simple, lab models can be troublesome with regard to the manipulation, control and recording of experimental variables. Interesting mechanical devices like the ballistic pendulum apparatus described by Wassel and experiments with variable 'g' force produced by means of an electromagnet (Kwasnowski and Murphy, 1984) are typical of such efforts (incidentally a very interesting circuit where Hall-effect sensors and flip-flop integrated circuits are used to sustain pendulum swing is shown by Karasz, 1980). Pendulum experiments based on computer-interface techniques are described by Nicklin and Rafert (1984), Priest (1986) and Squire (1986) among many others. These techniques allow the collection, processing and display of experimental data by means of sensors, I/O boards and computer software. However the issue of experiment control always remains.

The analog/hybrid computer is useful in creating an electronic analog from a pendulum's mathematical model. Analog simulation affords a way of setting up and observing pendulum experiments *without* hardware. Its utilization ranges from simple, even homemade, analog computers to large, expensive hybrid systems. Unfortunately, the analog/hybrid machine is now a nearly extinct breed. Its legacy remains in its descendent, the virtual analog/hybrid computer. Here we have chosen a few representative experiments demonstrate the utility of CDSS languages in this domain. Additional oscillator examples appear in Part 3.

We begin the technical discussion with the most fundamental pendulum mechanism, the free pendulum without friction. Its equation of motion is

$$m \ell^2 \, \ddot{\theta} \; = \; - \; m g \ell \sin \theta \tag{1}$$

The first tensor is the inertial moment

$$J \ddot{\theta} = m\ell^2 \ddot{\theta} \qquad (2)$$

which opposes $[d^2\theta/dt^2]$. The second term is the restoring moment due to gravity (opposing θ), that is, force = mg, arm = $\ell \sin \theta$ as shown in Figure 4.1.1. The pendulum's displacement is, for practical purposes, the horizontal distance x = $\ell \sin \theta$, *not* the traveled arc length s. Note that the tangential force due to gravity mg $\sin \theta$ is *not* a restoring force under this definition of displacement; the restoring (horizontal) force is F $\sin \theta$, where F is the tension on the (inextensible) string. The equilibrium point for the pendulum's mass is $\theta = 0°$.

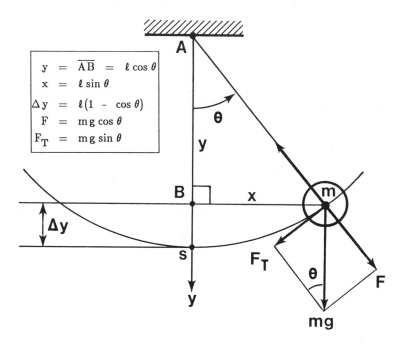

Figure 4.1.1   A physical realization of the fundamental free frictionless pendulum.

Division of both terms of Equation (1) by $m\ell^2$ and rearranging leads to the convenient form

$$\ddot{\theta} + \frac{g}{\ell} \sin \theta = 0 \qquad (3)$$

and by letting

$$\omega_0^2 = \left[\frac{g}{\ell} \right] \rightarrow \omega_0 = \left[\frac{g}{\ell} \right]^{\frac{1}{2}} \qquad (4)$$

where $\omega_0 = 2\pi f$ is the (undamped) radian natural frequency, Equation (3) takes the form

$$\ddot{\theta} + \omega_0^2 \sin \theta = 0 \tag{5}$$

This differential equation is nonlinear because of the restoring torque $\omega_0^2 \sin \theta$. For small θ values we can approximate $\sin \theta$ by the first term of the series (Taylor's theorem):

$$\sin \theta = \theta - \frac{\theta^3}{3!} + \frac{\theta^5}{5!} - \frac{\theta^7}{7!} + \dots \tag{6}$$

and therefore assume that

$$\sin \theta \approx \theta \tag{7}$$

Then Equation (5) is the linear fixed-coefficient differential equation

$$\ddot{\theta} + \omega_0^2 = 0 \tag{8}$$

We can solve Equation (8) by using the substitution

$$\theta(t) = e^{kt} \tag{9}$$

which generates the equation

$$k^2 + \omega_0^2 = 0 \quad \rightarrow \quad k = \pm j \omega_0, \quad j \triangleq \sqrt{-1} \tag{10}$$

Therefore, the *specific* solutions of Equation (8) are

$$\theta_1(t) = e^{j\omega_0 t}$$
$$\theta_2(t) = e^{-j\omega_0 t}$$

and the *general* solution of Equation (8) is the linear combination

$$\theta(t) = c_1 e^{j\omega_0 t} + c_2 e^{-j\omega_0 t} \tag{11}$$

We recall that exponential and circular functions are related by the remarkable Euler identity

$$e^{jx} = \cos x + j \sin x \tag{12}$$

Therefore, Equation (11) can be written as

$$
\begin{aligned}
\theta(t) &= c_1(\cos \omega_0 t + j \sin \omega_0 t) + c_2(\cos \omega_0 t - j \sin \omega_0 t) \\
&= j(c_1 - c_2) \sin \omega_0 t + (c_1 + c_2) \cos \omega_0 t
\end{aligned}
\tag{13}
$$

We now designate two arbitrary constants, A and B, so that

$$
A = j(c_1 - c_2)
\tag{14}
$$

and

$$
B = c_1 + c_2
\tag{15}
$$

and by substituting into Equation (13), the general solution (Equation 11) takes the form

$$
\theta(t) = A \sin \omega_0 t + B \cos \omega_0 t
\tag{16}
$$

The motion described by the linearized Equation (8) is harmonic. The cyclic frequency of the pendulum in the small θ range

$$
f = \frac{\omega}{2\pi} \quad \text{or} \quad f = \frac{1}{2\pi}\left(\frac{g}{\ell}\right)^{\frac{1}{2}}
\tag{17}
$$

depends only on its length ℓ (not on its mass), a property historically exploited in clock design. The period of the harmonic motion is

$$
T = \left(\frac{\omega}{2\pi}\right)^{-1} = \frac{2\pi}{\omega} \quad \text{or} \quad T = 2\pi\left(\frac{\ell}{g}\right)^{\frac{1}{2}}
\tag{18}
$$

and given T and ℓ we can solve for the gravitational acceleration

$$
g = \frac{4\pi^2 \ell}{T^2}
\tag{19}
$$

The general solution (Equation 16) under the initial conditions $\theta(0) = \theta_0$ (initial angular displacement) and $[d\theta/dt](0) = [d\theta_0/dt]$ (initial angular velocity) becomes

$$\theta(0) = A \cdot 0 + B \cdot 1 = \theta_0 \rightarrow B = \theta_0 \tag{20}$$

It is

$$\dot{\theta}(t) = \frac{d\theta(t)}{dt} = \omega_0 A \cos \omega_0 t - \omega_0 B \sin \omega_0 t \tag{21}$$

and therefore

$$\dot{\theta}(0) = \omega_0 A = \dot{\theta}_0 \rightarrow A = \frac{\dot{\theta}_0}{\omega_0} \tag{22}$$

From Equations (16), (20) and (22) we write

$$\theta(t) = \frac{\dot{\theta}_0}{\omega_0} \sin \omega_0 t + \theta_0 \cos \omega_0 t \tag{23}$$

or from Equation (4) we can write

$$\theta(t) - \dot{\theta}_0 \left[\frac{g}{\ell}\right]^{-\frac{1}{2}} \sin \left[\frac{g}{\ell}\right]^{\frac{1}{2}} t + \theta_0 \cos \left[\frac{g}{\ell}\right]^{\frac{1}{2}} t \tag{24}$$

We recall that the linear combination (sum) of a sine and a cosine wave (of the same period) is a simple harmonic motion. We write

$$\begin{aligned} \theta(t) &= A \sin \omega_0 t + B \cos \omega_0 t \\ &= C (\sin \omega t \cos \phi + \cos \omega t \sin \phi) \\ &= C \sin (\omega t + \phi) \end{aligned} \tag{25}$$

where C is the amplitude of the oscillation and ϕ is the phase (see also Section 4.10). It is

$$C = \sqrt{A^2 + B^2} \tag{26}$$

or from Equations (20) and (22)

$$C = \sqrt{\frac{\dot{\theta}_0^2}{\omega_0^2} + \theta_0^2} \tag{27}$$

and

$$\tan \phi \;=\; \frac{\omega_0 \theta_0}{\dot{\theta}_0} \tag{28}$$

By now the reader should recognize that the free, frictionless pendulum is the mechanical analog of the harmonic oscillator described in Section 3.2. The amplitude correction mechanism shown in HALT.sim and HALTA.sim can now be interpreted in the light of the foregoing discussion (especially Equation 23).

As a final note to this (intentionally long-drawn) introduction, let us point out some of the many different treatments of arriving at Equation (3)—all a matter of preference. For example, we can begin by applying Newton's law, so that

$$m \, \ddot{s} \;=\; - \, mg \sin \theta \tag{29}$$

and since the arc length s is written as

$$s \;=\; r \, \theta \quad \rightarrow \quad s \;=\; \ell \, \theta \tag{30}$$

Equation (29) can be written as

$$m \, \ell \, \ddot{\theta} \;=\; - \, mg \sin \theta \quad \rightarrow \quad \ddot{\theta} \;=\; - \, \frac{g}{\ell} \sin \theta \tag{3R}$$

Another approach begins by writing the system's kinetic and potential energy equations

$$E_K \;=\; \frac{1}{2} \, m \left(\ell \, \dot{\theta} \right)^2 \tag{31}$$

$$E_P \;=\; mg\ell \, (1 \,-\, \cos \theta) \tag{32}$$

In the case of a frictionless pendulum, there is no energy loss, and therefore $E_K + E_P = $ constant. Then

$$\frac{d}{dt} \, E_K \;+\; \frac{d}{dt} \, E_P \;=\; 0 \tag{33}$$

which, after the appropriate substitutions, is found to be Equation (3).

A more formalized approach involves the use of Lagrange's equation, having the advantage of requiring *only* the pendulum's speed (speed = the magnitude of the velocity or $|v| = \ell[d\theta/dt]$). The pendulum is frictionless; therefore the system is conservative. We write

$$\frac{d}{dt}\left(\frac{\partial T}{\partial \dot{\theta}}\right) - \frac{\partial T}{\partial \theta} + \frac{\partial U}{\partial \theta} = 0 \tag{34}$$

where T and U are, respectively, the kinetic and potential energy of the system (in standardized notation), so that the system's energy-geometry equations (see Figure 4.1.1) are

$$T = \frac{1}{2} m |v|^2 = \frac{1}{2} m (\ell \dot{\theta})^2 \tag{31R}$$

$$U = mg\Delta y = mg\ell(1 - \cos \theta) \tag{32R}$$

From Equation (34) and those above, it is

$$\frac{\partial T}{\partial \dot{\theta}} = m\ell^2\theta \quad \rightarrow \quad \frac{d}{dt}\left(\frac{\partial T}{\partial \dot{\theta}}\right) = m\ell^2\ddot{\theta} \tag{35}$$

$$-\frac{\partial T}{\theta} = 0 \tag{36}$$

$$\frac{\partial U}{\partial \theta} = mg\ell \sin \theta$$

$$\tag{37}$$

and therefore Equation (34) takes the form

$$m\ell^2\ddot{\theta} + mg\ell \sin \theta - 0 \quad \rightarrow \quad \ddot{\theta} + \frac{g}{\ell} \sin \theta = 0$$

Some textbooks prefer to define the Langrangian L where

$$L = T + U \tag{38}$$

and substitute into the equation

$$\frac{d}{dt}\left(\frac{\partial L}{\partial \dot{\theta}}\right) - \frac{\partial L}{\partial \theta} = 0 \tag{39}$$

with the same results. This abbreviated approach, however, may not be as useful pedagogically.

4.2   PENDULUM WITH CUBIC DAMPING TERM

The equation for the simple pendulum for small angular displacements (under the assumption $\sin \theta \approx \theta$) is

$$\ddot{\theta} = -\left(\frac{k}{\ell m}\right)\dot{\theta} - \left(\frac{g}{\ell}\right)\theta \qquad (1)$$

the damping force $(k/\ell m)[d\theta/dt]$ depends on both the constant $(k/\ell m)$ and the angular velocity $[d\theta/dt]$. If the damping term is proportional to some nth power of the angular velocity, the equation becomes

$$\ddot{\theta} = -\left(\frac{k}{\ell m}\right)\dot{\theta}^n - \left(\frac{g}{\ell}\right)\theta \qquad (2)$$

This interesting nonlinear differential equation is simulated by the block diagram of Figure 4.2.1 for n = 3, a cubic damping term (see also Strong and Hannauer, 1969).

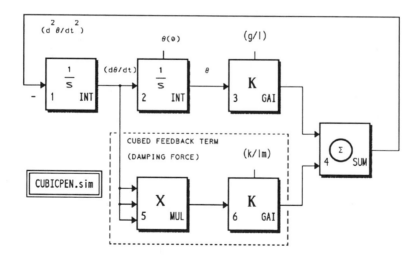

Figure 4.2.1   Simulating the pendulum with cubic damping term for $\sin \theta \approx \theta$.

4.3   PENDULUM WITH CUBIC DAMPING FOR LARGE θ

In this section we will simulate the equation

$$\ddot{\theta} = -\left(\frac{k}{\ell m}\right) \dot{\theta}^n - \left(\frac{g}{\ell}\right) \sin \theta \qquad (1)$$

that differs from the case of Section 4.2 because of the added term $\sin \theta$. The reader should investigate the differences between the two equations for a wide variety of theta values and different values of n. Figure 4.3.1 shows the simulator (see also Zilio, 1982).

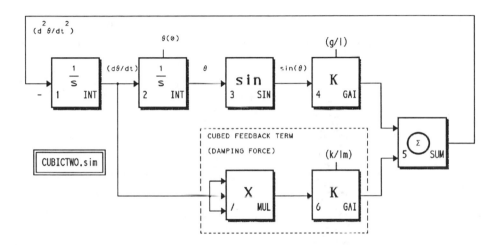

Figure 4.3.1   Simulating the pendulum with cubic damping term for large θ
(note the added block sin θ).

4.4   THE WILBERFORCE PENDULUM

Described and first investigated in 1894 by L. R. Wilberforce (1861-1944), this device is a fascinating demonstrator of coupled-system dynamics. Although it is a very valuable teaching tool, it is rarely discussed or referenced.

The Wilberforce pendulum, or Wilberforce spring, is a long and closely-wound helical spring loaded with a mass. The spring is suspended along the vertical axis and the loading body is symmetrical about an axis of revolution that coincides with that of the spring, as shown in Figure 4.4.1. Laboratory demonstration models show the load as a cylindrical mass having a radius greater than that of the flat spring helix. Masses m_1 and m_2 are symmetrically situated and adjustable. They are normally implemented as nuts on a fine-thread shaft, and they are used to *tune* the system.

This pendulum represents a mechanical system where a *single* body possesses *two* mechanically-coupled and dissimilar degrees of freedom. In the laboratory, it serves to demonstrate the weak coupling of two subsystems having separately the same natural frequency, resulting in a version of the *beats*. There are two natural modes of motion here. The first is a nearly pure rotational motion of the mass *about* the vertical axis. The second is a pure translational oscillation of the mass *along* the vertical axis. As the periods of both motions become almost equal, the small amount of coupling (weak coupling) results in a slow back-and-forth exchange of the system's kinetic energy between vertical and rotational oscillations.

The construction of a physical model of the Wilberforce pendulum is not easy, since the helical spring must be chosen carefully (Feather, 1961, p. 59-67; Walker, 1985). The author believes that the technical difficulties of realizing a working apparatus have contributed to its rarity of presence in the teaching laboratory. Analog computer simulation

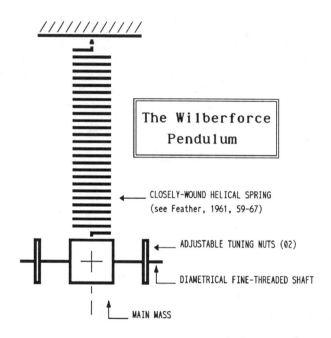

Figure 4.4.1   A physical realization of the Wilberforce pendulum.

or the use of a virtual analog computer in the form of a continuous dynamic system simulation language are viable and even superior alternatives to physical models. The Wilberforce pendulum equations are

$$\ddot{x} + x - b\theta = 0$$
$$\ddot{\theta} + \theta - ax = 0 \tag{1}$$

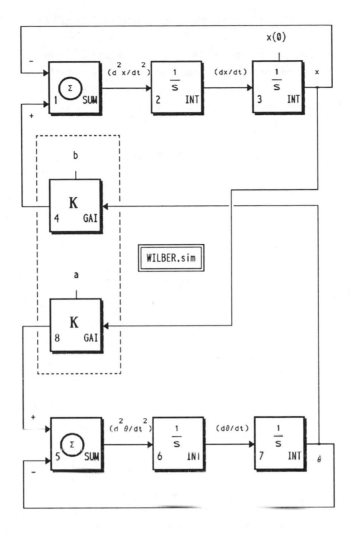

Figure 4.4.2   The block simulator of the Wilberforce pendulum.

It is assumed that the mass of the spring is negligible when compared to the mass of the load. The cross-coupling terms (-bθ) and (ax) determine the system's energy exchange characteristics. The block diagram of Figure 4.4.2 implements the system of Equations (1) and (2) so that the highest derivative is generated intentionally. Unlike an analog computer where computational amplifier conservation is the rule, CDSS languages allow the redundant mechanization and the monitoring of any block output in the simulated system. This feature makes these languages most suitable for teaching and research. Typical results may be obtained for b = 0.5 and a = 0.05 and 0.005, respectively. The experimenter may alter the cross-coupling coefficient values to allow for the investigation of any range or combination of variables.

4.5   PENDULUM WITH INCREMENTAL ERROR-CONTROLLED DAMPING

The pendulum with incremental error-controlled damping represents a large class of oscillatory mechanisms where an incremental output gain is generated proportional to some system variable. The pendulum equation for large amplitudes is modified to include a damping force F_d having a gain proportional to the error. We need

$$F_d = f(\dot{\theta}) \tag{1}$$

and, by relating to the proportionality $[dF_d/d(d\theta/dt)]$, it is

$$\left(\frac{dF_d}{d\dot{\theta}}\right) = k\,\dot{\theta} \tag{2}$$

or in general terms

$$\left[\frac{dF_d}{d\dot{\theta}}\right] = k\,|\dot{\theta}|\,\dot{\theta} \tag{3}$$

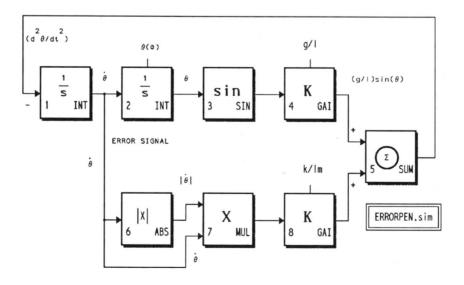

Figure 4.5.1   The block simulator of a pendulum with incremental error-controlled damping.

The equation of the pendulum with incremental error-controlled damping can now be written

$$\ddot{\theta} \;=\; - \left(\frac{k}{\ell m}\right) \dot{\theta}\,|\,\dot{\theta}\,| \;-\; \left(\frac{g}{\ell}\right)\,\sin\theta \tag{4}$$

Figure 4.5.1 shows the simulator. A variation on the theme is discussed by Netzer (1981), where the principle is used to improve the dynamic response of a servo amplifier system.

4.6   PENDULUM WITH LENGTH AS A FUNCTION OF TIME

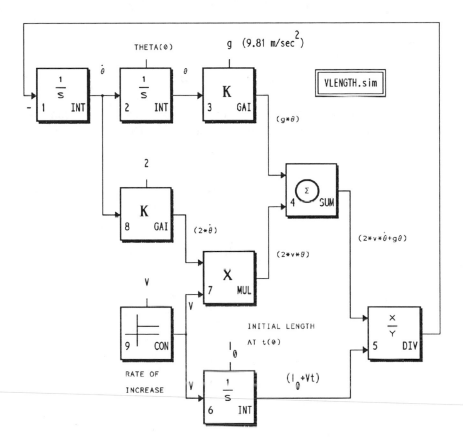

Figure 4.6.1   The block simulator of a pendulum with length as a function of time.

A pendulum with an initial length, ℓ_0, increasing linearly with time, so at a given time it is $\ell = \ell_0 + Vt$, is described by the equation

$$\ddot{\theta} = -\frac{2V\dot{\theta} + g\theta}{\ell_0 + Vt} \tag{1}$$

where $\theta < 15°$ and ℓ_0 is the initial length at t = 0. The small amplitude pendulum is simulated here as shown in Figure 4.6.1.

Analytically, solutions of this equation that includes a Coriolis-type term are in terms of Bessel and Neumann functions of first order (Relton, 1965). When the linear increase over a period is small compared to the initial length at t = 0, the analytic solution is a combination of Bessel and Neumann function of first order. This is called the adiabatic pendulum, a special case where the ratio of energy to frequency is constant (Wylen, 1971; Wylen and Schwarz, 1973).

4.7   THE WEIGHT-DRIVEN, DAMPED PENDULUM

The weight-driven, damped pendulum shown in Figure 4.7.1 consists of the pendulum mass, m, and the mass of the driving weight, m_w. The weight is attached to a

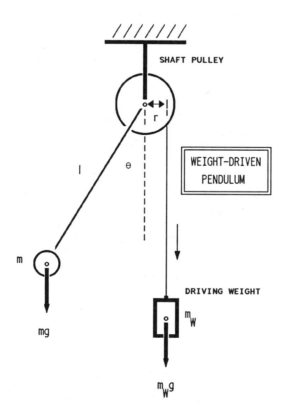

Figure 4.7.1 The physical model of a weight-driven, damped pendulum.

string wrapped about the shaft pulley of radius, r. The total torque has three components, to include the applied torque (T_a) due to the driving weight, the opposing torque (T) due to the pendulum itself, and the opposing damping torque (T_d) due to a damping coefficient, D. The system equations are

$$
\begin{aligned}
T_a &= m_w g r \\
T &= -T_c \sin \theta \\
&= m g \ell \sin \theta \\
T_d &= -D \dot{\theta}
\end{aligned}
\tag{1}
$$

where g is the gravitational acceleration.

The equation of motion is

$$
T_a + T + T_d = M \ddot{\theta}
\tag{2}
$$

where M is the total moment of inertia. From Equations (1) and (2) we write

$$
T_a - T_c \sin \theta - D \dot{\theta} = M \ddot{\theta}
\tag{3}
$$

The above equation is found in Rochlin and Hausma (1973). Falco (1976) rearranges it as shown below

$$
M \ddot{\theta} + D \dot{\theta} + T_c \sin \theta - T_a = 0
\tag{4}
$$

or

$$
\ddot{\theta} + \frac{D}{M} \dot{\theta} + \frac{T_c}{M} \sin \theta - \frac{T_a}{M} = 0
\tag{5}
$$

He then substitutes $\tau = (T_c/M)^{1/2} t$ so that Equation (5) becomes

$$
\left(\frac{d^2 \theta}{d\tau^2} \right) + A \left(\frac{d\theta}{d\tau} \right) + \sin \theta - B = 0
\tag{6}
$$

In Falco's equation time is now measured in units of $(T_c/M)^{1/2}$ so that $A = (D^2/MT_c)^{1/2}$ and $B = T_a/T_c$. The equation above leads to further investigations into position-dependent damping (quasiparticle-pair interference current) and into the Josephson weak link mechanisms (see Falco, 1976). Figure 4.7.2 shows the block diagram implementation of Equation (3) arranged for simulation like this:

$$\ddot{\theta} = \left(\frac{D}{M}\right)\dot{\theta} + \left(\frac{T_c}{M}\right)\sin\theta - \left(\frac{T_a}{M}\right) \qquad (7)$$

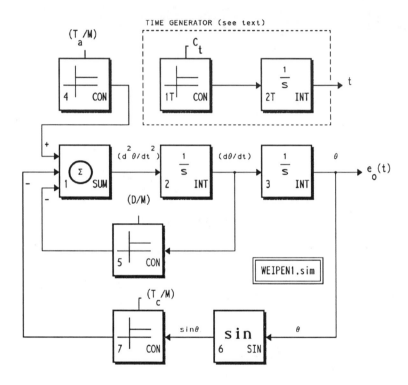

Figure 4.7.2   The block simulator of a weight-driven, damped pendulum.

Figure 4.7.3 is the simulator of Equation (5) rewritten as

$$\left(\frac{d^2\theta}{d\tau^2}\right) = B - A\left(\frac{d\theta}{d\tau}\right) - \sin\theta \qquad (8)$$

While Equation (7) is straightforward and easy to implement, Equation (8) is referenced in τ rather than t. In order to have a *valid comparison* of the results of Figures 4.7.2 and 4.7.3, a common time generator is used, rather than using TUTSIM's zero block.

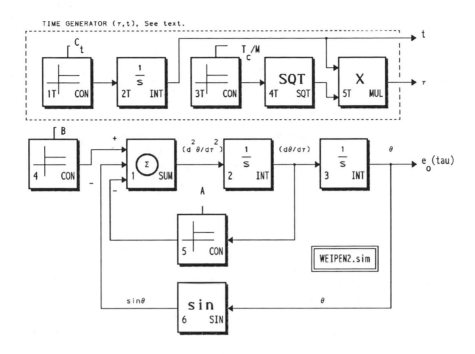

Figure 4.7.3 Alternate approach to the weight-driven, damped pendulum simulation (see Falco, 1976).

4.8 THE BOWDITCH CURVE (THE Y-SUSPENDED PENDULUM)

There is a rich historical background associated with this simulation. In 1815 James Dean published a paper on the effects of the librations of the moon on the apparent motion of the Earth as viewed from the moon. In the same volume of the *Memoirs of the American Academy of Arts and Sciences*, there was a contribution by Nathaniel Bowditch on the motion of a doubly-suspended pendulum. Influenced by Dean, who noted that the Earth's motion in the sky of the moon could be simulated by such a pendulum, Bowditch considered its motion and developed the curves known as Lissajous figures. Lissajous, however, was not the first to investigate the topic or draw these figures. An excellent historical and scientific account of the Y-suspended pendulum is by Crowell (1981).

The simulator of Figure 4.8.1 (BOWDITCH.sim) mechanizes the system of equations

$$x = a \sin(nt + d)$$
$$y = b \sin t$$

(1)

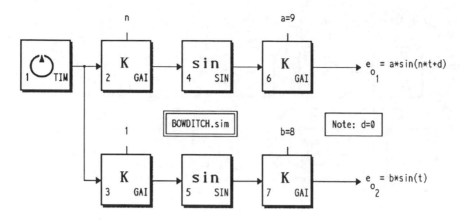

Figure 4.8.1   Block simulator of the Y-suspended pendulum (Bowditch or Lissajous curves).

as discussed by Lawrence (1972) using the following values: a = 9, b = 8 and d = 0. Readers should plot the Bowditch curve for n = 1/2, 1/3, 2/3, 1/4, 3/4, and 1/5. The Bowditch (Lissajous) figure has significance in electronics as a direct indicator of the magnitude of two sinusoidal signals and the phase angle between them. In-phase signals collapse the curve pattern to a straight line in the first and third quadrant.

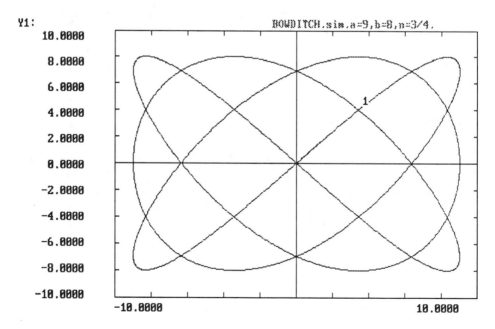

Figure 8.4.2   BOWDITCH.sim results for a = 9, b = 8, and n = 3/4.

If the signals are exactly 180° out of phase, the pattern is a straight line in the second and fourth quadrants (see also Byers, 1986). An excellent analytical exposition which includes examples of digital computation (BASIC) and mechanical analog computation is found in

Smith (1981) and in its companion article by Smith and Smith (1982). Also a microprocessor-based demonstration is discussed by MacLeod (1980). Figure 4.8.2 shows an example of the curve.

4.9   DEVELOPING PENDULUM MODELS

Traditionally, the pendulum has been used to study rotational motion, stability, energy transfer and nonlinearities, among a large list of topics. It all begins with the well-known formulation

$$m \ell \ddot{\theta} + D \ell \dot{\theta} + mg \sin(\theta) = f(t) \tag{1}$$

where

$$
\begin{array}{rcl}
m & = & \text{pendulum mass} \\
\ell & = & \text{length of the pendulum} \\
\theta & = & \text{angular displacement} \\
D & = & \text{frictional force per unit velocity} \\
g & = & \text{gravitational constant (32.2 ft/s}^2) \\
f(t) & = & \text{some excitation function applied at } t = 0.
\end{array}
$$

Equation (1) can be rearranged for the purpose of putting together a block diagram

$$\ddot{\theta} = \frac{1}{m \ell} f(t) - \frac{D}{m} \dot{\theta} - \frac{g}{\ell} \sin \theta \tag{2}$$

The block diagram of Figure 4.9.1 is then prepared using standard analog computer procedures. It is similar to that of the harmonic oscillator with one catch: an oscillator circuit starting up on initial conditions in reality has no input. As such, it is not amenable to a stability analysis via the e_0/e_i transfer function poles. This is not the case with the pendulum, even when it is made lossless, i.e., a purely conservative system initially energized by means of some input f(t). The point is moot and simply implies the *legal* existence of a complete transfer function rather than just a characteristic equation. Either way, it is easy to relate pendulum mechanisms to control systems and vice versa—a cardinal capability when teaching or learning these topics.

The linear model of Equation (1) is popular but is not adequately representative of the real pendulum. Squire (1986) shows that three damping terms must be included in the mathematical model, one quadratic and one linear on the velocity along with a velocity independent term, according to the equation

$$\ddot{\theta} + a \, |\dot{\theta}| \, \dot{\theta} + b \, \dot{\theta} + c \, \text{sgn} \, \dot{\theta} + \omega_0^2 \left(\theta - \frac{1}{6} \theta^3 \right) = 0 \tag{3}$$

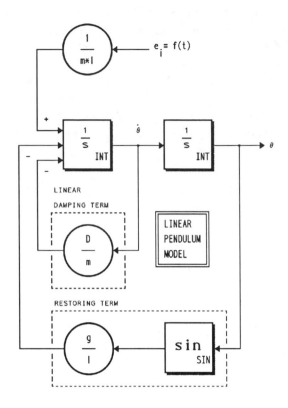

Figure 4.9.1   A popular model of the linear pendulum.

as simulated by the block diagram of Figure 4.9.2. The simple model of Equation (1) assumes that the damping torque is directly proportional to the angular velocity (recall that D was defined as frictional force per unit velocity). However, the dominant damping torque is due to the aerodynamic drag on the pendulum bob. The drag force equation

$$D \; = \; C_D \; \frac{1}{2} \; \rho \, V^2 \tag{4}$$

indicates that D is proportional to V^2, hence the quadratic damping term. Squire's work (1986) and the articles by Barratt and Strobel (1981) and de Castro (1986) easily convince us that the validity and reliability of a simulation is as good as the mathematical model itself. Then again, for a very complete model we must take into account the drag coefficient C_D of the bob, the air density ρ, the aerodynamic effects of the pendulum string or rigid support, etc., ad nauseam. The cutoff point should be defined by the requirements of the simulation itself, *not* by ill-conceived academic standards.

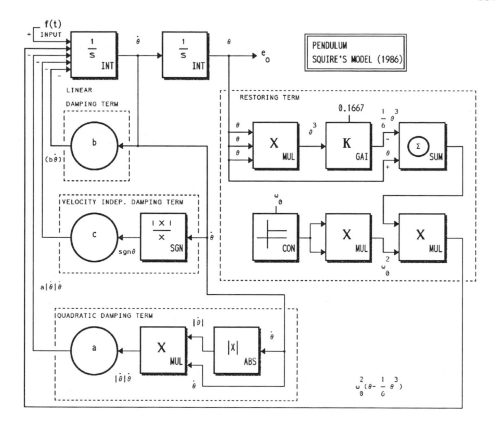

Figure 4.9.2 Squire's model (1986) of the pendulum.

Finally, the reader is directed to the work by Hartman (1986) on the dynamically shifted oscillator, the paper by Janssen et al. (1983) on the anharmonic oscillator and that by Tufillaro et al. (1984) on the Atwood Machine. All can be simulated with block diagram languages and will contribute to an in-depth understanding of pendulum mechanisms and of simulation concepts in general. Also the excellent general paper by Nelson et al. (1986) will be very useful in pendulum studies.

4.10   COMPLEX EXPONENTIAL FUNCTIONS

Earlier (in Section 4.1) we used Euler's identity to describe the motion of the frictionless pendulum. Somehow the example of a purely conservative system does not do justice to complex exponential functions and the Euler identity. These valuable analytical tools merit a further discussion, so let's consider the mechanical system of Figure 4.10.1. The equation of motion is written by considering the two active moments, the D'Alembert inertial torque $J[d^2\theta/dt]$ (opposing $[d^2\theta/dt^2]$) and the spring torque $k\theta$ opposing θ:

$$J\ddot{\theta} = -k\theta \tag{1}$$

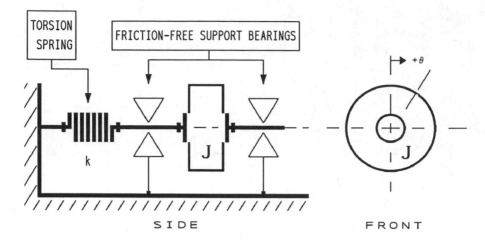

Figure 4.10.1   A physical realization of a torsional spring-mass system useful in the study of the Euler identity.

Intuitively we can see that the mass-spring system of Figure 4.10.1 exhibits both fundamental types of linear response (sinusoidal oscillation and exponential decay) in *combination*. We wish to express both exponential and sinusoidal responses in *homogeneous* mathematical terms, so we will use the complex number theory to extend the exponential function e^{st} (see also Section 6.2.3) so it describes both types of motion. *This is where Euler's formulation comes in.*

There are different ways to develop the Euler identity. One involves the use of power series; we write

$$\sin \phi = \sum_{k=0}^{\infty} (-1)^k \frac{\phi^{2k+1}}{(2k+1)!} \tag{2}$$

Differentiation of the above gives

$$\cos \phi = \sum_{k=0}^{\infty} (-1)^k \frac{(2k+1)\phi^{2k}}{(2k+1)!}$$

$$= \sum_{k=0}^{\infty} (-1)^k \frac{\phi^{2k}}{(2k)!} \tag{3}$$

Also it is

$$e^x = \exp x = \sum_{i=0}^{\infty} \frac{x^i}{i!} \tag{4}$$

or by expansion:

$$e^x = \sum_{k=0}^{\infty} \frac{x^{2k}}{(2k)!} + \sum_{k=0}^{\infty} \frac{x^{2k+1}}{(2k+1)!} \tag{5}$$

Now, we designate the purely imaginary number

$$x = j\phi \tag{6}$$

and substitute into Equation (5):

$$
\begin{aligned}
e^{j\phi} &= \sum_{k=0}^{\infty} \frac{(j\phi)^{2k}}{(2k)!} + \sum_{k=0}^{\infty} \frac{(j\phi)^{2k+1}}{(2k+1)!} \\
&= \sum_{k=0}^{\infty} \frac{(j^2)^k \phi^{2k}}{(2k)!} + \sum_{k=0}^{\infty} \frac{j(j^2)^k \phi^{2k+1}}{(2k+1)!} \\
&= \sum_{k=0}^{\infty} \frac{(-1)^k \phi^{2k}}{(2k)!} + \sum_{k=0}^{\infty} \frac{j(-1)^k \phi^{2k+1}}{(2k+1)!} \\
&= \sum_{k=0}^{\infty} (-1)^k \frac{\phi^{2k}}{(2k)!} + j \sum_{k=0}^{\infty} (-1)^k \frac{\phi^{2k+1}}{(2k+1)!}
\end{aligned}
$$

$$\tag{7}$$

From Equations (2), (3) and (7) we write the Euler identity

$$e^{j\phi} = \cos \phi + j \sin \phi \tag{8}$$

A popular form useful in electronics is

$$e^{j\omega t} = \cos \omega t + j \sin \omega t \tag{8R}$$

where clearly

$$\mathrm{Re}(e^{j\omega t}) \;=\; \cos \omega t \tag{9}$$

The complex conjugate of $e^{j\omega t}$ also expands as

$$e^{-j\omega t} \;=\; \cos \omega t \;-\; j \sin \omega t \tag{10}$$

Addition or subtraction of Equations (8) and (10) allows us to define cos ωt and sin ωt in complex exponential terms, so that

$$\cos \omega t \;=\; \frac{e^{j\omega t} + e^{-j\omega t}}{2} \tag{11}$$

and

$$\sin \omega t \;=\; \frac{e^{j\omega t} - e^{-j\omega t}}{2j} \tag{12}$$

Also it is

$$\begin{aligned}
|e^{j\omega t}| \;&=\; |\cos \omega t + j \sin \omega t| \\
&=\; \sqrt{\sin^2 \omega t + \cos^2 \omega t} \\
&=\; \sqrt{1} \\
&=\; 1
\end{aligned} \tag{13}$$

i.e., the magnitude of $e^{j\omega t}$ is always unity. This quantity can be seen as a phasor (we recall that a *complex vector* or *phasor* is a mathematical vector that describes a quantity in the complex plane, *not* a physical vector) of unit length (Figure 4.10.2) rotating counterclockwise with an angular velocity $\omega = 2\pi f$. The complex plane of Figure 4.10.3 helps us visualize the Euler's identity (Equation 8).

We define a phase angle ϕ from the relationship

$$t \;=\; \frac{\phi}{\omega} \tag{14}$$

Given a phasor amplitude A and a phase angle ϕ, the phasor $\overrightarrow{A} = A\,e^{j\omega t}$ resolves in the real component A cos ϕ and the imaginary j A sin ϕ. In the case where a phase angle is added to the forcing function as in

$$\theta(t) \;=\; A \sin(\omega t) + \phi \tag{15}$$

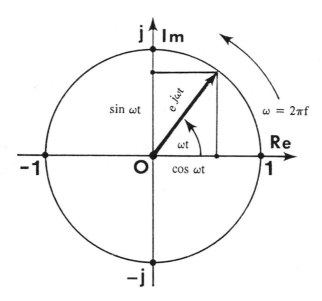

Figure 4.10.2   A unit-length phasor rotating counterclockwise in the complex plane.

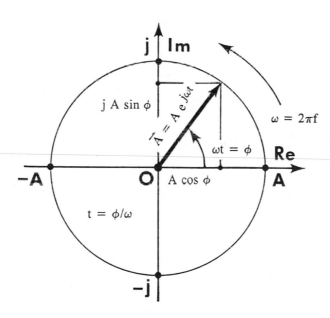

Figure 4.10.3   The complex plane as an aid to visualizing Euler's identity as per Equation (8).

(see also Equation 25, Section 4.1), the Euler identity is

$$
\begin{aligned}
A\,e^{j\,(\omega t + \phi)} &= A\,e^{j\phi}\,e^{j\omega t} \\
&= A\left[\cos\left(\omega t + \phi\right) + j\sin\left(\omega t + \phi\right)\right]
\end{aligned}
\tag{16}
$$

The concept is illustrated in Figure 4.10.4, where the length of the unit phasor $e^{\,j\omega t}$ is multiplied by A and the counterclockwise-rotating phasor $A\,e^{\,j(\omega t + \phi)}$ leads the unit phasor by an angle ϕ. The reader is referred to Section 3.2 and the harmonic oscillator experiment HARMOSC2.sim.

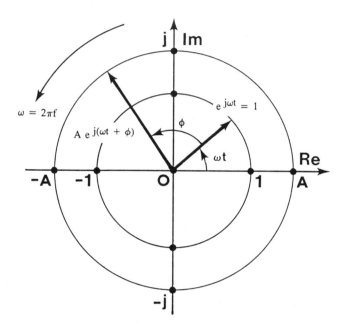

Figure 4.10.4   Visualizing a phasor leading another as per Equation (16).

It is of historical interest that the Euler identity of Equation (8) actually appears to be the work of English mathematician Roger Cotes (Smith, 1925). In 1714 Cotes published a theorem on complex numbers which states that

$$
j\,\theta = \log_e\left(\cos\theta + j\sin\theta\right)
\tag{17}
$$

That and many more fascinating facts are presented in the three-part series, "What's so natural about e," by John C. Finlay, which appeared in the 1980 volume of _Wireless World_. The reader is also referred to Section 6.2.2 on the hyperbolic functions $y = \cosh at$ and $\sinh at$.

5

TOPICS IN BALLISTICS

5.1   INTRODUCTION

The modelling and simulation of ballistic systems is of interest to many people, from among which the college physics student is the most visible. In this part we explore a few classical problems chosen for their suitability as programming paradigms. In Section 5.2 we demonstrate the use of the IFE block in simulating a discontinuous and nonlinear system involving a body's transition from upward to downward motion. Section 5.3 shows the REL block in action in the case of a body transitioning between media. A variant of the well-known cannon-fired projectile case is also discussed in Section 5.4. Block diagram languages are ideal for simulating complex ballistics problems involving discontinuities and nonlinearities of any type. So far, the author has not seen a ballistic problem that cannot be tackled.

5.2   THE BALLISTICS OF A VERTICALLY CATAPULTED LONG SLENDER CYLINDER WITH AERODYNAMIC DRAG

We wish to investigate the effect of aerodynamic drag on the vertical (both up and down) motion of a long and slender cylindrical body, when catapulted with an initial velocity $[dy/dt]_0$. It is assumed that the angle of attack is zero ($\alpha = 0°$), that is, the longitudinal axis of the body (e.g., an arrow) is parallel to its velocity vector. The catapulted body has no aerodynamic surfaces (e.g., fins) that could contribute to aerodynamic stabilization. This is a classical case of nonlinear and discontinuous system simulation and a favorite one for analog computer enthusiasts. James et al. (1966) propose two alternative analog circuit solutions, serving to illustrate the versatility of block diagram languages. We will approach the simulation in two ways, first by means of the IFE block (IF condition input 1, ELSE input 2) and second with the ABS (ABSolute value) Block.

The aerodynamic drag, D, of a long slender cylinder at zero angle of attack where the drag coefficient C_D is independent of Reynolds number (Re) and is assumed to be unity ($C_D = 1.0$), is

$$D = \left(\frac{C_D \, \rho \, S}{2} \right) \left(\frac{dy}{dt} \right)^2 \tag{1}$$

where ρ is the air density (lb-s^2/ft^4) and S is the frontal area of the body (ft^2). It is

$$k = \frac{C_D \gamma S}{2} \tag{2}$$

where k is a constant because C_D is independent of Re number. Now we write the differential equation of the system by applying Newton's second law:

$$\ddot{y} \pm \frac{k}{m} \dot{y}^2 = -32.2 \tag{3}$$

or

$$\ddot{y} + \frac{k}{m} \mid \dot{y} \mid \dot{y} = -32.2 \tag{4}$$

Equation (3) is two equations in one; the plus sign indicates upward motion and the minus sign is for the downward motion. The complete solution involves a system of two differential equations, because the system is *discontinuous*. If ℓ is the length of the cylinder and ρ_C its density, it is

$$\frac{k}{m} = \frac{C_D \rho S}{2 S \ell \rho_C} \tag{5}$$

Under the assumption of $C_D = 1.0$, the equation above becomes

$$\frac{k}{m} = \frac{\rho}{\rho_C} \tag{6}$$

Given that we are interested in the range $10^{-2} \leq k/m \leq 10^{-6}$ and that the cylinders's initial velocity is $[dy/dt]_0 = 300$ ft/s, we can implement and solve Equations (3) and (4) by means of two alternative TUTSIM setups.

First, Equations (3) and (4) are rewritten:

$$\ddot{y} = -32.2 \pm \frac{k}{m} \dot{y}^2 \tag{5}$$

$$\ddot{y} = -32.2 - \frac{k}{m} \mid \dot{y} \mid y \tag{6}$$

Equation (5) is implemented by using the IFE block as shown in Figure 5.2.1. The block diagram that represents Equation (6) is shown in Figure 5.2.2. Figure 5.2.3 shows a family

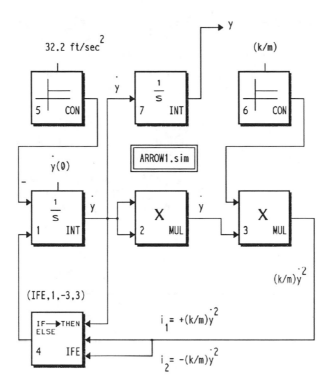

*Figure 5.2.1   Ballistic simulation of a vertically catapulted cylinder
with the IFE block (from Equation (5)).*

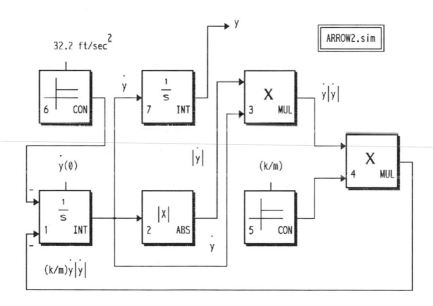

Figure 5.2.2 Alternate simulator of a vertically catapulted cylinder (from Equation (6)).

of solutions within the desired k/m range. Readers with analog/hybrid computer background can see that CDSS languages take the experimenter away from the voltage scaling required by traditional hardware methods. Also, there are no troublesome diode circuits, noisy potentiometers, or other experimenter's hazards. CDSS languages have made the patchboard a thing of the past.

The curves of Figure 5.2.3 are presented in a way that makes sense where the horizontal axis is assigned to the velocity [dy/dt] and the vertical axis is the height y. The velocity range is -500 to +500 ft/s and the zero threshold is marked by a vertical line (the Y command). Notice that the solution begins from the right (positive velocity) to the left. The height range is 0 to 1500 feet. The body's energy profile y - [dy/dt] is then shown for a k/m range of 10^{-2}, 10^{-3}, 10^{-4}, 10^{-5} and 10^{-6}. We notice the law of diminishing returns as (k/m) → 0 and the [dh/dt] - h profile shape as (k/m) is given a progressively large negative value.

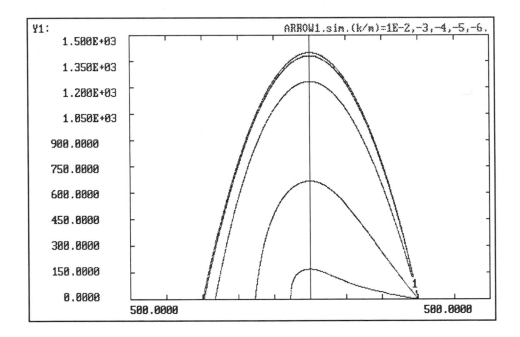

Figure 5.2.3   Velocity vs height curves for ARROW1.sim with
k/m = 1E-2, 1E-3, 1E-4, 1E-5 and 1E-6.

5.3   TRAJECTORY OF A BODY MOVING THROUGH A GRAVITATIONAL FIELD WITH VISCOUS DRAG PROPORTIONAL TO VELOCITY

This easy yet very instructive experiment was originally proposed by Wylen and Schwarz (1973). The simple trajectory problem is complicated by adding the effect of a viscous force proportional to the velocity. The differential equations of the system are

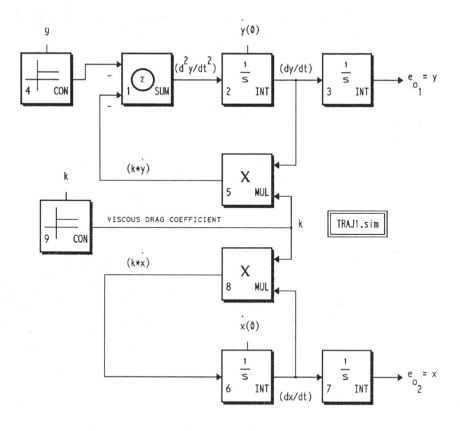

Figure 5.3.1   Simulation of a body moving through a gravitational field with viscous drag proportional to velocity.

$$\ddot{y} = - g k \dot{y} \tag{1}$$

$$\ddot{x} = - k \dot{x} \tag{2}$$

where g is the gravitational acceleration and k is the viscous drag coefficient. Figure 5.3.1 shows the simulator block diagram. The effect of k is investigated by using the MR command, resulting in the family of curves of Figure 5.3.2 (TRAJ1.sim).

Now, let's consider the more complicated case of the body transitioning from one medium to another, as in the case of a leaping dolphin. The result is a viscous drag coefficient that changes from k_2 to k_1 anytime the boundary h(0) is crossed as shown in Figure 5.3.3. The block diagram of Figure 5.3.4 simulates this by means of a REL block having the boundary h(0) as a parameter (the surface of the water). Its control input is supplied by integrator #3 that outputs y = h, the vertical displacement or altitude. One of the two situations may occur, depending upon the value of y = h. If y = h > P = h(0), REL output is from block #11. If y = h < P = h(0), REL output is from block #12. The method

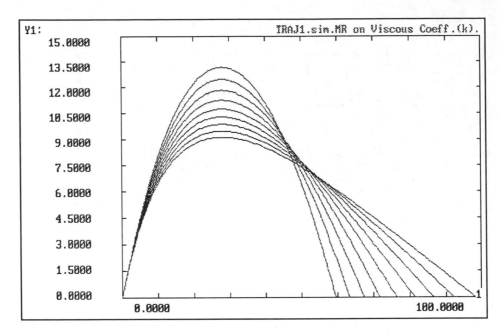

Figure 5.3.2   TRAJ1.sim results for a varying viscous drag coefficient.
The multirun (MR) command is used.

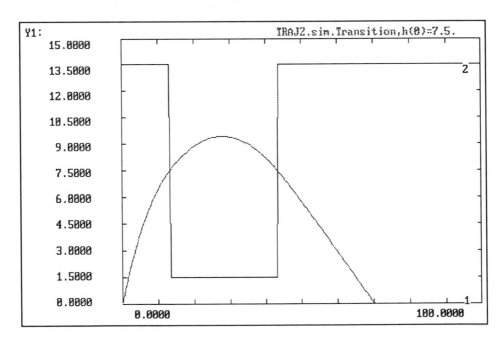

Figure 5.3.3   TRAJ2.sim results showing the transition from one viscous drag coefficient to another.

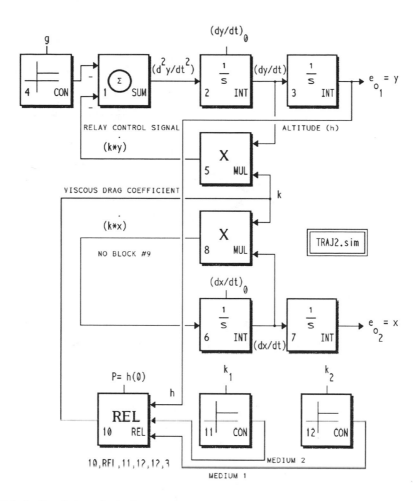

Figure 5.3.4 Simulation of a body transitioning from one medium to another with the REL block.

can be easily expanded for any number of boundaries. Albeit difficult to use in the beginning, the REL block is most useful for situations of this type.

5.4   CANNON PROJECTILE BALLISTICS

simulation of the two-dimensional trajectory of a cannon-fired projectile through the air is shown in Figure 5.4.1 where θ_0 is the elevation angle and V_0 is the muzzle velocity. The trajectory will be defined in terms of the rectangular Cartesian coordinates x and y originating at the cannon muzzle. Aerodynamic drag, D, opposes the instantaneous velocity vector, V, and mg is the weight of the projectile. It is

$$D \approx \rho V^2 = 4.7 \times 10^{-5} V^2 \, \ell b \tag{1}$$

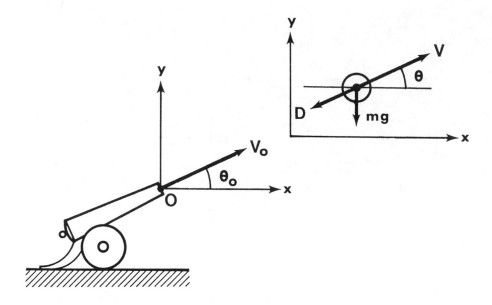

Figure 5.4.1   The physical setup of the two-dimensional cannon-fired projectile.

and

$$V^2 = \left(\dot{x}\right)^2 + \left(\dot{y}\right)^2 \tag{2}$$

$$\cos\theta = \frac{\dot{x}}{V} \tag{3}$$

$$\sin\theta = \frac{\dot{y}}{V} \tag{4}$$

where [dx/dt] and [dy/dt] are the constituent components of V and θ is the angle between the x-axis and V. We can now write the equations of motion

$$m\,\dot{x} = -D\cos\theta \tag{5}$$

$$m\,\dot{y} = -D\sin\theta - mg \tag{6}$$

or because of Equations (3) and (4)

$$m\,\dot{x} = -\frac{D}{V}\,\dot{x} \tag{7}$$

$$m\,\dot{y} = -\frac{D}{V}\,\dot{y} - mg \tag{8}$$

where g = 32.2 ft/s^2. Notice that D reduces the values of the velocity components [dx/dt] and [dy/dt]—therefore those of the coordinates. The formulation of Equations (7) and (8) bypasses the explicit use of both the sine and cosine terms without neglecting them, as they are built in the simulator of Figure 5.4.2. This is clever programming from the analog computer era where sine and cosine units were not always available.

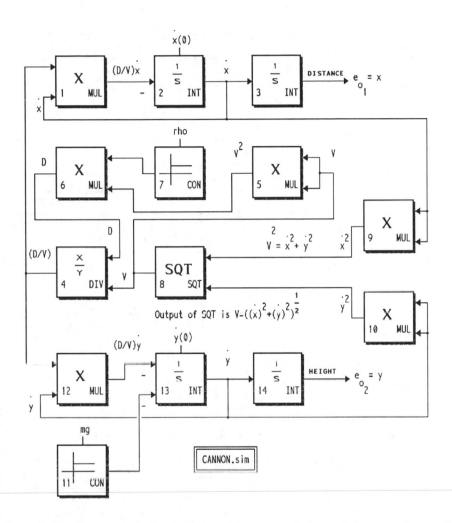

Figure 5.4.2   Cannon projectile simulation without the explicit use of trigonometric terms!

As an example, let's consider the case where $[dx/dt](0) = V_0 \cos \theta_0$, D = 0, $x(0) - y(0) = 0$, and $[dy/dt](0) = V_0 \sin \theta 0$. Given a mass m = 0.9315 slug, it is mg = 29.9943 slug-ft/s$^2 \simeq$ 30 lbs. Also, for V_0 = 800 ft/s and θ_0 = 20°, it is $[dx/dt](0)$ = 751.7540 and $[dy/dt](0)$ = 273.6161. The constant of block #7 is 0.000047. Figures 5.4.3 and 5.4.4, where 47 E-6 > ρ > 235 E-7 and 1.863 > m > 0.9315, show the effects of ρ and m, respectively. Both figures have grids prepared with the CON block (see Section 9 of the Appendix).

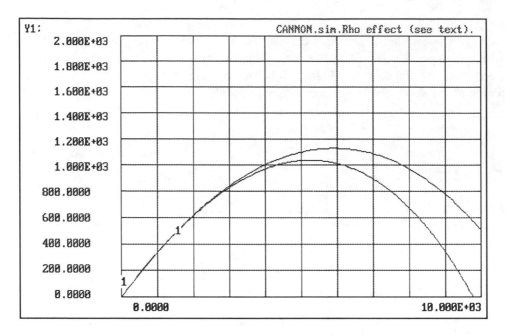

Figure 5.4.3   CANNON. sim results for different ρ values.

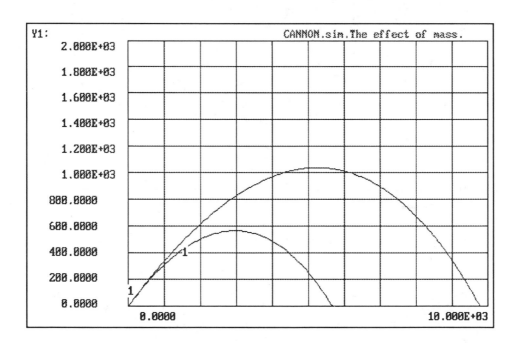

Figure 5.4.4   CANNON.sim results for different m values.

6 | BLOCK DIAGRAM LANGUAGES AND MATHEMATICS

6.1 INTRODUCTION

Block diagram languages are traditionally regarded as engineering tools and little else. By their very nature, however, they are ideally suitable for implementing *mathematics* in any discipline, be it general or applied. It is important to see the mathematical blocks of a CDSS language as equivalent dynamic substitutes of otherwise static mathematical expressions. Here we have chosen examples which attach to many disciplines and others that are somewhat unusual. The purpose of the material is many fold. First, to show techniques that facilitate the transition of equation-based mathematical models to block diagrams. Second, to demonstrate the use of block diagram techniques in the teaching (or researching) mathematical topics. In spite of its being an ideal teaching tool, block diagram languages are largely ignored by mathematicians. Yet these languages are *technically* and *philosophically* compatable with the mathematical sciences. The third purpose material is to help those transitioning from analog/hybrid computers to CDSS languages, although this requires a minimal effort because both are based on the same operating principles.

6.2 EXAMPLES OF MATHEMATICAL FUNCTION STUDIES

6.2.1 The Parabolic Function $y = kx^2$: A TUTSIM Investigation into Interdisciplinary Mathematics

In this section we embark on a somewhat lengthy discussion of the parabolic function. We will show how different technical philosophies can be equally useful in approaching the *same* problem and how block diagram languages augment the creative process by allowing the mechanization and testing of any given approach. The parabola is a conic section obtained by a cutting plane parallel to an element of a right-circular conical surface. It may also be defined as the locus of a point that moves so that its distance from a fixed line (the directrix) equals that from a fixed point (the focus). As Huntley (1970) writes, its study "involves a succession of discoveries of hitherto unsuspected truths" (p. 70). So let's investigate.

A unit parabola can be described in Cartesian form by the equation

$$X^2 = 2pY \tag{1}$$

117

where by letting $2p = 1$, a *squaring* characteristic may be obtained. Here we are using the shorthand created by Descartes (1596-1650) in his work unifying geometry and algebra.

In electronics the parabola may be realized by using an *analog multiplier* integrated circuit. The analog multiplier chip is a very significant building block in analog signal processing for both dc and frequency signals. It is a three-port device that accepts input signals e_x and e_y and yields their product, normally scaled down by a factor of ten, as shown in Figure 6.2.1.1(a). Tieing both inputs to a common signal e_i converts the multiplier to a squarer (Figure 6.2.1.1(b)). To control the speed at which the curve is generated, an integrator is added at the multiplier input. Speed can then be controlled by adjusting the integrator's time constant, normally by means of an input potentiometer (Figure 6.2.1.2(a)).

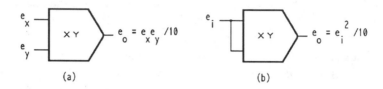

Figure 6.2.1.1 The analog multiplier (a) and its squaring configuration (b).

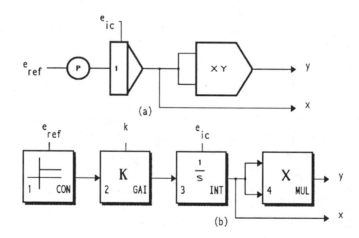

Figure 6.2.1.2 Analog computer parabola generator (a) and its equivalent block diagram (b).

Figure 6.2.1.2(b) shows the block diagram language mechanization of the concept. The effects of e_{ref} polarity change, the characteristic range limiting afforded via e_{ic} control, can be easily verified. If physical construction of the device is the ultimate goal, a block diagram language will help the designer develop valuable insight and understanding of the parametric model of the device. The greater the complexity of a design, the higher the value of a block simulator.

A parabola can also be generated by using the exponential decay technique, i.e., by setting up the exponential

$$X = e^{-t} \tag{2}$$

along with the equation

$$Y = e^{-kt} \tag{3}$$

where k is an arbitrary constant. For k = 2, Equation (3) becomes

$$Y = e^{-2t} \tag{4}$$

or

$$Y = \left(e^{-t}\right)^2 \tag{5}$$

From Equations (2) and (5), there is

$$Y = X^2 \tag{6}$$

which is the equation for the unit parabola. These simple manipulations describe the philosophy of the alternative mechanization based on the exponential decay technique. The electronic implementation is shown in Figure 6.2.1.3(a) where once the initial condition voltages are introduced, the curve is required to decay to zero value. The TUTSIM block diagram is shown in Figure 6.2.1.3(b). Typical results may be obtained by the reader for k = 0.1, 0.3, 0.6 and 0.9. The exponential function and its significance are discussed in Section 6.2.3 and the power raising mechanism is discussed in Section 6.3.3 (see also Figure 6.3.3.1).

Another approach to parabola design employs the characteristic projectile trajectory equation

$$Y = kX^2 \tag{7}$$

under the assumptions of a gravitational acceleration and initial horizontal and vertical velocities, so that

$$Y = Y(0) + \dot{Y}(0)t + \left(\frac{at^2}{2}\right) \tag{8}$$

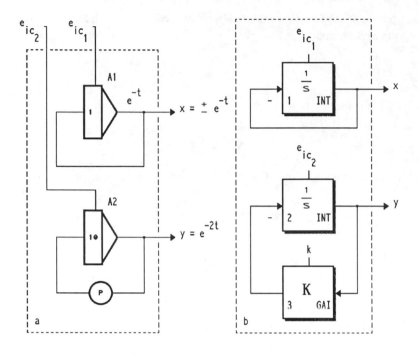

Figure 6.2.1.3   Parabola generation via the exponential decay technique with an analog circuit (a) and its equivalent block simulator (b).

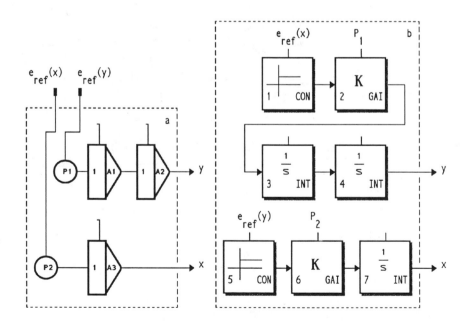

Figure 6.2.1.4   Generating a parabolic projectile trajectory with analog electronics (a) and a block diagram simulator (b).

Equation (8) describes the vertical projectile displacement. The horizontal displacement is expressed by the relationship

$$X = X(0) + \dot{X}(0)t \tag{9}$$

The electronic circuit setup is shown in Figure 6.2.1.4(a), where a -10V signal can be applied at the input of the integrator A1 and a +10V signal is applied at the input A3. Voltages $e_{ic}(1)$, $e_{ic}(2)$, and $e_{ic}(3)$ are initial-condition voltages for integrating amplifiers A1, A2, and A3, respectively. The TUTSIM implementation is shown in Figure 6.2.1.4(b). This is an interesting circuit binding algebra, geometry, physics and electronics together.

Now let us consider the system of the following two equations:

$$X = \sin t \tag{10}$$

$$Y = \sin^2 t \tag{11}$$

By virtue of a familiar trigonometric identity, Equation (1) can be rewritten as

$$Y = \frac{(1 - \cos 2t)}{2} \tag{12}$$

so Equations (10) and (11) can now have the form

$$X = \sin\left(\frac{t}{2}\right) \tag{13}$$

$$Y = \frac{(1 - \cos t)}{2} \tag{14}$$

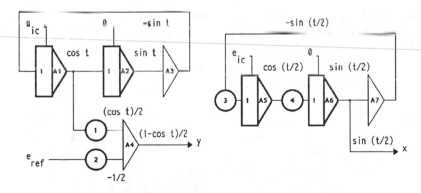

Figure 6.2.1.5   Parabolic function generation with analog computer elements mechanizing the system of Equations (13) and (14).

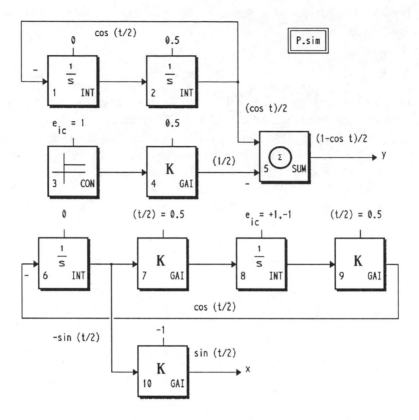

Figure 6.2.1.6   A parabola generator equivalent to that of Figure 6.2.1.5.

The system of Equations (13) and (14) can be mechanized as shown in Figure 6.2.1.5. This particular approach is an interesting one in which two sine-cosine oscillators are used and the parabolic function is produced by two oscillatory inputs applied on the horizontal and vertical axes of a plotter. Figure 6.2.1.5 shows a typical analog computer program (Karayanakis, 1988) that corresponds to the less cumbersome TUTSIM implementation of Figure 6.2.1.6. The reader should draw the first half of the curve by letting $e_{ic} = 1$ and then $e_{ic} = -1$ on integrator #8. Note that the sine-cosine oscillator yields negative sine which must be processed through a GAI block (#10).

6.2.2 The Hyperbolic Functions y = cosh at and sinh at

The problem of designing a function generator that outputs both sinh at and cosh at is similar to that of the harmonic oscillator (Section 3.2). The hyperbolic sine and cosine functions are associated with the hyperbola just like the circular functions sine ωt and cos ωt are associated with the unit circle. Sinh at and cosh at are closely related to both the exponential and circular functions and *share properties with both*.

With some reverse engineering in order, we begin by differentiating the desired outputs. The hyperbolic functions are defined as rational functions of the exponential function, and therefore we can differentiate them by using the sum and quotient rules. It is

$$\left(\frac{d}{dt}\right) \sinh at = \left(\frac{d}{dt}\right)\left(\frac{1}{2}\right)(e^{at} - e^{-at}) = a\frac{1}{2}(e^{at} + e^{-at}) = a \cosh at \tag{1}$$

Similarly,

$$\left(\frac{d}{dt}\right) \cosh at = \left(\frac{d}{dt}\right)\left(\frac{1}{2}\right)(e^{at} + e^{-at}) = a\frac{1}{2}(e^{at} - e^{-at}) = a \sinh at \tag{2}$$

Then we integrate the above equations:

$$\sinh at = a \int \cosh at\, dt \tag{3}$$

$$\cosh at = a \int \sinh at\, dt \tag{4}$$

The block diagram of Figure 6.2.2.1 implements the system of Equations (3) and (4). Parameter A is the initial condition to the INT block that yields A cosh at. The parametric coefficient a is a *time-scaling device*. The effect of a on sinh can be tested by the reader by letting a = 1 through 10 with the MR command.

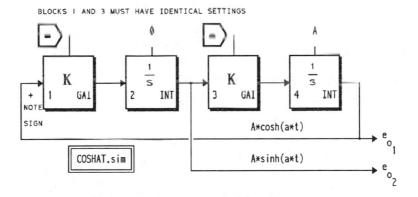

Figure 6.2.2.1   A hyperbolic sine and cosine generator.

In general, the formulas sinh x = $(1/2)(e^x - e^{-x})$ and cosh x = $(1/2)(e^x + e^{-x})$ are treated in many calculus and numerical methods texts. From a practical point of view, these curves are generated naturally by gravity, as in the case of a suspension bridge, a clothesline or a belt in a belt-driven mechanism. The cosh x or *catenary* curve (from catena, Latin for chain) and the other hyperbolic functions (see Abramowitz and Stegun, 1972) are very important in many engineering fields. The equation was discovered by Jacques Bernoulli (1654-1705). Christiaan Huygens (1629-1695) was the first to show its nonalgebraic nature in 1691. The geometrical definition of the catenary curve is the form of an inextensible and perfectly flexible chain of uniform density hanging from two supports (see also Lawrence, 1972). The curve is also found in the classical mathematical literature under the terms alysoid (from alysis, Greek for chain) and chainette.

An alternative approach to this simulation is to directly mechanize the system equation

$$\ddot{y} = a^2 y \tag{5}$$

We may solve Equation (5) analytically by first rearranging

$$\ddot{y} - a^2 y = 0 \tag{7}$$

then let

$$\dot{y} = m \tag{7}$$

so that Equation (6) becomes

$$m^2 - a^2 = 0 \tag{8}$$

Equation (8) has the roots

$$m = \sqrt{a^2} = \pm a \tag{9}$$

and therefore Equation (5) has the general solution

$$y = c_1 e^{at} + c_2 e^{-at} \tag{10}$$

where c_1 and c_2 are arbitrary coefficients. We can also write

$$y = A \cosh at + b \sinh at \tag{11}$$

(Many textbooks use ω instead of a or some other character. This is confusing to the student who associates omega with the radial frequency notation, rad/s. Needless to say, there is no periodicity here.)

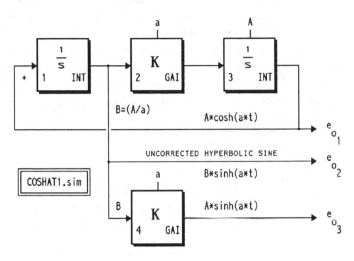

Figure 6.2.2.2   Alternate implementation of the hyperbolic function generator.

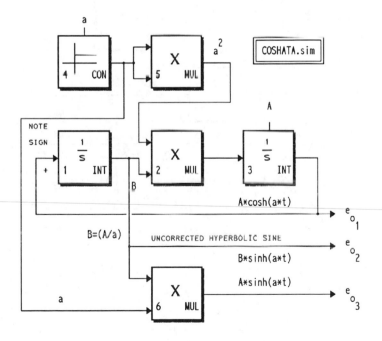

Figure 6.2.2.3   The hyperbolic function generator of Figure 6.2.2.2
with an added automatic correction mechanism.

Now we will consider a typical analog computer-type mechanization of Equation (5) like that found in the classical text by James et al. (1966, p. 124). The output of the integrator with the initial condition $y(0) = A$ is A cosh at. However, the output of the first integrator is (A/a) sinh at, that is B = (A/a) (Equation 11). The output $e_0(3)$ of Figure 6.2.2.2 (COSHAT1.sim) is the corrected signal A sinh at. This situation is similar to that encountered in the design of the harmonic oscillator circuit (Section 3.2), where the uncorrected sinewave amplitude appears as B = (A/ω). In this case, the automatic correction mechanism of Figure 6.2.2.3 (COSHATA.sim) may be used. In the case of Figure 6.2.2.4 (COSHAT2.sim), the output of the first integrator is aA sinh at and signal correction is made by routing it through the 1/a gain block.

It is interesting to note that the block diagrams of Figures 6.2.2.1, 6.2.2.2 and 6.2.2.4 are *mathematically equivalent*. However the last two generate confusing hyperbolic sine signals in need of correction. They are examples of the great analog computer struggle of the past, where amplifier conservation was the rule. As it appears, the configuration of Figure 6.2.2.4 is best for hardware implementation, as the signal Aa sinh at can be easily attenuated with a potentiometer (as opposed to using an active device to amplify).

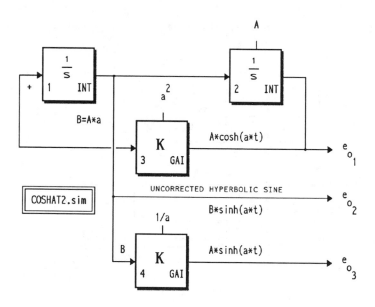

Figure 6.2.2.4   Another approach to generating the hyberbolic sine and cosine.

For those rusty on calculus, it is

$$\int \cosh t \; dt \;=\; \sinh t \qquad\qquad (12)$$

$$\int \sinh t \; dt \;=\; \cosh t \qquad\qquad (13)$$

$$\int \cosh at \; dt \;=\; \frac{1}{a} \sinh at \qquad\qquad (14)$$

$$\int \sinh at \; dt \;=\; \frac{1}{a} \cosh at \qquad\qquad (15)$$

$$\int A \cosh at \; dt \;=\; \frac{A}{a} \sinh at \qquad\qquad (16)$$

$$\int \sinh at \; dt \;=\; \frac{A}{a} \cosh at \qquad\qquad (17)$$

and

$$\int a^2 A \cosh at \; dt \;=\; a\,A \sinh at \qquad\qquad (18)$$

All of the above equations are seen at work here. Finally readers who would like to know a lot about hyperbolic functions are referred to the work by Shervatov (1966).

6.2.3 The Exponential Function $y = Ae^{\pm bt}$

This function is generated by differentiating the analytical function

$$y \;=\; A e^{-bt} \qquad\qquad (1)$$

so that

$$\dot{y} \;=\; - \, A b e^{-bt} \qquad\qquad (2)$$

From Equations (1) and (2) it is

$$\dot{y} = -by \qquad (3)$$

or

$$\dot{y} + by = 0 \qquad (4)$$

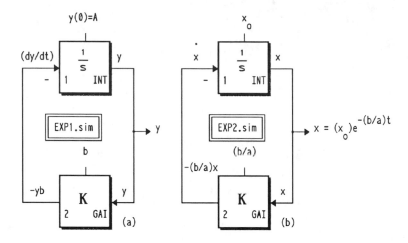

Figure 6.2.3.1   Two exponential function generators representing alternate thinking approaches.

The block diagram of Figure 6.2.3.1(a) is the simulator of Equation (4). Readers might want to draw some curves for a fixed A and a variety of b values. The scaling factor A is used so that the solution $y = Ae^{-bt}$ takes into account the scaling effects of y(0). Since $e^0 = 1$, the initial value of Ae^{-bt} is positive. Essentially, the function has a magnitude of A units at t = 0 and decays to a value of (A/e) in (1/6) time unit (see also Section 6.3.3.). Similarly the function

$$y = Ae^{bt} \qquad (5)$$

may be simulated by implementing the differential equation

$$\dot{y} - by = 0 \qquad (6)$$

The exponential function is very important in mathematical modelling and simulation, primarily because of its unique properties shown by the two equations

$$e^t = \frac{d(e^t)}{dt} \qquad (7)$$

$$e^t = \int_0^t e^t \, dt \tag{8}$$

That is, both its derivative and integral yield the function itself. In fact, *most signals that specify the transfer functions of physical systems can be expressed in some exponential form.* As a case in point, the outputs of the harmonic oscillator (see Section 3.2) can be expressed as

$$\sin \omega t = \left(\frac{1}{2j}\right) (e^{j\omega t} - e^{-j\omega t}) \tag{9}$$

$$\cos \omega t = \left(\frac{1}{2}\right) (e^{j\omega t} + e^{-j\omega t}) \tag{10}$$

A detailed discussion of Equations (9) and (10) is found in Section 4.10. Even the unit step function u(t) is a special case of the exponential function where the exponent has a zero coefficient or

$$e^{at} = u t \qquad (a = 0, t > 0) \tag{11}$$

The articles of Kammler and Lorrain (1969) and Corran and Gaal (1969) on the generation of the functions $1/t$ and $1/t^2$ are also of interest here (see Section 6.2.5).

Now we consider a mixing tank which receives fresh water at a flow rate, m, (gal/s) and discharges at the same rate. The liquid volume is V, a constant. The tank contains a saline solution; the amount of salt in it at any time, t, is n (lb). The mixture concentration at any time, t, is (n/V) (lb/gal). During any interval Δt the amount of escaping salt is

$$dn = - \left(\frac{n}{V}\right) m \, dt \tag{12}$$

and by rearranging

$$\frac{dn}{dt} + \left(\frac{m}{V}\right) n = 0 \tag{13}$$

or

$$V\dot{n} + mn = 0 \tag{14}$$

The expression above is a linear, homogeneous differential equation of the first order having constant coefficients. Its general form is

$$a\dot{x} + bx = 0 \tag{15}$$

Variations of this equation are found throughout the physical world. Its simulation model can be best explained by considering the following analytical steps. The explicit solution for the derivative is

$$\dot{x} = -\frac{b}{a}x \tag{16}$$

if

$$x = k\,e^{qt} \tag{17}$$

where k is an arbitrary constant. It is

$$\dot{x} = k\,q\,e^{qt} \tag{18}$$

Substituting Equations (17) and (18) into Equation (16) gives

$$k\,q\,e^{qt} = -\frac{b}{a}\,k\,e^{qt} \tag{19}$$

or

$$q = \frac{-b}{a} \tag{20}$$

Substituting Equation (20) into Equation (17) gives

$$x = k\,e^{-(b/a)t} \tag{21}$$

Now we must evaluate k in order to have a complete solution. This is done by expressing it in terms of the initial value of x so that $x = x_0$ at $t = 0$. It is

$$x_0 = k \tag{22}$$

and by substituting the above into Equation (21) we get

$$x = x_0\,e^{-(b/a)t} \tag{23}$$

Equation (16) is simulated as shown in Figure 6.2.3.1(b). This time we can investigate results for a fixed (b/a) gain (e.g., 0.5) and a variety of x_0 values (e.g., 1 through 10).

As a numerical example, let us consider again the mixing tank. If $V = 10$ gallons, $m = 20$ (gal/s) and the initial amount of salt $n_0 = 5$ gallons, the system equation is

$$10\,\dot{n} + 20\,n = 0 \quad (n_0 = 5) \tag{24}$$

having the solution (see Equation (23))

$$n = 5\,e^{-2t} \quad (\ell b) \tag{25}$$

Note that if $n_0 = 0$ (or $x_0 = 0$ in Equation (16)), the equation has the trivial solution $x = 0$, a valid solution resulting from the absence of a forcing function. At all times the solution curve begins with the initial condition value and decreases exponentially to become an asymptote of zero.

It is of interest to note the equation

$$L\,\dot{i} + R\,i = 0 \quad (i_0 > 0) \tag{26}$$

representing a closed loop RL circuit (discussed in detail in Section 8.2.3) and the equation

$$C\,\dot{v} + \frac{1}{R}\,v = 0 \quad (v_0 > 0) \tag{27}$$

are also of the same form. For example, if $v_c = v_0 = 5V$, $R = 0.05\ \Omega$ and $C = 10$ F, Equation (27) becomes

$$10\,\dot{v} + 20\,v = 0 \quad (v_c = v_0 - 5\,V) \tag{28}$$

The RC system so described is exactly analogous to the mixing tank system of Equation (24) and n is analogous to v. Of course, the solution is

$$v = 5\,e^{-2t} \quad (V) \tag{29}$$

The block diagram simulation of the series RC and RL circuits are discussed in detail in Section 8.2.

Another significant application of the exponential function is in transport delay simulation, discussed in detail in Section 6.7. Here we will establish the connection between transport delay and exponential notation. The equation

$$e_0(t) = e_i(t - \tau) \tag{30}$$

indicates a process where the input signal, $e_i(t)$, is delayed by a time, τ. The Laplace transform of Equation (30) is

$$e_0(s) = \int_0^\infty e_i(t - \tau) e^{-st} dt \tag{31}$$

and by letting

$$t - \tau = h \tag{32}$$

Equation (31) is rewritten as

$$e_0(s) = \int_{-\tau}^\infty e_i(h) e^{-s(\tau + h)} dh \tag{33}$$

We note that $e_i(h) = 0$ when $h < 0$, so we change the lower limit and rewrite

$$e_0(s) = \int_0^\infty e_i(h) e^{-s(\tau + h)} dh \tag{34}$$

or

$$e_0(s) = e^{-s\tau} \int_0^\infty e_i(h) e^{-sh} dh \tag{35}$$

or

$$e_0(s) = e^{-s\tau} e_i(s) \tag{36}$$

and therefore

$$T(s) = \frac{e_0}{e_i}(s) = e^{-s\tau} \qquad (37)$$

Finally the reader is directed to Section 12.14 where the exponential function is used to simulate a most important statistical signal processor yielding the exponentially-mapped past estimate of the mean.

6.2.4 The Inverse Function $y = f^{-1}(x)$

We say that two functions f and g are inverse if $f(g(x)) = x$ for each x in the g-domain and if $g(f(x)) = x$ for each x in the f-domain. Then we write $g = f^{-1}$. The generalized notation $f^{-1}(x)$ refers to the inverse of the function f, not the reciprocal. Inverse functions are useful in simulation and when linearizing signals (Weiner, 1972). They may be used to create a new function or linearize a given function by generating its mirror image curve, a reflection of the original curve in the line $y = x$. Note that according to the reflective property of inverse functions, the f curve contains the point (a,b) if and only if the f^{-1} curve contains the point (b,a).

Traditionally, inverse functions are implemented by piecewise-linear approximation methods (i.e., via diode function circuits). Whenever possible, the use of the logarithmic technique shown in Figure 6.2.4.1 is recommended. This approach is used with logarithmic circuits (section 6.5) or multifunction converters (Section 8.5). In the simulator of Figure 6.2.4.1 it is $f(x) = Ae^{-bt}$. Readers may visualize the concept by plotting both input and output functions and their sum (see also Section 12.10).

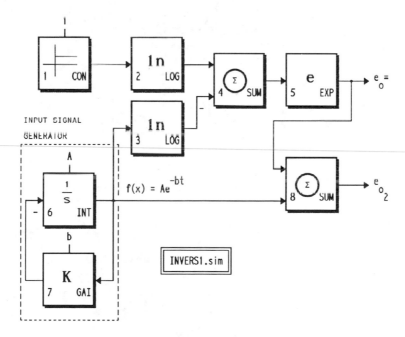

Figure 6.2.4.1 A setup for the investigation of inverse functions.

6.2.5 The Function f(t) = 1/t

This useful analytic function is generated from its describing differential equation

$$\frac{df}{dt} = -f^2 \tag{1}$$

Assuming some constant a where $t > a$, it is

$$f(a) = a^{-1} \tag{2}$$

(see also Gilliland, 1967; Kammler and Lorrain, 1969; and Corran and Gaal, 1969). In the block diagram of Figure 6.2.5.1 (F.sim), the CON block (#4) supplies the initial conditions to the integrator in the form of a wirable input to the circuit (see Section 1.5).

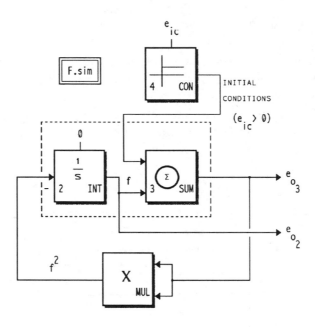

Figure 6.2.5.1   Generating the analytic function f(t) = 1/t.

6.2.6 Circles and Some Cyclic Curve Functions

The circle is represented in Cartesian form by the equation

$$X^2 + Y^2 = r^2 \tag{3}$$

and in polar form (of interest here) by the system of parametric equations

$$X = r \cos t$$
$$Y = r \sin t \tag{4}$$

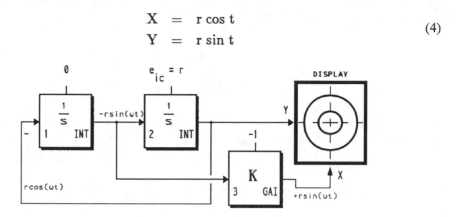

Figure 6.2.6.1 Implementing the circle equations with a harmonic oscillator.

Its traditional analog implementation is shown in Figure 6.2.6.1, where a harmonic oscillator (see also Section 3.2) is used with initial conditions $e_{ic} = r$ and $\omega = 1$. The first integrator generates -r sin t because the INT block is noninverting (unlike the typical analog computer opamp integrator).

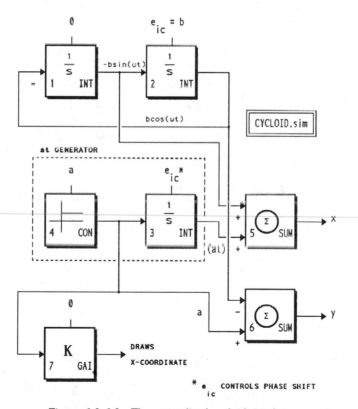

Figure 6.2.6.2 The generalized cycloid simulator.

A cycloid can be described as the path of a point situated within a circle of radius a at a distance b from the circle's center when the circle rolls along a horizontal surface. The generalized cycloid is described by the following system of parametric equations

$$X \;=\; at \;-\; b \sin t \tag{5}$$

$$Y \;=\; a \;-\; b \cos t \tag{6}$$

The block diagram implementation is shown in Figure 6.2.6.2. A cycloid curve for a = 0.3, b= 1 may be drawn (use a horizontal scale of 0 - 15). Blocks #3 and #4 form the (at) generator and the gain block (#7) is used with a zero parameter to generate the x-coordinate.

The generalized limaçon of Pascal is described by the following system

$$X \;=\; 4a \cos t \;-\; k \cos 2t \tag{7}$$

$$Y \;-\; 4a \cos t \;-\; k \sin 2t \tag{8}$$

It can be visualized as the trace of a point fixed within a circle which is rolling upon a fixed circle of equal radius. Figure 6.2.6.3 shows a block simulator structured with TUTSIM's function generators. As an exercise, we can draw the curve for the case 2a =k (Karayanakis, 1980, 1985b, 1986; Pedoe, 1976).

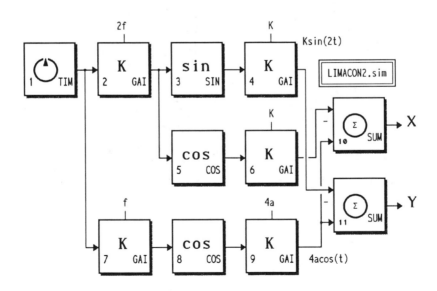

Figure 6.2.6.3   The generalized limaçon of Pascal simulator.

Hypocycloids are special cases of the cyclic curve, which is a higher plane curve. The hypocycloid can be visualized as the trace of a fixed point within a circle of radius r rolling around the inside of a fixed circle of radius R. The *generalized* hypocycloid is described by the following system of parametric equations:

$$X = (R - r) \cos t + r \cos \frac{(R - r)t}{r} \tag{9}$$

$$Y = (R - r) \sin t + r \sin \frac{(R - r)t}{r} \tag{10}$$

Different values of R and r will yield special cases. The block diagram of Figure 6.2.6.4 implements Equations (1) and (2) to form a generalized simulator.

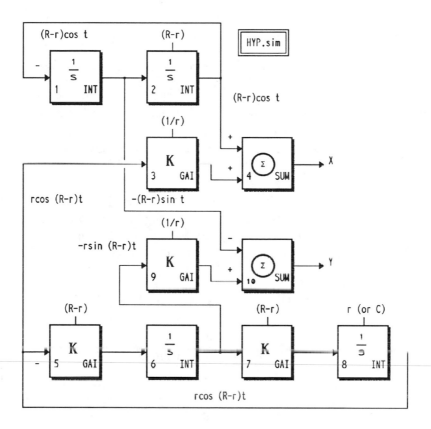

Figure 6.2.6.4 The generalized hypocycloid simulator.

The hypocycloid of four cusps is a special case of the hypocycloid curve formed when the radius of the fixed circle is four times that of the one rolling inside, or R = 4r. It is described by the system of parametric equations

$$X = (R - r) \cos t + C \cos \frac{(R - r)t}{r} \tag{11}$$

$$Y = (R - r) \sin t - C \sin \frac{(R - r)t}{r} \tag{12}$$

When $C > r$, a *prolate* hypocycloid is drawn. When $C = r$, the cusps of the cycloid will be inscribed inside the fixed circle. When $C < b$, a *curtate* hypocycloid will appear. The *asteroid* is also a hypocycloid of four cusps, formed with $R = 4r$. In this case, the system of the generalized Equations (1) and (2) becomes

$$X = \left(\frac{R}{4}\right) (3 \cos t + \cos 3t) \tag{13}$$

$$Y = \left(\frac{R}{4}\right) (3 \sin t - \sin 3t) \tag{14}$$

Readers can plot an asteroid by letting $R = 4r$ and $r = 1$ (-5,+5 on both axes). Theoretically, a hypocycloid having *any* number of cusps can be generated by applying the generalized system of Equations (1) and (2). Readers could generate a seven-cusp trace by letting $r = 2$ and $R = 4r$.

Like hypocycloids, epicycloids are special cases of the cyclic curve. Epicycloids are formed when a circle of radius r rolls around the *outside* of a fixed circle of radius R and a point on the circumference of the moving circle traces out the curve. The generalized epicycloid is described by the following system of parametric equations:

$$X = (R + r) \cos t - r \cos \frac{(R - r)t}{r} \tag{15}$$

$$Y = (R + r) \sin t - r \sin \frac{(R - r)t}{r} \tag{16}$$

The block diagram simulator of this system is left as an exercise for the reader. Different values for R and r will yield special cases like those of the *cardioid* and *nephroid*. Note also that, in the case where the tracing point is situated along a radial line of the moving circle and at some distance C from center, if C is larger than the diameter, the epicycloid is described by the system:

$$X = (R + r) \sin t - C \sin \frac{(R - r)t}{r} \tag{17}$$

$$Y = (R + r) \cos t - C \cos \frac{(R - r)t}{r} \tag{18}$$

The cardioid is an epicycloid of *one* cusp formed when R = r and is described by the system

$$X = R(2 \cos t - \cos 2t) \tag{19}$$

$$X = R(2 \sin t - \sin 2t) \tag{20}$$

The nephroid is an epicycloid of *two* cusps formed when R = 2r and is described by the system

$$X = r(3 \cos t - \cos 3t) \tag{21}$$

$$Y = r(3 \sin t - \sin 3t) \tag{22}$$

6.3 THE SIMULATION OF HIGH-ORDER ALGEBRAIC EQUATIONS

6.3.1 Introduction: Generating Integral Powers

The technical solution to the simulation of an algebraic equation of the nth degree (with real and complex roots) of the form

$$y(x) = a_0 x^n + a_1 x^{n-1} + \ldots + a_{n-1} x + a_n \tag{1}$$

rests in generating powers of x. High-order algebraic equations are easily mechanized with linear multipliers or multifunction converter (mfc) integrated circuits (see Section 8.5). However, this approach is costly because an equation of the nth degree requires (n-1) linear multiplier or mfc chips. In simulation, the generalized polynomial implementation problem is best seen as one of raising a single quantity to various powers, rather than multiplying quantities. This philosophy leads to an alternate powerful solution based on the indefinite integral algebraic functions

$$\int u^n \, du = \frac{u^{n+1}}{n+1} \tag{2}$$

(see Tuma, 1979, p. 254; and Petit Bois, 1964). In this expression, the constant of integration is omitted and u = f(c), n ≠ -1 (a constant). We are interested in time as the independent variable, so we substitute dt for du, so that

$$u^n = n \int_0^t u^{n-1} \, dt \tag{3}$$

that is, repeated integrations of a constant yield *any* integral power of that constant ($u \geq 0$) so that

$$u \;=\; \int_0^t 1 \; dt$$

$$u^2 \;=\; 2 \int_0^t u \; dt \tag{4}$$

$$u^3 \;=\; 3 \int_0^t u^2 \; dt$$

and so on. The concept is represented by the block diagram of Figure 6.3.1.1. This technique has limitations, to include the large number of integrators required to implement a polynomial (one per power) and the inability to simulate nonintegral powers.

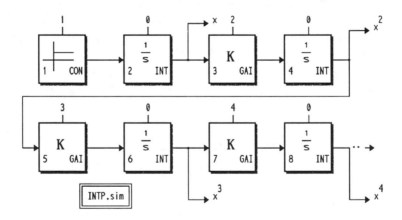

Figure 6.3.1.1　Generating polynomial powers by repeated integrations of a constant.

The complete solution of a polynomial requires *two* computer runs—one to find all the positive real roots and another for the negative real roots. By definition, real roots ar the values of x for which y = 0. The complete solution is found by letting t = x (the output of the first integrator) and arranging a four-quadrant display with the CB command, where H = 2, -1, 1, Y1 = 2, -1, 1, Y2 = 4, -1, 1 and so on. the first run outputs the *first quadrant* portion of the solution for y = f(1) where the parameter of the CON block (#1) is unity. The second run completes the solution in the second quadrant portion for y = f(-1), where the CON parameter is -1 and the setting for the GAI (#3 block) is -2.

6.3.2 Some Examples

The quartic function

$$y(x) = Ax^4 + Bx^3 + Cx^2 + Dx + E \tag{1}$$

where x ≠ 0 can be simulated by generating its powers as shown in Figure 6.3.1.1 and using gain blocks to set the A, B, C, D, E values. The straightforward implementation of Figure 6.3.2.1 involves the additional five GAI blocks and a summer.

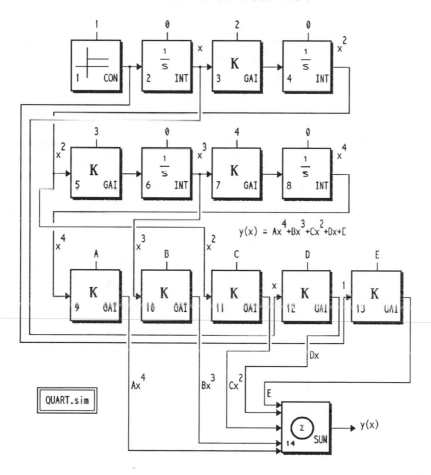

Figure 6.3.2.1   Simulating a quartic function according to the method of Figure 6.3.1.1.

A different viewpoint emerges if we set x = t and consider the time function

$$y(t) = At^4 + Bt^3 + Ct^2 + Dt + E \qquad (2)$$

which can be differentiated successfully with respect to time so that

$$y = At^4 + Bt^3 + Ct^2 + Dt + E$$
$$\dot{y} = 4At^3 + 3Bt^2 + 2Ct + D$$
$$\ddot{y} = 12At^2 + 6Bt + 2C$$
$$\frac{d^3y}{dt^3} = 24At + 6B \qquad (3)$$
$$\frac{d^4y}{dt^4} = 24A$$

This suggests the remarkably simple implementation of Figure 6.3.2.2, where the constant value of the fourth derivative is the input of the first integrator. The tutorial implementation of Figure 6.3.2.3 uses integrators with hardwired conditions (see Section 1.5) so that only the values of A, B, C, D, E are entered rather than the explicit $[d^3y/dt^3] = 24A$, and so on. This simulator uses TUTSIM time; therefore it can only output the first half of the solution curve, the function f(1). In contrast, the simulator of Figure 6.3.2.1 can produce both halves of the curve. Given a desired solution range f(-a,a), the first half is the realization of f(a) and the second half is for f(-a). Note that the proper sign on the E constant (GAI #13) ensures continuity of the solution curve.

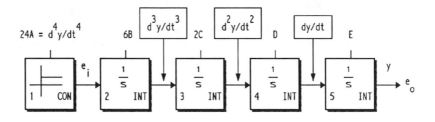

Figure 6.3.2.2   An alternate approach to quartic generation.

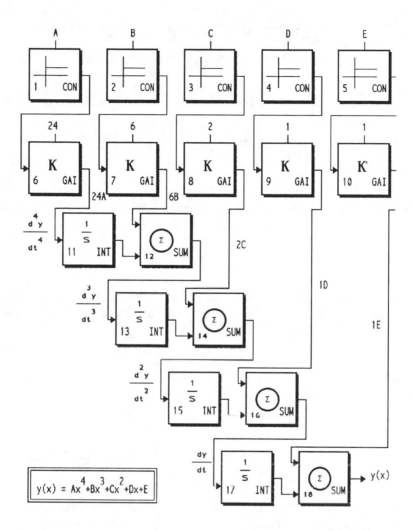

Figure 6.3.2.3   Generating a quartic with the method of Figure 6.3.2.2.

6.3.3   Solving Nonintegral Cases

In Sections 6.3.1 and 6.3.2 methods for finding the real roots of equations having integral powers were discussed. Here we describe another pure analog technique having great computational utility, thereby providing a universal approach to the simulation of algebraic polynomials with *nonintegral, integral* or *mixed* powers. Originally described by Forrest (1965), the technique allows easy operational amplifier mechanization of polynomials.

Mathematically, this technique is based on the relationship

$$x = x_0 e^{-t} \tag{1}$$

which, when raised to the nth power, becomes

$$x^n = x_0^n e^{-nt} \tag{2}$$

The block diagram simulator of the above equation is implemented from the relationship

$$\frac{d}{dt}\left(x_0^n e^{-nt}\right) = -n x_0^n e^{-nt} \tag{3}$$

without the requirement that n be an integral. In contrast to the approach of Section 6.3.1, only those powers of x required by a given equation need be generated. This results in an overall reduction of computing blocks, something relevant to hardware designers. Note that, like before, a complete solution requires two runs.

When the final goal is the design of an operational amplifier circuit, overloading considerations call for the adoption of scaling constants k and a, so that Equations (1), (2) and (3) become, respectively,

$$x = k x_0 e^{-at} \tag{4}$$

$$x^n = k^n x_0^n e^{-nat} \tag{5}$$

$$\frac{d}{dt}\left(k^n x_0^n e^{-nat}\right) = -n a k^n x_0^n e^{-nat} \tag{6}$$

It is recommended that the reader become familiar with the exponential function simulation technique of Section 6.2.3 and the application to parabolic function of Section 6.2.1. Figure 6.3.3.1 provides a synoptic view of the power generation mechanism.

The quadratic

$$y(x) = x^2 - 6x + 5 \tag{7}$$

is implemented by the exponential power generation method as shown in Figure 6.3.3.2 (QUAD2.sim). This approach requires only six blocks! Conceptually, we may write Equation (6) in the pertinent form

$$y(x) = k^2 x_0^2 e^{-2at} - 6 k x_0 e^{-at} + 5 \tag{8}$$

If we are designing operational amplifier circuits, we may choose the value of scaling factor a so that the product (na) (see Equation 5) is within 0.1 and 10, thus avoiding excessive

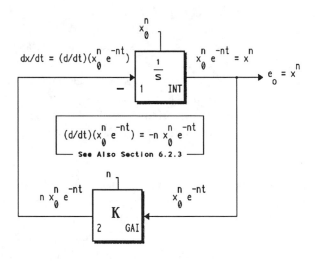

Figure 6.3.3.1 The principle of nonintegral power generation.

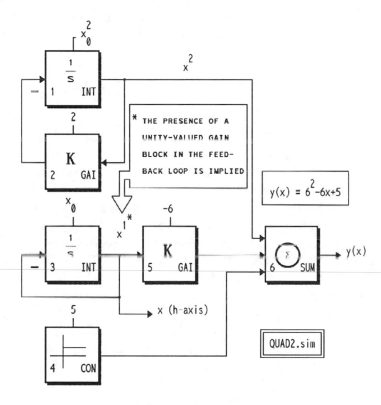

Figure 6.3.3.2 Implementing a quadratic with the method of Figure 6.3.3.1.

circuit gains. The location of the roots is not affected by the magnitude of a. In this simulation we chose a = 1 and k = 1. Also, physical circuit design calls for considering the opamp saturation level and choosing a suitable k value. The circuit is simulated in two halves. In the example, we chose to find the real roots of y lying in the interval $-10 \leq x \leq 10$. The first half of the simulation deals with the interval $10 \leq x \leq 0$ and the original conditions of the integrators are - (-10) = 10 for x_0 and $(-10)^2 = 100$ for $x_0{}^2$. The second half $0 \leq x \leq 10$ calls for the original conditions $-(+10)^2 = -10$ for x_0 and $(+10)^2 = 100$ for $x_0{}^2$. The numerical values of the two roots can be read by using TUTSIM's SN command.

Most people believe that the simulation of algebraic equations and polynomials is normally a job for specialized software. However, the universal block diagram approach in conjunction with a CDSS language provides a dynamic and flexible point of view. Most of all, it provides the in-between steps required toward the building of actual hardware.
We urge the reader to become familiar with the simulation techniques discussed here, as they offer unlimited potential in many tough problem mechanizations calling for the generation of decimal, fractional and mixed-number powers (see also the method by Hundel, 1977). Of course, the PWR block is very handy, although the scheme shown here is very useful when translating the mathematical block to real hardware with operational amplifiers only and *without* expensive logarithmic generator, multiplier or multifunction converter integrated circuits.

6.4   DIFFERENTIAL EQUATIONS

6.4.1   Introduction

The general-purpose block diagram language is an assembly of mathematical, logical, and specialized function blocks which are then interconnected to form mathematical models. These models are often based on one or more differential equations which, once restated in block diagram form, are solved for a variety of specified conditions. Just like analog computers, the equations most suitable for solution with a CDSS langugage are dfqs with only one independent variable represented by time. Special techniques also allow the solution of algebraic equations and partial dfqs.

It is important to remember that, unlike analog computers where modules like multipliers, dividers, arbitrary function generators, and so on, are often a luxury and a very finite commodity, block diagram languages have no such limitations. Thus, they are ideal tools for investigating both linear and nonlinear differential equations which can be solved for any steady or *unsteady* state conditions. The following examples speak for themselves.

6.4.2   Solving Linear Ordinary Differential Equations

The classical differential equation programming technique of Lord Kelvin (Thomson, 1876a and 1876b) is found in all analog computer literature. It is an indispensable tool in the creation of a mathematical block diagram from an equation or an equation system. Of interest here is the case of the constant-coefficient linear ordinary differential equation (LODE) of the form

$$a_0(x) \frac{d^n y}{dx^n} + a_1(x) \frac{d^{(n-1)} y}{dx^{n-1}} + \ldots + a^{n-1}(x) \frac{dy}{dx} + a_n(x) y = f(x)$$

(1)

As in analog computer programming, we substitute the independent variable x for time t to produce signals that correspond to the dependent variables and their derivatives. By letting t be the independent variable and according to the notation $[d^n y/dt] = y^{(n)}$ we rewrite Equation (1):

$$a_0 y^{(n)} + a_1 y^{(n-1)} + \ldots + a_{n-1} y^{(1)} + a_n y = f(x)$$

(2)

Lord Kelvin's method calls first for setting the highest order derivative equal to all the other equation terms, so we write

$$y^{(n)} = - \left[\frac{a_1}{a_0} y^{(n-1)} + \ldots + \frac{a_{n-1}}{a_0} y^{(1)} + \frac{a_n}{a_0} y - \frac{1}{a_0} f(x) \right]$$

(3)

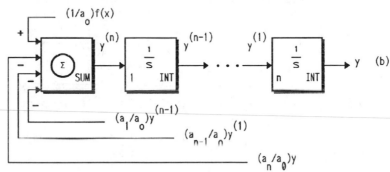

Figure 6.4.2.1   Illustrating Lord Kelvin's method of LODE programming.

Then we draw a number of integrators equal to the order of the equation as shown in Figure 6.4.2.1(a). The output of each integrator is, by definition, a *state variable*. It is assumed that the highest-order derivative $y^{(n)}$ is available and it is the input to the first block. Finally, we establish the loops by connecting the appropriate lower order terms according to the equation being modelled. Equation (3) suggests step (b) of Figure 6.4.2.1 leading naturally to the final block diagram of Figure 6.4.2.2. The summing block ahead of the first integrator is redundant; the signals may be summed directly into the integrator. However, in this case, the highest order derivatve will not be available for recording or observation.

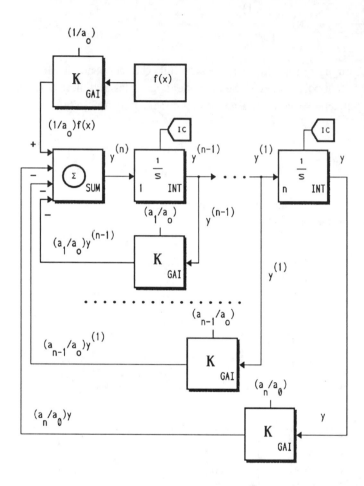

Figure 6.4.2.2   The block simulator of a generalized LODE (Eq. 3) according to Lord Kelvin's method.

An alternate approach involves the use of multiplier blocks. The block simulator of Figure 6.4.2.3 allows the direct entry of a_1, a_{n-1}, a_n and $1/a_0$ rather than calculating the ratios a_1/a_0, etc. This setup is expensive in blocks but rich in experimental advantages. In the case of analog computers where multipliers are a rare commodity, this approach constitutes a luxury or even an impossibility. Notably there are many ways to implement a block simulator. Of course, the final step always involves the entry of arbitrary constants, the setup of forcing function(s) and the introduction of initial conditions to integrators (if every integrator has an initial condition, the problem has a unique solution). In the case of systems having numerous equations, the entire procedure is repeated for each equation and the connecting loops are again established with the equations themselves as wiring guides.

There are several examples of this procedure throughout the book (e.g., the case of coupled systems in Section 8.4). The classical method of Lord Kelvin is indeed easy and efficient, and is preferred by many over the more elaborate state-equation approach to simulation. This is, however, a matter of preference, style and need.

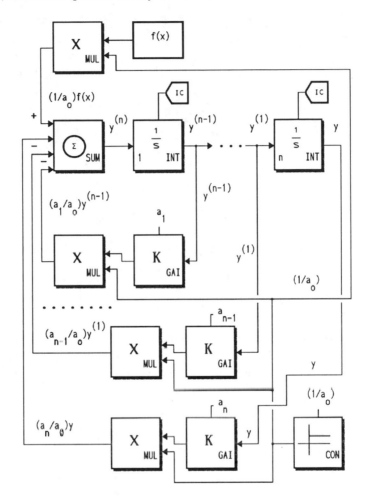

Figure 6.4.2.3 An alternate LODE simulation approach with multiplier blocks.

Let us consider the generalized nth order LODE

$$a_0(t) \frac{d^n y}{dt^n} + a_1(t) \frac{d^{n-1} y}{dt^{n-1}} + \ldots + a_{n-1}(t) \frac{dy}{dt} + a_n(t) y = f(x) \quad (4)$$

From a practical point of view, the dynamic system represented by Equation (1) has n energy storage regions (the same as the order of the equation that describes it). Therefore, the system requires n integrators for its block diagram model. Solving Equation (1) for the highest derivative and according to the notation $[d^n y/dt] = y^{(n)}$, it is

$$y^{(n)} = - \left[\frac{a_1}{a_0} y^{(n-1)} + \ldots + \frac{a_2}{a_0} y^{(n-2)} + \ldots + \frac{a_{n-1}}{a_0} y^{(1)} + \frac{a_n}{a_0} y - \frac{1}{a_0} f(x) \right]$$

(5)

To reiterate, the output of each integrator is a state variable (a coordinate in phase-space). We designate the state variables y_i so that

$$y = y_1$$

$$\frac{dy}{dt} = y_2$$

$$\frac{d^2 y}{dt^2} = y_3$$

$$\ldots$$

$$\frac{d^{n-2} y}{dt^{n-2}} = y_{n-1}$$

$$\frac{d^{n-1} y}{dt^{n-1}} = y_n$$

(6)

The dependent variable y is defined as the first state variable, its first derivative is as the second state variable, and so on. The (n-1) derivative is finally defined as the nth state variable according to the ascending order of Equation (3). Then Equation (2) can be written *as a system of n first-order simultaneous equations*:

$$\frac{dy_1}{dt} = y_2$$

$$\frac{dy_2}{dt} = y_3$$

$$\ldots$$

$$\frac{dy_{n-1}}{dt} = y_n$$

$$\frac{dy_n}{dt} = \frac{1}{a_0} f(x) - \frac{a_n}{a_0} y_1 - \frac{a_{n-1}}{a_0} y_2 - \ldots - \frac{a_2}{a_0} y_{n-1} - \frac{a_1}{a_0} y_n$$

(7)

The system above is the *state-space* or *phase-space* representation of the original Equation (1). Its implementation is similar to that of the classical method of Lord Kelvin (which also involves state variables). However, the state equation approach embodies the concept of the phase-portrait representation and links block language simulation with mathematical analysis. The utility of the phase-space diagram is discussed in Section 6.4.5. Generally there is no unique way in choosing state variables, in developing state equations and therefore in impelementing a simulator. A simulator based on state equations is structurally different from one formed by the conventional higher-order derivative method, although the results are, of course, identical.

6.4.3 Nonlinear Ordinary Differential Equations

The study of nonlinear ordinary differential equations (NODEs) and their systems provides a fascinating but often prohibitive topic for the scientist, the engineer and even the mathematician. The opening statement by Jordan and Smith (1987) in their highly acclaimed book, *Nonlinear Ordinary Differential Equations*, states that generally it is is not possible to obtain analytic solutions to an arbitrary differential equation. Not only do we lack complete means of expressing solutions, but often, even if an analytic solution exists, its equation is far too complicated and detracts from the essential features of the solution. Qualitative solution techniques seek to deduce the essential features of solutions *without* solving the original equation (this applies to both LODE and NODE categories). Mathematicians use a geometrical device, the *phase plane*, to obtain information about the stability and the behavior of nonlinear equations. CDSS languages are useful here as they allow the block buildup of a mathematical model of the LODE or NODE under study and the subsequent plotting of the phase-plane solution trajectories. The phase-plane diagram is discussed in Section 6.4.5 (see also the book on mathematical models by Beltrami, 1987).

We cannot overemphasize that once a mathematical block model is built, CDSS languages allow investigations with different coefficients, initial conditions or forcing functions. The dynamic simulation approach permits the generation of the solution trajectories under *any* conditions thought by the experimenter. Therefore, block diagram languages represent the ultimate tool in investigating nonlinear equations and systems. Unfortunately this approach is rarely found in the teaching or research of mathematics. Another interesting observation on the block language approach is that an equation or a system of simultaneous equations acquire physical essence. This is important in conceptualizing and applying the concept behind the symbols. As a case in point we chose the van der Pol equation. An important thing to remember is that once in block diagram form, a differential equation can be easily seen and treated as a *feedback system*.

Van der Pol's equation represents an oscillator with nonlinear damping. As Guckenheimer and Holmes (1983) point out, energy is dissipated at large amplitudes and generated at low amplitudes. In 1927, van der Pol discussed the forced oscillations of a triode oscillator having negative resistance. The original article (van der Pol, 1927) is reprinted in the Dover edition of Bellman and Kalaba (1964). The van der Pol oscillator is an archetypal model of systems having limit cycle, because of nonlinear damping. An excellent discussion of nonlinear damping appears in Jordan and Smith's book (1987) on nonlinear differential equations, along with an extended discussion of the van der Pol equation. An early interesting treatment appears in Rockard's *Theorie des Oscillateurs* (1941). Another interesting experiment is described in a paper entitled, "Frequency Demultiplication" (van der Pol and van der Mark, 1927), involving a neon bulb RC relaxation oscillator driven by a sinusoidal voltage source. The circuit is described and analyzed in the paper by Kennedy and Chua (1986).

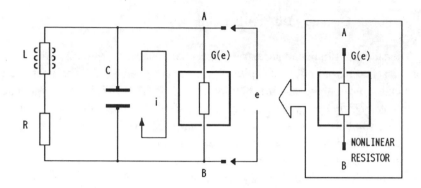

Figure 6.4.3.1   An LRC resonant circuit connected to a nonlinear resistor.

Prior to discussing the van der Pol triode oscillator, it is important to address the oscillator of Figure 6.4.3.1. It consists of a resonant circuit (the LRC network) connected to a nonlinear two-terminal network (a nonlinear resistor) representing the function i = G(e).

$$i \simeq ae + be^3 \tag{1}$$

The circuit equation is

$$LC\ddot{e} + \left[L\,\frac{dG(e)}{de} + RC \right] \dot{e} + e + RG(e) = 0 \tag{2}$$

An excellent analysis of the circuit of Figure 6.4.3.1 appears in Vojtášek (1969) and Vojtášek and Janáč (1969) (see also Minorsky, 1962; and Andronov et al., 1966).

The oscillator of Figure 6.4.3.2 is one version of the van der Pol triode circuit. Notably, there are many variations on the theme, especially when discussing the van der Pol equation itself. For example, discussions with analog computer simulations are found in Jackson (1960), Rogers (1966), Peterson (1967), Chao and Vines (1971) and Jamshidi (1971) among many others. Mathematical treatments of the van der Pol equation are found in Guckenheimer and Holmes (1983); Tondl et al. (1970); Guterman and Nitecki (1984); Tomita (1986); Jordan and Smith (1987); Glass and Mackey (1988) and Mohler (1991), among many others.

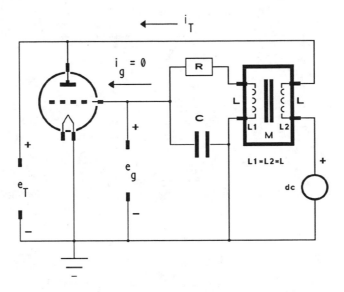

Figure 6.4.3.2 A version of the van der Pol triode circuit.

The nonlinear characteristic of the triode is approximated by the equation

$$i_T \simeq g_T \left(e_g - \frac{1}{3\, e_{SAT}^2}\, e_g^3 \right) \tag{3}$$

where i_T is the tube current, g_T is the tube conductance, e_{SAT} is the characteristic saturation voltage and e_g is the grid voltage as shown in Figure 6.4.3.2 (see also Cole, 1968 and Chao and Vines, 1971). The circuit equation is

$$R\, i_C + e_g + L \left(\frac{d\, i_C}{d\, t} \right) - M \left(\frac{d\, i_T}{d\, t} \right) = 0 \tag{4}$$

Also it is

$$i_C = C \left(\frac{d\, e_g}{d\, t} \right) \tag{5}$$

From Equations (3), (4) and (5) we write

$$\frac{d^2}{d\, t^2} \left(\frac{e_g}{e_{SAT}} \right) - \left(\frac{M g_T - R C}{L C} \right) \left[1 - \left(\frac{M g_T}{M g_T - R C} \right) \left(\frac{e_g}{e_{SAT}} \right)^2 \right] \frac{d}{d\, t} \left(\frac{e_g}{e_{SAT}} \right) + \frac{1}{L C} \left(\frac{e_g}{e_{SAT}} \right) = 0 \tag{6}$$

We let

$$\frac{e_g}{e_{SAT}} = e \tag{7}$$

$$\frac{Mg_T - RC}{LC} = k_1 \tag{8}$$

$$\frac{Mg_T}{Mg_T - RC} = k_2 \tag{9}$$

and

$$\omega_0 = \frac{1}{\sqrt{LC}} \rightarrow \omega_0^2 = \frac{1}{LC} \tag{10}$$

where ω_0 is the circuit's natural frequency. After substitution, Equation (6) becomes

$$\ddot{e} - k_1 (1 - k_2 e^2) \dot{e} + \omega_0^2 e = 0 \tag{11}$$

Both ω_0 and k_2 have dimensions in T^{-1}, while k_1 and e are now dimensionless. By letting (Chao and Vines, 1971)

$$\tau = \omega_0 t \rightarrow \omega_0 = \frac{\tau}{t} \tag{12}$$

and

$$x = \sqrt{k_2}\, e \rightarrow e = \frac{x}{\sqrt{k_2}} \tag{13}$$

Substitution of Equations (12) and (13) into Equation (11) yields the normalized dimensionless equation

$$\frac{d^2}{dt^2} \left(\frac{x}{\sqrt{k_2}} \right) - k_1 \left[1 - k_2 \left(\frac{x}{\sqrt{k_2}} \right)^2 \right] \frac{d}{dt} \left(\frac{x}{\sqrt{k_2}} \right) + \frac{\tau^2}{t^2} \left(\frac{x}{\sqrt{k_2}} \right) = 0 \tag{14}$$

or, after multiplying both terms by $\sqrt{k_2}$,

$$\frac{d^2}{dt^2} x - k_1 (1 - x^2) \frac{dx}{dt} + \frac{\tau^2}{t^2} x = 0 \qquad (15)$$

We divide Equation (15) by $\omega_0^2 = \tau^2/t^2$ and set $k_1/\omega_0^2 = \epsilon$ so that

$$\frac{d^2}{d\tau^2} - \epsilon(1 - x^2)\dot{x} + x = 0 \qquad (16)$$

Equation (16) is one of the many forms of the van der Pol equation. This format is found in Chao and Vines (1971) who also discuss an analog simulation and numerical methods used in digital computer simulation.

A physical interpretation of the van der Pol equation may begin with the *conservative* system

$$\ddot{x} + f(x) = 0 \qquad (17)$$

(see also Section 3.2) in which the total energy E_T is constant and

$$E_T = E_K(\dot{x}) + E_P(x) \qquad (18)$$

An added nonlinear *damping* term, $g(x)\dot{x}$, where $g(x) \geq 0$ modifies Equation (17) so that

$$\ddot{x} + g(x)\dot{x} + f(x) = 0 \qquad (19)$$

Equation (19) describes a *nonconservative* system and if $f(x) = x$ and $g(x) = -\epsilon(1-x^2)$ ($\epsilon > 0$), it becomes

$$\ddot{x} - \epsilon(1 - x^2)\dot{x} + x = 0 \qquad (20)$$

which is often found in the popular form

$$\ddot{x} - \epsilon(1 - \mu x^2)\dot{x} + \omega_0^2 x = 0 \qquad (21)$$

Mohler (1991) provides an excellent analytical treatment of Equation (20) and a discussion on the nonconservative system. Figure 6.4.3.3 (VANDERP.sim) shows the simulator of Equation (20). A phase plot may be prepared by letting $e_{ic}(x) = 1$ (the system will not be set in motion without some nonzero initial condition) and $\epsilon = 1$. It allows the observation of the periodic limit cycle solution. The oscillations are *self-sustained*; they are independent of any external peridic forcing functions. They arise because of the way energy is exchanged between states—a characteristic of the system's internal structure. Readers may wish to investigate this system further by introducing various forcing functions and for a variety of ϵ values.

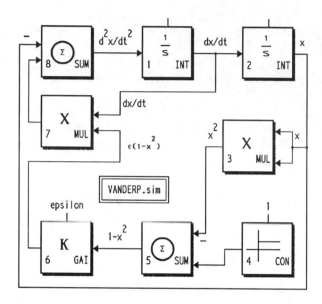

Figure 6.4.3.3   The simulator of the generalized van der Pol equation (Eq. 20).

Finally, the modified van der Pol equation by Kaplan and Yaffe (1976)

$$\ddot{x} + \omega_0^2 x = \epsilon\left[1 - \frac{1}{4}\mu\left(x^2 + \frac{\dot{x}^2}{\omega_0^2}\right)\right]\dot{x} \tag{22}$$

represents an oscillator with better amplitude stability. The reader is referred to the original work for further details. Just like any dfq model, the various versions of the van der Pol equation can be seen and treated as a closed-loop system. To reiterate this important point, a suitable arrangement of the constituent function blocks can reveal the physical essence of a feedback structure. Then the dynamic system entrapped in an equation escapes the severely limiting world of mathematical analysis and can be seen for what it is.

6.4.4   A Few Words on the Utility of the Phase-Plane Diagram

Anyone familiar with differential equations has encountered phase-plane diagrams (or phase portraits) during the study of the second-order, linear, homogeneous, constant-coefficient system

$$\dot{x} = a_1 x + b_1 y \tag{1}$$

$$\dot{y} = a_2 x + b_2 y \tag{2}$$

Essentially, the phase portrait involves the geometric representation of the solutions of the system. It provides much qualitative information about the system and is invaluable in stability studies (see for instance Leighton, 1966; and Guterman and Nitecki, 1984). Here, is regarded as a parameter; the solution curves are plotted in the Cartesian x-y plane (the phase plane).

The value of phase plane diagrams or phase portraits rests on the beholder's ability to extrapolate system behavior from the solution trajectories. Notably, characteristic patterns of phase portraits clearly identify the operating modes of the system under study. Phase plane work is of fundamental importance in the study of nonlinear differential equations (Jordan and Smith, 1988) and system dynamics in general. Unlike mathematical analysis, block diagram modelling techniques allow the explicit mechanization of a complex nonlinear system, and thus the plotting of its phase portrait. Continuous dynamic simulation languages fill serious gaps in mathematical and systems research; by degree, they should be regarded as necessary mathematical tools (see Minorsky, 1962).

In the case of the friction-free (undamped) spring-mass oscillator or its electrical analog, the harmonic (sine-cosine) oscillator (Section 3.2), the *phase trajectories* are circles. Phase trajectories are also known as *phase paths* or *integral curves*. The position of the mass (displacement = x) is represented on the horizontal axis and its velocity (dx/dt) on the vertical axis. Given some initial condition that sets the system in motion, the point $(d, [d^2 x / dt^2])$ moves along a circular trajectory (see Figure 3.2.4). In this experiment we observe this motion and map the trajectory (or trajectories) as the exchange between kinetic and potential energies take place. The system's energy is purely kinetic when the $(x, [d^2 x / dt^2])$ point is momentarily situated on the vertical axis, and purely potential when on the horizontal axis. In all cases, the pair $(\theta, [d^2 \theta / dt^2])$ represents the *state* of the system and the phase trajectories show the *evolution of any state in time* (although the time variable does not appear in the diagram). Phase portraits incorporate arrows indicating the *direction* of the phase trajectories and allow the complete qualification of a system's motion without explicitly solving the governing differential equation. As a mathematical tool, we can't do any better than that.

Usually the characteristic patterns of phase-space plots are formed around a *singular point* in the system response, a point in which the derivatives of the system variable are zero. In the case of the system of Equations (1) and (2), the point (x=0,y=0) is where both [dx/dt] and [dy/dt] vanish, or

$$\left(\frac{dx}{dt}\right)^2 + \left(\frac{dy}{dt}\right)^2 = 0 \tag{3}$$

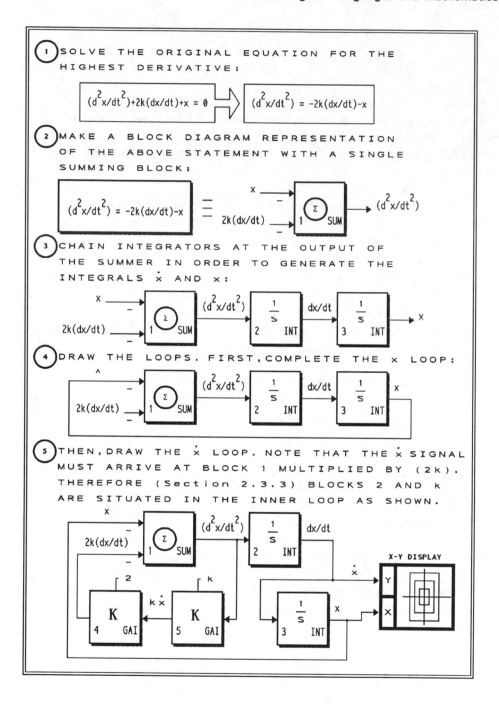

Figure 6.4.4.1   Guidelines for dfq block diagram modelling.

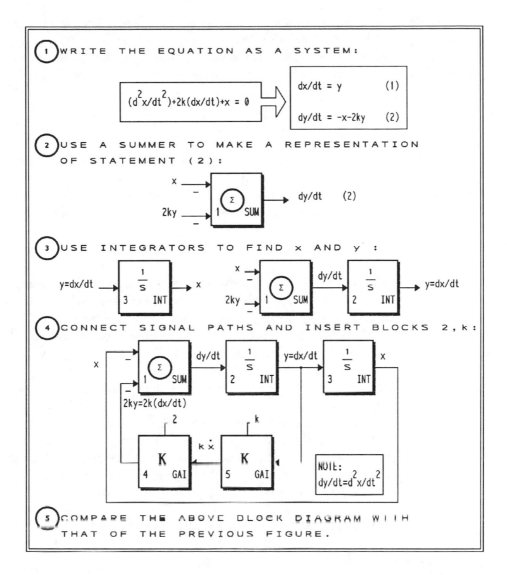

Figure 6.4.4.2 An alternate approach to dfq block diagram modelling.

This is the *equilibrium* point of the system of Equations (1) and (2). It makes sense that singular points *always* appear on the horizontal axis of a phase plane. In our case, if the determinant is not zero, the origin (0,0) is the *only* equilibrium point of the system. Both the spring-mass system and the harmonic oscillator are responding as conservative systems.

If damping or some frictional force exists as a function of the velocity, the general equation is

$$\ddot{x} + 2d\dot{x} + x = 0 \qquad (4)$$

The phase portrait allows us to obtain information about the three solution cases that depend on d values: 1) exponentially decreasing (or increasing if the damping is negative) oscillations, 2) exponential response without oscillation, and 3) critical damping (the boundary between 1 and 2). Again, Equation (4) can be written as a system of two first-order equations:

$$\dot{x} = y \tag{5}$$

$$\dot{y} = -x - 2dy \tag{6}$$

However, for the purpose of block diagram modelling, Equation (4) is sufficient. Figures 6.4.4.1 and 6.4.4.2 allow the comparison between the two approaches and even shedding some light on the analytical process itself (for more insight on the subject see Sections 6.4.2.1 and 6.4.2.2).

In his very interesting paper on the rapid production of system phase-plane portraits on the EAI 380 hybrid/analog computer, Kerr (1977) discusses several examples of phase portrait generation. Anderson and Walsh (1990) show how the elementary theory of central orbits is developed in terms of the phase plane. An excellent discussion of phase-plane diagrams is found in the author's favorite book on mathematical models in biology by Leah Edelstein-Keshet (1988) and in the excellent, but hard-to-find, book on biological oscillators by Pavlidis (1973). The use of phase portraits in nonlinear system dynamics is exemplified by Mohler (1991) in the first volume of his work on nonlinear systems. Also the interested reader is referred to the article on analyzing nonlinearity by Hale and LaSalle (1963) and the work on computer simulation in nonlinear circuit analysis by Chao and Vines (1971). The advanced reader will find the works by Guckenheimer and Holmes (1983) and Vojtášek and Janáč (1969) most interesting. Without doubt, a small book can be written on phase-space diagrams, adjacent concepts and the numerous examples from many disciplines.

6.5   LOGARITHMIC TECHNIQUES IN SIMULATION

6.5.1   Introduction

Logarithmic functions of the form

$$y = \log_b w \tag{1}$$

(read "y equals the logarithm of base b of w") are very useful in setting up clean and simple subsystem simulators. The exponential function will also be considered here, where

$$x = b^w \tag{2}$$

It is

$$x = \log_b^{-1}(w) = b^w \tag{3}$$

that is, the exponential function is by definition the antilogarithm or inverse of the logarithm. There are two systems of logarithms in use, one to the base 10 and another to the base e (2.718...). The basic premise of Equation (3) holds true for both systems. If

$$w = \log_{10} y \tag{4}$$

then

$$y = 10^w \tag{5}$$

And if

$$w = \log_e y = \ell n\ y \tag{6}$$

then

$$y = e^w \tag{7}$$

TUTSIM provides both natural logarithm ℓn (LOG) and exponential (EXP) function blocks. When using either one must remember that an exponent is an antilogarithm. Simulations with log and antilog blocks are subject to range restrictions, since in Equation (4) there must always be $y > 0$ (because $w \rightarrow -\infty$ as $y \rightarrow 0$). Nevertheless, log/antilog techniques offer alternatives to sensitive algorithms and may eliminate block redundancy. The following examples show a few implementations of the concept. For information about actual hardware implementation of logarithmic calculations, readers are referred to Graeme (1973 and 1977), Sheingold (1976), Wait et al. (1975) and Wong and Ott (1976).

6.5.2   Multiplication and Division

Single quadrant multiplication according to the equation

$$z = xy \tag{1}$$

can be performed as shown in Figure 6.5.2.1 where x,y are problem variables. Here

$$\ell n\ x + \ell n\ y = \ell n\ xy \tag{2}$$

$$e^{\ell n\ xy} = xy \tag{3}$$

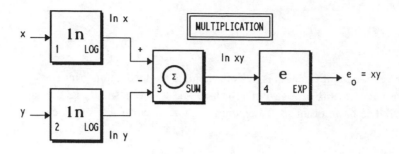

Figure 6.5.2.1   Multiplication using logarithms.

Also, the equation

$$z = \frac{x}{y} \tag{4}$$

is simulated as shown in Figure 6.5.2.2 according to the equations

$$\ell n\ x - \ell n\ y = \ell n\ \frac{x}{y} \tag{5}$$

$$e^{\ell n\ (x/y)} = \frac{x}{y} \tag{6}$$

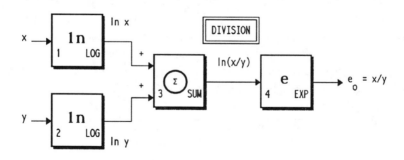

Figure 6.5.2.2   Division using logarithms.

6.5.3   Power Generation

The equation

$$z = x^y \tag{1}$$

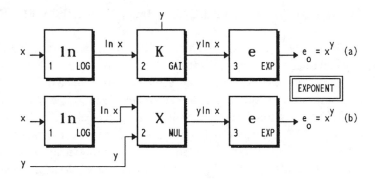

Figure 6.5.3.1 Power generation using logarithms.

is simulated as shown in Figures 6.5.3.1(a) and 6.5.3.1(b) where the GAI block is replaced by a multiplier. In both cases it is

$$(\ell n \ x)\, y \;=\; y \ \ell n \ x \tag{2}$$

and

$$e^{y \, \ell n \ x} \;=\; x^y \tag{3}$$

The concept is readily adaptable to complex nonlinear function generation involving nonintegral powers (see also Section 8.5).

6.5.4 Inverse Generation

The function

$$y \;=\; \frac{1}{f(x)} \;=\; f^{-1}(x) \tag{1}$$

can be simulated according to the equations

$$\ell n \ (1) \ - \ \ell n \ [f(x)] \;=\; \ell n \ \frac{1}{f(x)} \;=\; \ell n \ [f^{-1}(x)] \tag{2}$$

and

$$e^{\ell n[\, f^{-1}(x)\,]} \;=\; f^{-1}(x) \tag{3}$$

The simulation is discussed in detail in Section 6.2.4.

6.6   TECHNIQUES IN GRAPHICAL COMPUTATION OF FUNCTIONS

The computer implementation of mathematical problems is a most important activity in both teaching and research. During the 60s and 70s we saw many analog/hybrid computer applications in mathematics, but somehow this activity eclipsed. The 80s were the era of the desktop digital computer (see Kolomyjec, 1983; Lether, 1986; Walton and Walton, 1987; and Flanders, 1988) and the trend-setting decade in computer-based mathematics education. The versatility of the BASIC language was demonstrated in many interesting articles (Stick and Stick, 1985; Lether, 1986; and Montaner, 1987; among many others). Calculator techniques and specialized software followed (see for example, Waits and Demana, 1989; White, 1988; and Levy, 1990) and are firmly entrenched in today's schools, universities and research establishments.

The graphical computation of mathematical functions is essential in problem solving. There are, undoubtedly, many ways to do this—from the many specialized teaching software to the new (and most impressive) symbolic tools. Block diagram languages allow the conceptualization of a mere formula as a mathematical model and provide the versatility of 'what if' investigations. Furthermore, since the typical CDSS language is more of less 'an analog/hybrid computer in a box,' we can revive many early computational techniques from the analog computer past. All this connects well with dynamic system simulation, control system design, electronics and a myriad of other things involving mathematics. As a case in point, we consider the equation

$$f(x) \ = \ x(x - 1) + \sin x^2 \tag{1}$$

which is investigated by Levi (1990), who uses the popular software Mathcad. Figure 6.6.1 shows the block model structure (EQU1.sim) which is a straightforward implementation of Equation (1). Figures 6.6.2(a), (b) and (c) show a graphical exploration which is indeed *much* easier and faster than that of Mathcad. The first four blocks of the EQU1.sim model constitute a cosine wave generator, so x is swept within the range $-A \leq x \leq A$, where A is a user-defined amplitude value (it is x = f(t) = A cos 2πft).

A second example is the equation

$$g(x) \ = \ \tan x - x \tag{2}$$

also found in Levi's paper (1990). Figure 6.6.3 shows the block simulator (EQU2.sim). Note that in the absence of a tan block, the function is implemented according to the relationship tan x = sin x/cos x. Figure 6.6.4 displays the tangent curves for the range $-2\pi \leq x \leq 2\pi$ and the output of block #8 is the function g(x) (Figure 6.6.5). Note that in both figures, the vertical lines are drawn by the simulator as the input x = f(t) sweeps through assigned range.

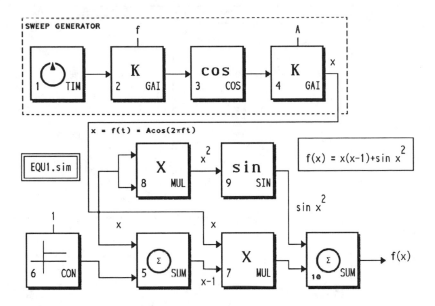

Figure 6.6.1   The simulator of Equation (1).

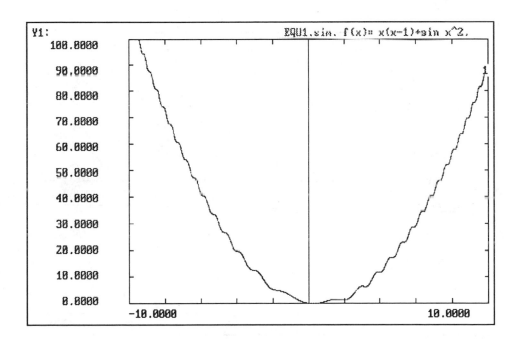

Figure 6.6.2(a)   Results of the EQU1.sim.

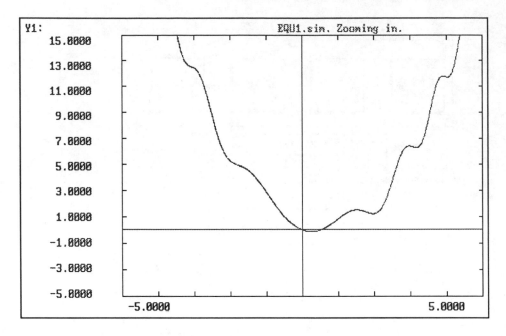

Figure 6.6.2(b)   Zooming in on the curve of Figure 6.6.2(a).

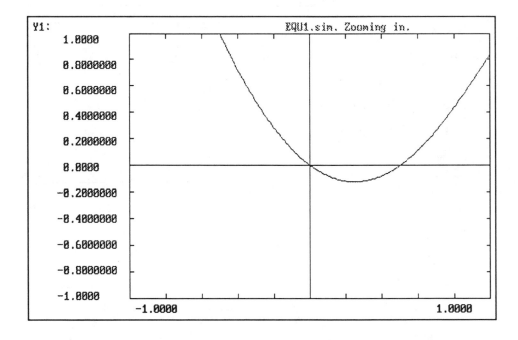

Figure 6.6.2(c)   Detail inspection of the curve of Figure 6.6.2(a).

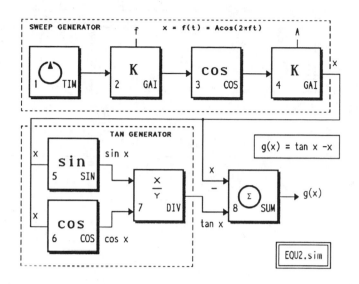

Figure 6.6.3   The simulator of Equation (2).

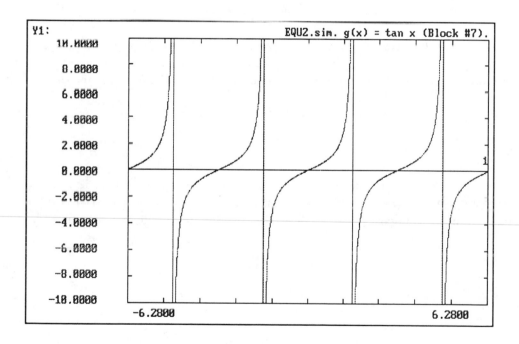

Figure 6.6.4   Tangent curves for the range -2π ≤ x ≤ 2π generated by the EQU2.sim.

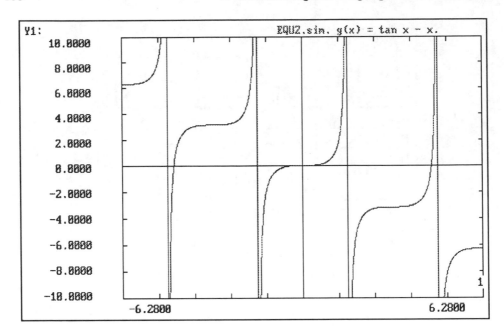

Figure 6.6.5   The solution curve g(x) for the EQU2.sim.

These two examples illustrate the versatility of the block diagram language as a graphing tool in mathematics. For precise results, zooming in and out, paning and the insertion of reference lines are combined with the inherent flexibility of the simulator.

6.7   TRANSPORT DELAYS

6.7.1   Introduction

Real world dynamic processes often involve the constant or variable delayed response of one or more variables to a stimulus input. This delayed response is known as transport delay, transport lag or deadtime. The time-domain definition of an ideal delay is

$$T = f(t - \tau) \tag{1}$$

having the Laplace transform (see also Section 6.2.3)

$$T(s) = \mathcal{L}[f(t - \tau)] = F(s)\,e^{-\tau s} \tag{2}$$

where F(s) is the Laplace transform of f(t) and τ is the delay time constant.   The strict implementation of Equation (1) requires a storage device. However, Equation (2) redefines the problem to approximate the function $e^{-\tau s}$ so that the delay can be easily varied over a wide range of time while maintaining a constant amplitude. In the frequency domain (s = jω)

we write

$$T(j\omega) = e^{-j\omega\tau} \tag{3}$$

indicating that the *pure time delay* is characterized by zero signal attenuation and a *pure phase shift*.

Transport delays are important in simulation as they are found in many diverse systems. Some examples are pneumatic networks, material moving operations with conveyor belts and pipes, electrical and electronic signal delays, chemical processes, control systems, human-machine control systems, biological processes and social or financial systems involving use of delayed information. There are many approaches to time delay simulation. The analytic approach based on some mathematical approximation for $e^{-\tau s}$ is popular and useful in analog computation and dynamic system simulation languages like TUTSIM. For example, let us consider the Taylor series expansion

$$e^{-\tau s} = 1 - \tau s + \frac{(\tau s)^2}{2!} - \frac{(\tau s)^3}{3!} + \frac{(\tau s)^4}{4!} - \dots \tag{4}$$

Equation (4) presents difficult mechanization problems as it requires sequential differentiation. The rate of convergence of the Taylor series is slow for large values of the argument τs rendering it unsuitable for high frequencies and long delay values. Another approach uses the approximation

$$e^{-\tau s} = \lim_{n \to \infty} \left[\frac{1}{1 + \frac{\tau s}{n}} \right]^n \tag{5}$$

Given any finite n, Equation (5) generates a pole of order n situated on the negative real axis of the s plane at $(-n/\tau)$. Mechanization of Equation (5) calls for n-cascaded first-order lags with n as large as possible (small n values result in poor approximation), as in the case of Chien et al. (1952) where n = 80 was used! The most popular delay approximation is one developed by Padé (1892) using rational function representation; it is also discussed by Wall (1931) in the context of positive definite power series. Convergence of sequences of Padé approximations is found in Wall (1931) and Bellman and Straus (1949). The mechanization of the Padé time delays are discussed by Hohmann (1972), Holst (1969), Roth and Reschke (1974), Stewart (1960), Sullivan (1978) and Teasdale (1953).

Bessel delay functions are applied by Deliyannis (1970) and Storch (1954). Chebyshev functions are used by Deliyannis (1970), Hausner and Furlani (1966) and Stojamovic and Radmanovic (1978). Even- and odd-order polynomial approximations are shown in Hepner (1965), Mirou (1968) and Ziegler (1964). Least-squares techniques are discussed by Crane and Klopfenstein (1979), McAvon (1968), Tomlinson (1965) and Wilson and Papamichael (1981 and 1983). Various hybrid and digital techniques are shown by Heller

(1963), Keats and Leggett (1972), Mutharasan (1971) and Mutharasan and Coughanowr (1972). The reader is also directed to the following sources: Anday (1972), Cereijo (1975), Dvorak (1976), Hojberg (1966), King and Rideout (1962), Kogan and Chernyshev (1966), Mazanov and Tognetti (1974), Mesch (1966), Schwarze et al. (1963), Skala (1971) and Vichnevetsky (1964). Variable delay is discussed by Holst (1969), Nilsen and Levine (1970), Seddon (1968) and Stone and Dandl (1957). The following reviews of transport delay simulation techniques are highly recommended: Ammon (1961), Davies (1972), King (1961), Knowles and Leggett (1972) and Stubbs and Single (1954). The reference list is not exclusive. It merely shows what the author considers primary references in a vast topic of significance to dynamic system simulation. In addition to those found above, many old analog computer books provide valuable insight into the simulation and application of transport delays.

6.7.2   The Padé Formulation

In 1892 Padé published his famous thesis *Sur la Représentation Aprochée d'une Fonction par des Fractions Rationelles* at the Ecole Normalle. He shows how a delay is approximated by rational fraction where the numerator and denominator are polynomials. Without doubts, Padé's work is still timely and significant. It is

$$e^{-\tau s} \cong \frac{P_a(s)}{Q_b(s)} = P_{a,b} \tag{1}$$

where a and b are the degrees of the polynomials P and Q, respectively. The generalized expression is given by

$$P_a(s) = 1 - \frac{ax}{(a+b)\,1\,!} + \frac{a(a-1)x^2}{(a+b)(a+b-1)\,2\,!}$$
$$- \ldots + \frac{(-1)^a\, a(a-1)\ldots 2\bullet 1\, x^a}{(a+b)(a+b-1)\ldots(b+1)\,a\,!}$$

and

$$Q_b(s) = 1 + \frac{bx}{(b+a)\,1\,!} + \frac{b(b-1)x^2}{(b+a)(b+a-1)\,2\,!}$$
$$+ \ldots + \frac{b(b-1)\ldots 2\bullet 1\, x^b}{(b+a)(b+a-1)\ldots(a+1)\,b!}$$

$$\tag{2}$$

The approximation is completely defined by choosing the orders a and b of the two polynomials. In the simplest case, letting a = b = 1 defines the first-order Padé approximation

$$P_{1,1}(s) = \frac{1 - \frac{\tau}{2} s}{1 + \frac{\tau}{2} s} \tag{3}$$

The simulator of Equation (3) can be developed from the original transfer function by algebraic rearrangement. It is

$$P_{1,1}(s) = \frac{1 - \frac{\tau s}{2}}{1 + \frac{\tau s}{2}} = \frac{2 - 1 \frac{\tau s}{2}}{1 + \frac{\tau s}{2}} = \frac{2}{1 + \frac{\tau s}{2}} - 1 = 2 \frac{2}{\tau s + 2} - 1 \tag{3R}$$

and, finally

$$P_{1,1}(s) = 2 \left(\frac{\tau}{\tau s + 2} \right) \frac{2}{\tau} - 1 \tag{4}$$

The block diagram development is shown in Figure 6.7.2.1. This approach is useful in mechanizing difficult transfer function problems. Knowledge of the block diagram protocol (see Part 2) and some algebraic imagination are the only requirements. The TUTSIM block diagram of Figure 6.7.2.2 (PADE1ST.sim) may be investigated for $\tau = 0.5$, 1.0, and 2.0 using sinusoidal and step inputs. According to Gilliland (1967), the first-order approximation works reasonably well for a delay $\phi \leq 0.6$ radians. Since

$$\phi = \omega \tau \tag{5}$$

where ω is the radian frequency, it is

$$\tau \leq \frac{0.6}{\omega} \tag{6}$$

Therefore, the first-order Padé approximation can provide relatively large time delays at *very low* frequencies. However, this approximation is regarded as primitive by many, a thing of the past. There are, of course, higher-order Padé delays. For example, the second-order approximation is found by letting a = b = 2 in the generalized formulation of Equation (2), so that

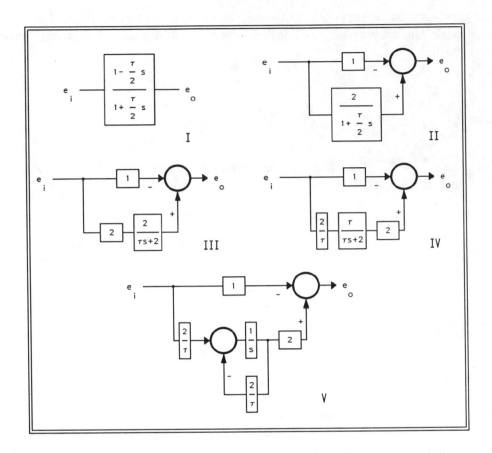

Figure 6.7.2.1　Systematic development of the Padé $P_{1,1}(s)$ simulator.

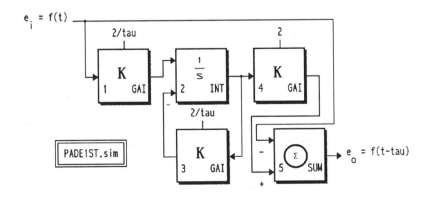

Figure 6.7.2.2　The $P_{1,1}(s)$ simulator.

$$P_{2,2} = \frac{1 - \dfrac{\tau s}{2} + \dfrac{\tau^2 s^2}{12}}{1 + \dfrac{\tau s}{2} + \dfrac{\tau^2 s^2}{12}} \tag{7}$$

or, after some algebra work

$$P_{2,2} = \frac{12 - 6\tau s + \tau^2 s^2}{12 + 6\tau s + \tau^2 s^2} \tag{8}$$

This approximation works well for a delay $\phi \leq 18$ radians (Gilliland, 1967). Higher-order approximations can be developed in a similar fashion. The reader should remember that TUTSIM's delay function block (DEL) is generally the most expedient, accurate and economical way (in block count) to implement time delays.

7 NONLINEAR DYNAMIC SYSTEMS: SELECTED EXAMPLES

7.1 INTRODUCTION

The topic of nonlinear systems is vast and fascinating, especially for the user of block diagram languages. In this part we show a few representative examples, and emphasis is placed on chaotic systems. As chaos is a topic of current interest, our primary goal here is to show applied CDSS language techniques. We recommend that readers become familiar with the generalized methods of Section 6.4 prior to reading this material. Interested readers will find that working with block diagram models and languages validates their mathematical background and leads to the discovery of important segments of knowledge lost in the labyrinth of ineffective mathematical analysis tools. It is best that one works with a couple of good modelling-oriented math books on hand, so we recommend the work on differential equation models by Braun et al. (1983) and the book on mathematics of dynamic modelling by Beltrami (1987).

7.2 THE MATHIEU EQUATION

7.2.1 Introduction

The Mathieu equation is a time-varying equation of the form

$$\ddot{y} + [a + b\,f(t)]\,y = 0 \tag{1}$$

which is a particular form of the Hill equation

$$\ddot{y} + a(t)\,y = 0 \tag{2}$$

Equation (1) designates a large number of nonlinear physical systems of heterogeneous nature and is invaluable in stability investigations. An excellent mathematical analysis of Mathieu's equation and a discussion on equations with periodic coefficients (Floquet theory) is found in Jordan and Smith (1987), along with the procedure for determining stability via solution perturbation. There are many variations of Equation (1), where f(t) is a periodic function of time, normally a sine or cosine function (Jackson, 1969; Jordan and Smith, 1987; Mohler, 1991; Peterson, 1967; and Ricci, 1972). Yorke (1978) uses a square-wave model for a pendulum with oscillating support (Sections 7.2.4 and 7.2.5) as a replacement for the sinusoidal model, thus permitting a matrix solution. However the Mathieu equation of the popular form

$$\ddot{y} + (a - 2p \cos \omega t)y = 0 \qquad (3)$$

puzzles scientists, engineers and classroom teachers who then largely avoid it. The reason rests in the truculent nature of the equation which is unstable for certain combinations of the a and p constants. In fact, an a-p plot reveals a complex geometrical pattern of stability regions (Mohler, 1991; Ricci, 1972; Rocard, 1960; and Stocker, 1950).

In the Mathieu equation case, mathematics fail the application-oriented practitioner who must determine conditional oscillatory behaviors and stability conditions. Simulation techniques are very useful here. Analog and hybrid computers are naturally suited to the task. Ricci (1972) shows how this equation is solved and the stability (a-p) plot is created using parallel logic components and hybrid programming. The Mathieu equation is readily programmable on any small analog computer and is naturally suited to continuous dynamic simulation techniques on the digital machine. What follows are a few application examples that provide insight in the applied aspects of the Mathieu equation. It is recommended that readers review Sections 8.2 and 8.3 prior to reading the LC and LRC cases. To reiterate, the Mathieu equation is useful in investigating systems of borderline stability or those having unstable regions. Examples of these systems are vibrating strings, membranes, waveguides, containers with sloshing liquids, synchronous motors operating under varying loads, etc.

7.2.2 The LC Circuit Revisited

The series LC circuit discussed in Section 8.3.2 is described by the homogeneous differential equation

$$L\ddot{q} + \frac{1}{C} q = 0 \qquad (1)$$

If we introduce a small variation in capacitance ΔC so that $C = C_0 f^{-1}(t)$ where $f(t)$ is a periodic time function, the response of the system will depend on $f(t)$ and if

$$f(t) = 1 - \Delta C \cos \omega_1 t \qquad (2)$$

the coefficient $1/C$ of Equation (1) becomes

$$\frac{1}{C} = \frac{1}{C_0} (1 - \Delta C \cos \omega_1 t) \qquad (3)$$

Equation (1) now has the form

$$L\ddot{q} + \frac{1}{C_0}(1 - \Delta C \cos \omega_1 t)q = 0$$

$$LC_0\ddot{q} + (1 - \Delta C \cos \omega_1 t)q = 0 \tag{4}$$

$$\ddot{q} + \frac{1}{LC_0}(1 - \Delta C \cos \omega_1 t)q = 0$$

The mean resonant frequency ω_0 of the system (Section 8.3.2) is

$$\omega_0 = \sqrt{\frac{(1/C)}{L}}$$

or, in terms of C_0

$$\omega_0 = \frac{1}{\sqrt{LC_0}} \rightarrow \omega_0^2 = \frac{1}{LC_0} \tag{5}$$

Substitution in Equation (4) gives

$$\ddot{q} + \omega_0^2(1 - \Delta C \cos \omega_1 t)q = 0 \tag{6}$$

By letting

$$\omega_0^2 = a \tag{7}$$

and

$$\frac{\omega_0^2 \Delta C}{2} = p \tag{8}$$

in Equation (6), we get the Mathieu equation

$$\ddot{q} + (a - 2p \cos \omega_1 t)q = 0 \tag{9}$$

in the form of Equation (3) of Section 7.2.1. The simulator of Figure 7.2.2.1 (MATHIEU.sim) should be investigated for $q(0) = 0.1$, $\omega_0 = 1.6 \rightarrow a = 2.56$, $p = 0.64$, $\omega_1 = 1.8$ and $\Delta C = 0.5$.

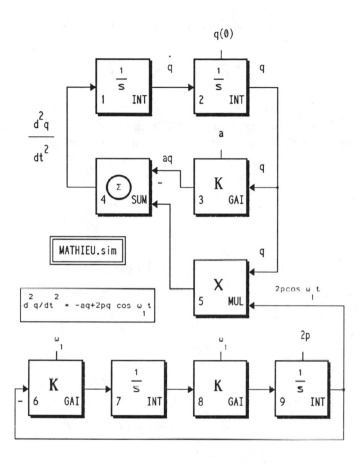

Figure 7.2.2.1 Simulating the Mathieu equation.

A complete study of the Mathieu equation appears as early as 1932 with a paper by M. J. O. Strult in *Ergebnisse der Math. Wissensch* (Rocard, 1960). An early analog computer study performed with the then noted Darmstadt repetitive differential analyzer is reported by Dhen (1956) and is also discussed by Tomovic and Karplus (1970).

7.2.3 The LRC Circuit Revisited

The inclusion of a series resistor in the LC circuit of Section 7.2.2 forms a series RCL network described by the equation

$$LC_0\ddot{q} + RC_0\dot{q} + (1 - \Delta C \cos \omega_1 t)\, q = 0$$

$$\ddot{q} + \frac{R}{L}\dot{q} + \frac{1}{LC_0}(1 - \Delta C \cos \omega_1 t)\, q = 0 \tag{1}$$

$$\ddot{q} + \frac{R}{L}\dot{q} + \omega_0^2 (1 - \Delta C \cos \omega_1 t)\, q = 0$$

This is the Mathieu equation describing a series RCL circuit with a variable rotary capacitor. Another variation on the theme can be constructed from the forced equation

$$LC\left(\frac{d^2 e_C}{dt^2}\right) + RC\left(\frac{d e_C}{dt}\right) + e_C = e_s(t)$$

$$\frac{d^2 e_C}{dt^2} + \frac{R}{L}\left(\frac{d e_C}{dt}\right) + \frac{1}{LC}e_C = \left(\frac{1}{LC}\right) e_s(t) \tag{2}$$

$$\frac{d^2 e_C}{dt^2} + \frac{R}{L}\left(\frac{d e_C}{dt}\right) + \omega_0^2 e_C = \omega_0^2 e_s(t)$$

Given that

$$e_s(t) = e_0 \cos \omega_1 t \tag{3}$$

then Equation (2) takes the form

$$\frac{d^2 e_C}{dt^2} + \frac{R}{L}\left(\frac{d e_C}{dt}\right) + \omega_0^2 (e_C - e_0 \cos \omega t) = 0 \tag{4}$$

also of the Mathieu form.

7.2.4 The Simple Pendulum with Oscillating Support

Let us consider a simple pendulum having mass m with length ℓ. Its pivot point moves vertically in response to a periodic forcing function

$$u(t) = U \cos \omega t \tag{1}$$

The motion equation when the pendulum support is fixed is

$$\ddot{\theta} + \frac{g}{\ell} \sin \theta = 0 \tag{2}$$

or, under the assumption of a small θ where $\sin \theta \approx \theta$,

$$\ddot{\theta} + \frac{g}{\ell} \theta = 0 \tag{3}$$

When the pivot point moves *vertically* in response to forcing function (1), there is an added acceleration component on the pendulum mass and the total *effective* acceleration (effective g) is

$$g_E + g + \ddot{u} = g - \omega^2 U \cos \omega t \tag{4}$$

Then Equation (2) becomes

$$\ddot{\theta} + \left[\frac{g}{\ell} - \frac{\omega^2 U}{\ell} \cos \omega t \right] \theta = 0 \tag{5}$$

which is a form of the Mathieu equation.

7.2.5 The Inverted Pendulum with Oscillating Support

In the case of the inverted pendulum where the center of gravity is situated above the pivot point, it is $(\sin \theta \approx \theta)$

$$m\ell\ddot{\theta} - mg\theta = 0 \tag{1}$$

This equation describes a totally unstable system (Rocard, 1960). If the pivot point is subjected to a vertical motion in response to a forcing function (see also Section 7.2.4)

$$u(t) = U \cos \omega t \tag{2}$$

Equation (1) becomes

$$m\ell\ddot{\theta} + m(-g + \omega^2 U \cos \omega t)\theta = 0$$

$$\ddot{\theta} + \left[-\frac{g}{\ell} + \frac{\omega^2 U}{\ell} \cos \omega t \right] \theta = 0 \tag{3}$$

$$\ddot{\theta} - \left[\frac{g}{\ell} - \frac{\omega^2 U}{\ell} \cos \omega t \right] \theta = 0$$

This equation differs from Equation (5) of the previous section only in the sign of the second term (due to the negative coefficient -a = -g/l) which, of course, is to be expected since the system is unstable. Otherwise the properties of the Mathieu equation remain unaltered (see also Rao, 1990). The block diagram of Figure 7.2.5.1 (MPEN.sim) will simulate both the conventional and the inverted pendulum, depending upon the choice of signs for the inputs of the first integrator. The simulation of the function $U\omega^2 \cos(\omega t)$ is explained in detail in the Appendix. A common mistake in simulations like this one is the use of heterogeneous units, e.g., we must decide whether we will use degrees or radians (1 degree is equal to 0.017453 rad), feet or meters, express g in proper units, etc. Readers are left to experiment on their own.

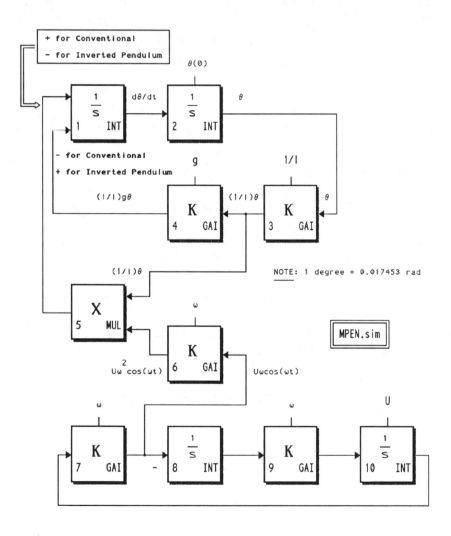

Figure 7.2.5.1 A block diagram useful in the simulation of both conventional and inverted pendulum models.

7.3 CHAOS

7.3.1 Introduction

A series of important mathematical discoveries fueled the topic of chaos in the 70s, prompting the subsequent appearance of many books and research articles. Although labeled 'a new science' (Gleick, 1987), chaos emerges from the work of Henri Poincaré (1854-1912). Poincaré argued against the Laplacian outlook of the 17th century, according to which total determinism and complete predictability are implied by the laws of nature (excellent introductory discussions are by Crutchfield et al., 1986; and Jensen, 1987). Modern nondeterministic viewpoints accept that arbitrarily small uncertainties acting to influence a system's state may become large enough in time to seriously affect the system. Thus, predicting a system's future state is impossible (see also Pippard, 1985). The property of randomness is called chaos (from the Greek χάος, a state of unpredictable flux, disorder, confusion). Random behavior exists even in *very simple* dynamic systems (May, 1976). Much of this theory was established long ago (Poincaré, 1880-90; Bendixson, 1901). The reader is also urged to read the discussion on Poincaré stability (also referred to as stability of paths or orbital stability) in Jordan and Smith (1988). See also Guckenheimer and Holmes (1983) for an exposition of the Poincaré-Bendixson Theorem and Bendixson's Criterion.

In 1927, van der Pol and van der Mark published their well-known works on frequency demultiplication (van der Pol, 1927; van der Mark, 1927, reprinted in Bellman and Kalaba, 1964). They describe a triode valve (tube) circuit having nonlinear chaotic response (see Section 6.4.3.3). The papers by Ruelle and Takens (1971), and Feigenbaum (1979 and 1980) deal with chaotic phenomena in turbulence and are classics. The famous work on deterministic nonperiodic flow by Lorenz (1963) is discussed in more detail in Section 7.3.3. In this book we discuss three- and four-dimensional chaotic systems, chosen as a cross-section of examples in chaotic dynamics. Section 7.3.2 presents a brief overview of chaos research intended to guide the newcomer. Chaos exists in all systems and it is discussed in journals of all disciplines. The topical treatment here is limited by the scope of this work and is geared to providing examples of utilization for block diagram modelling and CDSS languages.

7.3.2 A Brief Review of Chaos Research

A prospective researcher of chaos will do well to begin with the book on nonlinear oscillations, dynamical systems and bifurcations of vector fields by Guckenheimer and Holmes (1983). It is no less than an outstanding mathematical exposition of modern chaos research. Another excellent work in the same category but with a biological orientation is that by Glass and Mackey (1988). The collected works on chaos edited by Holden (1986) is also a must. Holden is also the coauthor of a very good book on chaos in biological systems (Degn et al., 1987). Cvitanovic's (1984) collected works and Devancey's (1989) book on chaotic dynamical systems are also of interest here. Thompson and Steward (1986) apply geometrical methods in nonlinear dynamics and chaos and Schuster (1984) discusses stochastic phenomena and chaotic behavior in complex systems. An excellent book on chaotic vibrations is by Moon (1987).

Chaotic-like motion is discussed by Mendelson and Karioris (1991). It is recommended that the excellent work by Bohr (1951) on almost periodic functions is read by anyone interested in chaotic-like oscillatory phenomena. Of related interest are the chapter on periodically forced nonlinear oscillators (Tomita, 1986) and the early article by Cartwright (1948). Although not a book on chaos per se, Mohler's work on nonlinear systems (1991) is pertinent here. Rietman's book (1989) discusses the computer modelling of chaos, fractals, cellular automata and neural networks with BASIC. To reiterate, the literature on chaos is vast. There are many useful books and articles which could not be referenced here. Most of the works listed include large bibliographies. The books by Pickover (1990) and that by Gleick (1987) offer an excellent introduction to the topic of chaos. Also Pickover's work on pattern formation and chaos in networks (Pickover, 1988) offers insight on the unusual network topology of some chaotic systems.

In the electronics field there are many ramifications of chaos, especially in the cases of some nonlinear systems. The reader is strongly urged to read the article by Jefferies et al. (1989). These nonlinear systems have unusual outputs which are neither multiples nor subharmonics of the driving frequency. Often there is no apparent relation between input and output. Chaotic circuits are presented and analyzed by Lindsay (1981), Test et al. (1982), Rollins and Hunt (1982), Brorson et al. (1983), Matsumoto (1984) Perez (1985) and many others. Of great interest is the Chua circuit (Matsumoto et al., 1984; Matsumoto, 1987). The Chua circuit is the simplest autonomous electrical circuit enabling the observation of a chaotic attractor. Chua's circuit (Figure 7.3.2.1) is a third-order, reciprocal nonlinear circuit. It has a single nonlinear element, a piecewise-linear resistor with only three segments

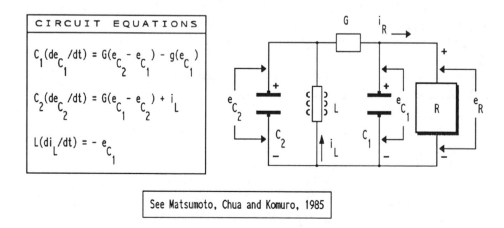

CIRCUIT EQUATIONS

$$C_1(de_{C_1}/dt) = G(e_{C_2} - e_{C_1}) - g(e_{C_1})$$

$$C_2(de_{C_2}/dt) = G(e_{C_1} - e_{C_2}) + i_L$$

$$L(di_L/dt) = -e_{C_1}$$

See Matsumoto, Chua and Komuro, 1985

*Figure 7.3.2.1   Chua's third-order reciprocal nonlinear circuit
enabling the observation of a chaotic attractor.*

(see also the article by Chua and Kang, 1977, on section-wise piece-wise-linear functions). Chua's circuit is also discussed by Weldon (1990) who uses an active equivalent having an active inductor and an opamp nonlinear function generator. The following papers form a good reading sequence (Prof. Chua is the coauthor of all but the first): Zhong and Ayrom (1985); Matsumoto et al. (1985); Matsumoto et al. (1986); Kennedy and Chua (1986), Chua et al. (1986) which is a key paper in the theory of chaos (the paper is divided into two parts dealing with the rigorous proof of chaos and the rigorous analysis of bifurcation phenomena, respectively), Tanaka et al. (1987), and Chua and Madan (1988).

Newcomb and Sathyan (1983) discuss an RC opamp chaos generator. Another chaos demonstrator circuit using opamps and one multiplier is found in Mishina et al. (1985). Briggs (1987) presents five simple nonlinear systems exhibiting chaotic dynamics. These are the Feigenbaum machine circuit, the diode-inductance circuit, the spinning magnet, the Duffing oscillator and the bouncing ball. Also Mello and Tufillaro (1987) present an excellent analysis on the strange attractors of a bouncing ball. Ballico and Sawley (1990) discuss a bipolar motor case. An unusual oscillating system (saline oscillator) is shown by Yoshikawa et al. (1991). Olsen (1984) discusses the chaotic motion of an enzyme reaction. Mees (1986) discusses chaos in feedback systems.

7.3.3   Three-Dimensional Chaotic Systems

In this section we will examine briefly the Lorenz butterfly, the Rössler attractor and chaos in chemical kinetics. There were many attempts to model and predict weather phenomenon in the 50s and 60s. These models involved linear equations and data. To the best of Newtonian metaphysics, it was believed that more data improve predictability. Of course, it is not so. The model of two-dimensional convection introduced by Lorenz (1963) is a remarkable three-dimensional nonlinear system of autonomous differential equations. In spite of its deceptive simplicity, the system exhibits chaotic behavior (see also Lorenz, 1980). Prof. C. Sparrow (of Cambridge University fame) has written extensively on the Lorenz equations and their significance (Sparrow, 1982, 1983, 1986). As Sparrow notes, systems of this nature were hardly heard of in 1963 and Lorenz's work was largely ignored for about a decade.

The simulation of the Lorenz strange attractor is a favorite among CDSS language users. Its equations are:

$$
\begin{aligned}
\dot{x} &= \sigma \, (y - x) \\
\dot{y} &= \rho \, x - y \, xz \\
\dot{z} &= xy - bz
\end{aligned}
\tag{1}
$$

Lorenz's work is based on earlier research by Salzmann (1962) involving the Oberbeck-Boussinesq equations of fluid connection in a two-dimensional layer heated from below. The Lorenz equations represent three modes, one in velocity and two in temperature (see also

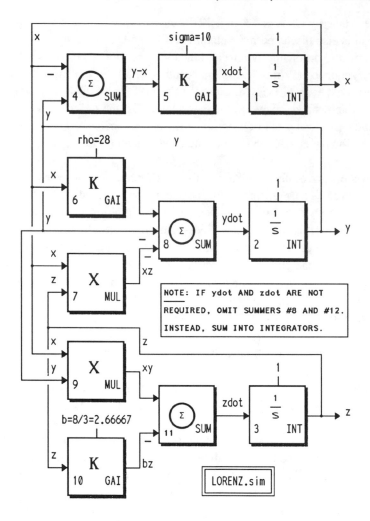

Figure 7.3.3.1   The simulator of the Lorenz strange attractor.

Guckenheimer and Holmes, 1983) whose parameters are the Prandtl number σ, the Rayleigh number ρ and the aspect ratio b. Note that normally σ, ρ,b > 0. The Lorenz system is often studied for different ρ values within the range $0 < \rho < \infty$ using constant σ and b. Lorenz's original 1963 paper shows trajectories for $\sigma = 10$ and b = 8/3. Figure 7.3.3.1 (LORENZ.sim) shows the simulator. The Lorenz *butterfly* trajectory projected on the y-z plane is shown in Figure 7.3.3.2 where $\rho = 28$, $\sigma = 10$, b = 8/3 (see also Sparrow, 1986, p. 126, Figure 6.8).

It is advantageous to observe three-dimensional attractors in their proper coordinate cube (x,y,z) as in Holden and Muhamad (1986). However, readers may simply choose to

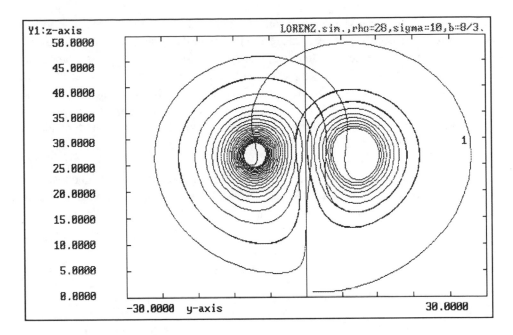

Figure 7.3.3.2   The Lorenz butterfly trajectory projected on the y-z plane ($\rho = 28$, $\sigma = 10$, $b = 8/3$).

project on the xy, yz, and xz planes for some fascinating trajectories. Incidentally, the word *trajectory* signifies the change in the system state variables over time. As such, trajectory plots allow the visualization of dynamic system characteristics (see also Section 6.4.5 on phase-plane diagrams and Section 6.4.2 on state variables). An *attractor* is a point or set of points toward which a trajectory of a system tends over a period of time. The attractor may be a single point denoting a local minimum or a closed trajectory in the case of periodicity. In the case of chaotic systems, attractors appear to wander randomly in the phase space and are called *strange* attractors. A mathematical definition of the terms *attractor* and *strange attractor* in terms of the Lebesgue measure appears in Guckenheimer and Holmes (1983). The Lorenz attractor is also simulated by Rietman with BASIC (1989).

In 1976 Rössler described a chaotic system with only one cross term:

$$
\begin{aligned}
\dot{x} &= -(y + z) \\
\dot{y} &= x + ay \\
\dot{z} &= b + z(x - c)
\end{aligned}
\tag{2}
$$

where a, b, and c are constants (Rössler, 1976, 1979c). The Rössler system models the flow around a single loop of the Lorenz attractor (which has two cross terms). Chaos is shown when c = 5.7 (use a = b = 1/5); the flow forms a Möbius band (see also Holden and Muhamad, 1986). Notably, this is a very simple model of a truncated Navier-Stokes equation (Rietman, 1989). The Rössler system simulator is left to the reader as an exercise.

Chaos in chemical kinetics is a somewhat specialized and relatively new topic on chaos, where it is assumed that readers are familiar with the basic oscillatory dynamics of chemical systems. An excellent and very readable treatment of this topic appears in Edelstein-Keshet's book (1988) on mathematical models in biology. The first theoretical work was performed by Lotka (Lotka, 1920). Like the Lotka-Volterra model (see Lotka, 1956) discussed in Section 12.12, the Lotka chemical kinetics model is *structurally unstable*, implying that the system exhibits neutral cycles sensitive to minor changes in dynamics (see Gurel and Gurel, 1983; and Edelstein-Keshnet, 1988).

The abstract reaction mechanism considered here is described by Willamowski and Rössler (19870) and discussed by Holden and Muhamad (1986). It involves chemical reactions which are at most second order. The system is

$$\dot{x} = x(a - k_1 x - z - y) + k_2 y^2 + a_3$$
$$\dot{y} = y(x - k_2 y - a_5) + a_2 \qquad (1)$$
$$\dot{z} = z(a_4 - x\, k_5 z) + a_3$$

where a_i are concentrations of reactants that are held constant and where k_i are rate constants. That is $a_i, k_i > 0$. Holden and Muhamad (1986) show system trajectories in the xy, yz and zx planes for $k_1 = 0.25$, $k_2 = 0.001$, $k_s = 0.5$, $a_1 = 30$, $a_2 = a_3 = 0.01$, $a_4 = 16.5$ and $a_5 = 10$. Readers will find that the xy-plane trajectories resemble those of the classical Lotka-Volterra prey-predator problem discussed in detail in Section 12.12. An excellent exposition on chemical oscillations and a collection of strange attractors are found in Gurel and Gurel (1983).

7.3.4   Four-Dimensional Chaotic Systems

Strange attractors of four-dimensional chaotic systems belong to the hyperchaos category (see Rössler, 1979b and 1983). In a three-dimensional system, sensitivity to initial conditions in indicated by the single Liapunov exponent (Holden and Muhamad, 1986). A four-dimensional system may exhibit two positive Liapunov exponents, thus having solution trajectories more irregular than chaos (i.e., hyperchaos). Rössler (1979a, 1979b and 1983) describes the simple four-dimensional system

$$\dot{x} = -y - z$$
$$\dot{y} = x + 0.5y + w$$
$$\dot{z} = 3 + xz \qquad (1)$$
$$\dot{w} = -0.5z + 0.05w$$

The practical problem with this system is, of course, visualization. Ideally we must be able to create 3-d plots in the xyz, xyw and zxw spaces.

7.3.5   The Forced Duffing's System

Forced nonlinear dynamic systems are of interest as chaotic generators. Forced nonlinear oscillators provide the simplest nontrivial examples that exhibit both kinematically complex and chaotic behavior (see Tomita, 1986). A nonlinear oscillator with a cubic term is described in the original paper by Duffing (1918). His equation

$$\ddot{x} + b\dot{x} - x + 4ax^3 = c \cos \omega t \qquad (1)$$

represents both electrical and mechanical forced systems (see also Stoker, 1950). The Duffing equation is found in the literature in different forms. Jordan and Smith (1987) provide an excellent mathematical analysis of the basic Duffing equation expressed in dimensionless form

$$\ddot{x} + k\dot{x} - x + x^3 = \Gamma \cos \omega t \qquad (2)$$

Veda (1979 and 1980) discusses the Duffing equation of the form

$$\ddot{x} + a\dot{x} + x^3 = b \cos(t) \qquad (3)$$

where $a, b > 0$ and $a < 1$ with $b < 25$ (see also Holden and Muhamad, 1986). Also Moon and Holmes (1979 and 1980) show that the Duffing equation having the form of Equation (2) represents the simplest possible model of the magnetoelastic beam subjected to forced vibrations. This is a slender elastic steel beam situated in the nonuniform field of two fixed

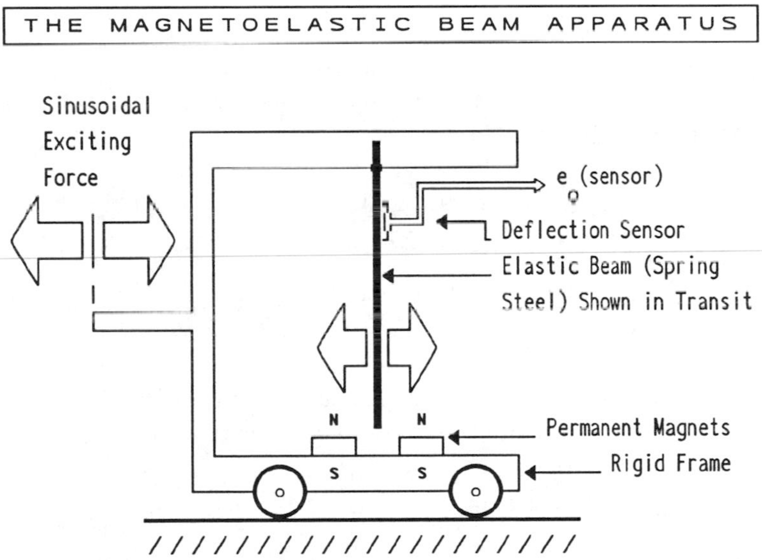

Figure 7.3.5.1   A physical representation of the magnetoelastic beam.

permanent magnets as shown in Figure 7.3.5.1 (see also the excellent book by Moon on chaotic vibrations, 1987). Guckenheimer and Holmes (1983) also include a discussion of the magnetoelastic beam in their book. Notably the magnitude of each magnet's attractive force exceeds that of the beam's elastic force. Without the magnets, elastic forces keep the steel beam straight. However the presence of the force fields cause the beam to rest with the lower end close to one of the magnets. The two magnetic forces cancel each other in an unstable central equilibrium which Guckenheimer and Holmes (1983) describe as a *potential barrier* separating the two domains of attraction. This potential which has two minima, is modelled by the symmetric one-dimensional field equation

$$V(x) = \frac{x^4}{4} - \frac{x^2}{2} \tag{4}$$

Since the force acting on the beam depends on the V gradient, Newton's law suggests that

$$\ddot{x} = - \text{ grad } V \tag{5}$$

and therefore

$$\ddot{x} - x + x^3 = 0 \tag{6}$$

(see also Section 4.9, Equation (3)). Equation (6) is a simple model of the beam. The inclusion of a linear velocity-dependent term k[dx/dt] allows the modelling of friction, aerodynamic and magnetic damping. Then Equation (6) takes the form

$$\ddot{x} + k\dot{x} - x + x^3 = 0 \tag{7}$$

Equation (7) is the unforced version of Equation (2). The reader might want to add coefficients representing realizable radian frequencies and experiment with the various forms of the Duffing equation. One such form is

$$\ddot{x} + \omega_0^2 x \pm a x^3 = F \cos \omega t \tag{8}$$

discussed in detail in the text on mechanical vibrations by Rao (1990) who examines both the damped and undamped cases.

Duffing's equation is also discussed in mathematical detail by Holmes and Whitley (1983 and 1984). Readers are also referred to the Sections 11.6 and especially 11.7 for further discussions on the various spring restoring force functions and the cubic nonlinearity. If we consider the modified equation

$$\ddot{x} = - \frac{1}{m}[- k\dot{x} + bx + a x^3] + f(t) \tag{9}$$

where f(t) is a forcing function, we can easily relate the Duffing system to the linear case. Here the restoring force is $(bx + ax^3)$ and, depending upon the sign of a, we have a *hard spring* (the restoring force characteristic slopes upward) when $a > 0$. If $a < 0$, the characteristic slopes downward defining a *soft spring* (see also SPRING1.sim, Section 11.6). Figure 7.3.5.2 is the block simulator of Equation (9). Readers should plot the phase portrait for $a = (4)(0.25) = 1$, $b = 5$, $k = 0.15$, $f(t) = c \cos 2\pi 2t$ ($c = 0.5$, $\omega = 4\pi \rightarrow f = 2$ on #2) and $(1/m) = 1$.

Another interesting mechanical system is the Duffing oscillator based on the Euler strut (Briggs, 1987). It consists of an inverted pendulum with a top mass supported by a spring steel beam. The top mass is slightly greater than the critical value that induces an unstable vertical equilibrium. The inverted pendulum is driven by a conventional pendulum of larger mass to which it is coupled by a spring. The driving force is approximately sinusoidal. In this device, the gravitational force exceeds the beam's elastic force (without

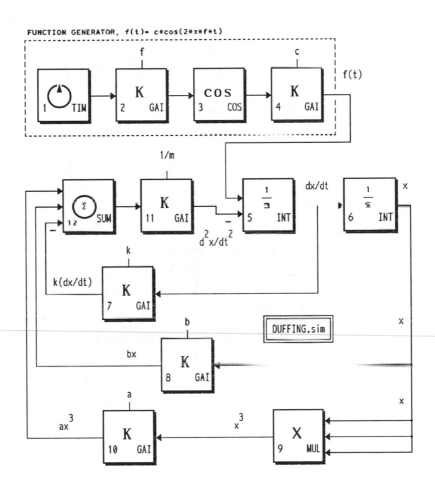

Figure 7.3.5.2   The simulator of Equation (9) of the Duffing form.

the top mass, elastic forces keep the beam straight). Figure 7.3.5.3 shows the basic apparatus. Briggs (1987) uses a knife-edge support for the driving pendulum. He also uses a reference pointer situated behind the inverted pendulum and rigidly coupled to the driving pendulum. The pointer provides a reference phase for visual comparison. Note that the tension adjustment screw is used to relieve the inverted pendulum of any force when both pendula are vertical.

The electrical system shown in Figure 7.3.5.4(a) is an RL circuit with a nonlinear inductor consistency of several turns of insulated wire wound on an iron core. The resistor R represents the coil resistance. The relationship between flux Φ (in Webers, Wb) and current for the saturating element is described by the equation

$$ i = \frac{1}{L_0} \Phi + b \Phi^3 \tag{10} $$

Faraday's law states that

$$ e_L = N \frac{d\Phi}{dt} \tag{11} $$

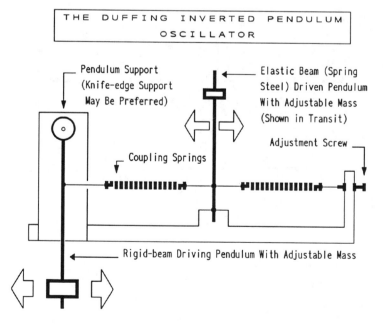

Figure 7.3.5.3   A physical representation of the Dufffing inverted pendulum oscillator.

where N is the number of coil turns and [dΦ/dt] is in Wb/s. According to Kirchoff's law, it is

$$e_L + e_R = e_s \tag{12}$$

and therefore, from Equations (10), (11) and (12) it is

$$N\dot{\Phi} + \left(\frac{1}{L_0}\Phi + b\Phi^3\right) = e_s$$

$$\dot{\Phi} = \left(\frac{1}{N}\right) e_s - \frac{R}{N}\left[\frac{1}{L_0}\Phi + b\Phi^3\right] \tag{13}$$

which can be easily put in a block model form. The circuit of Figure 7.3.5.4(b) is described by the equation

$$e_L + e_C = E \sin \omega t \tag{14}$$

We rewrite after the appropriate substitutions

$$N\dot{\Phi} + \frac{1}{C}\dot{q} = E \sin \omega t \tag{15}$$

and differentiate

$$N\ddot{\Phi} + \frac{1}{C}\dot{q} = E \omega \cos \omega t \tag{16}$$

From Equations (16) and (10) and since [dq/dt] = i, we write

$$N\ddot{\Phi} + \frac{1}{C}\left[\frac{1}{L_0}\Phi + b\Phi^3\right] = E\omega \cos \omega t$$

$$\ddot{\Phi} + \left(\frac{1}{N}\right) E \omega \cos \omega t - \frac{1}{CN}\left[\frac{1}{L_0}\Phi + b\Phi^3\right] \tag{17}$$

Equation (17) is also easily put in a block model form. It describes a forced Duffing system. The governing equation of the same circuit but with an added resistor can also be easily written.

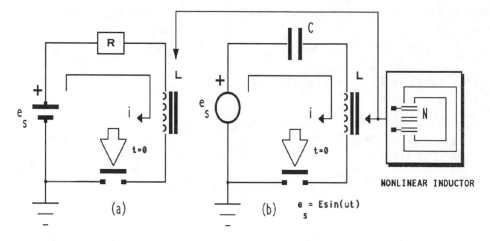

Figure 7.3.5.4   A nonlinear RL circuit described by an equation of the Duffing form (Equation (17)).

7.3.6   The Forced Negative Resistance Oscillator

Negative resistance oscillators are well known as systems of great kinematical complexity and as chaos generators. The system

$$\dot{x} = y$$
$$\dot{y} = a(1 - x^2)y - x^3 + b \cos (ft) \tag{1}$$

is described by Veda and Akamatsu (1981) and discussed by Holden and Muhamad (1986). The system is oscillatory without forcing (unlike the Duffing oscillator of Section 7.3.5). The generalized static characteristic of tunnel diodes shows a region of negative resistance and as a result, tunnel diode oscillators are known to exhibit complex behavior. An excellent analysis of this type of circuit and a hybrid computer simulation are found in Vojtášek and Janáč (1969). Of interest is the paper by Pasupathy (1973) and the analysis by Spasov and Enikova (1973). A negative resistance LRC oscillator and an opamp negative resistor circuit are discussed by Lewis (1976).

The topic of negative resistance (NR) and its applications is most interesting, especially within the context of system stability and chaos. The following papers are of interest: the current-controlled NR circuit by Stanley and Ager (1970); the two-transistor NR circuit by Nishikawa (1971); the N-type NR circuit by Iyer and Sharma (1972); the current-controlled NR by Shafai (1972); the N-type NR generator with two Darlington pairs by Gupta and Nath (1973); the current-controlled S-type NR circuit by Sharma (1974); the current-controlled NR device by Al-Charchafchi (1975); the paper on simulated inductors using NR by Al-Charchafchi and Abdulrahman (1977); the two-transistor current-controlled two-terminal NR network by Al-Charchafchi and Dehlavi (1975); the voltage-controlled NR circuit by Al-Charchafchi et al. (1977); the NR circuit having a NPN and a FET transistor by Andrew (1977); the key paper on the generation of NR by three-pole circuits by Genin and Brezel (1977); the circuit by Lewis (1976); and the NR circuit by Balakrishnan (1978). There are many more papers on the topic. What is mentioned here only represents the author's collection. Negative resistance can be simulated in the CDSS environment by using user-defined piecewise-linear approximation blocks or by implementing the polynomial of the i-e characteristic.

7.3.7 The Brusselator System

The Brusselator is a nonlinear system first proposed by Prigogine and LeFever (1968). Prigogine is the recipient of the 1977 Nobel prize in chemistry for work in nonlinear systems and thermodynamics (see also Prigogine and Nicolis, 1967). The Brusselator, named after the city of Brussels, is the formal set of chemical reactions

$$
\begin{aligned}
A &\rightarrow X \\
B + X &\rightarrow Y + D \\
2X + Y &\rightarrow 3X \\
X &\rightarrow E
\end{aligned}
\tag{1}
$$

and represents an abstract model of the spatially nonuniform chemical patterns of an autocatalytic, nonequilibrium system. It is hypothetical because it involves trimolecular reactions which are implausible, serving only to introduce nonlinearity (see also Holden and Muhamad, 1986; Edelstein-Keshet, 1988; and Rietman, 1989). The Brusselator is discussed by Babloyantz (1986) and Danby (1985).

By letting all kinetic constants equal to unity, the system of Equation (1) is written as

$$
\begin{aligned}
\dot{x} &= A + x^2 y - Bx - x \\
\dot{y} &= Bx - x^2 y
\end{aligned}
\tag{2}
$$

which has a single steady-state solution which is unstable when $B > A^2 + 1$ (Holden and Muhamad, 1986). Then a stable-limit cycle appears with x,y representing concentrations of X and Y of a formal chemical oscillator (Prigogine and Nicolis, 1967). An interesting version of the Brusselator is the forced system by Tomita and Kai (1978):

$$
\begin{aligned}
\dot{x} &= A + x^2 y - Bx - x + g(t) \\
\dot{y} &= Bx - x^2 y \\
g(t) &= a \cos (ft)
\end{aligned}
\tag{3}
$$

Of interest is the similar Schnakenberg system (Schnakenberg, 1979; also discussed by Edelstein-Keshet, 1988, p. 356-360). The block simulator of Equation (2) is shown in Figure 7.3.7.1 (BRUSSEL.sim). The reader should investigate the system's response for A = 1 and B = 3. The self-organizing nature of the system is evident.

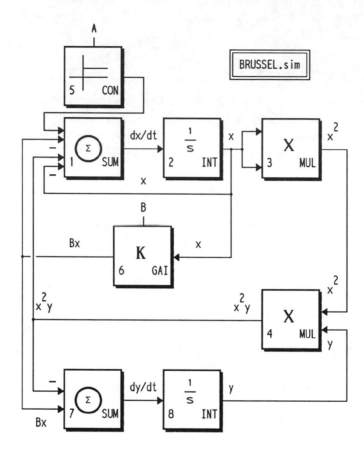

Figure 7.3.7.1 The simulator of the Brusselator system.

7.3.8 Glycolytic Oscillations

Our final example is the simplified model of the generalized glycolytic oscillator

$$\dot{x} = f(t) - xy^2$$
$$\dot{y} = xy^2 - y$$

(1)

where $f(t) = a + b \cos \omega t$, as described by Holden and Muhamad (1986). The block diagram implementation of this system is straightforward and is left as an exercise for the reader.

8 THE SIMULATION OF ELECTRICAL CIRCUITS AND DEVICES—I

8.1 INTRODUCTION

When people talk of electrical circuit and device simulation, special purpose software or custom programs come to mind. There are excellent circuit design and analysis software with schematic editors, large libraries and many features. Some are variants of the SPICE language, with or without schematic editors. Just as this book is not a substitute for specialized textbooks, block diagram languages are not replacements for specialized circuit analysis software. There are, however, tactical advantages to using the mathematical model approach rather than that of a schematic editor. *Block diagram modelling allows the viewing of circuits and devices as dynamic systems rather than mere schematics*. This is important when we seek insight on how things work. Writing SPICE code or working with a schematic editor-based program does not promote insight building as readily. Techniques discussed encourage interdisciplinary thought via the concept of direct analogy. Throughout the book the force-voltage relationship is used to promote a unified system approach that makes sense.

8.2 FIRST-ORDER CIRCUITS AND THEIR ANALOGS

8.2.1 Introduction

Physical systems able to store energy in *only one form and location* are classified as *first order* systems. They are modelled by ordinary differential equations with constant coefficients that include a single variable and the first derivative. In general it is

$$c_1 \dot{x} + c_0 x = f(t) \tag{1}$$

where c_1 and c_0 are the coefficients, x is the variable and $f(t)$ is an input or disturbance known as a *forcing function*. If $f(t) = 0$, the response of the represented system is its *natural motion*, the response of the *unforced* (or *homogeneous*) equation

$$c_1 \dot{x} + c_0 x = 0 \tag{2}$$

If $f(t)$ exists, the response is the linear sum of the natural motion and the motion due to $f(t)$ or *forced motion*. The natural motion (or homogeneous solution) has the general form Ae^{kt} where A and k are constants. A is determined the *initial conditions* and by $f(t)$, while k is a property of the system itself, characterizing its natural motion.

In the following sections we will look at some examples of first-order electrical systems, their simulation and some of their analogs. There are numerous excellent circuit books in the international market that address circuit design at all levels. It should be emphasized that this part deals with the simulation aspects of the topic and it is *not* a substitute for specialized books.

8.2.2   The Series RC Circuit

First we will examine the RC circuit of Figure 8.2.2.1(a), simulate it, compare it with the hydraulic network of Figure 8.2.2.1(b) and explain why it lacks a mechanical analog. The series RC circuit has two parameters, R and C, both positive constants. R is the resistance (in ohms) and C is the capacitance (in farads). When the switch closes the loop at $t = 0$, current begins to flow supplied by source e_s. It is:

$$e_R + e_C = e_s \ , \ \ e_s = f(t) \tag{1}$$

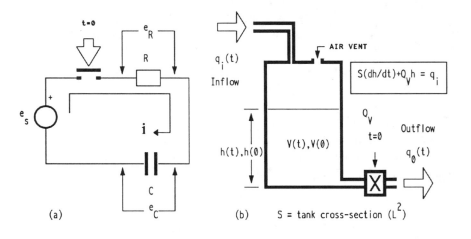

Figure 8.2.2.1   A series RC circuit (a) and a directly analogous hydraulic system (b).

If q is the charge on the capacitor (in coulombs), it is

$$e_R = R\,\dot{q} \tag{2}$$

and

$$e_C = \frac{1}{C}\,q \tag{3}$$

The describing first-order differential equation is

$$R\dot{q} + \frac{1}{C} q = e_s \tag{4}$$

Since

$$q = \int_{t_0}^{t} i\, dt \tag{5}$$

and therefore

$$\dot{q} = \frac{dq}{dt} = i \tag{6}$$

Equation (4) can be rewritten as

$$e_R + \frac{1}{C} \int_{t_0}^{t} i\, dt = e_s \tag{7}$$

from Equations (1) and (7) it is

$$e_C = \frac{1}{C} \int_{t_0}^{t} i\, dt \tag{8}$$

and since Ohm's law states

$$i = \frac{e_R}{R} \tag{9}$$

Equation (8) can take the form

$$e_C = \frac{1}{C} \int_{t_0}^{t} \frac{e_R}{R}\, dt \tag{10}$$

Or by differentiating

$$\dot{e}_C = \frac{1}{CR} e_R \qquad (11)$$

By definition

$$\tau = RC \qquad (12)$$

and Equation (9) can be written as

$$\dot{e}_C = \frac{1}{\tau} e_R \qquad (13)$$

Also from Equation (1) it is

$$e_R = e_s - e_C \qquad (14)$$

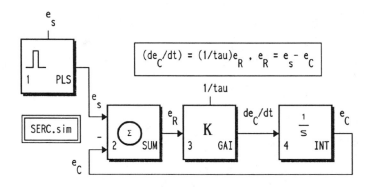

Figure 8.2.2.2   *A simulator of the series RC circuit.*

The system of Equations (13) and (14) is simulated by the block diagram of Figure 8.2.2.2 (SERC.sim) (see also the response equation in Section 9.1). The setup allows us to investigate the time behavior of voltages e_R and e_C for any time constant τ and any forcing function $e_s = f(t)$. Readers should experiment first with a forcing function (1,P,LS,1,2,1) and $\tau = 0.5$ ($1/\tau = 2$ entered as the parameter of block #3). Then the pulse can be replaced with a constant and the response of the simulator can be investigated for various τ values.

Let us now consider an RC circuit described by a homogeneous equation (no forcing function). There is an initial capacitor charge $q(0) = q_0$ and current begins to flow when the switch closes the loop at $t = 0$. The capacitor discharges through the resistor and the circuit equation is

$$e_C + e_R = 0$$

$$\frac{1}{C} q + Ri = 0$$

$$\frac{1}{C} q + R\dot{q} = 0 \tag{15}$$

$$C\dot{q} + \frac{q}{R} = 0$$

or for the purpose of simulation

$$\dot{q} = - q \left(\frac{1}{R}\right) \left(\frac{1}{C}\right) \tag{16}$$

The circuit's response is

$$q(t) = q_0 e^{-(1/RC)t} = q_0 e^{-t/\tau} \tag{17}$$

The system can be simulated by substituting the known values for C and R into Equation (16). For example if $C = 5F$ and $R = 0.1\Omega$, Equation (16) becomes

$$\dot{q} = - 2q \tag{18}$$

and if $q(0) = 10$ coulombs, the simulator of Figure 8.2.2.3 (RC1.sim) will provide the q or $i = [dq/dt]$ curves for the circuit. However, the simulator of Figure 8.2.2.4 implements Equation (16) *directly* and component values can be assigned *directly*. Employing the integrator of Section 1.5 (Figure 1.5.6) allows the introduction of capacitor charge via a wired input to the summer (as opposed to parameter entry), so that intermittent or unusual conditions may be introduced from another subsystem.

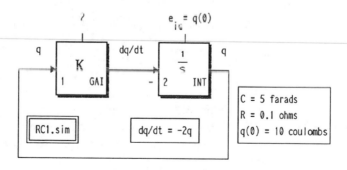

Figure 8.2.2.3   Simulating Equation (18).

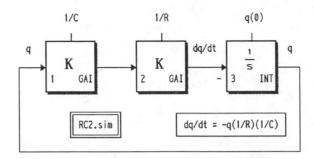

Figure 8.2.2.4   An alternate simulator of the series RC circuit.

A direct hydraulic analogy exists between the RC circuit and a ventilated holding tank discharging its fluid content through a valved outlet. The fluid content (equivalent to the capacitor charge) discharges through the outlet at a rate determined by the valve setting. The valve is equivalent to the electrical variable resistor (potentiometer) that acts to restrict current flow. The tank is equivalent to the capacitor holding the charge and the time constant of the system is directly proportional to both the fluid volume and the valve setting (see also the mixing tank problem and the comments on the RC circuit in Section 6.2.3). The initial condition is $V(0) = V_0$ where V is the volume and the forcing function is $q_i(t) = 0$ for $e_s = 0$.

The response of Equation (17) is obvious in the case of the hydraulic system. As for the RC circuit, anytime a resistor is present (as in RC, RL and RCL circuits) a potential exists across it so that, according to Ohm's law,

$$e(t) \;=\; R\,i(t) \tag{19}$$

There is power dissipation in heat form according to Joule's law

$$W(t) \;=\; R\,i(t)^2 \tag{20}$$

Therefore, the total energy of the system does not remain constant.

A curious property of the RC circuit is its lacking of a mechanical analog. Amazingly enough, only one dfq book was found that addressed this important detail (Trahanas, 1989). Induction is the electrical equivalent of a mass (L → m). The circuit lacks an inductive element and, of course, a mechanical system cannot be realized without a mass.

The holding tank of Figure 8.2.2.1(b) provides a good starting point for the study of liquid-level systems. The liquid level (or head) h defines the system's potential that induces the outflow $q_0(t)$. The inflow $q_i(t)$ is equivalent to the electrical $e_s(t)$. Here q denotes volumetric flow rate (L^3/s, L = any suitable unit of length), and it is assumed that $q_0(t)$ is directly proportional to h. The value regulates the constant Q_V (the cross-sectional area of the discharge orifice) so that

$$q_0(t) = Q_V h \tag{21}$$

Therefore, Q_V is a proportionality constant equivalent to a potentiometer setting. If S is the tank's cross-sectional area (in L^2), is

$$\Delta q(t) = q_1(t) - q_0(t) = S \dot{h} \tag{22}$$

From Equations (21) and (22), we write the differential equation of the system (Figure 8.2.2.1(b))

$$S \dot{h} + Q_V h = q_i \tag{23}$$

Earlier is was mentioned that $q_0(t)$ is assumed directly proportional to h, because the outflow-inducing pressure is assumed directly proportional to the head (a convenient assumption that doesn't influence the quantitative results significantly). Without belaboring the point, there are different approaches in determining the performance of a tank discharging its fluid content through a short, narrow horizontal tube. The Poiseuille equation allows us to see the problem as one of hydrostatics, although others use Bernoulli's equation and Torricelli's theorem and treat it form a hydrodynamic point of view, taking into account the acceleration of the liquid as it moves from the tank to the outlet tube.

8.2.3   The Series RL Circuit

Let us consider the series RL circuit governed by the equation

$$e_L + e_R = e_s \tag{1}$$

Faraday's law states that the voltage drop across an inductor is proportional to the inductance and to the derivative of the current flowing through it, or

$$e_L = L \left(\frac{di}{dt} \right) \tag{2}$$

Since $i = e_R/R$, Equation (2) is written

$$e_L = L \left(\frac{d}{dt} \right) \left(\frac{e_R}{R} \right) = \frac{L}{R} \left(\frac{d\, e_R}{dt} \right) \tag{3}$$

By definition it is

$$\tau \;=\; L\left(\frac{1}{R}\right) \tag{4}$$

and Equation (3) becomes

$$\dot{e}_R \;=\; \frac{1}{\tau}\, e_L \tag{5}$$

From Equation (1) we have

$$e_L \;=\; e_s \;-\; e_R \tag{6}$$

The system of Equations (5) and (6) is easily simulated as in the case of the RC circuit. Readers should build and compare this simulator with that of the RC circuit (Figure 8.2.2.2). Given identical τ and e_s, the two circuits produce identical curves where the $e_R(t)$ and $e_C(t)$ responses of the RC circuit match the respective $e_L(t)$ and $e_R(t)$ outputs of the RL circuit. The direct mechanical analog of the series RL circuit is described by the equation

$$m\,\frac{du}{dt} \;+\; du \;=\; F_s \;,\quad F_s \;=\; f(t) \tag{7}$$

representing a network having a body of mass, m, moving under the influence of some friction (or viscous) force, d, proportional to its velocity, u. Equation (1) can be rewritten as

$$L\,\frac{di}{dt} \;+\; R\,i \;=\; e_s \;,\quad e_s \;=\; f(t) \tag{8}$$

and a direct comparison can be made between Equations (7) and (8). First, *an electric potential (or electromotive force) is directly analogous to a mechanical force*, or

$$e_s(t) \quad\rightarrow\quad F_s(t) \tag{9}$$

and *electric current is directly analogous to velocity*, or

$$i(t) \;=\; \dot{q}(t) \quad\rightarrow\quad u(t) \;=\; \dot{x}(t) \tag{10}$$

We recall from the previous section that

$$L \quad\rightarrow\quad m \tag{11}$$

that is, *an inductance is seen as an 'electric inertia' coefficient, directly analogous to a mechanical mass.* Then Equation (2) is said to correspond exactly to the inertial law (Newton's second law of motion)

$$F = m \left(\frac{du}{dt} \right) \tag{12}$$

We know (Section 8.22, Equations 19 and 20) that energy dissipates in heat form through R. In the mechanical network, energy dissipates due to friction, so that *electrical resistance is directly analogous to mechanical friction*, or

$$R \rightarrow d \tag{13}$$

An inductor stores up an electromagnetic energy

$$E_L = \frac{1}{2} L i^2 \tag{14}$$

which is directly analogous to the kinetic energy

$$E_k = \frac{1}{2} m u^2 \tag{15}$$

or

$$\frac{1}{2} L i^2 \rightarrow \frac{1}{2} m u^2 \tag{16}$$

The homogeneous equation

$$L \frac{di}{dt} + R i = 0 \tag{17}$$

has the natural response

$$i(t) = A e^{-(R/L)t} \quad (i(0) = i_0) \tag{18}$$

or

$$i(t) = A e^{-t/\tau} \tag{19}$$

where $A = i(0) = i_0 > 0$, thus indicating that the current dissipates exponentially to a level (1/e) of its original value with a time constant $\tau = LR^{-1}$.

In the case where e_s is a constant, the circuit has the forced solution

$$i(t)_{forced} \;=\; \frac{e_s(t)}{R} \tag{20}$$

plus the natural solution of Equation (19), which becomes

$$i(t)_{nat} \;=\; A\,e^{-t/\tau} \tag{19R}$$

Then, at the closing of the switch ($t = 0$), it begins to output the curve-solution

$$i(t) \;=\; A\,e^{-t/\tau} \;+\; \frac{e_s}{R} \tag{21}$$

or if $i_0 = 0$

$$i(t) \;-\; \frac{e_s}{R}\left(1 \,-\, e^{-t/\tau}\right) \tag{22}$$

indicating that the current rises asymptotically to the level e_s/R.

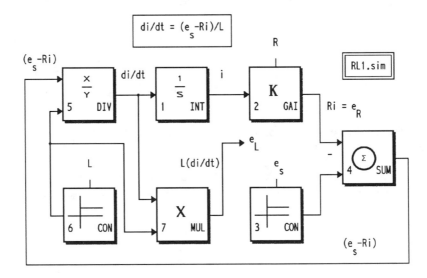

Figure 8.2.3.1   A series RL circuit simulator which allows the direct entry of L and R values.

The block diagram of Figure 8.2.3.1 (RL1.sim) implements the rearranged equation

$$\frac{di}{dt} \;=\; \frac{e_s - R\,i}{L} \tag{23}$$

and allows the direct entry of L and R values. For example, given L = 4H, R = 200Ω and e_s = 12V, we can readily obtain the i(t) response. It is

$$i(t) = i_R(t) = i_L(t) \tag{24}$$

and i(t) is the output of the INT (#1) block. The time constant of the circuit is $\tau = (4H/200Ω) = 0.02s$. Therefore, it takes 0.02s for i(t) to reach 63.2% of the maximum current, $i_{max} = (12V/200Ω) = 0.06A$, or 0.03792A. This is verified by rescaling the output as shown in Figure 8.2.3.2. Both $e_L(t)$ and $e_R(t)$ are available from blocks #7, where $e_L(t) = L(di/dt)$ and #2, where $e_R(t) = Ri$. An alternative simulator can be constructed based on the relationship

$$\frac{di}{dt} = \frac{1}{L}\left(e_s - Ri\right) \tag{25}$$

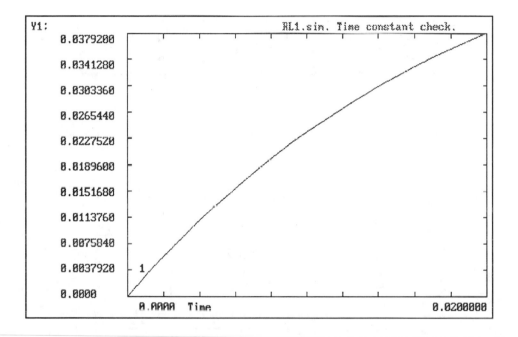

Figure 8.2.3.2   Time constant verification of the RL1.sim example. It takes 0.02 s for i(t) to reach 63.2% of the i_{max} or 0.03792 A.

The RL circuit can be tested for a square or rectangular wave input. The waveform generator (Figure 8.2.3.3) consists of blocks #6 through #10. It is a modified consinusoidal generator outputing $e_s(t) = A\, sgn(sin\, 2\pi ft)$. The output of Figure 8.2.3.4 shows the case for f = 10, A = 12V, L = 4H and R = 200Ω. Note that often it is necessary to bypass the first few cycles until the circuit stabilizes. Readers will find experimentation with other values (e.g., f = 100, 500) very instructive. Sharpe (1969) provides an excellent discussion on the analog computer simulation of first-order systems with emphasis on RC and RL circuit problems.

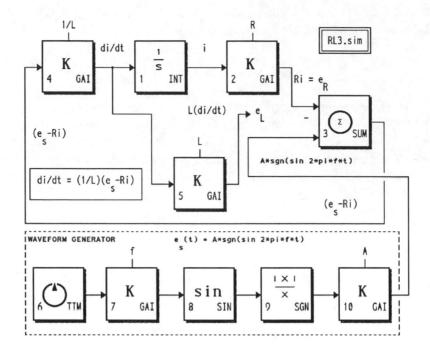

Figure 8.2.3.3   Testing the RL circuit for a square or rectangular wave input.

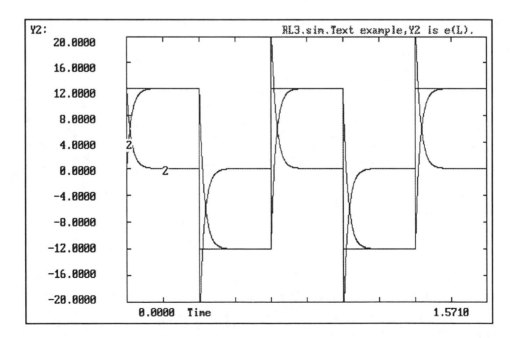

Figure 8.2.3.4   The results of RL3.sim.

8.3 SECOND-ORDER CIRCUITS AND THEIR ANALOGS

8.3.1 Introduction

The homogeneous second-order differential equation

$$c_2 \ddot{x} + c_1 \dot{x} + c_0 x = 0 \tag{1}$$

describes physical systems capable of storing energy in two different forms, as in the case of the mass-spring-dashpot mechanical system (potential and kinetic energies) or the series LRC electrical system (electrical and electromagnetic energies described in Section 8.3.2.). Problems of this category are simulated by setting up a block diagram that represents the explicit equation for the highest-order derivative

$$\ddot{x} = - \left(\frac{c_1}{c_2} \right) \dot{x} - \left(\frac{c_0}{c_2} \right) x \tag{2}$$

This is a popular analog computer technique used to conserve coefficient potentiometers. However this programming approach does not suit investigations where independent adjustments of c_2, c_1 and c_0 are normally expected. Instead, we rearrange the terms of Equation (2) so that

$$\ddot{x} = - \frac{1}{c_2} \left(c_1 \dot{x} + c_0 x \right) \tag{3}$$

The block diagram of Figure 8.3.1.1 leads to the simulator of Figure 8.3.1.2 as the direct implementation of Equation (3), where the three coefficients are recognized as individually adjustable dependent variables.

Physical systems represented by Equation (1) have a mean resonant frequency

$$\omega_0 = \omega_n - \sqrt{\frac{c_0}{c_2}} \tag{4}$$

which is the undamped natural frequency ω_n of the system or the frequency at which the system oscillates when $c_1 = 0$. Also the relative damping ratio of the system is

$$\varsigma = \frac{c_1}{2\sqrt{c_0 c_2}} \tag{5}$$

The parameters ω and ζ have great physical significance and contribute to mathematical simplification.

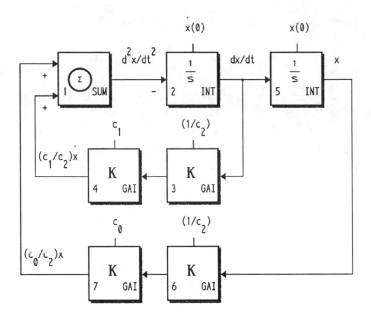

Figure 8.3.1.1 Simulating Equation (1).

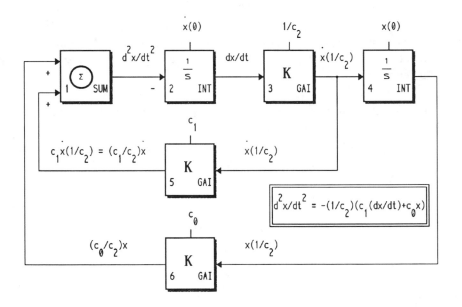

Figure 8.3.1.2 A final simulator of Equation (1).

In its general form, Equation (1) is

$$c_2\ddot{x} + c_1\dot{x} + c_0 x = f(t) \tag{6}$$

and therefore the generalized transfer function of a second-order system can be written in the frequency domain as

$$\frac{x(s)}{F(s)} = \frac{1}{c_2 s^2 + c_1 s + c_0} \tag{7}$$

Some algebra will help us express the transfer function in terms of ζ and ω_n. It is

$$\frac{1}{c_2 s^2 + c_1 s + c_0} = \frac{\dfrac{1}{c_2}}{s^2 + \dfrac{c_1}{c_2} s + \dfrac{c_0}{c_2}} = \frac{\dfrac{1}{c_0} \dfrac{c_0}{c_2}}{s^2 + c_1 \dfrac{1}{c_2} s + \dfrac{c_0}{c_2}}$$

$$= \frac{1}{c_0} \frac{\dfrac{c_0}{c_2}}{s^2 + c_1 \dfrac{1}{\sqrt{c_2}} \dfrac{1}{\sqrt{c_2}} s + \dfrac{c_0}{c_2}}$$

$$= \frac{1}{c_0} \frac{\dfrac{c_0}{c_2}}{s^2 + c_1 \dfrac{1}{\sqrt{c_2}} \dfrac{1}{\sqrt{c_2}} \sqrt{c_0} \dfrac{1}{\sqrt{c_0}} s + \dfrac{c_0}{c_2}}$$

$$= \frac{1}{c_0} \frac{\dfrac{c_0}{c_2}}{s^2 + c_1 \dfrac{1}{\sqrt{c_0 c_2}} \dfrac{\sqrt{c_0}}{\sqrt{c_2}} s + \dfrac{c_0}{c_2}}$$

$$= \frac{1}{c_0} \frac{\left(\sqrt{\dfrac{c_0}{c_2}}\right)^2}{s^2 + 2\left(\dfrac{c_1}{2\sqrt{c_0 c_2}}\right)\left(\sqrt{\dfrac{c_0}{c_2}}\right) s + \left(\sqrt{\dfrac{c_0}{c_2}}\right)^2} \tag{8}$$

By substitution from Equations (4) and (5), we get the popular form

$$\frac{x(s)}{F(s)} = \frac{1}{c_0} \frac{\omega_n^2}{s^2 + 2\varsigma\omega_n s + \omega_n^2} \tag{9}$$

Apologies are extended to those offended by the lengthy algebraic manipulations used to derive Equation (9). However many people (engineers or engineering/technology students) experience difficulty in moving form Equation (7) to Equation (9) despite their having successfully completed several college-level mathematics courses.

The characteristic equation of the system is

$$s^2 + 2\varsigma\omega_n s + \omega_n^2 = 0 \tag{10}$$

from which

$$s = -\varsigma\omega_n s \pm \omega_n (\varsigma^2 - 1)^{\frac{1}{2}} \tag{11}$$

The transient response of the system depends on the roots of Equation (10) and therefore it is uniquely defined by the damping ratio, ς. The roots are

$$\begin{aligned}
&\text{complex for } \varsigma < 1 \\
&\text{real and equal for } \varsigma = 1 \\
&\text{real and unequal for } \varsigma > 1
\end{aligned}$$

When $\varsigma = 0$ the system is *undamped* (an oscillator). When $\varsigma < 1$ the system is *underdamped*. The only natural mode is an oscillatory mode having the form

$$\exp(-\varsigma\omega t) \sin(\nu t + \epsilon) \tag{12}$$

where $\varsigma\omega$ is the damping index and $\nu = \omega(1 - \varsigma^2)^{\frac{1}{2}}$ is the angular frequency. When $\varsigma = 1$, the natural mode is *critically damped*. By definition, critical damping is the value of ς required to produce real and equal roots from the system's characteristic equation. When $\varsigma > 1$, the system is *overdamped*, with two separate exponential modes of the form $\exp(-s_1 t)$, $\exp(-s_2 t)$ where $(-s_1)$ and $(-s_2)$ are the real roots of the characteristic equation.

8.3.2   The Series LC Circuit

The series LC network is described by the circuit equation

$$e_L + e_C = f(t) \tag{1}$$

or the homogeneous differential equation $(f(t) = 0)$

$$L \frac{di}{dt} + \frac{1}{C} \int_{t_0}^{t} i \, dt = 0 \qquad (2)$$

$$\rightarrow \quad L\ddot{q} + \frac{1}{C}q = 0 \quad \rightarrow \qquad (3)$$

$$\rightarrow \quad \ddot{q} + \frac{1}{L_C}q = 0 \qquad (4)$$

Equation (4) describes a resonant system where the charge oscillates periodically between capacitor plates with a mean resonance frequency

$$\omega_0 = \frac{1}{\sqrt{LC}} \rightarrow \omega_0^2 = \frac{1}{LC} \qquad (5)$$

If we apply a voltage $e_C(t)$ across the capacitor, a charge q develops where

$$q(t) = C \, e_C(t) \qquad (6)$$

or

$$e_C(t) = \frac{1}{C} q(t) \qquad (7)$$

as reflected in Equation (2). The equivalent mechanical equation is

$$F = kx \qquad (8)$$

because *a capacitor's electrostatic charge is analogous to the mechanical displacement (or position) x and capacitance corresponds to the spring's inverse stiffness k^{-1} (or C^{-1} corresponds to the spring constant k),* so we write

$$q(t) \rightarrow x(t) \qquad (9)$$

$$C \rightarrow k^{-1}, \quad C^{-1} = k \qquad (10)$$

Also resistance is equivalent to a mechanical friction coefficient, normally represented by the viscous friction coefficient d (Section 8.2.3).

The analogy between q and x can be further derived from the analogy between i and [dx/dt] (Section 8.2.3), since it is

$$i = \frac{dq}{dt} = \dot{q}, \quad \dot{x} = \frac{dx}{dt} \tag{11}$$

This is consistent with the statement that voltage dropped across a capacitor is proportional to the integral of the current flowing through it, or

$$e_C(t) = \frac{1}{C} \int_{t_0}^{t} i(t)\, dt \tag{12}$$

The capacitor stores a charge energy (or electrostatic energy)

$$E_C = \frac{1}{2}\left(\frac{1}{C}\right) q^2 \tag{13}$$

directly analogous to a spring's strain (potential) energy

$$E_{SP} = \frac{1}{2} k x^2 \tag{14}$$

From Equations (4) and (5), we write

$$\ddot{q} + \omega_0^2 q = 0 \tag{15}$$

where $q(0) = q_0$, $[dq/dt](0) = i(0) = 0$ are the initial conditions corresponding to some initial capacitor charge occuring at $t = 0$ (open for $t < 0$) and no initial current flow. Equation (2) is then analogous to the mechanical equation

$$m\ddot{x} + k x = 0 \tag{16}$$

representing a frictionless mass-spring or an undamped pendulum mechanism having an undamped natural frequency

$$\omega_0 = \sqrt{\frac{k}{m}} \tag{17}$$

at which, by definition, the system oscillates when damping (or viscosity) is zero.

The expected output of the LC circuit is

$$e_0(t) \;=\; q(t) \;=\; q_0 \cos \omega_0 t \tag{18}$$

We observe that the law of energy conservation

$$E_T \;=\; E_K + E_P \tag{19}$$

can be established for both the electrical and the mechanical networks (E_T = total system energy) by considering the analogies

$$\frac{1}{2} k x^2 \;\;\rightarrow\;\; \frac{1}{2} \left(\frac{1}{C}\right) q^2 \tag{20}$$

for the potential energy E_P and

$$\frac{1}{2} m \dot{x}^2 \;\;\rightarrow\;\; \frac{1}{2} L i^2 \tag{21}$$

for the kinetic energy E_K. Substitution of Equations (20) and (21) into Equation (19) provides the equation of the total electrical (electrocstatic and electromagnetic) energy of the LC circuit:

$$E_T \;=\; \frac{1}{2} \left(L i^2 + \frac{q^2}{C} \right) \tag{22}$$

The first term represents the 'kinetic' *electromagnetic* field energy occurring when current flows through the inductor coil. The 'potential' *electrostatic* energy of the second term is held as a capacitor charge. Differentiation of Equation (22) produces Equation (2), the original homogeneous differential equation of the system.

8.3.3   The LRC Circuit and Its Mechanical Analog

There are many approaches to setting up a dynamic simulation for the LRC circuit of Figure 8.3.3.1(a). The first case involves a voltage source $e_s(t)$ and current flow begins at the closing of the switch at $t = 0$. The second case involves a charged capacitor. If $e_s(t) = 0$, it is

$$e_L(t) + e_R(t) + e_C(t) \;=\; 0 \tag{1}$$

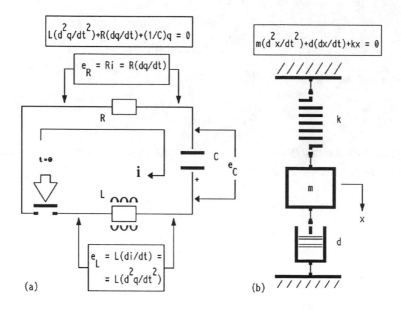

Figure 8.3.3.1   An LRC circuit (a) and an equivalent mass-spring-damper mechanical system (b).

Since

$$i_C(t) \;=\; i_R(t) \;=\; i_C(t) \;=\; i \tag{2}$$

and

$$i_C(t) \;=\; C\left(\frac{d\,e_C}{d\,t}\right) \tag{3}$$

we can write

$$e_L(t) \;=\; L\left(\frac{d\,i}{d\,t}\right) \;=\; LC\left(\frac{d^2 e_C}{d\,t^2}\right) \tag{4}$$

$$e_R(t) \;=\; R\,i \;=\; RC\left(\frac{d\,e_C}{d\,t}\right) \tag{5}$$

$$e_C(t) = \frac{1}{C} \int_{t_0}^{t} i \, dt \tag{6}$$

Substitution of Equations (4), (5) and (6) into Equation (1) gives the system equation expressed in terms of i, where

$$L \left(\frac{di}{dt}\right) + Ri + \frac{1}{C} \int_{t_0}^{t} i \, dt = 0 \tag{7}$$

or in terms of e_C where

$$LC \left(\frac{d^2 e_C}{dt^2}\right) + RC \left(\frac{d e_C}{dt}\right) + e_C = 0 \tag{8}$$

The last two equations are generalized expressions of Ohm's law or Kirchhoff's second law, whereby the sum of electromotive forces and differences in potential across the elements within a closed loop equal the source (or equal zero if the source is zero). Another popular form is in terms of e_C and ω_0. From Equation (8) it is

$$\frac{d^2 e_C}{dt^2} + \frac{R}{L} \left(\frac{d e_C}{dt}\right) + \frac{1}{LC} e_C = 0 = \frac{d^2 e_C}{dt^2} + \frac{R}{L} \left(\frac{d e_C}{dt}\right) + \omega_0^2 e_C \tag{9}$$

Also given that

$$i - \frac{dq}{dt} = \dot{q} \tag{10}$$

Equation (7) can be written in terms of q, where

$$L \, \ddot{q} + R \, \dot{q} + \frac{1}{C} q = 0 \tag{11}$$

with the initial conditions $q(0) = q_0$ and $[dq/dt](0) = 0$ (the lack of a forcing function implies that all system excitations exist in the form of initial conditions). Unlike the LC circuit of Section 8.3.2, the total energy of the system dissipates because of the resistor ($\omega = Ri^2$). This is best seen through the expression

$$\frac{d\left(\frac{1}{2} Li^2\right)}{dt} + \frac{d\left(\frac{1}{2} \frac{q^2}{C}\right)}{dt} = \frac{d\left(-R_i^2\right)}{dt}$$

which, when differentiated, becomes the original system equation.

The mass-spring-damper mechanical system of Figure 8.3.3.1(b) is described by the equation

$$m\ddot{x} + d\dot{x} + kx = 0 \qquad (12)$$

where d and k are functions of [dx/dt] and x but with time invariant. The equation above is directly analogous to Equation (11). Contrary to a popular belief, Equation (12) is NOT directly analogous to Equation (7). Mechanical displacement is directly analogous to electrical charge, not current. *Direct* analogies facilitate unquestionable mathematical equivalency between physical systems and their simulators, thus establishing the validity of an often questioned process. Rigorous *mathematical equivalency* must exist in order for a direct analogy (and thus corresponding behavior) to exist. Figure 8.3.3.2 depicts some directly analogous electrical and mechanical quantities. We justify our approach to analogies (there are others the author considers invitations to confusion, if not fundamentally incorrect) by reverting to the fundamental laws of physics, mechanics, electricity and thermodynamics. These laws, based on empirical observation, are expressed in terms of temporal changes or, specifically, in terms of rate of change of the pertinent variables. Cases in point are Faraday's law

$$e_L(t) = L\left(\frac{di}{dt}\right) \qquad (13)$$

or Newton's second law

$$F(t) = m\left(\frac{du}{dt}\right) \qquad (14)$$

mentioned throughout the text. Fourier's heat law, Fick's law of diffusion and the law of conservation of mass and energy are also pertinent here.

Contrary to the methods used in this book, Cannon (1967) sates that when working from the equation of motion, it is pedagogically sound to consider that velocity is analogous to voltage. We take a very strong exception to this statement. Cannon's choice of the inverse (force → current) analog as opposed to the direct (force → voltage) analog (see also Raven,

DIRECT ANALOGIES BETWEEN MECHANICAL AND ELECTRICAL QUANTITIES	
MECHANICAL	ELECTRICAL
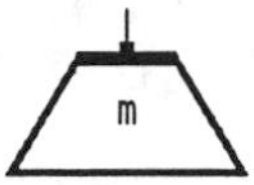 Mass, m	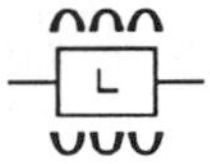 Inductor, L
 Dashpot: Damping, Friction or Viscous Force Coefficient, d	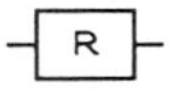 Resistor, R
Spring Constant, k	Inverse Capacitance, C^{-1}
Spring Inverse Stiffness, k^{-1}	 Capacitance, C
Displacement, x	Charge, q
Velocity, $\dot{x} = dx/dt$	Current, i
	Rate of Change of Charge, $\dot{q} = dq/dt = i$
Force, F	Voltage, e
Kinetic Energy, $E_K = (1/2)m\dot{x}^2$	Energy Stored by an Inductor, $E_L = (1/2)Li^2$
Potential (Strain) Energy Stored by a Spring, $E_{SP} = (1/2)kx^2$	Charge Energy Stored by a Capacitor, $E_c = (1/2)(1/C)q^2$

Figure 8.3.3.2 Some directly analogous quantities.

1987) violates the concept of **direct analogy** which is essential in simulation. The inverse analog is popular with traditional control system authors seeking to establish analogous nodal topologies. Perhaps the most elegant explanation on behalf of the direct analogy approach is by Rosenberg and Karnopp (1983) who introduce the words *effort* and *flow* and define voltage as effort and current as flow. They state that the choice of voltage as effort is natural, since voltage is electromotive force. Rosenberg and Karnopp go on to point out that when we say *the current flows*, we immediately establish an analogy to velocity. In his remarkable book on differential equations, Trahanas (1989) supports the direct analogy approach, as also do Rocard in his classic book, *Dynamique Générale des Vibrations* (1960), and Ogata (1978).

To reiterate, the author believes that only direct analogies are useful in simulation. Inverse analogies are constructs traditionally used to denote equivalent nodal topologies. Unlike the concept of centrifugal force which is a mythical but useful construct (imagine an outwardly-directed force required to sustain rotational motion!), inverse analogies are **reverse truth**. As such they are harmful and pedagogically unsound.

8.4   COUPLED SYSTEMS

The topic of coupled dynamic systems is vast and often specialized. This section focuses on basic electrical and mechanical coupled systems and is only intended as a conceptual introduction. A logical starting point is the electrical transformer model in which two wire coils are immersed in common flux linkages (we assume no iron core effects). The electrical characteristics of the coils depend on the linking flux and therefore the coils are magnetically coupled. In Figure 8.4.1, L_1 and L_2 are the *self-inductances* of the two coils and M is the *mutual inductance*. This simple device model is described by the following system of differential equations:

$$e_1 \; = \; L_1 \, \frac{d i_1}{d t} \; \pm \; M \, \frac{d i_2}{d t}$$

$$e_2 \; = \; L_2 \, \frac{d i_2}{d t} \; \pm \; M \, \frac{d i_1}{d t} \tag{1}$$

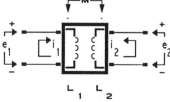

Figure 8.4.1   An electrical transformer model described by the system of Equation (1).

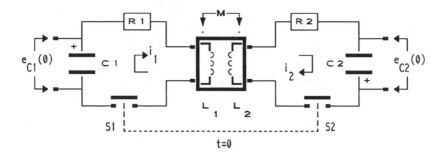

Figure 8.4.2   Two circuits coupled by mutual inductance.

The dots indicate the dependence of the mutual flux orientation on the coil winding direction. A dual-coil transformer may involve any of the sixty-four possible combinations of the two voltages references, two current references and the two flux sense dots, so caution is advised in modelling specific transformer devices. (Note that the algebraic signs of the mutual inductances depend on the relative winding senses). Caution is also advised in the modelling of mutually-coupled circuits other than transformers. Figure 8.4.2 shows an example of two circuits coupled by mutual inductance. The following are given: L_1, L_2, R_1, R_2, C_1, C_2, M (in H), $e(C_1)_0$, $e(C_2)_0$, $i_1(0) = i_2(0) = 0$. We also know (Section 8.3.3) that

$$q = C\, e_C \quad \rightarrow \quad e_C = \frac{q}{C}, \quad i = \frac{dq}{dt}$$

The system equations (Kirchoff's law) are

$$L_1 \frac{d^2 q_1}{dt^2} + M \frac{d^2 q_2}{dt^2} + R_1 \frac{dq_1}{dt} + \frac{q_1}{C_1} = 0$$

$$(2)$$

$$L_2 \frac{d^2 q_2}{dt^2} + M \frac{d^2 q_1}{dt^2} + R_2 \frac{dq_2}{dt} + \frac{q_2}{C_2} = 0$$

If we wish, we can rewrite the equations without q, or some other variable, so we can obtain the simulation model of our choice (the generalized method of simulating coupled dynamic systems is discussed later on this section).

The coupled circuits of Figure 8.4.3 do not involve mutual inductance. Here we have R_1, R_2, L_1, L_2, C_1, C_2, $i_1(0)$ and $i_2(0)$. We can apply Kirchoff's law to write the loop current equations of the system:

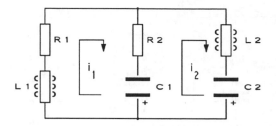

Figure 8.4.3   An example of coupled circuits (Equations 6 and 7).

$$L_1 \frac{d\,i_1}{d\,t} + (R_1 + R_2)\,i_1 + \frac{1}{C_1} \int_0^t i_1\,dt - R_2\,i_2 - \frac{1}{C_1} \int_0^t i_2\,dt = 0$$

$$L_2 \frac{d\,i_2}{d\,t} + R_2\,I_2 + \left[\frac{C_1 + C_2}{C_1 C_2}\right] \int_0^t i_2\,dt - R_2\,i_1 - \frac{1}{C_1} \int_0^t i_1\,dt = 0 \tag{3}$$

Then we differentiate both equations:

$$L_1 \frac{d^2 i_1}{d\,t^2} + (R_1 + R_2) \frac{d\,i_1}{d\,t} + \frac{1}{C_1}\,i_1 - R_2 \frac{d\,i_2}{d\,t} - \frac{1}{C_1}\,i_2 = 0$$

$$L_2 \frac{d^2 i_2}{d\,t^2} + R_2 \frac{d\,i_2}{d\,t} + \left[\frac{C_1 + C_2}{C_1 C_2}\right]\,i_2 - R_2 \frac{d\,i_1}{d\,t} - \frac{1}{C_1}\,i_1 = 0 \tag{4}$$

We may simulate the system of Equations (4) to find the responses $i_1(t)$ and $i_2(t)$. The two solution curves depend on the initial condition $i_1(0)$ and $i_2(0)$ only. The simulator block diagram is prepared by solving both equations for the highest derivative and mechanizing them according to Figure 8.4.4. The simulation equations are

$$\frac{d^2 i_1}{dt^2} = -\left[\frac{R_1 + R_2}{L_1}\right]\frac{di_1}{dt} - \left[\frac{1}{C_1 L_1}\right]i_1 + \left[\frac{R_2}{L_1}\right]\frac{di_2}{dt} + \left[\frac{1}{C_1 L_1}\right]i_2$$

$$\frac{d^2 i_2}{dt^2} = -\left[\frac{R_2}{L_2}\right]\frac{di_2}{dt} - \left[\frac{C_1 + C_2}{C_1 C_2 L_2}\right]i_2 + \left[\frac{R_2}{L_2}\right]\frac{di_1}{dt} + \left[\frac{1}{C_1 L_1}\right]i_1$$

$$(5)$$

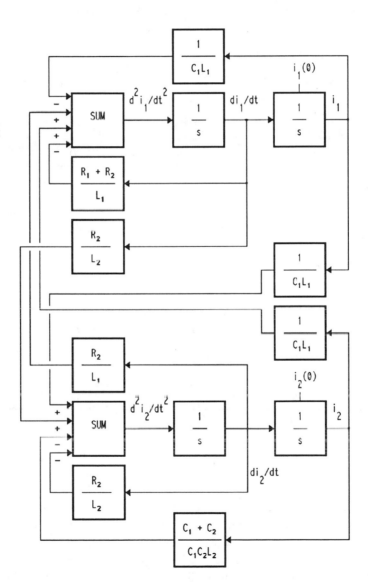

Figure 8.4.4   The block model of the circuit of Figure 8.4.3.

Unless the highest derivative is needed, summing is done directly into the first integrator. As is, the simulator uses two summers, four integrators, and 8 gain blocks, for a total of fourteen computational blocks. A possible modification involves the use of multiplier blocks so a repeat gain value (say $1/C_1L_1$) is entered only once by means of a CON block.

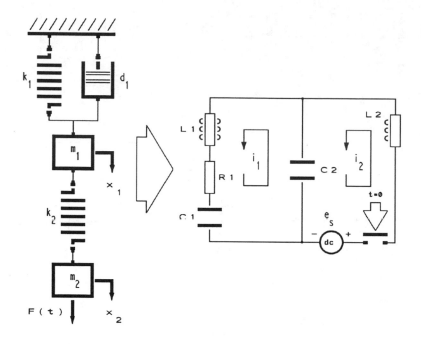

Figure 8.4.5   A coupled circuit and its direct mechanical analog.

Another coupled circuit and its mechanical analog are shown in Figure 8.4.5. This time we begin by writing the mechanical system equations (Newton's second law) for each mass:

$$\ddot{x}_1 + d\,\frac{\dot{x}_1}{m_1} + \left(\frac{k_1 + k_2}{m_1}\right)x_1 - \frac{k_2 x_2}{m_1} = 0$$

$$\ddot{x}_2 + k_2\,\frac{x_2}{m_2} - k_2\,\frac{x_1}{m_2} - \frac{F(t)}{m_2} = 0 \qquad (6)$$

Note that d is the damping coefficient (not to be confused with the differential operator d), and x_1, x_2 are the displacements of m_1 and m_2 from the equilibrium (down = positive). We can also develop the electrical system equations directly from the system above by using the direct analogy concepts discussed throughout Part 8. We recall that $k \to C^{-1}$, $m \to L$, $x \to q$ and $F(t) \to e_s(t)$, where the arrow implies a direct analogy. Therefore, for example,

$$\left(\frac{k_1 + k_2}{m_1}\right) x_1 \quad \rightarrow \quad \left[\frac{\left(\dfrac{1}{C_1} + \dfrac{1}{C_2}\right)}{L_1}\right] q_1 \quad = \quad \left[\frac{1}{C_1} + \frac{1}{C_2}\right] \frac{q_1}{L_1}$$

and the two system equations are

$$\ddot{q}_1 + \frac{R_1}{L_1} \dot{q}_1 + \frac{q_1}{L_1}\left[\frac{1}{C_1} + \frac{1}{C_2}\right] - \frac{q_2}{C_2 L_1} = 0$$

$$\ddot{q}_2 + \frac{q_2}{C_2 L_2} - \frac{q_1}{C_2 L_2} - \frac{e_s(t)}{L_2} = 0 \qquad (7)$$

The system above may be simulated like the case of Figure 8.4.3. The equations may be rewritten for current rather than charge by recalling that i = [dq/dt]. Finally, the directly analogous system of Figure 8.4.6 is left as an exercise for the interested reader. (Clue: we have added a second damper, d_2, in parallel with spring k2, corresponding to the addition of R_2 in the circuit.) The reader might also try building up the simulators by direct substitution as per Section 9.1.2.

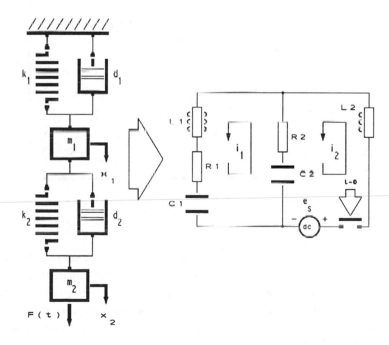

Figure 8.4.6   Another coupled circuit and its direct mechanical analog.

8.5 THE SIMULATION OF A MULTIFUNCTION CONVERTER INTEGRATED CIRCUIT

The multifunction converter (mfc) integrated circuit is used in analog signal conditioning and computation. Known as 'a single chip analog computer,' it is an uncommitted analog circuit with the basic transfer function

$$e_0 = e_y \left(\frac{e_z}{e_x} \right)^m \tag{1}$$

The mfc chip can be configured to perform linear and nonlinear computations including products, ratios, power or root functions, trigonometric functions like sine, cosine, arctangent and vector, magnitude, true RMS and log. Its configuration depends on a few external passive components so that a circuit designer is offered an unlimited spectrum of possibilities (Burr-Brown, 1975; Counts and Pouliot, 1972; Sheingold, 1976). Mfc chips are made by Analog Devices, Burr-Brown, and National Semiconductor.

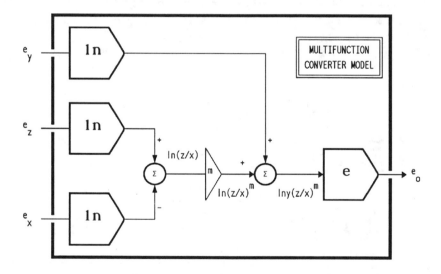

Figure 8.5.1   A model of the multifunction converter.

This device is of interest here for two reasons. First, as a good simulation exercises using TUTSIM's logarithmic (LOG) block and the specialized computational techniques associated with it. Second, a useful mfc simulator can help in the design and qualification of circuits through TUTSIM. Circuit design with mfc chips is a viable alternative to the often troublesome piecewise linear approximation techniques and the modern but wasteful multiplier techniques (Wong and Ott, 1976).

Essentially, the computational advantage of mfc rests in its logarithmic block architecture as shown in Figure 8.5.1. The desired transfer function is realized by converting the three input signals into their logarithmic values, therefore reducing multiplications to additions, divisions to subtractions and powers or roots to a simple gain operation! Then antilog reconversion produces the output (see also Section 3.5). The direct block diagram implementation of the mfc architecture can easily be implemented. Reconversion of the logarithmic signals is achieved by the EXP (ℓn^{-1}) block. The only limitation here is the published $-30 < \Sigma$in $< +30$ limit of the EXP or LOG block. In practice, the exponent m of Equation (1) is $0.25 < m < 5$ for Analog Devices, $0.20 < m < 5$ for Burr-Brown and $0.1 < m < 10$ for National Semiconductor chips (see also Counts and Pouliot, 1972 and Graeme, 1982).

THE SIMULATION OF ELECTRONIC DEVICES AND CIRCUITS—II

9.1 GENERALIZED PASSIVE CIRCUIT SIMULATION TECHNIQUES

9.1.1 Transform Impedance Techniques

A convenient method of creating mathematical models of electrical networks involves the s-domain, where a circuit's R, C and L elements are expressed in terms of transform impedance. First we define the Laplace transforms

$$\mathcal{L}\,[e(t)] \;=\; E(s) \tag{1}$$

$$\mathcal{L}\,[i(t)] \;-\; I(s) \tag{2}$$

$$\mathcal{L}\,[z(t)] \;=\; Z(s) \tag{3}$$

where E(s), I(s) and Z(s) are the voltage, current and impedance in the s-domain, and s is the Laplace operator (s = [d/dt] with dimensions of s^{-1}). By definition (Ohm's law) it is

$$Z(s) \;=\; \frac{E(s)}{I(s)} \tag{4}$$

In Section 8.3.3 we developed the time domain equation for the series LRC circuit. Expressed in terms of i(t) it is

$$e_i(t) \;=\; L\left[\frac{di}{dt}\right] \;+\; R_i(t) \;+\; \frac{1}{C}\int_{t_0}^{t} i(t)\,dt \tag{5}$$

Given zero initial conditions we write the Laplace transform of Equation (5):

$$\mathcal{L}\,[e_i(t)] \;=\; \mathcal{L}\left[L\left[\frac{di}{dt}\right] \;+\; R_i(t) \;+\; \frac{1}{C}\int_{t_0}^{t} i(t)\,dt\right] \tag{6}$$

or

$$E_i(s) = sLI(s) + RI(s) + \frac{1}{Cs} I(s)$$

$$= I(s) \left[Ls + R + \frac{1}{Cs} \right] \qquad (7)$$

From Equations (7) and (4) it is

$$Z(s) = sL + R + \frac{1}{Cs} \qquad (8)$$

that is the transform impedance of a resistor is

$$\frac{E(s)}{I(s)} = R \quad \text{(Ohms)} \qquad (9)$$

while for an inductor it is

$$\frac{E(s)}{I(s)} = Ls \quad \text{(Ohms)} \qquad (10)$$

and for a capacitor it is

$$\frac{E(s)}{I(s)} = \frac{1}{Cs} \quad \text{(Ohms)} \qquad (11)$$

It is important to remember that *all* network rules apply in the frequency domain. Since R, C and L are seen as impedance elements according to Equations (9), (10) and (11), they can be combined in series, in parallel or in both according to the known rules (Figure 9.1.1.1). The network of Figure 9.1.1.2 has the total transfer impedance

$$Z(s) = \frac{R_L + R_1 (R_L Cs + 1)}{R_L Cs + 1} \qquad (12)$$

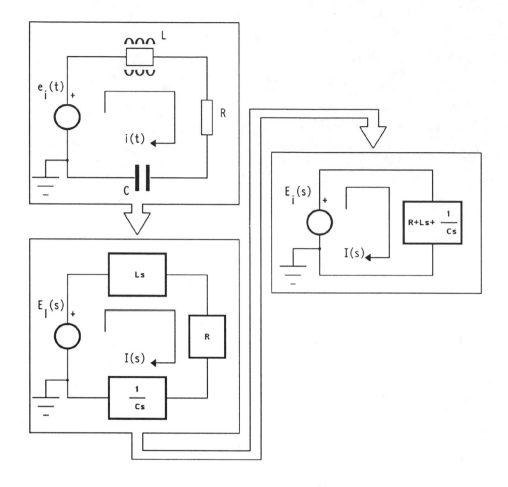

Figure 9.1.1.1 An RCL network expressed in transform impedance terms.

Then rewriting Equation (4)

$$E_i(s) \;=\; \frac{R_L \;+\; R_1\,(R_L\,Cs \;+\; 1)}{R_L\,Cs \;+\; 1}\; I(s) \tag{13}$$

We notice that the output signal $E_0(s)$ is measured across nodes N1 and N2 (Figure 9.1.1.2), so that

$$E_0(s) \;=\; I(s)\left[\frac{R_L}{R_L\,Cs \;+\; 1}\right]$$

$$I(s) \;=\; E_0(s)\,(1 \;+\; R_L\,Cs)\,\frac{1}{R_L} \tag{14}$$

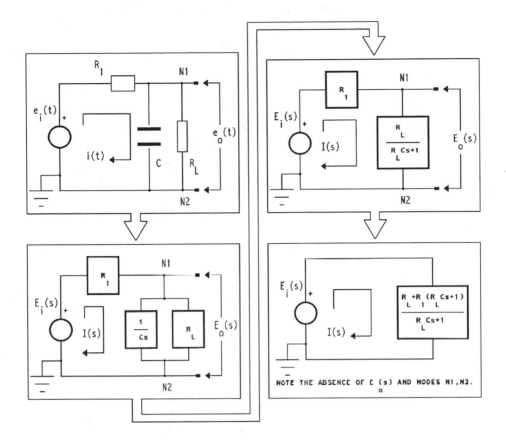

Figure 9.1.1.2   Another example of applying transfer impedance techniques (see text).

Substitution of Equation (14) into Equation (13) produces the transfer function of the network

$$E_i(s) = \frac{R_L + R_1 (R_L Cs + 1)}{R_L} E_0(s)$$

$$\frac{E_0(s)}{E_i(s)} = \frac{R_L}{R_L + R_1 (R_L Cs + 1)} \qquad (15)$$

$$= \frac{1}{1 + \dfrac{R_1}{R_L} + R_1 Cs}$$

By letting $a = [1 + (R_1/R_L)]$ and $\tau = R_1 C$, the transfer function above takes the form

$$T(s) = \frac{1}{\tau s + a} \tag{16}$$

We recognize a simple feedback system with input e_i, output e_0, a forward element $G(s) = 1/\tau s$ and a gain feedback element $H(s) = a$ (Figure 9.1.1.3). The network simulator is easily developed as shown in Figure 9.1.1.3. The simulator's output e_0 represents the voltage measured across C or R_L (Figure 9.1.1.2) as per Equation (14).

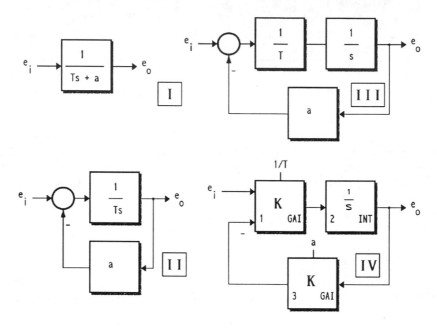

Figure 9.1.1.3 From transfer function to block diagram simulator.

A better explanation of the process rests in the voltage divider principle (Figure 9.1.1.4), according to which

$$\frac{E_0(s)}{E_i(s)} = \frac{\dfrac{R_L}{R_L C s + 1}}{\dfrac{R_L + R_1 (R_L C s + 1)}{R_L C s + 1}} \tag{15R}$$

$$= \frac{R_L}{R_L + R_1 (R_L C s + 1)}$$

Note that the capital letter formality $e(t) \rightarrow E(s)$ used here is not always observed in the book.

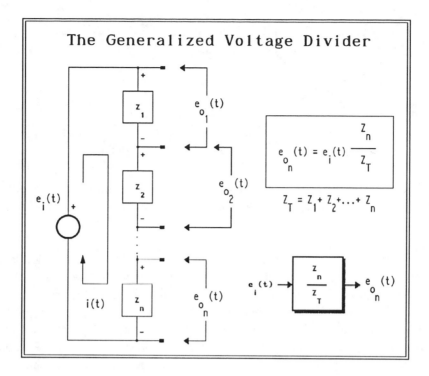

Figure 9.1.1.4   The generalized voltage divider principle from a block diagram point of view.

As a final note, let us consider the Laplace operator s. In the *time* domain we substitute s for [d/dt], a rate of change. In the *frequency* domain we write $s = j\omega$. Remember, however, that this substitution is valid *only* for sinusoidal excitations. Our proof results from differentiating the cosine function twice

$$y \;=\; \cos \omega t \tag{17}$$

so that

$$\dot{y} \;=\; -\,\omega \sin \omega t \tag{18}$$

and

$$\ddot{y} \;=\; -\,\omega^2 \cos \omega t \tag{19}$$

Substitution of (17) into (19) gives

$$\ddot{y} \;=\; -\,\omega^2 y \tag{20}$$

or since $s^2 = [d^2/dt^2]$,

$$s^2 y = - \omega^2 y \qquad (21)$$

Solving for s gives

$$s = \sqrt{- \omega^2}$$
$$= j\omega \qquad (22)$$

This limitation can be bypassed easily through expression of a nonsinusoidal function as a sum of sine and cosine terms by using Fourier series or the various Fourier integral expansions.

It is interesting to note that in 1892, Oliver Heaviside (1850-1925) developed the operational calculus while investigating the preservation of Morse pulses sent through a cable. The concept of transfer functions as we now it today emerged from Heaviside's operational calculus technique. The operational notation provides a direct interpretation of a system in a physical terms, because the operator $s = [d/dt]$ represents a real dynamic condition and an operational analysis is valid for excitations of *any* form. However the steady-state analysis approach ($s = j\omega$) is necessary for electrical and electronic networks involving frequency and phase responses, although it may be obscuring the physical reality of a nonelectrical physical system or those of a control system mechanism. Generally speaking, the choice of mathematical modelling tools affects the structure of the simulator itself—and therefore the simulator's utility and the interpretation of the results.

9.1.2   Direct Simulation

In contrast to the various circuit simulation techniques already discussed, the direct simulation approach allows a simulator setup without writing the system's dynamic equations! So far we have focused on the differential equation representation of circuits (Sections 8.2 and 8.3) and in transform impedance techniques (Section 9.1.1). Direct simulation is based on Kirchoff's two laws which state:

1. The sum of the voltages around a closed loop is zero.

2. The sum of the currents flowing to a junction is zero.

In previous examples we have use nodal voltage and branch current equations in alternative proofs and formulations. Here, Kirchoff's laws are used in conjunction with representations of the passive L, R and C elements in their *integral causal form* based on the concept of direct analogy as discussed and justified in Section 8.3.3. Based on material already presented, we can easily form Figure 9.1.2.1. It shows the three passive elements, their analog computer simulator, the TUTSIM L, C, R block diagrams and their equivalent

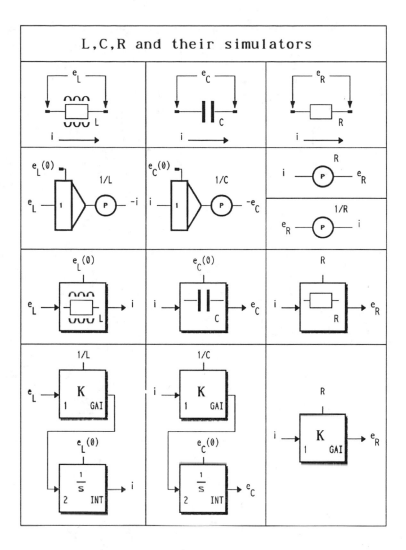

Figure 9.1.2.1   L,C,R and their block simulators.

redundant TUTSIM simulators. The method is facile, as it involves direct substitution according to Figure 9.1.2.1.

In 1954 Larrowe described the direct simulation technique, also discussed in the articles by Yates (1965), Gilliland and Billinghurst (1966), Lalli (1976) and in the classic Systron-Donner handbook of analog computation (Gilliland, 1967). The RC circuit of Figure 9.1.2.2(I) (see Section 8.2.2) can be simulated by direct substitution. The analog computer schematic (II) shows an inverting integrator. The equivalent block diagram (III) includes one integrator and two gain blocks (or *attenuation* (ATT) blocks so R and C can be entered

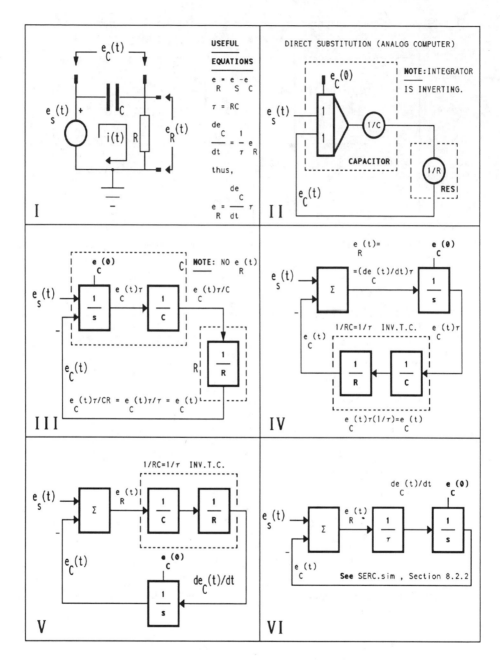

Figure 9.1.2.2　Developing the block simulator of an RC circuit.

directly). This simulator provides $e_C(t)$ only. If we wish to have the $e_R(t)$ solution also, we must input $-e_C(t)$ and $e_s(t)$ to a summing block *preceding* the integrator. Then the summer's output is $e_R(t)$. Some block rearrangement and the inclusion of a summer allow the different perspective of panel IV, subsequently arriving via step V to the simulator SERC.sim (Section

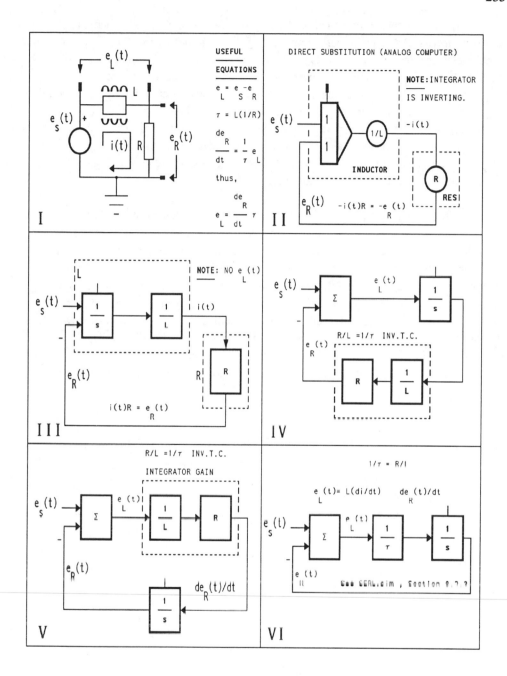

Figure 9.1.2.3 Developing the block simulator of an RL circuit.

8.2.2). A second example employing the RL circuit is developed in a similar fashion in Figure 9.1.2.3. Note that the output of the integrator in III and IV is $\int e_L(t)dt$ and therefore the output of the (I/L) block is $i(t) = (1/L) \int_{t0}^{t} e_L(t)dt$. Finally, block diagram VI satisfies the system equation $L[di(t)/dt] = e_s(t) - Ri(t)$ (see Section 8.2.3).

The direct substitution method demonstrated in the examples above is applicable to complex circuits also. The analog simulation of electrical networks with direct substitution techniques was very popular prior to the advent of portable digital-computer circuit analysis software like SPICE. Today specialized software with good schematic editors are inherent to any design, analysis and testing effort. However using a continuous dynamic simulation language in which a mathematical block setup is involved (rather than an electronic schematic) allows an in-depth mathematical look at the system level. Then circuits are seen as dynamic systems rather than cookbook recipes, something that makes block diagram languages ideal in the teaching of electricity, electronics and signal processing in general. For best results, the author teaches with both types of software.

When using the direct simulation approach with complex networks having a junction of three or more similar energy-storing elements, the situation of excess integrators emerges. When loop or node analysis is used, the number of integrators often exceed the order of the describing differential equation. To reiterate, Larrowe (1954) recommends the use of Kirchoff's laws instead (nodal voltages and branch currents). Using an analog computer extra integrators introduce an extraneous root in the characteristic equation if not perfectly matched. However this consideration is not pertinent to simulation languages, although it behooves the intent reader to read the articles by Otterman (1957, 1958), Scott (1957), Walters (1953) and Giloi (1962). Of course, direct simulation is not limited to electrical circuits; the concept is easily extensible to mechanical, thermal and other networks.

9.2   ACTIVE CIRCUIT SIMULATION

9.2.1   The Fundamental Inverting Operational Amplifier

The operational amplifier block in Figure 9.2.1.1(a) has an open loop gain -A and a very high input impedance z_A. It is shown here combined with external input and feedback impedances z_i and z_f. The voltage at junction J is e_{vg}. It is

$$e_0 = (- A) \ e_{vg} \tag{1}$$

Since

$$| - A | \ \to \ \infty \tag{2}$$

we can write

$$e_{vg} = - \frac{e_0}{A \ \to \ \infty} \tag{3}$$

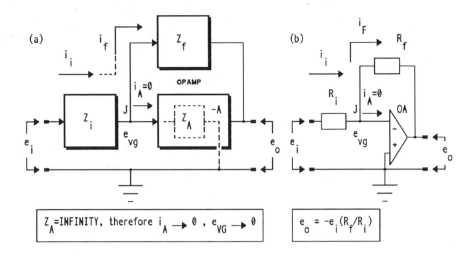

Figure 9.2.1.1 The inverting OA configuration as a block diagram (a) and as an electronic circuit (b).

or

$$e_{vg} \;\rightarrow\; 0 \tag{4}$$

The voltage e_{vg} at junction J is the virtual ground potential which is, for all practical purposes, zero. Also any current between the virtual ground function J and the operational amplifier is insignificant. For all practical purposes no current flows into the amplifier, or

$$i_A \;=\; 0 \tag{5}$$

Referring to the schematic we write

$$e_i - e_{vg} \;=\; i_i z_i \tag{6}$$

$$e_{vg} - e_0 \;=\; i_F z_F \tag{7}$$

or because of Equation (4)

$$e_i \;=\; i_i z_i \;\rightarrow\; i_i \;=\; \frac{e_i}{z_i} \tag{8}$$

$$- e_0 \;=\; i_F z_F \;\rightarrow\; i_F \;=\; \frac{- e_0}{z_F} \tag{9}$$

Since nothing flows into the operational amplifier of Equation (5), it is

$$i_i = i_F \tag{10}$$

and therefore from Equations (8), (9) and (5)

$$\frac{e_i}{z_i} = \frac{-e_0}{z_F}$$

$$e_0 = -e_i \frac{z_F}{z_i} \tag{11}$$

This is a working equation for the inverting operational amplifier configuration of Figure 9.2.1.1(a) and the equivalent electronic circuit of Figure 9.2.1.1(b) where

$$e_0 = -e_i \frac{R_F}{R_i} \tag{12}$$

Equation (12) suggests that if $R_F = R_i$ the output equals minus input. If $R_f > R_i$ the input is multiplied by a constant (system gain $-k = -(R_f/R_i)$ and when $R_f < R_i$ there is attenuation or division.

The operational amplifier (OA) is the most significant building block in analog circuit design. Combinations of operational amplifiers and passive components are used to implement countless different signal processing functions. Excellent books on the subject abound, among them those by Franco (1988) and Graeme (1973 and 1977) and the classic texts by Roberge (1975), Smith (1971) and Wait et al. (1975).

9.2.2 From Transfer Functions to Operational Amplifier Circuits

Consider the familiar lag transfer function

$$\frac{e_0(s)}{e_i(s)} = \frac{A}{1 + bs} \tag{1}$$

$$A e_i(s) = (1 + bs) e_0(s)$$

$$b e_0(s)s + e_o(s) - A e_i(s) = 0 \tag{2}$$

Since s = [d/dt], Equation (2) is written in the time domain as

$$b \frac{d e_0}{dt} + e_0 - A e_i = 0$$

$$\frac{d e_0}{dt} = \frac{A}{b} e_i - \frac{1}{b} e_0$$

(3)

If A = 10 and b = 0.01, the original transfer function is

$$\frac{e_0(s)}{e_i(s)} = \frac{10}{1 + 0.01 s}$$

(4)

and the corresponding differential equation according to Equation (3) is

$$\frac{d e_0}{dt} = 1000 e_i - 100 e_o$$

(5)

which is implemented with the diagram of Figure 9.2.2.1(a). The analog computer mechanization of Figure 9.2.2.1(b) uses the potentiometers P1 and P2 for setting up A and b. The resistance R_{p1} is the input resistance R_i to the integrator, and R_{p2} is the feedback resistance R_f, as shown in the equivalent electronic schematic of Figure 9.2.2.2. The conditions of Equation (5) are met when $R_f = 10 R_i$. If we choose $R_f = 100 k\Omega$, it is $R_1 = k\Omega$. Since a time constant of $\tau = = 0.01$ is desired, and the time constant of the operational amplifier circuit is $\tau = R_f C$, it is C = 0.1μF.

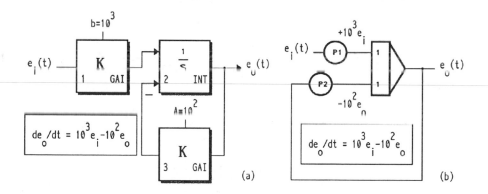

Figure 9.2.2.1 Block diagram (a) and analog computer (b) implementation of a dfq representing the transfer function $e_0(s)/e_i(s) = 10/(1 + 0.01s)$.

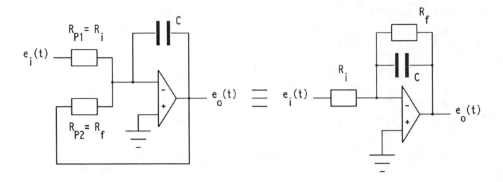

Figure 9.2.2.2   Two equivalent electronic schematics.

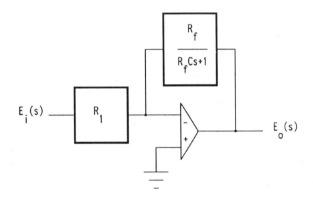

Figure 9.2.2.3   An OA transfer impedance example (see text).

We can apply the transform impedance techniques of Section 9.1.1 to find the equivalent s-domain representation of Figure 9.2.2.3 where

$$z_F(s) \;=\; \frac{R_F \dfrac{1}{Cs}}{R_F + \dfrac{1}{Cs}} \;=\; \frac{R_F}{R_F Cs + 1} \tag{6}$$

From the Section 9.2.1 we know that

$$e_0(s) \;=\; -\,\frac{z_F(s)}{z_i(s)}\, e_i(s) \tag{7}$$

Therefore, from Equations (6) and (7) it is

$$\frac{e_0(s)}{e_i(s)} = - \frac{R_F}{R_i} \frac{1}{R_F C s + 1} \qquad (8)$$

By letting $R_F/R_i = A$ and $\tau = R_F C = b$, the transfer function above is the same as Equation (1)—but with a phase inversion (i.e., the minus sign) due to the inverting operational amplifier. The techniques demonstrated here are applicable to any case regardless of circuit complexity.

9.2.3 Modelling and Simulation of the Operational Amplifier

The ubiquitous operational amplifier (OA) is an active frequency-selective device of high gain. Here we will examine the open-loop operational amplifier in the context of continuous dynamic simulation. There are hundreds of OA integrated circuits and many simulation models such as those of SPICE. Our model must have dynamic face validity so that it will be used as a replacement of the pure gain block in simulations like that of Section 9.2.1.

The most important dynamic characteristic of the open loop OA is its amplitude-frequency response. A typical OA exhibits a gain fall of -20 dB/decade. We recall that the decrease

$$\frac{e_o}{e_i} = \frac{1}{10}$$

is expressed in dB as

$$\frac{e_0}{e_i} \ (dB) = 20 \log_{10} \left(\frac{1}{10}\right) = -20\,dB$$

Thus for a rate of gain decline of -20 dB/decade, the gain falls -20 dB for each decade of frequency. (The frequency-gain or Bode plot of a specific device is available from its manufacturer.) We can approximate the -20 dB response with the transfer function

$$H(s) = A \frac{1}{1 + s \frac{1}{\omega_0}} = \frac{A \omega_0}{s + \omega_0} \qquad (1)$$

where A is the dc (or zero frequency) gain and ω_0 is the corner *radian* frequency (also referred to as the -3 dB frequency, half-power frequency, cutoff frequency or break). It is the point at which the gain-frequency characteristic drops 3dB (0.707 of its peak value), or the *pole* of the transfer function. The frequency ω_0 establishes the *bandwidth* of the operational amplifier and is inversely related to the time constant $\tau = RC$:

$$\omega_0 = \frac{1}{\tau} \tag{2}$$

Therefore Equation (1) can be written as

$$H(s) = A\,\frac{1}{\tau s + 1} \tag{3}$$

Some textbooks prefer Equation (1) where the gain-bandwidth product $A\omega_0$ appears in the numerator. Equation (2) suggests that *high bandwidth is characterized by a quick time response*. The larger the ω_c value, the further away from the origin a pole is situated, and therefore the system's transient response decays faster. The single-pole OA model of Figure 9.2.3.1 can be readily simulated with the FIO block. The FIO block simulates the low pass

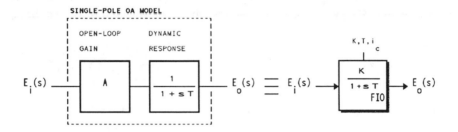

Figure 9.2.3.1   A block representation of a single-pole OA model.

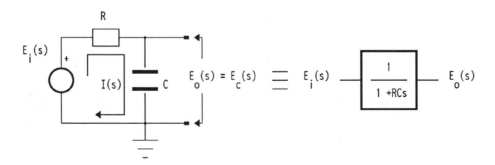

Figure 9.2.3.2   A single block representation of a passive RC filter.

filter of Figure 9.2.3.2. It is important here to understand this circuit well. As a review (see also Sections 8.2 and 9.1, let us develop the filter's equation and its transfer function. If we apply an input voltage $e_i(t)$ and assume that no current flows to the output, it is

$$e_i(t) = R\,i(t) + \frac{1}{C} \int i(t)\,dt \tag{4}$$

and since

$$\mathcal{L}\left[e_C(t)\right] = E_C(s) = \frac{1}{C}\frac{I(s)}{s} = \frac{1}{Cs}\,I(s) \tag{5}$$

$$\mathcal{L}\left[e_R(t)\right] = E_R(s) = R\,I(s) \tag{6}$$

we can write

$$E_i(s) = \left(R + \frac{1}{Cs}\right)I(s) \tag{7}$$

We are looking at the output across the capacitor, or $E_o(s) = E_C(s)$. From Equation (5) it is

$$I(s) = Cs\,E_0(s) \tag{8}$$

and by substituting into Equation (7)

$$E_i(s) = \left(R + \frac{1}{Cs}\right)Cs\,E_0(s) = (RCs + 1)\,E_0(s) \tag{9}$$

Then the circuit's transfer function is

$$H(s) = \frac{E_0(s)}{E_i(s)} = \frac{1}{1 + RCs} \tag{10}$$

or, given that $\tau = RC$,

$$H(s) = \frac{1}{\tau s + 1} \tag{11}$$

This transfer function is frequently seen as

$$H(s) = \frac{\dfrac{1}{RC}}{s + \dfrac{1}{RC}} \tag{12}$$

In the frequency domain recall that the period T of a signal is related to its cyclic frequency f, or

$$T = \frac{1}{F} \tag{13}$$

and since

$$T = \frac{2\pi}{\omega} \tag{14}$$

the *radian* frequency (rads/s) is related to the *cyclic* frequency (Hz) by the equation

$$\omega = 2\pi f \rightarrow f = \frac{\omega}{2\pi} \tag{15}$$

We also recall that for cosinusoidal signals it is $s = j\omega$ and $\tau = 1/\omega_0$. Transfer function 11 is often found in the literature written in the frequency domain. For example:

$$H(j\omega) = \frac{1}{1 + j\omega\tau} = \frac{1}{1 + j\dfrac{\omega}{\omega_0}} = \frac{\omega_0}{j\omega + \omega_0} = \frac{1}{1 + j\dfrac{\omega}{2\pi f_0}}$$

Multiplying any of the above times A gives the single-pole OA model. It has the magnitude response

$$|H(j\omega)| = \frac{|A|}{|1 + j\dfrac{\omega}{\omega_0}|} = \frac{|A|}{\sqrt{1 + \left(\dfrac{\omega}{\omega_0}\right)^2}} \tag{16}$$

and its phase response over all ω is

$$\arg[H(j\omega)] = \phi(\omega) = \phi(A) - \tan^{-1}\frac{\omega}{\omega_0} \tag{17}$$

The 3 dB frequency of this filter is

$$f_0 \;=\; \frac{1}{2\pi\tau} \tag{18}$$

An operational amplifier model may have one, two or three poles (Figure 9.2.3.3). Each stage is seen as an ideal amplifier in series with a low-pass RC filter. Each stage provides a distinct pole frequency. Frequency rolloff characteristics of all stages combine to form the desired overall response of the system. Note that the overall gain of the system is the product of the cascaded gain; the decibel value is the *sum* of the individual values.

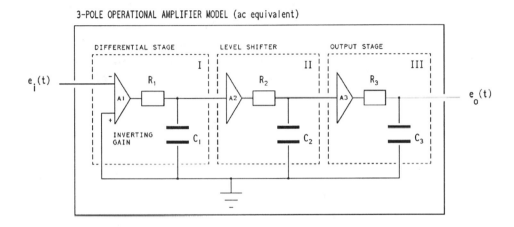

Figure 9.2.3.3 A 3-pole OA model.

Essentially the first pole is the dominant one and, in most situations, it is the only significant pole. A second pole may be used to model the effects of higher frequencies. The transfer function of a two-pole OA model is

$$H(s) \;=\; \frac{A}{(\tau_1 s \,+\, 1)(\tau_2 s \,+\, 1)} \tag{19}$$

which is simulated by two cascaded FIO blocks. The reader is cautioned that in spite of their ubiquitous nature, operational amplifiers are specialized integrated circuits. Successful application in circuit design is deceptively easy and demands special knowledge and skills. Most OA texts like those by Coughlin and Driscoll (1987), Franco (1988), Gayakwad (1988), Irvine (1981), Johnson and Jayakumar (1982) and Stanley (1989a) to name a few, focus on the applied aspects of the major categories of operational amplifiers and their use in linear circuit design. The text by Kennedy (1988) is a bit more theoretical and discusses single and multiple pole OA models. Roberge (1975) has a strong control system and Laplace transform orientation while Mastascusa (1988) discusses OA models in the context of computer simulation. Useful information on OA models and their extended application in analog filter design is found in the text by Van Valkenburg (1982).

9.3   NOISE REDUCTION IN FEEDBACK CIRCUITS AND CASCADED GAIN SYSTEMS

Often circuit design practice is based on control system principles, as is the case of most operational amplifier networks. Noise in linear feedback circuits with cascaded gains is of interest here. The block diagram/continuous simulation approach helps us acquire the big picture. The fact that deliberately injected or inadvertently introduced noise affects the signal to noise (S/N) ratio of operational amplifier circuits is well known. However noise may enter a network from many different locations; each case can differ from another in the effects the intruding signal has on circuit operation. In 1972 Darbie explained some of the issues involved. We use the transfer function and block diagram approach to model and examine a few series gain networks. For simplification we consider the operational amplifier to be a pure gain element (see also the comments on the FIO block at the end of this section).

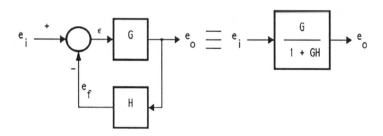

Figure 9.3.1   Basic feedback system representations.

Our starting point is the system of Figure 9.3.1, used here to establish the necessary conventions and the proper continuity. The forward block G is a gain element, block H represents the feedback network, e_F is the negative feedback signal arriving at the summing junction and ϵ is the system error. It is

$$e_F \;=\; H\, e_0 \tag{1}$$

$$\epsilon \;=\; e_i \,-\, e_F \tag{2}$$

$$e_0 \;=\; G\, \epsilon \tag{3}$$

and therefore

$$e_0 = G(e_i - H e_0) \tag{4}$$

$$\frac{e_0}{e_i} = \frac{G}{1 + GH} \tag{5}$$

Equation (5) is the well-known representation of a closed-loop control system.

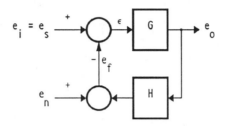

Figure 9.3.2   Introducing noise ahead of the feedback element.

The block diagram of Figure 9.3.2 has inputs $e_i = e_s$ (the signal) and e_n (the noise). Both e_s and e_n contribute to the output, so we designate the two constituent components of e_0, e_{0s} and e_{0n} so that

$$e_0 = e_{0s} + e_{0n} \tag{6}$$

Since we wish to study the propagation of e_n, we set

$$e_s = 0 \tag{7}$$

and therefore Equation (6) becomes

$$e_0 = e_{0n} \tag{8}$$

The two summing nodes of Figure 9.3.2 can be consolidated and the system looks like that of Figure 9.3.1 again, but with e_n in the place of e_i, so that

$$\frac{e_{0n}}{e_n} = \frac{G}{1 + GH} \tag{9}$$

Therefore, noise entering the feedback path ahead of the feedback element (Figure 9.3.2) is seen by the circuit like any other normal input signal.

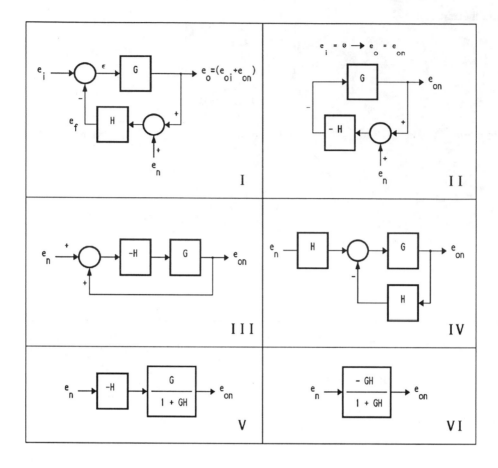

Figure 9.3.3 *A more complicated case of noise introduction.*

The case of Figure 9.3.3 is not intuitively obvious without the use of block diagram techniques. After some rearrangement, we write the system equations for circuit III ($e_i = 0 \rightarrow e_o = e_{0n}$) as follows

$$e_n + e_{0n} = e \tag{10}$$
$$e_{0n} = - e\,GH$$

$$e = - \frac{e_{0n}}{GH} \tag{11}$$

and therefore

$$e_n + e_{0n} = - e_{0n} \frac{1}{GH}$$

$$\frac{e_{0n}}{e_n} = - \frac{GH}{1 + GH}$$

(12)

Step-by-step block diagram development is shown in Figure 9.3.3. The negative feedback control loop is *iconical*, created for the convenience of analysis. In reality a feedforward (positive feedback) loop exists (see circuit III of Figure 9.3.3). Transfer function 12 indicates that the noise will appear at the output somewhat *attenuated*, depending upon the values of G and H. Usually $H \ll 1$ and if $H = 0.5$, $G = 1$ it is $e_{0n} = - 0.33333\ e_n$. If $H = 0.5$ and $G = 0.1$ then $e_{0n} = -0.04762\ e_n$ (these are somewhat extreme values but illustrate the point well). Thus we have identified an interesting but obscure noise reduction mechanism.

The case of cascaded (series) gains G_1, G_2, ..., G_n is straightforward (Figure 9.3.4) and the system transfer function is

$$\frac{e_0}{e_i} = \frac{G_1 G_2 \ \cdots \ G_n}{1 + G_1 G_2 \ \cdots \ G_n H}$$

(13)

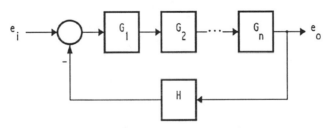

Figure 9.3.4   A feedback system with series gains situated in the forward path.

Let us now consider the system of Figure 9.3.5 having four cascaded gain sections with three noise injection points between them. For the purpose of analysis, we designate the error signals as ϵ, ϵ_1, ϵ_2 and ϵ_3. If $e_i = e_n(2) = e_n(3) = 0$, the bock diagram can be redrawn as per Figure 9.3.6. Then it is

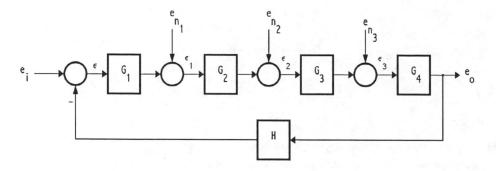

Figure 9.3.5   Forward path gains with noise injection points between them.

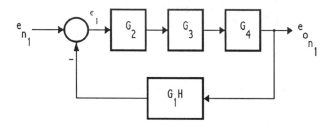

Figure 9.3.6   Redrawing the block diagram of Figure 9.3.5 when $e_i = e_n(2) = e_n(3) = 0$.

$$\frac{e_{0n_1}}{e_{n_1}} = \frac{G_2\,G_3\,G_4}{1 + G_1\,G_2\,G_3\,G_4\,H} \tag{14}$$

The procedure is then repeated for $e_0(n2)$ and $e_0(n3)$ and we obtain the transfer functions

$$\frac{e_{0n_2}}{e_{n_2}} = \frac{G_3\,G_4}{1 + G_1\,G_2\,G_3\,G_4\,H} \tag{15}$$

and

$$\frac{e_{0n_3}}{e_{n_3}} = \frac{G_4}{1 + G_1\,G_2\,G_3\,G_4\,H} \tag{16}$$

The three equations above tell us that any noise introduced at the later stages of a negative feedback network having cascaded forward gains is *attenuated* by the gains that *precede* the noise injection point. On the contrary, noise occurring at the earlier stages is *enhanced* by the gains that *follow*.

When cascading forward gains, there are questions of system stability. These complex issues are addressed in the vast operational amplifier circuit literature. TUTSIM is suitable for investigating and qualifying the system design methodology for operational networks. The reader might want to use the First Order function (FIO) block to represent an operational amplifier. It is a very useful block having the transfer function

$$T(s) \; = \; \frac{K}{1 \; + \; s\tau} \tag{17}$$

and the additional property of breaking an algebraic loop without affecting a problem's steady state solution. Given well-chosen parameters, the FIO block serves well as a low-end frequency selective device (Section 9.2.3). Figures 9.3.7 (OAN1.sim) and 9.3.8 (OAN2.sim) are typical investigations of signal processing in cascaded-gain systems. TUTSIM's noise block (NOI), a generator of uniformly distributed pseudorandom noise, is used here.

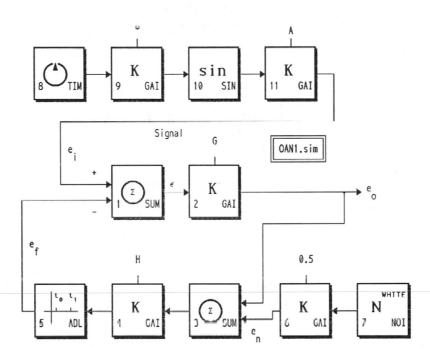

Figure 9.3.7 An initial investigation of signal processing in cascaded-gain systems.

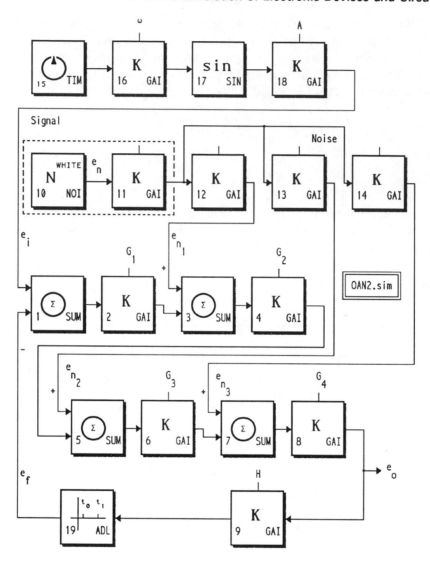

Figure 9.3.8   A further investigation of signal processing in cascaded-gain systems.

9.4   THE SIMULATION OF DIODES AND DIODE CIRCUITS

There are many different ways to approach the simulation of semiconductor diodes and their circuits with a continuous system simulation language. Diode simulators can be implemented from detailed mathematical models similar to those used in the SPICE circuit simulation language and its variants. We seek, however, to maximize the utility of the language. Mechanizing the detailed mathematical model of a passive component clearly transcends the purpose and the very spirit of this type of simulation. Instead, working linear approximations are used with hardly any functional penalty. After all, even a detailed model

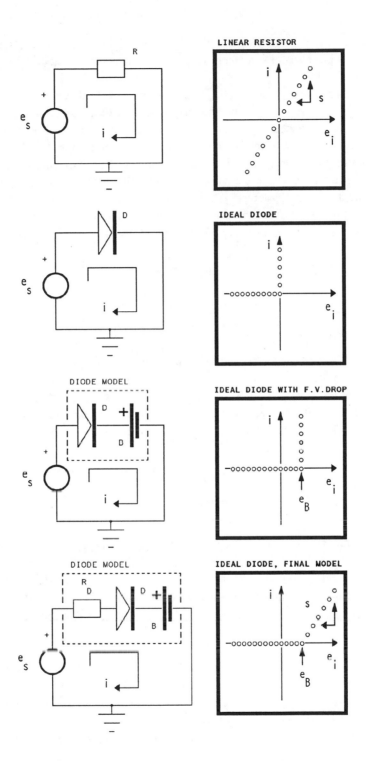

Figure 9.4.1 The e-i characteristics of a linear resistor and three ideal diode models.

demands qualification by assigning values. These are ballpark figures drawn from solid state texts or manufacturer's books in an effort to approximate a given diode family or type.

Expressing the current-to-voltage transfer function of a diode involves an exponential expression with an empirical constant that enters the basic diode equation, the slope equation and the dynamic resistance expression. This constant, known as the exponential ideality factor, affects the curvature of the characteristic and complicates things further. From a functional point of view, the generalized pn junction can be seen as a *nonlinear resistor* with impedance dependent on the direction of the current flowing through it. There are several diode equivalent circuits of interest in simulation (or, in circuit analysis, for that matter). The *ideal* diode of Figure 9.4.1 has no internal resistance and no voltage drop so that the current achieves its maximum value instantly when the diode is forward biased. It is instructive to compare the transfer characteristic (e_i-i_0 plot) of a linear resistor to that of the ideal diode. The resistor's e_i-i_0 plot is its *conductance* (the ratio of current to voltage) and its slope, s, is

$$s \; = \; \frac{\Delta i}{\Delta e_s} \; = \; \frac{1}{R} \tag{1}$$

where e_s is the source voltage. In contrast the nonlinear transfer plot of the ideal diode shows that any positive (forward) voltage is limited to zero and the slope of the characteristic approaches *infinity* ($s \rightarrow \infty$). Then $R = 0$ and the diode acts as a short circuit (ON state). A negative voltage results in a zero current and a *zero* slope, because the diode is acting as an open circuit (OFF state), where $R = \infty$. In the ideal case it is

$$z \; \triangleq \; \begin{cases} R_{min} \; = \; 0 & e_i \; > \; 0 \\ R_{max} \; = \; \infty & e_i \; < \; 0 \end{cases} \tag{2}$$

In reality the *forward* resistance R_{min} has typical values between 1 - 100Ω and R_{max} is 100kΩ to 1MΩ so that $Rmax \gg R_{min}$. The diode approximates a *switching action* modelled by the scheme of Figure 9.4.2. By definition a switch is a device with resistance that can be changed from a very small value (ON) to a very high value (OFF). *Essentially then, the primary function of a diode as a design component is to allow current flow in one direction only.*

The second diode model of Figure 9.4.1 shows the diode in series with a source e_B. The source represents the barrier potential (0.2 - 0.3V for Ge diodes and 0.5 - 0.7V for Si diodes) that must be overcome before any substantial current is passed onto the load. This implies that a Si diode with a typical forward conducting (turn-on) voltage $e_b = 0.7$V can be seen as a switch that closes only when the 0.7V threshold is reached, that is

$$z \; \triangleq \; \left\{ R_{min} \; = \; 0 \quad e_i \; > \; 0.7 \, V \right. \tag{3}$$

SWITCHING DIODE MODEL

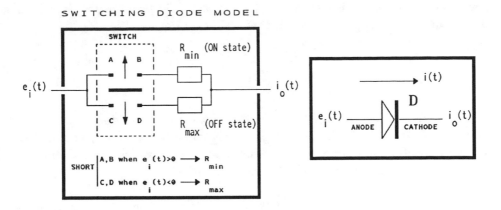

Figure 9.4.2 The diode as a switching device.

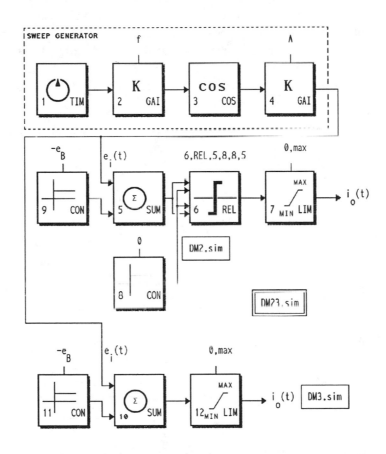

Figure 9.4.3 A quasi-dynamic diode simulator (DM2.sim) and a static simulator (DM3.sim).

A better ideal diode model is synthesized by adding the equivalent resistance R_d. Now, the transfer plot shows a sloping characteristic where, as per Equation (1), it is

$$s = \frac{\Delta i}{\Delta e_s} = \frac{1}{R_d} \tag{4}$$

Both Δi and Δe_s are found from a diode's performance graph and the *dynamic resistance* R_d is determined from Ohm's law. In reality not only do infinite slope response models not exist, they are also not realizable (even in simulation). They are just the transitory steps of a logical approach to a useful piecewise-linear diode model.

The two principal ways of approaching the diode modelling task are shown in Figure 9.4.3 (DM23.sim). The first model (DM2.sim) is a quasi-dynamic simulator built around a REL block operating as a polarity-sensitive comperator. It actually imitates the switching action of the diode. The second model (DM3.sim) is a static simulator. Rather than simulating diode switching dynamics, the transfer characteristic is synthesized in a piecewise-linear manner. *Both* models show the response of Figure 9.4.4 and the transfer plot of Figure 9.4.5. *Either* model can be modified to include slopes other than unity by adding a GAI block after the limiter. Note, however, that the contribution of R_d is insignificant when circuit resistances are large compared to the equivalent resistance of the diode. This, of course, is the case in most functional real world circuits where $R_d << R_L$ (R_L = load resistance).

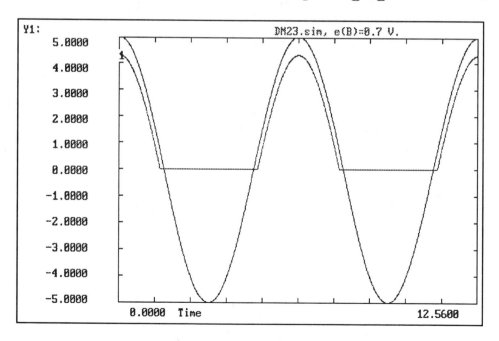

Figure 9.4.4   *The results of both DM2.sim and DM3.sim models with $e_B = 0.7$ V.*
Curves are superimposed.

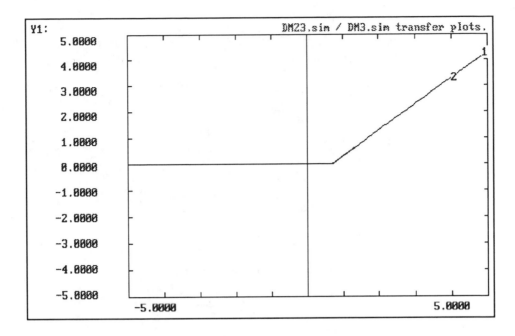

Figure 9.4.5   The superimposed transfer plots of DM2.sim and DM3.sim.

The quantity e_B is also useful in the small voltage range, where the diode voltage drop is nontrivial. On the other hand, this forward voltage drop (the effect of the barrier potential) may be ignored as insignificant in the presence of relatively high voltages. A more compact diode model can be made with the IFE block. Figure 9.4.6 (a) and (b) show the simulation of both forward- and reverse-biased diodes. The performance of these models is compatible to the sophisticated ones found in specialized circuit analysis software.

Contrary to the apparent ease of things, there are a few words of caution. In general, result circuits where the input is isolated from the output are easy to simulate and link. Then a *unidirectional* (A → B) cause-and-effect relationship exists. The actual buildup of complex integrated circuits is possible because of this property. There are, however, cases where one or more events occurring during circuit operation affect the operation (and thus the outcome) of one or more preceding sections of that circuit. These bidirectional cause-and-effect relationships are hard to simulate and more specialized software are necessary. An example of a bidirectional cause-and-effect case is that of a forward-biased diode becoming reverse-biased at some point during circuit operation because of, say, a charged output capacitor.

To reiterate, there are many ways to approach diode circuit simulation with CDSS languages. A positive limiter, for example, can be simulated with a REL and a CON block (Figure 9.4.7). The control input is the signal $e_i(t)$ itself. When it is $e_i(t) > P$ the relay's output is the reference signal e_{ref} (note that e_{ref} is also the parameter P of the REL block). When $e_{ref} < P$, the output is the input signal itself.

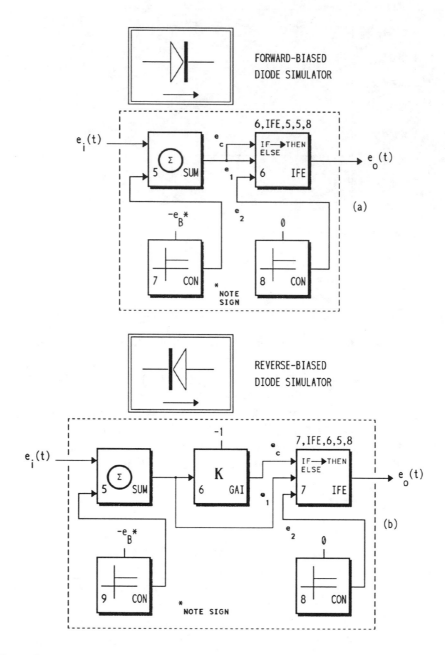

Figure 9.4.6 *Simulating the forward-biased (a) and the reverse-biased (b) diode functions.*

Often it is necessary to use diodes in conjunction with resistors, as in the circuit of Figure 9.4.8, where R_1 and R_L form a voltage divider network. In this example we set $R_1 = 1k\Omega$, $R_L = 10k\Omega$ and a diode drop of 0.7V. The input signal is $e_i(t) = A \sin \omega t$ ($A = 5V$). The results of the simulation (DCIR1.sim) are shown in Figures 9.4.9 and 9.4.10. The LIM block used here is but one way of approaching the simulation task.

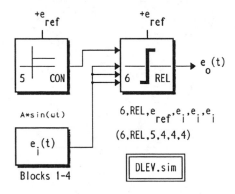

Figure 9.4.7   A positive limiter simulator.

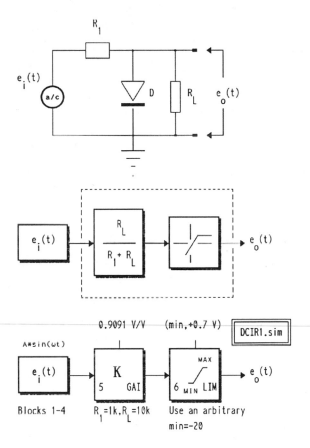

*Figure 9.4.8   The simulation of a diode circuit used in conjunction with resistors
(a voltage divider network).*

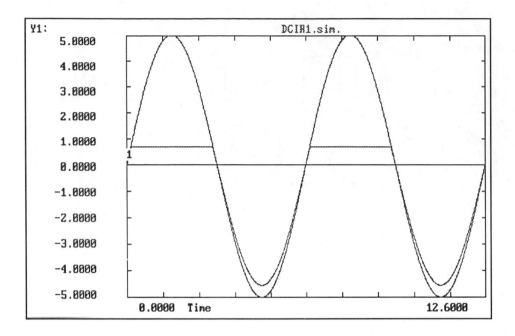

Figure 9.4.9   The results of DCIR1.sim.

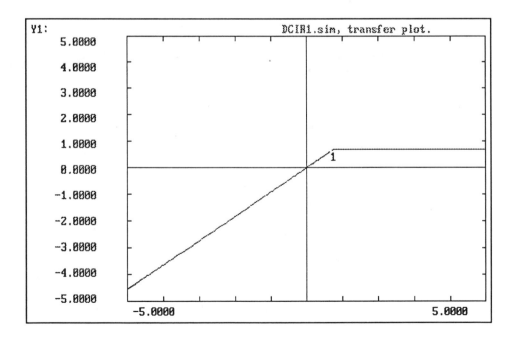

Figure 9.4.10   The transfer plot of DCIR1.sim.

Occasionally, things get difficult in diode circuit simulation. The clamping circuit of Figure 9.4.11 is a case in point. It is one of the most misunderstood simple circuits, often given poor exposure in textbooks. The circuit works like this: Given a square wave input, there are *two* circuit states, one for the positive half-cycle ($0 > t > T/2$) and another for the negative half-cycle ($T/2 > t > T$), as shown in Figure 9.4.11. During a positive half-cycle, the diode conducts and appears as a short. Since the resistor R is shorted out, it is $e_0(t) = 0$ and the capacitor charges up. The circuit's time constant is very small and therefore C charges up near instantaneously to the level $e_C(0) = + e_i$.

During a negative half-cycle, the diode acts as an open switch. Current flows through R and *the RC network is enabled*. The capacitor charge exists as an initial condition at the onset of the negative half cycle. When the input goes positive again, the activity of the RC network cases. the capacitor-source loop is re-established, and so on. We begin to look at the circuit by considering its first state (Figure 9.4.11 II) when the diode conducts and shorts the resistor R out, so that $e_0(t) = e_R(t) = 0$. The capacitor begins to change at $t_0 = 0$ through an implied residual resistance r. The circuit equation is

$$\begin{aligned}
e_i &= e_r + e_C \\
&= ir + e_C \\
&= rC \frac{de_C}{dt} + e_C
\end{aligned}$$

$$\begin{aligned}
\frac{de_C}{dt} &= \frac{e_i - e_C}{rC} \\
&= - \frac{(e_C - e_i)}{rC}
\end{aligned} \tag{5}$$

Since e_i is a constant, we can write

$$\frac{de_i}{dt} = 0 \tag{6}$$

and therefore the first term of Equation (5) can be written as

$$\frac{de_C}{dt} = \frac{de_C}{dt} + \frac{de_i}{dt} = \frac{d(e_C - e_i)}{dt} \tag{7}$$

From Equations (5) and (7), we write the equation

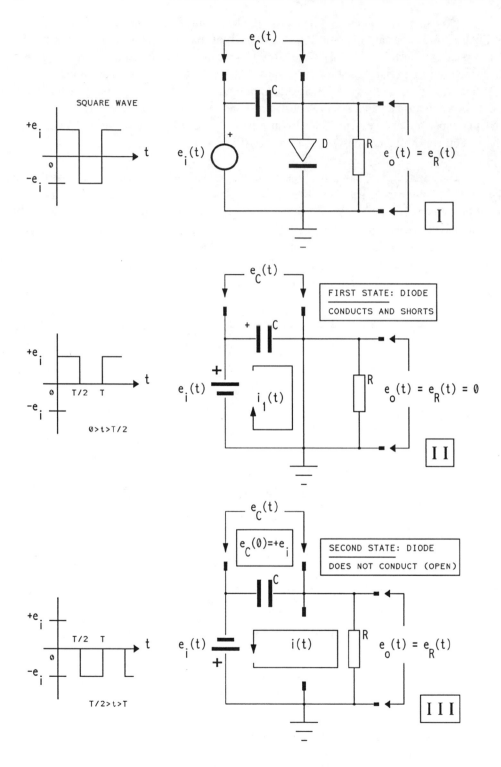

Figure 9.4.11 Simulating a diode clamping circuit.

$$\frac{d\left(e_C - e_i\right)}{dt} = -\frac{\left(e_C - e_i\right)}{r\,C}$$

$$\frac{d\left(e_C - e_i\right)}{e_C - e_i} = -\frac{dt}{r\,C}$$

(8)

and then integrate

$$\int \frac{d\left(e_C - e_i\right)}{e_C - e_i}\, d\left(e_C - e_i\right) = \int_{t_0}^{t} -\frac{dt}{r\,C}\, dt$$

(9)

To solve Equation (9), we take the following steps:

$$\ell n \frac{d\left(e_C - e_i\right)}{e_C - e_i} = -\frac{t}{r\,C}$$

(10)

$$\frac{e_C - e_i}{e_C - e_i} = e^{-t/r\,C}$$

(11)

$$e_C - e_i = \left(e_C - e_i\right) e^{-t/r\,C}$$

(12)

By definition $r\,C = \tau$, so we write

$$e_C - e_i = \left(e_C - e_i\right) e^{-t/\tau}$$

$$e_C \left(1 - e^{-t/\tau}\right) = e_i \left(1 - e^{-t/\tau}\right)$$

(13)

and since from Equation (6) itself it is $e^{-(t/\tau)} = 1$, Equation (13) becomes

$$e_C = e_i \left(1 - e^{-t/\tau}\right)$$

(14)

Since $r \to 0$, it is $\tau \to 0$ and therefore the capacitor charges *very fast*. (This calculus session supplements the discussion of Section 8.2.2 on the series RC circuit also.)

The second circuit state is entered when $e_i(t)$ goes negative and the diode ceases to conduct, acting as an open switch. Then the RC network of Figure 9.4.12 springs into existence. By then, C is fully charged so that $e_C(0) = +e_i$. Essentially then, the second

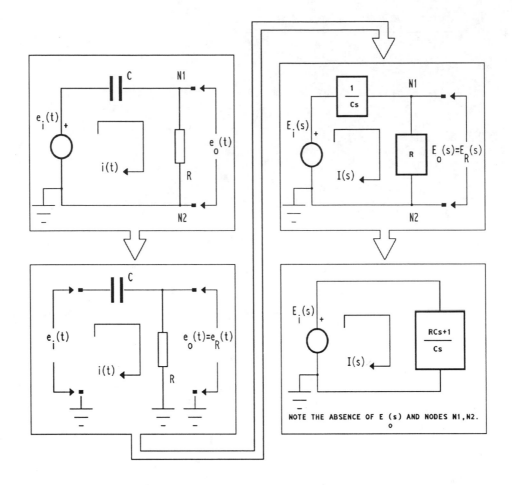

Figure 9.4.12   Applying transform impedance techniques on an RC differentiator.

circuit state involves a simple RC high pass filter, a differentiating circuit having a negative voltage e_i for an input and a charged capacitor.

We apply the transform impedance techniques of Section 9.1.1 and write

$$E_i(s) \;=\; I(s) \left[\frac{RCs + 1}{Cs} \right] \tag{15}$$

$$E_0(s) \;=\; R\,I(s)$$

$$I(s) \;=\; E_0(s) \left[\frac{1}{R} \right] \tag{16}$$

and therefore

$$E_i(s) = \left[\frac{RCs + 1}{Cs}\right] \left[\frac{1}{R}\right] E_0(s)$$

$$T(s) = \frac{e_0(s)}{E_i(s)} = \frac{RCs}{RCs + 1} \tag{17}$$

and since $RC = \tau$, it is

$$T(s) = \frac{\tau s}{\tau s + 1} \tag{18}$$

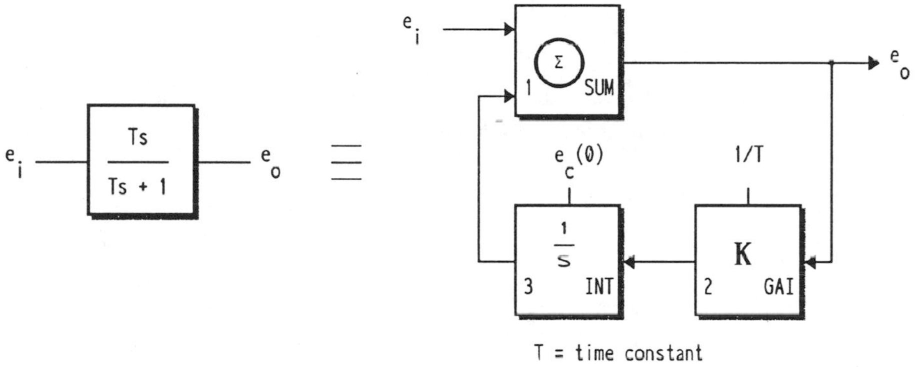

Figure 9.4.13   The block simulator of transfer function (18) (see text).

This transfer function is simulated by either the block diagram of Figure 9.4.13 or that of 9.4.14. The latter uses a wirable initial condition scheme (Section 1.5) allowing the delivery of $e_c(0)$ at the onset of the negative-going input signal. The improved setup of Figure 9.4.15 (RCNET.sim) uses a reset control in conjunction with a resettable integrator (RIN) block so that signal regeneration is avoided. (The reader is urged to test this simulator with a negative-going pulse input with and without reset and different τ values). Note that the GAI, RIN and SUM blocks form an excellent and most versatile integrator with wired reset and initial condition signal paths (see also Section 1.7). The complete circuit is simulated in Figure 9.4.16. It is offered here as an example of a flexible and semi-intuitive approach to dynamic simulation. There are, of course, other ways of approaching the subject.

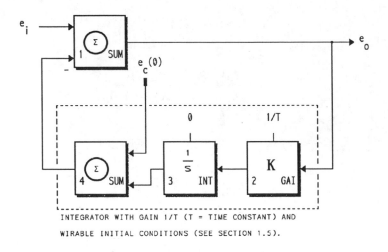

Figure 9.4.14 Another approach to the simulation of transfer function 18 using a wirable initial condition scheme.

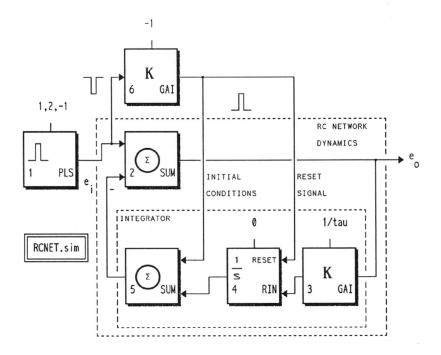

Figure 9.4.15 An intermediate step toward simulating the clamping circuit.

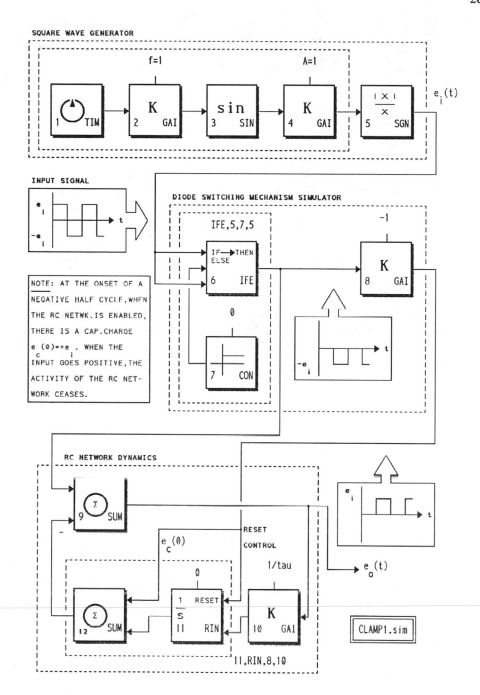

Figure 9.4.16   The final simulator of the clamping circuit.

10   AEROSPACE VEHICLE SIMULATION AND HUMAN-MACHINE CONTROL SYSTEMS

10.1   INTRODUCTION

Aerospace network simulation is easy and interesting with block diagram languages. Their utility far exceeds that of the expensive analog/hybrid machines traditionally employed by experimenters in this multidimensional field. Once a mathematical model is established, it is possible to implement a simulation with much less trouble with CDSS languages for the following reasons. First, time and amplitude scaling is not required here. It is, however, a cardinal requirement of all analog/hybrid computers, because their amplifier-based units are subject to saturation (see also Section 1.6). Second, the analog/hybrid computer has a finite number of computational elements. Once we have run out of integrators, that's it. This important limitation does not exist in CDSS languages. Third, the inverting nature of the physical amplifier always increases the number of computational units required for a problem setup. With CDSS languages signal inversion is not imposed on the experimenter. Fourth, nonlinear units like multipliers and dividers and various function generators are a pure luxury on analog/hybrid systems. Even when available, there are very few. Not so in block diagram languages where we are not obligated to employ small angle approximations. Fifth, auxiliary units like strip chart recorders, x-y plotters, voltmeters and periodic function generators are not required in the virtual lab. Trace and x-y displays, hard copy and precision readout capabilities and the function generator blocks are precision virtual substitutes for this hardware. Some other languages also provide three dimensional plotting facilities.

In this part we have considered the need for simple vehicle models which can be used when experimenting with control systems, human operator models, and the like. Often simplified vehicle representations which are understood by the nonspecialist are very useful in preliminary research. More complex mathematical models normally described by large differential equation systems are readily put in block diagram form by using Lord Kelvin's method (Section 6.4.2.1) or state variables (Section 6.4.2.2). Both are traditional analog computer techniques. Of course, nonlinear terms and arbitrary function generators can be used throughout the model. The latter may involve the FNC block which allows the implementation of a piecewise-linear function. All CDSS languages feature arbitrary function generators. TUTSIM's FNC block allows a maximum of 100 parameter pairs. Some functions can be synthesized with polynomial techniques (see Sections 6.3.1, 6.3.2 and especially 6.3.3) and with various explicit or implicit mechanizations (Section 11.2).

268

10.2   A SIMPLE REPRESENTATION OF FIXED-WING LONGITUDINAL DYNAMICS

To approach a simulation of fixed-wing longitudinal dynamics from a generalized mathematical point of view we consider the ordinary quartic dfq with constant coefficients of the form

$$s^4 + A_3 s^3 + A_2 s^2 + A_1 s + A_0 = 0 \tag{1}$$

as discussed in the paper by Karayanakis (1985). It is well known that the fixed-wing longitudinal motion consists of two modes, the short-period response and phugoid (long-period) response. The first is shown primarily in terms of angle of attack (α) changes while the phugoid manifests itself in terms of perturbation of the aircraft's velocity vector. The characteristic Equation (1) can be factored into the product of two quadratics, one representing the short-period response and the other representing the phugoid mode. Then we write

$$\left(s^2 + 2\varsigma_{SP}\omega_{SP}s + \omega_{SP}^2\right)\left(s^2 + 2\varsigma_{LP}\omega_{LP}^2\right) = 0 \tag{2}$$

where ω_i is the undamped natural frequency and ς_i is a measure of damping. It should be noted that the two modes are well separated from each other in terms of frequency content, so that normally it is

$$\omega_{SP} >> \omega_{LP}$$

and

$$1 > \varsigma_{SP} > \varsigma_{LP}$$

Much understanding can be gained by looking at these quadratics from an analogies point of view. The familiar damped linear oscillator equation

$$\ddot{x} + \frac{d}{m}\dot{x} + \frac{k}{m}x = 0 \tag{3}$$

is useful here with roots

$$x_{1,2} = \frac{d}{2m} \pm j\left[\frac{k}{m} - \left(\frac{d}{2m}\right)^2\right]^{\frac{1}{2}} \tag{4}$$

In the case where $\omega = 0$, there is no oscillation and the imaginary part vanishes, so that

$$\frac{k}{m} = \left(\frac{d}{2m}\right)^2 \tag{5}$$

The damping that corresponds to a condition of no oscillation is called *critical damping*, d_c, and is expressed as:

$$d_c = 2(km)^{\frac{1}{2}} \tag{6}$$

Then oscillator damping (d) can be measured as a percentage of critical damping where ς is the ratio of damping to critical damping or

$$\varsigma = \frac{d}{d_c} \tag{7}$$

If $d = 0$ there is an undamped oscillation where the undamped natural frequency ω can be written as

$$\omega = \left(\frac{k}{m}\right)^{\frac{1}{2}} \tag{8}$$

Substitution of the above definitions into Equation (3) gives

$$\ddot{x} + 2\varsigma\omega\dot{x} + \omega^2 x = 0 \tag{9}$$

which is the form of each of the constituent parts of Equation (2) (see also Karayanakis, 1985).

Modelling methodology shown here is useful when a generalized but relevant experimental setup is required, as opposed to a highly detailed simulation. An example is found in Muckler et al. (1961 a, b and c) in conjunction with transfer of training research. The block model can be easily structured from Equation (9) according to the procedure discussed in Section 6.4.2 (see also Section 10.5 on the lateral/directional case).

10.3   GENERALIZED LONGITUDINAL DYNAMICS FOR THE STUDY OF FIXED-WING SHORT-PERIOD RESPONSE

Often we wish to observe the short-period response of the longitudinal mode of a conventional subsonic fixed-wing aircraft. Assuming zero acceleration along the flight path, we exclude the phugoid mode from the model. The torque equation about the lateral axis is

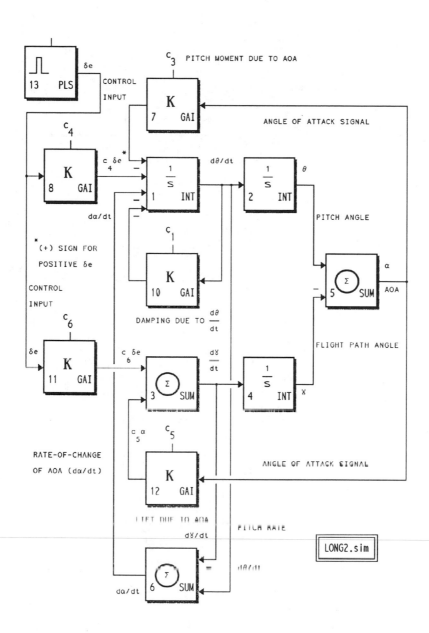

Figure 10.3.1 A generalized short-period longitudinal dynamics simulator.

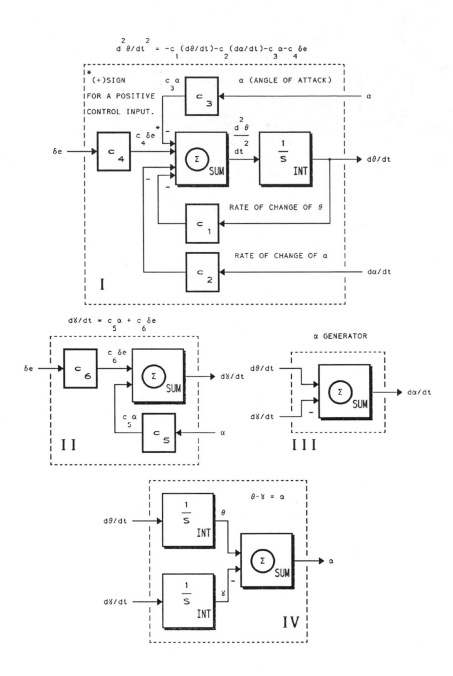

Figure 10.3.2   Macro-blocks (I-IV) leading to the synthesis of LONG2.sim of Figure 10.3.1.

$$s^2\theta + c_1 s\theta + c_2 s\alpha + c_3\alpha + c_4\delta e = 0 \qquad (1)$$

where θ is the pitch angle, α is the angle of attack, δe is the deflection of the elevator control, c_n denotes a proportionality constant and s is the complex variable. The normal force equation is

$$c_5\alpha + c_6\delta e - s\gamma = 0 \qquad (2)$$

where γ is the flight path angle. Also it is

$$\theta = \alpha + \gamma \qquad (3)$$

The pitch-to-elevator transfer function is found from Equations (1), (2) and (3):

$$\frac{s\theta}{\delta e}(s) = \frac{\dot{\theta}}{\delta e}(s) = \frac{[(c_4 - c_2 c_6)\, s + (c_4 c_5 - c_3 c_6)]}{[s^2 + (c_1 + c_2 + c_5)\, s + (c_3 + c_1 c_5)]} \qquad (4)$$

The system of Equations (1), (2) and (3) is simulated in Figure 10.3.1 (LONG2.sim) with the following c-coefficient values: $c_1 = 1.0$, $c_2 = 0.053$, $c_3 = 4.32$, $c_4 = 15.2$, $c_5 = 0.9$, and $c_6 = 0.364$. A few runs will verify that the system's undamped natural frequency ω_n depends heavily on c_3 (the pitching moment due to angle of attack). The damping ratio ζ is primarily determined by c_5 (the lift due to angle of attack) and secondarily by c_1 (the damping due to pitching velocity). This simulation approach allows the study of aircraft dynamic characteristics by relating the various c-coefficients to the functional parameters of the problem. Finally, Figure 10.3.2 shows how the simulator of Figure 10.3.1 came about. The buildup technique used here is straightforward, based on individual mechanization and then connection of subsystems representing Equations (1), (2) and (3).

10.4 THE LONGITUDINAL SHORT-PERIOD TRANSFER FUNCTION

The pitch-to-elevator transfer function for the short-period mode of a fixed-wing aircraft (see Equation (4) of Section 10.3) describes a system of characteristic second-order dynamics between δe and $[d\theta/dt]$, with derivative action in the numerator. We can express the undamped natural frequency ω_n as

$$\omega_n \equiv \left(c_3 + c_1 c_5\right)^{\frac{1}{2}} \qquad (1)$$

The damping ratio ζ can be written as

$$\zeta \equiv \frac{c_1 + c_2 + c_5}{2\omega_n} \tag{2}$$

and the steady-state gain $C_0 = [d\theta/dt]/\delta e$ is

$$c_0 \equiv \frac{c_4 c_5 - c_3 c_6}{c_3 + c_1 c_5} \tag{3}$$

Then we designate a coupling coefficient c_7 so that

$$c_7 = \frac{c_4 - c_2 c_6}{c_3 + c_1 c_5} \tag{4}$$

Substitution of Equations (1), (2), (3) and (4) into Equation (4) of Section 10.3 produces a functional form of the short-period transfer function:

$$\frac{\dot{\theta}}{\delta e}(s) = \frac{-(c_7 s + c_0)}{\left[\left(\dfrac{s}{\omega_n}\right)^2 + 2\zeta\left(\dfrac{s}{\omega_n}\right) + 1\right]} \tag{5}$$

The following observations can be verified on the simulator:

1) Coefficient c_3 (the pitching moment due to α) has a significant effect on ω_n.
2) Coefficient c_5 (the lift due to α) influences ζ.
3) The damping ratio is also influenced by c_1 (the damping due to pitching velocity).
4) The pitching velocity per elevator deflection (steady-state gain) c_0 is influenced heavily by the product $c_4 c_5$.
5) The derivative coefficient c_7 is influenced by c_4.
6) c_0 shapes the steady-state change of θ for a pulse input of δe.

This simulation approach allows the setup of transfer function based parametric studies for research in aircraft dynamics and control, handling qualities research, analog pilot benchmarking, and many other related topics. Figure 10.4.1 shows the TUTSIM simulator (LONGTF.sim). A more detailed description of this method is found in Jex and Cromwell (1962).

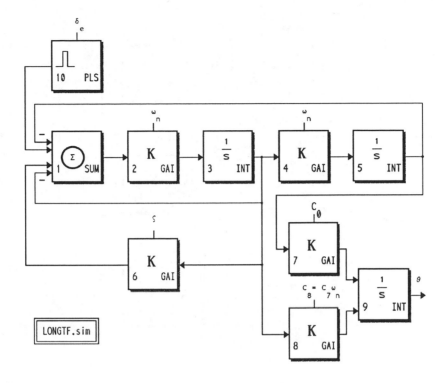

Figure 10.4.1   The simulator of the longitudinal short-period transfer function (5).

10.5   A VERY SIMPLE LATERAL/DIRECTIONAL SIMULATION

The simple simulator of fixed-wing lateral/directional dynamics described here provides a quick setup alternative over more elaborate schemes. Basically, we seek a response

$$\frac{\phi}{(\delta ai + \delta ai_{TRIM})} \qquad \frac{1}{s + k_1} \tag{1}$$

where ϕ is the bank angle, δai is the pilot's aileron control input and δai_{TRIM} is the aileron trim control setting. We also desire a ψ output (heading) so that

$$\frac{\psi}{(\delta ai + \delta ai_{TRIM})} = \frac{k_2}{s \ (s + k_1)} \tag{2}$$

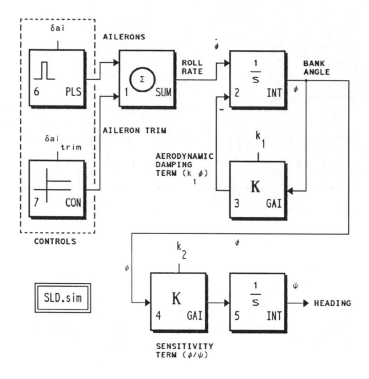

Figure 10.5.1   A simple lateral/directional dynamics simulator.

where k_2 is a $[(d\phi/dt)/\psi]$ sensitivity parameter. Transfer functions (1) and (2) are simulated as shown in Figure 10.5.1 (SLD.sim). It is instructive to consider first the system response for $k_1 = 0$. A pulse δai (2,5,1) effects an increase in ϕ and the system maintains the ϕ value present when the control input is removed. Given a $k_2 = 0.5$, ψ continues to depart, a scenario that describes early VTOL vehicles well (see also Sections 10.8 and 10.12).

The condition $k > 0$ implies the existence of aerodynamic stability where a steady aileron input is required to maintain a steady bank angle. When δai is removed, the aircraft recovers (as in the case of a stable airplane with a strong dihedral effect). The CON block added in parallel with the PLS block provides for the simulation of out-of-trim conditions. Its function is illustrated by Figure 10.5.2 where $k_1 = 1$, $\phi/\psi = 0.5$, $\delta ai = 0$, $\delta ai_{TRIM} = 0.1$. Essentially, this simulator represents an inertial system with damping and in spite of simplicity, it is quite realistic in terms of expected response from a pilot's point of view. Various degrees of instability may be simulated when $k_1 < 0$.

Another generalized approach to the simulation of lateral/directional dynamics is based on the quintic characteristic equation

$$s^5 + A_4 s^4 + A_3 s^3 + A_2 s^2 + A_1 s + A_0 = 0 \qquad (3)$$

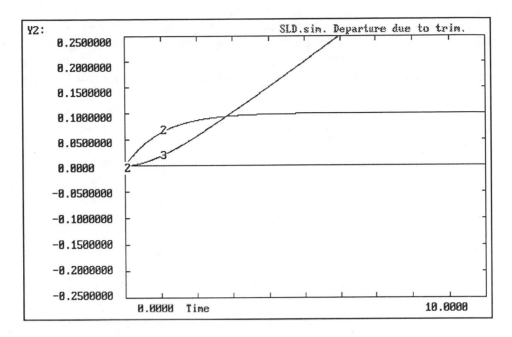

Figure 10.5.2   Response of the SLD.sim (see text).

which describes an aircraft's lateral motion in a fashion similar to that of Section 10.2. Essentially lateral motion consists of *three* modes (see also Karayanakis, 1985). The first two and foremost are the *Dutch roll* and the *spiral divergence*. The Dutch roll is a damped oscillation involving both rolling and yawing motions. It gets its name from its resemblance to a Dutchman merrily ice skating down a canal. Both the damping and the natural frequency of the Dutch roll vary with aircraft and flight conditions. Light damping of this mode is often a problem, especially when combined with a high natural frequency. Under such circumstances it is impossible to dampen the Dutch roll mode manually; artificial means are necessary to ensure flight safety. The spiral divergence is a mild divergence where the airplane tends to roll into a turn leading to a spiral condition. This divergence is of no serious consequence since the pilot can easily deal with its unusually very large time constant. The third mode is the *roll subsidence* or damping-in roll mode represents one of the four nonzero roots of the characteristic equation. It is a very heavily damped convergence and can be simply described as the rolling response of the aircraft to an aileron input. Its heavy damping makes it not readily discernible to the pilot. All three lateral modes are found in modern aircraft and can be simulated by modelling the characteristic Equation (3) just as the longitudinal case of Section 10.2. Notably, the quintic has a complex pair of roots that represent the Dutch roll—one negative real root representing roll subsidence and a very small real (often positive) root representing the spiral divergence mode. The lateral characteristic equation resembles the longitudinal one (Equation (1) Section 10.2) with the exception of zero root in s. For practical purposes, the quintic is reduced often to a quartic with a unity coefficient of the highest power.

The use of generalized dfq-based mathematical models should involve an informed choice of the experimenter. Such models are easy to implement and their mathematical face validity is always an asset. However, there are alternate approaches involving the solution of pertinent simultaneous equations or the mechanization of transfer functions. Finally, a little-mentioned, but very real phenomenon, is adverse yaw effect due to aileron drag. A realistic simulator may also incorporate the p-factor effect (propeller-induced yawing motion which is a function of pitch angle and power).

10.6   AN INTRODUCTION TO VTOL AIRCRAFT CONTROL

Vertical takeoff and landing (VTOL) aircraft provide a fascinating research facet in aeronautical, control and human factors engineering. There are many different VTOL configurations. Each shows many variants. Despite widely different physical and operating characteristics, VTOL aircraft (other than rotorcraft, not considered here), have a powerful common denominator: handling under full manual control is a difficult if not an impossible task. A VTOL machine is a hard-to-fly aircraft. This section uses TUTSIM to investigate the dynamics of the generalized hovering maneuver. Hovering is a unique capability of VTOL machines, where the aircraft maintains a fixed position with respect to a ground reference for some time period. The vehicle is supported and controlled through its powered lift system. Without the benefit of forward velocity, a hovering VTOL aircraft has no restoring aerodynamic forces or moments. This is to say that the machine lacks both *attitude* and *path* stability. Attitude stability pertains to the aircraft's degrees of rotation, while path stability involves translational motion (for a more detailed discussion, see Karayanakis, 1990).

Of specific interest here is the one-dimensional hovering transition from one ground reference point to another. In our generalized vehicle, one or more reaction powerplants generate a resultant thrust force T_R so that the aircraft hovers in reference to a ground plane. The hovering transition maneuver is done by introducing a control input δe that makes the vehicle rotate by a pitch angle θ. The resulting horizontal component of thrust T_H induces the longitudinal acceleration required for horizontal motion. Modelling the fundamental VTOL control structure is the first step. If $K_{\delta e}$ is the control input gain and x is the longitudinal motion of the aircraft, it is

$$\ddot{\theta} \;=\; K_{\delta e}\,\delta e$$
$$\ddot{x} \;=\; K_\theta\,\theta$$

(1)

The system of Equation (1) describes the one-dimensional hovering transition problem for a very small θ. Clearly the parameter θ that corresponds to a specific controller input δe can be found by integrating twice. Then the displacement x is found after two more integrations (Figure 10.6.1). Therefore the transfer function of the system is

$$\frac{x}{\delta e} = \frac{K_{\delta e} K_\theta}{s^4} \tag{2}$$

That is, vehicle travel is proportional to the fourth integral of the control input. This peculiar situation is evaluated by letting $K_{\delta e} = K\theta = 1$ in the block diagram of Figure 10.6.1 and running the simulation (VTOL1.sim). The results show that, for an impulse-type control input of unity amplitude, system output is a cubic parabola.

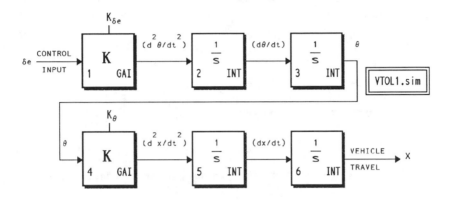

Figure 10.6.1 An introductory experiment in VTOL simulation.

It can be safely concluded that the vehicle is impossible to fly because any control input results in a continuously growing departure. Control input must be proportional to the fourth derivative of x(t); that is, we are asking the controller to generate the fourth derivative of an infinite amplitude signal—clearly an impossibility! The inherent instability of the system can be remedied by altering the dynamics of the system itself. What comes to mind is feedback, as we are interested in reducing the sensitivity to both controller inputs and ambient disturbances (i.e., atmospheric turbulence). Also we wish to modify the natural frequencies of the system so that its response time is altered. Ideally a specific δe causes a specific body attitude which, in turn, induces a specific translational motion. So let's experiment.

The basic system has a fourth-order pole at s = 0 by virtue of transfer function (3), where the four cascaded integrators make the denominator vanish. As a result any input excitation (controller input or noise disturbance) induces a continuously growing response in x(t). Figure 10.6.2 (VTOL2.sim) shows a first attempt to improve vehicle dynamics by adding two negative feedback loops. The system's new transfer function is

$$\frac{x(s)}{\delta e(s)} = \frac{K_{\delta e} K_\theta}{s^2 (s^2 + as + bK_\theta)} \tag{3}$$

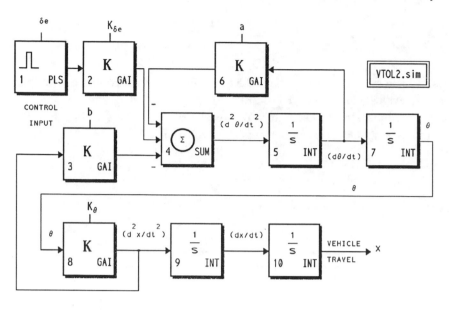

Figure 10.6.2   An attempt to improve VTOL vehicle dynamics by adding two feedback loops.

We can now investigate the vehicle's response to pulse and step inputs respectively, having common settings of a = b = 10. The results tell a story of significantly improved dynamic behavior. There are now four natural frequencies, two equaling zero and two depending on parameters a and b. The vehicle exhibits an exponential decay response now, rather than a behavior of constant departure.

Of course there are many other things we can do toward improving the aircraft's handling characteristics. For example, a challenging task would be to reshape the control input itself. The reader is referred to the classic works by Franke and Döpner (1963), Goldberger (1966), Elkind et al. (1968), Fry et al. (1969), Baron et al. (1970), Frost (1972), Greif et al. (1972), and Corliss et al. (1978). The subject of VTOL stability and control is a vast one and many references can be found in aeronautical and control journals, government documents and university or other research reports.

10.7   THE XV5A SIMULATOR

The XV5A is a classical lift-fan VTOL aircraft built by Ryan in the early 60s. Its being one of the most documented aircraft of its type led to the adoption of various XV5A simulation models in research. The model chosen here allows the simulation of a hovering control task with the XV5A in the fan mode, dealing with the control of displacement along the longitudinal axis (both altitude and lateral/directional motion are suppressed). Much of the optimal control research in human-machine system funded by AFFDL in the 60s and 70s is based on this model (as cases in point, see Elkind et al., 1968; and Baron et al., 1970).

A very detailed simulation model can be found in Goldberger (1966) and the complete linearized equations of motion are in Elkind et al. (1968) along with the hovering stability derivatives.

The equations of motion for the simplified hovering problem are

$$
\begin{bmatrix} \dot{u} \\ \dot{x} \\ \dot{q} \\ \dot{\theta} \end{bmatrix} = \begin{bmatrix} X_u & 0 & 0 & -\bar{g} \\ 1 & 0 & 0 & 0 \\ M_u & 0 & M_q & 0 \\ 0 & 0 & 1 & 0 \end{bmatrix} \begin{bmatrix} u \\ x \\ q \\ \theta \end{bmatrix} + \begin{bmatrix} 0 \\ 0 \\ M_{NF} \\ 0 \end{bmatrix} \delta_\theta \tag{1}
$$

where u is the incremental velocity and x is the incremental displacement along the longitudinal axis, q is the pitch rate (the angular velocity about the y-axis), θ is the pitch angel, δ_θ is the pitching moment control input, X is the force along the x-axis and M is the moment about the y-axis. In this simulation we use values found in Elkind et al. (1968): mass, m = 28.5 slugs; converted gravitational constant, $\bar{g}$ = g/157.3 = 0.561 ft/deg-s; drag damping, $x_u = (1/m)(\partial x/\partial u) = -0.111s^{-1}$; velocity stability, $M_u = (1/Iy)(\partial M/\partial u)$ = 0.51 deg/ft-s, in which the moment of inertia Iy about the y-axis is 15.139 slug-ft^2; pitch damping, $M_q = (1/Iy)(\partial M/\partial q) = -0.0704$ s^{-1}; and pitching moment control coefficient, $M_{NF} = 2.66$ s^{-2} (the value 0.106 is used in XV5A.sim). Figure 10.7.1 (XV5A.sim) shows the simulator. Readers will enjoy investigating the system's θ, x and u responses to pulse and step inputs, respectively.

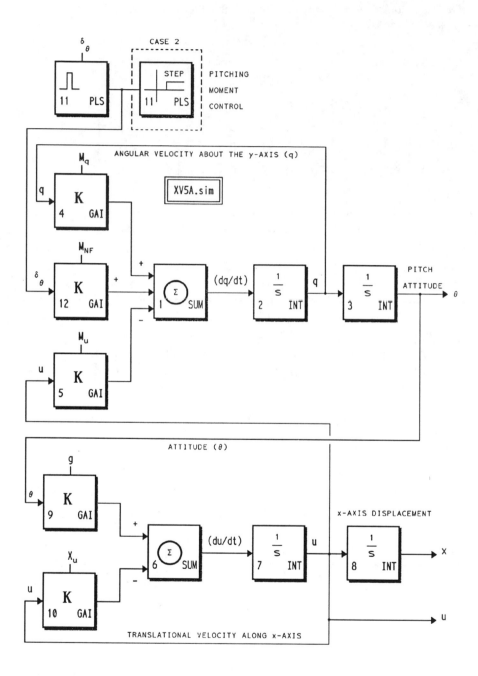

Figure 10.7.1   The XV5A simulator.

11 NONLINEAR FUNCTIONS AND CONTROL SYSTEMS: SELECTED EXAMPLES

11.1   ABOUT NONLINEARITIES

Most natural systems are nonlinear to some extent; that is, their behavior cannot be described by linear differential equations having constant coefficients. Often there is deliberate use of nonlinearities in system design. Introducing one or more nonlinear characteristics in a system may improve its performance. Nonlinearities are found everywhere, and it is logical that those who study and model systems of any kind (biological, economic, electronic, mechanical, and the like) be aware of the principal nonlinearities, their characteristics and the outcome of their combinations. In simulation it is frequently necessary to mechanize nonlinear transfer characteristics. CDSS languages provide users with a variety of linear and nonlinear blocks. The setup of Figure 11.1.1 is used to plot out the transfer

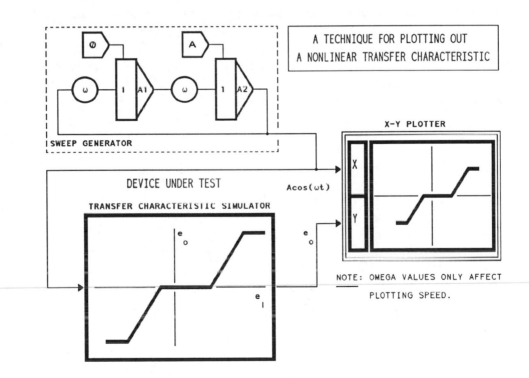

Figure 11.1.1   A setup for the plotting of transfer characteristics.

283

characteristic of a block or a device. The harmonic oscillator may be substituted by TUTSIM's TIM-GAI-SIN(COS)-GAI function generator. The best way to become familiar with the various blocks of any CDSS language is to plot their transfer characteristics first and then investigate the input and output waveforms. The following sections examine a few continuous and switching nonlinearities. These simulation examples demonstrate the versatility of TUTSIM can serve as expandable and modifiable devices and provide paradigms of technique.

11.2   DEADZONE

The deadzone is a discontinuous nonlinearity having the transfer characteristic of Figure 11.2.1. Its mathematical description is

$$f(x) = \begin{cases} 0 & a \leq x \leq b \\ x - b & x > b \\ x - a & x < a \end{cases} \tag{1}$$

It is also known as the threshold, deadband, inert zone and region of no sensitivity. The characteristic can be synthesized as shown in Figure 11.2.2. This simulation approach requires the use of the *time derivative* of the input, that is $[de_i/dt]$ instead of e_i (Cox, 1970). This simulator allows user-defined breakpoints, slope control, x-shift control and sign. Delivery of initial conditions via a summer (see Section 1.5) and replacement of the GAI (#6) block with a multiplier will allow remote reconfiguring of the transfer characteristic.

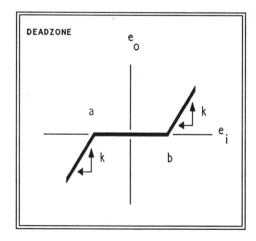

Figure 11.2.1   The generalized deadzone transfer plot.

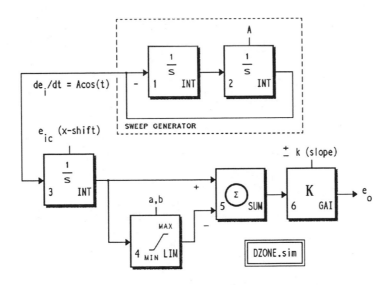

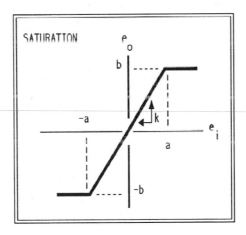

Figure 11.2.2   Deadzone synthesis according to Cox (1970).

11.3   SATURATION

Saturation or slope limiting is the discontinuous nonlinearity shown in Figure 11.3.1. Its transfer characteristic can be generated from an integrator (linear slope) and a deadzone (Figure 11.3.2) as described by Freeman and Cox (1967). The simulator of Figure 11.3.2 allows independent adjustment of breakpoints, slope control and horizontal shift. Also quadrant reversal occurs with a negative k-value. Like the previous deadzone circuit, this design requires the time derivative of the input.

Figure 11.3.1   The generalized saturation transfer plot.

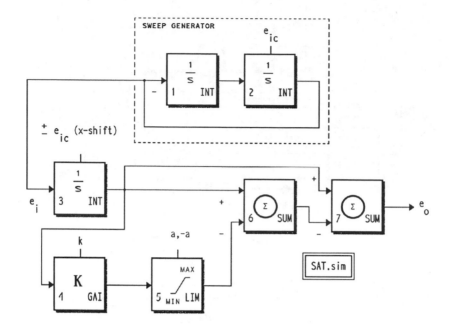

Figure 11.3.2   Saturation synthesis according to Freeman and Cox (1967).

TUTSIM's limiter (LIM) block provides a conventional characteristic with a *unity* slope and user defined minimum and maximum limits. Its use with a unity gain block at the output allows quick quadrant reversal. Using the *output* gain block for the overall restructuring of the characteristic calls for caution, because it affects both the slope and the limits. The output gain may be used as a slope control and the limiter parameters are adjusted accordingly. An *input* gain block can be used to adjust the slope without affecting limits. This allows the easy synthesis of asymmetric saturation , discussed in the following section.

11.4   AN ASYMMETRIC SATURATION CHARACTERISTIC

The transfer characteristic of Figure 11.4.1 can be synthesized as shown in Figure 11.4.2 by taking advantage of the LIM and GAI block properties. The first quadrant portion of the characteristic has an upper limit b set by the LIM block #5 by letting min = 0 and max = b. The slope, k_1, is determined by the GAI block preceding the limiter. We know that the slope of the LIM block characteristic is unity. The *input* GAI block affects the slope only, not the values of the limit parameters. The third quadrant portion of the curve is then implemented the same way. The two sections are summed to produce the complete transfer plot.

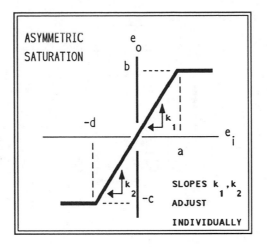

Figure 11.4.1   Defining the asymmetric saturation parameters.

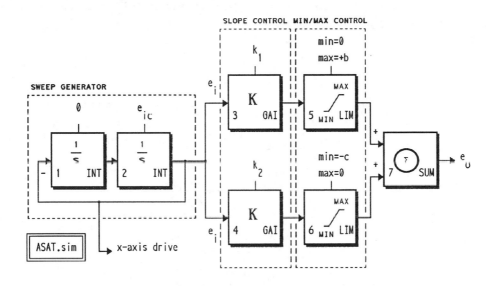

Figure 11.4.2   Synthesis of a fully-controllable saturation nonlinearity.

11.5   INPUT-CONTROLLED GAIN: SIMULATING THE EQUATION $y = kx^n \, \text{sgn} \, x$

The block diagram of Figure 11.5.1 simulates the equation

$$y = kx^n \, \text{sgn} \, x \tag{1}$$

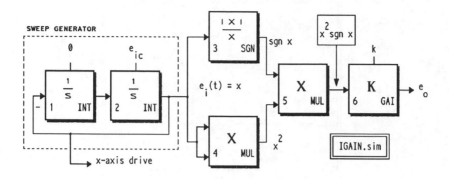

Figure 11.5.1   The simulator of the input-controlled gain equation (see text).

A useful exercise is to plot the transfer characteristic for n = 2 and k = 1, 0.5, 0.1. This nonlinear characteristic is useful in control system simulation. It is presented here as an example of a wide class of functions where

$$e_0 = f(e_i) \tag{2}$$

and where a proportionality $de_0/df(e_i)$ is related to the input by a constant k, so that

$$\left| \frac{d\,e_0}{d\,f(e_i)} \right| = k\,e_i \tag{3}$$

and therefore

$$e_0 = \begin{cases} k\,(e_i)^2 & e_i > 0 \\ -\,k\,(e_i)^2 & e_i < 0 \end{cases} \tag{4}$$

or in general,

$$e_0 = k\,f(e_i)\,\mathrm{sgn}\,e_i \tag{5}$$

TUTSIM's SGN block is useful here, although the sgn x function can be easily implemented according to the relationship

$$\text{sgn } x \;=\; \frac{|x|}{x} \tag{6}$$

at the expense, of course, of two blocks. The characteristic can be used to represent the nonlinear restoring moment on an aerodynamic surface as a function of angle of attack (Abramson, 1958). It is often implemented in its simpler form

$$y \;=\; k\,|x|\,x \tag{7}$$

where

$$y \;=\; k\,x^2\,\text{sgn } x \;=\; k\,x^2\,\frac{|x|}{x} \;=\; k\,|x|\,x \tag{8}$$

as the absolute value square circuit or absquare (Netzer, 1981). Tomovic and Karplus (1962) show an example of a mechanical system simulation with an original reference to Rideout et al. (1956) who appear to be the earliest users of this circuit (see also Section 4.5).

11.6   SOFT, HARD AND ASYMMETRICAL SPRING RESTORING FORCE FUNCTIONS

Often it is necessary to simulate the restoring force action of a *nonlinear* spring. Typical spring nonlinearities are found in *soft* or *hard* springs having *symmetrical* or *asymmetrical* restoring force characteristics. The simulator of Figure 11.6.1 (SPRING1.sim) is based on the equation

$$f(y) \;=\; cx \;+\; \epsilon x^3 \tag{1}$$

and generates a symmetrical restoring force characteristic. Soft spring action is simulated when $\epsilon < 0$ as the restoring force weakens with spring extension. Hard action occurs when $\epsilon > 0$ as the restoring force stiffens with spring extension. Typical plots for $c = 0.7, 1, 1.5$ and $\epsilon = 1$ and $\epsilon = -1$ will acquaint the reader with both cases.

An asymmetrical spring force action is simulated as shown in Figure 11.6.2 (SPRING2.sim) where the equation

$$f(y) \;=\; cx \;-\; \epsilon x^2 \tag{2}$$

is implemented. When $\epsilon < 0$ the first quadrant segment provides soft spring action and the third quadrant hard. When $\epsilon > 0$ the opposite occurs.

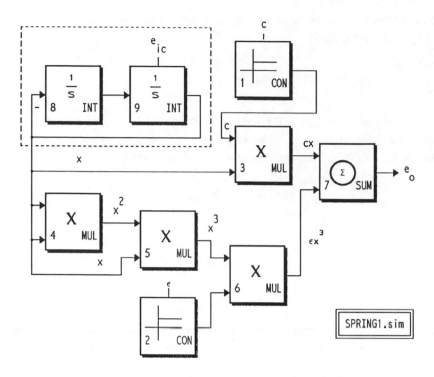

Figure 11.6.1 Simulation of the restoring force function of symmetrical springs.

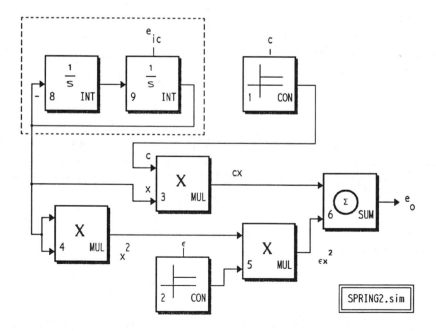

Figure 11.6.2 Simulation of the restoring force function of asymmetrical springs.

11.7 INVESTIGATING THE SATURATING INTEGRATOR NONLINEARITY $x = \dot{y} + y^3$

The nonlinear differential equation

$$x = \dot{y} + y^3 \tag{1}$$

describes the response of a saturating old-fashioned tube integrator circuit. For small y-values the cubed term is negligible, the nonlinearity is slight and the characteristic approximates that of the integration process. However, as y becomes large,, the cubed term predominates and the transfer plot looks like a nonlinear gain. The reader can experiment with the simulator of Figure 11.7.1. First try $e_i = x = 0.1$ using the output $e_0(2)$ as a reference trace. This nonlinearity and its effects on control system performance are discussed by Kolk (1973).

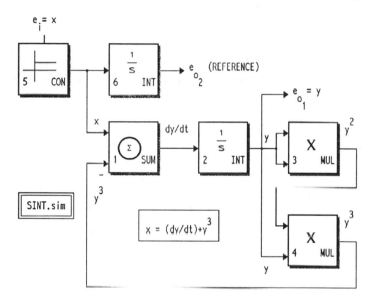

Figure 11.7.1   The simulator of the saturating integrator nonlinearity.

11.8   HYSTERESIS

In general terms, hysteresis is an input-output transfer response lag where the curve resulting from an input signal of *increasing* amplitude is not the same as that of a *decreasing* signal. Hysteresis is found in electronic comparators, in inductor circuits (Kiess, 1990) and in ferromagnetic cores. Backlash, found in gear mechanisms, is a form of mechanical hysteresis. There are many hysteretic phenomena in nature where essentially one value of input results in two possible output values.

The block diagram of Figure 11.8.1 shows an adaptation of the saturation-with-hysteresis mechanical model by Garon (1969). This simulator uses an LME (Euler limited

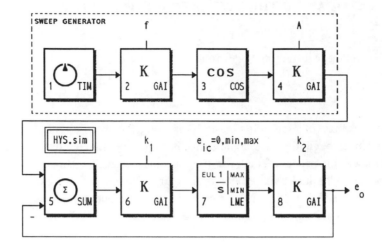

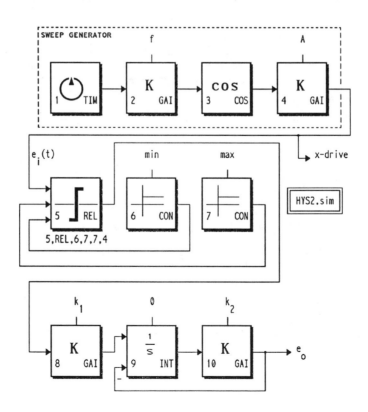

Figure 11.8.1 Synthesis of the hysteresis characteristic based on the saturation-with-hysteresis mechanical model by Garon (1969).

Figure 11.8.2 Another way to simulate hysteresis.

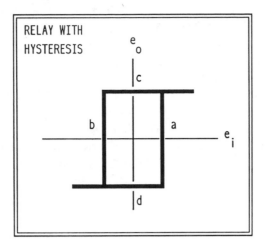

Figure 11.8.3   The transfer plot of the relay-with-hysteresis nonlinearity.

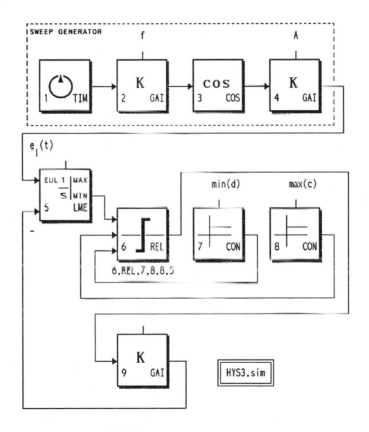

Figure 11.8.4   The simulator of the relay-with-hysteresis nonlinearity.

integrator) block with a negative feedback loop. The simulator of Figure 11.8.2 (HYS2.sim) employs a REL block. The relay response is integrated and the output is fed back into the integrator, resulting in a hysteretic response. Here try $k_1 = 1$, $k_2 = 7$ and f = 1, A = 12 so that $e_i(t) = 12 \cos 2\pi t$.

The transfer characteristic of Figure 11.8.3 represents a relay with hysteresis. It is simulated by the setup of Figure 11.8.4 (HYS3.sim), where constants 7 and 8 determine the maximum (c) and minimum (d) levels. An LME block is used to control points a and b. Like all hysteresis simulators shown here, some trial and error is necessary to obtain the desirable geometry. The transfer plot of Figure 11.8.5 was made with the following settings: block #5 LME = -2,2;   #7 CON = 3;   #8 CON = -3;   #9 GAI = 0.8;   and $e_i(t)$ (sweep signal) = 10 cos 2πt.

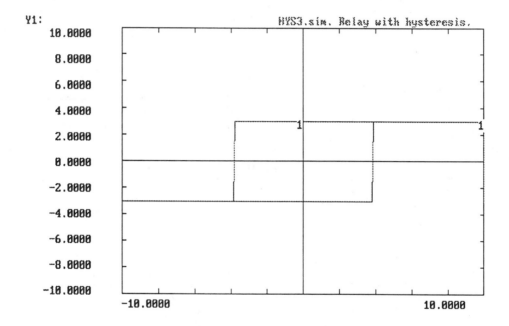

Figure 11.8.5   Results of the HYS3.sim (see text for parameter values).

11.9   THE NONLINEARITY f(x) = γ sin μx - sin x

The nonlinear function

$$f(x) \;=\; \gamma \sin \mu x \;-\; \sin x \qquad (1)$$

for $0.9 < \gamma\mu < 1.1$ and $\gamma > 0$, $\mu > 0$ as proposed by Teodorescu (1971) is an example of a symmetric continuous nonlinearity of importance in simulation. The simulator of Figure 11.9.1 (NLT1.sim) generates the characteristic of Figure 11.9.2 for $\mu = 0.5$ and $\gamma = 2.2$.

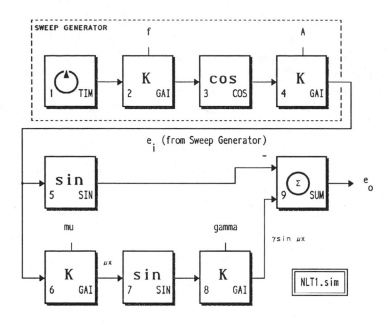

Figure 11.9.1   Simulation of a symmetric continuous nonlinearity (see also Teodorescu, 1971).

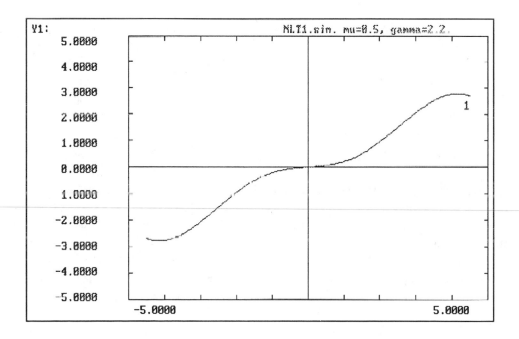

Figure 11.9.2   Results of NLT1.sim for $\mu = 0.5$ and $\gamma = 2.2$.

11.10   DUAL THRESHOLD DETECTOR

Often the simulation of on-off control systems and relay servomechanisms in general requires special relay analogs. The REL block is used to simulate ideal conventional relays, comparators and inverters. It also serves as a versatile building block for more elaborate relay-based functions. Transfer plot I of Figure 11.10.1 represents a *dual-threshold detector* or a *relay with deadzone* having a fully controllable *symmetrical* transfer characteristic.

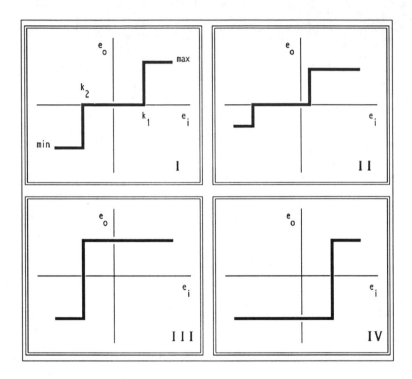

Figure 11.10.1   Various threshold detector characteristics discussed in the text.

It is synthesized by the simulator of Figure 11.10.2 (DREL.sim) where $k_1 < 0$, $k_2 > 0$, $|k_1| = |k_2|$,   max > 0,   min < 0, $|min| = |max|$.   When $|k_1| \neq |k_2|$ and $|min| \neq |max|$, any *asymmetrical* characteristic may be synthesized, as shown in transfer plot II. For a *symmetrical* response try $k_1 = -2$, $k_2 = 2$, max $= 2$, min $= -2$. The third transfer plot of Figure 11.10.1 results when $k_1 = k_2 = x$, $x > 0$. Transfer plot IV is generated when $k_1 = k_2 = x$, $x < 0$. Of course, these extreme cases of the DREL.sim example are simply generated by a REL block preceded by a summing junction.

Both the input and a positive or negative constant are summed. However, a *signal-controlled characteristic* where CON blocks #9, #14, #7 and #13 are replaced with 'hardwired' signal paths is possible here, thus allowing the *remote reconfiguration* of the device. Also the addition of a SUM block past the limited (#15) allows the *shifting* of the

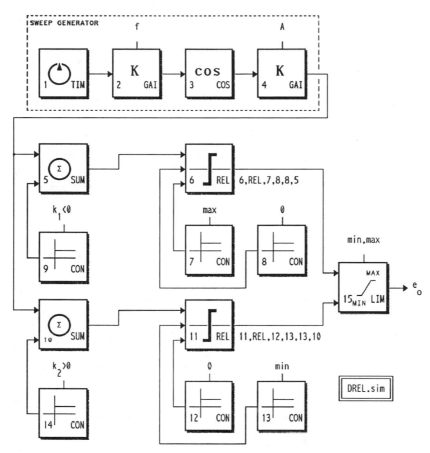

Figure 11.10.2   A generalized simulator of the various threshold detector nonlinearities.

response characteristic along the e_0 axis by a value determined by a CON block parameter or by some external signal. As a case in point, we can modify the file DREL.sim to DREL1.sim by adding (#16, SUM, #15, #17) and then (#17, CON). The arbitrary values $k_1 = -3$, $k_2 = 1$, max $= 3$, min $= -2$ and CON (#17) $= 1$ will generate an asymmetrical response characteristic (its plotting is left as an exercise). The reader is probably aware that the LIM block (#15) of Figure 11.10.2 is unnecessary since a SUM block will do. It was, however, used by the author in a simulation where *final device limits* had to be set in a signal-controlled environment.

11.11   MAGNITUDE DETECTOR

Another useful switching circuit is the *magnitude detector*. The circuit's behavior is independent of the sign or polarity of the input. It has zero output when the input is within a reference range. When the input is outside the range, a specified (large) output appears. The transfer plot I of Figure 11.11.1 represents a symmetrical magnitude detector. All six characteristics are implemented directly from the block diagram of Figure 11.11.2

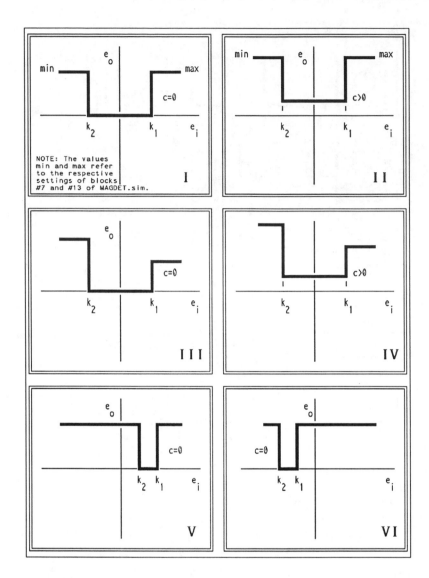

Figure 11.11.1   Various magnitude detector characteristics discussed in the text.

(MAGDET.sim) by assigning appropriate values and signs to blocks #9, #14, #7, #13 and #16. For a symmetrical response try the values $k_1 = -2$, $k_2 = 2$, max = min = 2 and $c = 0$. The input and output waveforms should also be inspected. The reader should investigate the transfer plots for $c = 1$, $k_2 = -k_1$, max = -min of Case 1, and max = 2 and min = 3 of Case 2.

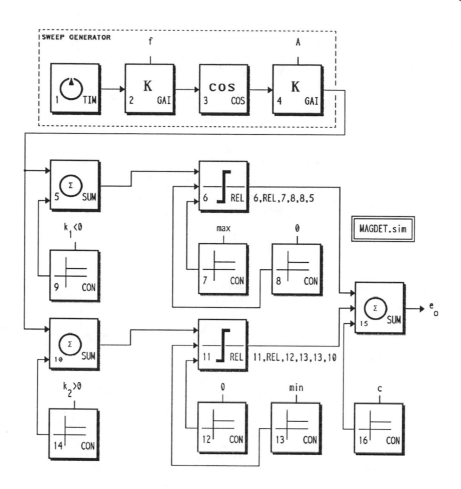

Figure 11.11.2 A generalized simulator of the various magnitude detector nonlinearities.

11.12   SECOND-ORDER SYSTEM WITH TIME-VARYING FEEDBACK

The concept of time-varying feedback is very appealing. The step response of a second-order system is improved if the damping signal is low at the onset of the step response and increases with time. In this simulation, a simple second-order system is considered, described by the transfer function

$$G(s) \;=\; \frac{1}{s^2} \tag{1}$$

The feedback loop carries the signal $(k\dot{x} + x)$, where $k\dot{x}$ is the time-varying velocity feedback component. The factor k is a time variant-coefficient generated by an integrator having a constant a as its input so that $k = a/s$ (Figure 11.12.1). The simulator of Figure 11.12.2 (TDUMP1.sim) is a preliminary setup where we see an exceptional time-dependent

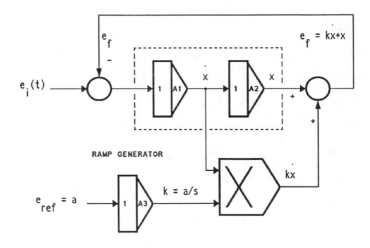

Figure 11.12.1　Analog representation of the second-order system with time-varying feedback.

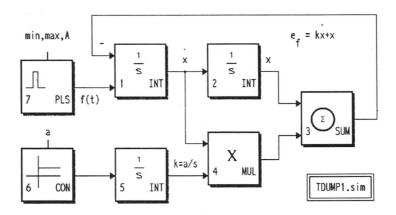

Figure 11.12.2　The preliminary setup for investigating time-dependent nonlinear damping.

nonlinear damping mechanism at work. We should now investigate the superimposed responses to a pulse forcing function for $a = 0$ and $a = 1$, respectively. The reader should also try testing for intermediate values like $a = 0.2$ and $a = 0.4$.

The system is interesting, so we proceed with the more elaborate setup of Figure 11.12.3 (TDUMP2.sim). Here a REL block triggers the k ramp as the leading edge of the pulse occurs. This configuration does not perform as well as the first one where the integrator begins to operate *prior* to the arrival of the disturbance (although TDUMP1.sim is somewhat unrealistic, since we do not know when to trigger the k ramp). The recovery performance of TDUMP2.sim is, however, excellent and the concept of time-varying

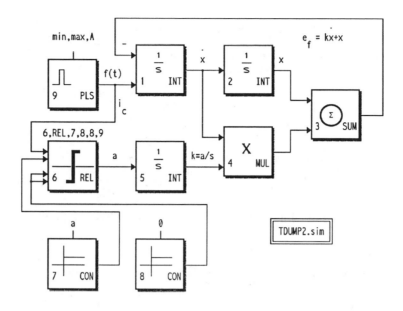

Figure 11.12.3 Simulator of the second-order system with time-varying feedback.

feedback holds great promise. The initial transfer function of the system (TDUMP2.sim) when the feedback signal e_f is unity (a = 0 at the output of the REL block):

$$\frac{e_0(s)}{e_1(s)} = \frac{1}{s^2 + 1} \qquad t_0 < t < t_{R_1} \tag{2}$$

where $t_R(1)$ is the instant the REL activates. The system is then an oscillator. Immediately after the relay turns on, it is

$$\frac{e_0(s)}{e_i(s)} = \frac{1}{s(s + k) + 1} \qquad t_{R_1} < t < t_{R_2} \tag{3}$$

where $t_R(2)$ is the instant the REL deactivates. Since

$$k = \frac{a}{s} \tag{4}$$

Equation (3) can be written as

$$\frac{e_0(s)}{e_i(s)} = \frac{1}{s^2 + a + 1} \qquad {}^t R_1 < t < {}^t R_2 \qquad (5)$$

At the instant the relay turns off the output of integrator #5 levels off, so that from now on k = a (constant). Now the system's transfer function is

$$\frac{e_0(s)}{e_i(s)} = \frac{1}{s + a + 1} \qquad {}^t R_2 < t \qquad (6)$$

Another application of the time-varying damping concept found in Karybakas (1966) who uses an interesting time-varying gain circuit made with op amps and diodes.

11.13 THE STREUDING RATE-OF-CHANGE LIMITER FOR QUANTIZED SIGNALS

The circuit block diagram of Figure 11.13.1 is an analog rate limiter for quantized signals designed by Streuding (1977). It allows the smoothing of the change between the levels of quantized signal without affecting the signal's fidelity. The circuit can be also used as a noise filter with excellent results, since it rate limits noise pulses. The simple nonlinear control system of Figure 11.13.1 acts to limit the rate of change of its output. It can be easily

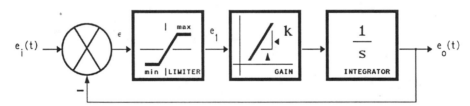

Figure 11.13.1   System-level representation of an analog rate limiter for quantized signals according to Streuding (1977).

implemented with an operational amplifier and a few passive components. Its applications range from D/A interface tasks to noise filtering and sample-data control systems. Although the author is aware of various other software- and hardware-based smoothing techniques (Ganesan, 1983; Grossblatt, 1984; Hester, 1984; Jess, 1968; Nielsen, 1979; Wagner, 1980), the Streuding circuit has been proven easy to implement and very useful in simulations (Karayanakis, 1991).

Figure 11.13.2 shows the simulator diagram (STREUDING.sim) where the quantized test signal is formed by generating a sinusoidal waveform (blocks #1 through #4) and sending it through a sample-and-hold (SPL) block. The resulting quantized waveform is then imputed into the rate-of-change limiter (blocks #6 through #9). It can be seen that the

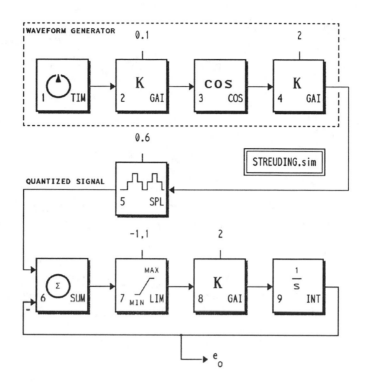

Figure 11.13.2 The simulator of the Streuding circuit.

limiter (block #7) bounds the error single *before* it is integrated to produce the output e_0. By virtue of the unity gain feedback loop, it is $e_0 \simeq e_i$ and therefore the error is a time derivative of the input. Limiting the error signal results in limiting the maximum rate of change of e_0. The circuit smoothes the quantized input waveform. The reader should investigate this useful device for the values shown in Figure 11.13.2 by plotting c_0 and the quantized signal first and then by plotting e_0 and the original waveform so the phase error is assessed.

11.14   THE GENERATION OF z-PLANE DAMPING RATIO CURVES

Sampled data (SD) systems involve system state transition according to a sampled sequence $f^*(t)$ having a Laplace transform $F^*(s)$ so that

$$F^*(s) = \sum_{n=0}^{\infty} f(nT)\, e^{-nTs} \tag{1}$$

where T is the sampling period. If we define

$$z = e^{Ts} \tag{2}$$

we can write the z-transform of $f^*(t)$ as

$$F(z) \; = \; F^*(s) \tag{3}$$

or

$$F(z) \; = \; \sum_{\mu=0}^{\infty} f(nT)\, z^{-n} \tag{4}$$

and thus define the z-plane, viewing z as a function of s according to Equation (2). Like the s-plane in the analog domain, the z-plane is useful in the design of discrete (sampled data) systems.

Here we are interested in the z-plane damping ratio curves as related to root locus techniques for SD systems. The relationships between the root locus techniques of analog and SD systems are established by considering the damping factor ζ, the frequency ω and the damping ratio δ as shown in the s-plane (Figure 11.14.1) where

$$\psi \; = \; \cos^{-1} \delta \tag{5}$$

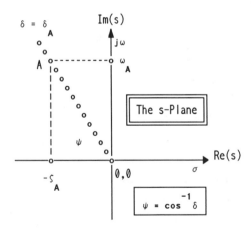

Figure 11.14.1   Defining the s-plane parameters.

The above relationship defines a family of δ-lines and the s-plane root locus may be easily constructed. In the case of the z-plane, we map the s-plane into the z-plane according to Equation (2). The line defined by $Re(s) = \sigma = $ constant maps into the circle in the z-plane with radius $r = e^{\sigma T}$. The line defined by $Im(s) = \omega = $ constant maps into the ray in the z-plane at angle ω (radians). When $s = j\omega$, then

$$z \; = \; e^{j\omega T} \tag{6}$$

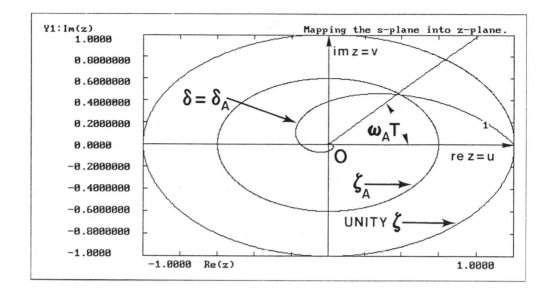

Figure 11.14.2   Illustrating the process of mapping the s-plane into z-plane.

that is, z is a unit magnitude phasor at an angle $\theta = \omega T$. Therefore, the jω-axis in the s-plane becomes the unit circle in the z-plane as shown in Figure 11.14.2. Essentially, the stable region of the s-plane (left half) maps into the interior of the unit circle in the z-plane, and the right half of the s-plane maps into the exterior of the unit circle. The radial ωT lines and the concentric ζ circles define the δ damping ratios. The damping ratio lines of the s-plane map into logarithmic spirals on the z-plane according to the equation

$$z = \exp \left| - \frac{\sigma}{\sqrt{1 - \delta^2}} \, \omega T \right| \exp(j\omega T) \tag{7}$$

Equation (7) is simplified by substituting

$$\frac{\delta}{\sqrt{1 - \delta^2}} = k \tag{8}$$

and

$$\omega T = t \tag{9}$$

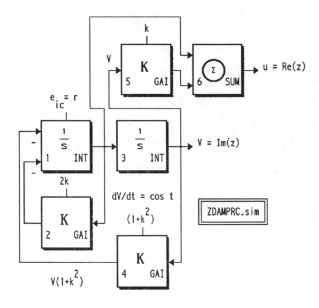

Figure 11.14.3   The mechanization of Equation (14) (see text).

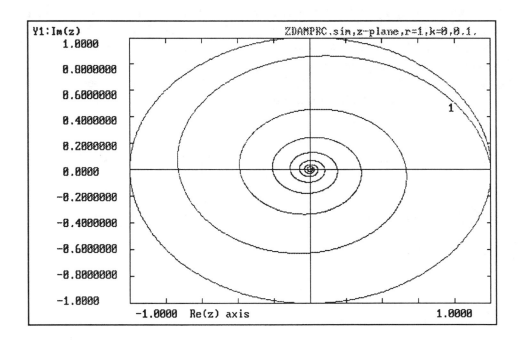

Figure 11.14.4   Output of ZDAMPRC.sim (z-plane) for $e_{ic} = r = 1$
with $k = 0$ (circle) and 0.1 (converging spiral).

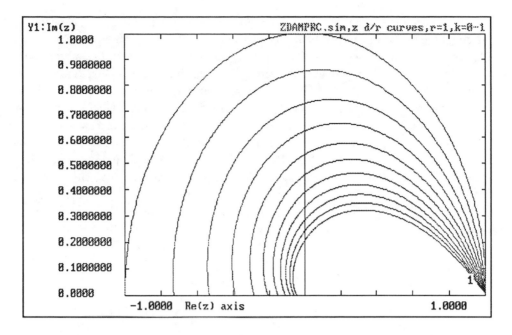

Figure 11.14.5   A group of z-plane damping ratio curves (k = 0 - 1) (from ZDAMPRC.sim).

so that

$$z = e^{-kT} e^{jT} \tag{10}$$

or

$$
\begin{aligned}
z &= e^{-kt} (\cos t + j \sin t) \\
&= e^{-kt} \cos t + j e^{-kt} \sin t
\end{aligned}
\tag{11}
$$

Therefore, the complex variable z has the real part

$$\mathrm{R}\,e(z) = e^{-kt} \cos t = u \tag{12}$$

and the imaginary part

$$\mathrm{I}\,m(z) = e^{-kt} \sin t = v \tag{13}$$

Differentiating Equation (13) twice yields the second-order differential equation

$$\ddot{v} = -2k\dot{V} - (1 + k^2)v \tag{14}$$

which can be easily mechanized as shown in Figure 11.14.3 (ZDAMPRC.sim). Note that the initial condition $e_{ic} = r$ is arbitrary. It represents the radius of the unit circle when $k = 0$ (Figure 11.14.4). Actually the block diagram of Figure 11.14.3 (ZDAMPRC.sim) represents a harmonic oscillator similar to that of Section 3.2 but with rate damping. Integrator #1 generates the term cos t and integrator #3 outputs sin t (the integrator with the initial conditions generates the cosine, always. The explanation for this is simple: only the cosine may have nonzero initial conditions. Therefore, it is easy to generate ν and μ using Equations (12) and (13) and to plot the z-plane damping ratio curves of Figure 11.14.5. The more 'automated' setup of Figure 11.14.6 (ZDRC1.sim) is a useful modification of the previous simulator as it works with the MR command. This interesting and instructive simulation was first performed on an analog computer by Cook and Willems (1967). The block diagram language simulation approach used here provides considerable versatility over the analog computer and allows us to reexamine useful mathematical techniques like that of Cook and Willems in the light of modern simulation techniques.

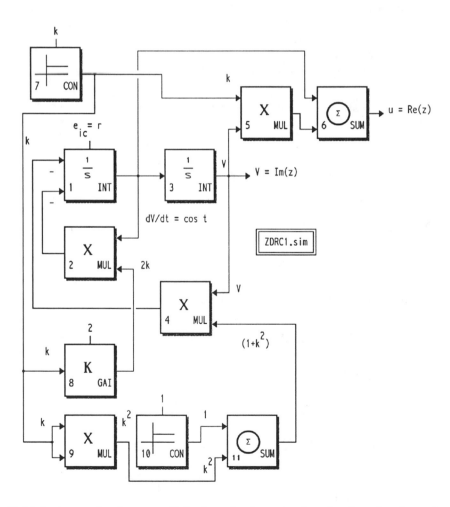

Figure 11.14.6   A somewhat 'automated' simulator for the generation of z-plane damping ratio curves.

12 | SOLVING PROBLEMS FROM DIVERSE DISCIPLINES

12.1   INTRODUCTION

The simulation topics in this part of the book have been selected to point out an unusual simulation approach, a useful technique or an obscure application. One of the author's goals is to revive analog/hybrid computer applications lost in time. The sections on conformal mapping are of considerable importance, especially since they are within the simulation capability of TUTSIM's student version. Perhaps some future simulation work in airfoil design and airflow visualization with block diagram languages will result. Although some of the topics and the supporting mathematical tools are somewhat specialized, it is hoped that the section will appeal to a sophisticated reader.

12.2   CONFORMAL MAPPING AND THE JOUKOWSKI AIRFOIL

A very interesting category of problems suitable for implementation with CDSS languages is that of conformal mapping. The technique relates functions in the z-plane where

$$z = x + iy \tag{1}$$

to another plane ω where

$$w = u + iv \tag{2}$$

by the transformation

$$w = f(z) \tag{3}$$

so that a complex region can be mapped into a simple coordinate system, thus allowing for an easier approach to solving boundary value problems. During the transformation the shape of the infinitesimal (but not the finite) elements is not altered. Angular relationships are maintained in the immediate region of a transformed point, given that f(z) is analytic at the point and $\dot{f}(z) \neq 0$.

If Equation (3) represents a nonviscous and irrotational potential flow pattern and equation

$$w \; = \; g(\varsigma) \tag{4}$$

represents another flow pattern, where ς is a complex variable so that

$$\varsigma \; = \; \xi \; + \; i\eta \tag{5}$$

the conformal transformation from the z-plane to the ς-plane is described by the equation

$$f(z) \; = \; g(\varsigma) \tag{6}$$

where x and y are the z-plane coordinates and ξ and η are the coordinates of the ς-plane. As Abbot and Von Doenhoff (1959) explain, plotting the known (z-plane) flow function on the ς-plane involves solving an equation of the form

$$\varsigma \; = \; h(z) \tag{7}$$

Then a circle can be transformed into an airfoil (wing section) by substitution of the variable

$$\varsigma \; = \; z \; + \; \frac{a^2}{z} \tag{8}$$

into the equation of flow about a cylinder (see Glauert, 1924; Theodorsen and Garrick, 1933; Tominson et al., 1955).

The Joukowski airfoil is mapped by considering the extended Joukowski transformation

$$\frac{\varsigma \; - \; nc}{\varsigma \; + \; nc} \; = \; \left(\frac{z \; - \; c}{\varsigma \; + \; c}\right)^n \tag{9}$$

written in the form

$$\varsigma \; = \; nc \left[\frac{(z \; - \; c)^n \; + \; (z \; + \; c)^n}{(z \; + \; c)^n \; - \; (z \; - \; c)^n}\right] \tag{10}$$

and then expanded into a binomial series

$$\varsigma \; = \; z \; + \; \frac{n^2 \; - \; 1}{3} \; \frac{c^2}{z} \; + \; \cdots \tag{11}$$

This is an infinite series as n is seldom an integer.

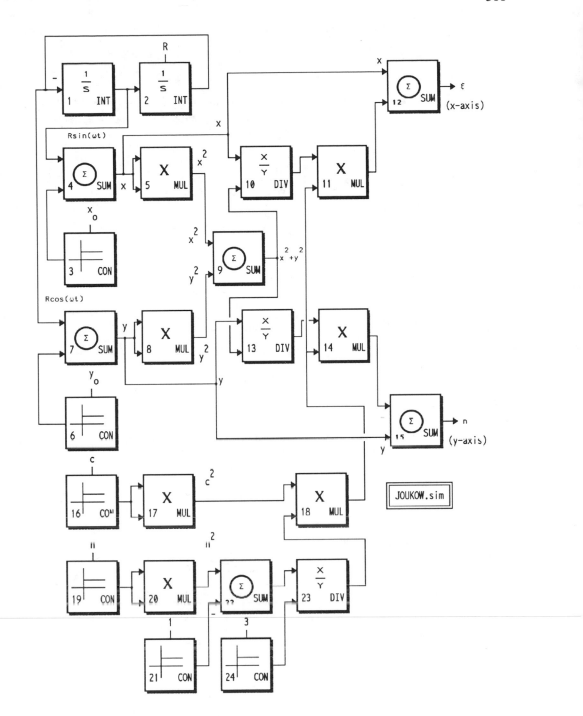

Figure 12.2.1   Implementation of Equations (13) through (16).

For any given point, the function

$$\varsigma \;=\; \varsigma\,(z) \tag{12}$$

determines the value of ς that defines a point on the ς-plane. Therefore by substituting Equations (1) and (5) into Equation (11) and then separate the real and imaginary parts, it is

$$\xi \;=\; x \;+\; \left(\frac{n^2 - 1}{3}\, c^2 \right) \frac{x}{x^2 + y^2} \;+\; \cdots \tag{13}$$

and

$$\eta \;=\; y \;-\; \left(\frac{n^2 - 1}{3}\, c^2 \right) \frac{y}{x^2 + y^2} \;+\; \cdots \tag{14}$$

The parametric equations of circle in the z-plane are

$$x \;=\; x_0 \;+\; R \sin \omega t \tag{15}$$

$$y \;=\; y_0 \;+\; R \cos \omega t \tag{16}$$

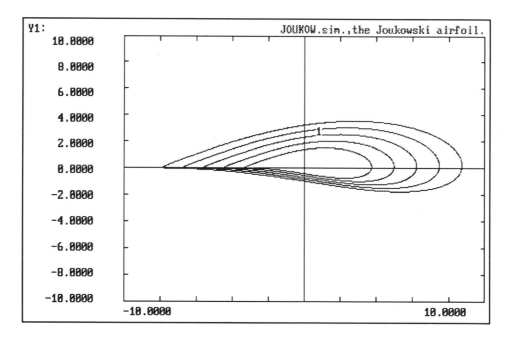

Figure 12.2.2 Joukowski profiles (R = 3, x_0 = 0.6, y_0 = 0.4, c = 1 and n = 4).

Therefore if x and y are within the value range specified by the system of Equations (15) and (16), the transformation Equations (13) and (14) will map these values into any given airfoil shape. An excellent discussion of the Joukowski profile development is by Abbot and Von Doenhoff (1959). Also, the books by Carrier et al. (1966) and Mathews (1988) provide rich information on the functions of a complex variable.

The block diagram of Figure 12.2.1 (JOUKOW.sim) is used to implement Equations (13), (14), (15) and (16). The harmonic oscillator circuit of Section 3.2 is used to generate the circle equations. Joukowski profiles of Figure 12.2.2 result for $R = 3$, $x_0 = 0.6$, $y_0 = 0.4$, $c = 1$ and $n = 4$. Two additional multipliers (not shown in Figure 12.2.1) driven by a scaling constant block were used to generate the profiles under a MR command.

12.3 THE HEINHOLD CONFORMAL MAPPING METHOD

Conformal mapping is realizable by the Heinhold method (Heinhold, 1959; Tomovic and Karplus, 1962) whereby the complex variable is represented in the form

$$z = x + iy \tag{1}$$

without the introduction of explicit polar coordinates. We therefore consider the mapping

$$w = f(z) = u(x,y) + iv(x,y) \tag{2}$$

and since time is the desired independent variable, the problem variables must take the form (Tomovic and Karplus, 1962)

$$z = x + iy$$
$$= x[\phi(t),\psi(t)] + iy[\phi(t),\psi(t)] \tag{3}$$

$$z = z(t) = x(t) = iy(t) \tag{4}$$

$$u = u[x(t),y(t)] = u(t) \tag{5}$$

$$v = v[x(t),y(t)] = v(t) \tag{6}$$

Then, Equation (2) can be rewritten in the form

$$w(t) \equiv f[z(t)]$$
$$= u[x(t),y(t)] + iv[x(t),y(t)] \tag{7}$$

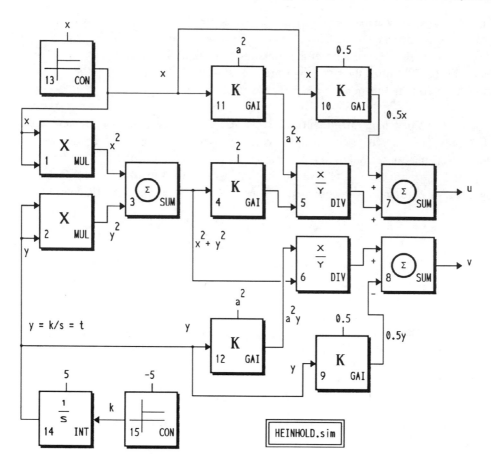

Figure 12.3.1   Implementation of the system of Equations (10) and (11).

or, from Equations (5) and (6) as

$$w(t) \;=\; u(t) \;+\; i\,v(t) \tag{8}$$

Given

$$w \;=\; \frac{1}{2}\left[z \;+\; \frac{a^2}{z}\right] \qquad\qquad a^2 \;<\; 1 \tag{9}$$

it is

$$u \;=\; \frac{x}{2} \;+\; \frac{a^2 x}{2\left(x^2 \;+\; y^2\right)} \tag{10}$$

and

$$v = \frac{y}{2} - \frac{a^2 y}{x^2 + y^2} \qquad (11)$$

The system of Equations (10) and (11) is simulated by the block diagram of Figure 12.3.1 (HEINHOLD.sim) where $y = k/s = t$. The u-v plot of Figure 12.3.2 is made with $a = 1$ and $x = 1, 0.8, 0.6$, and 0.4 The reader may want to investigate the effects of a when $a < 1$ or $a > 1$, assign additional scaling factors at the outputs and consider the adoption of a constant $b \neq a$ for the numerator of Equation (11) (block #12 in Figure 12.3.1).

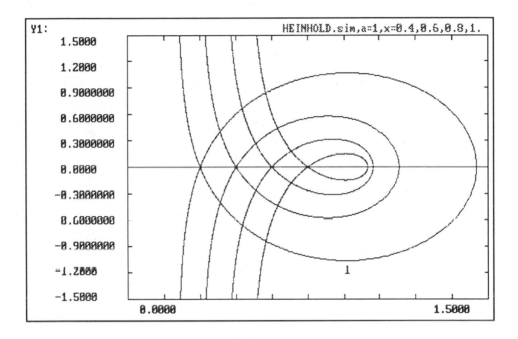

Figure 12.3.2   The results of HEINHOLD.sim   (u-v plot) for $a = 1$ and $x = 1, 0.8, 0.6$ and 0.4.

12.4   AN ELEMENTARY LUNG SIMULATION

The simple lumped element lung model of Figure 12.4.1(a) is described by the equation

$$R_f q + k \int_0^t q \, dt = P \qquad (1)$$

where R_f is the fluid resistance in the bronchi (air viscance), q is the volumetric flow rate of air and k is the spring constant due to the compressibility of the air. The constant P is

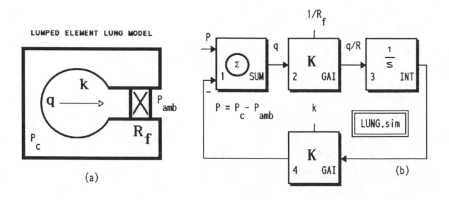

Figure 12.4.1   A lumped element lung model (a) and its simulator (b).

defined as the difference between the pressure P_c within the chest cavity (assumed identical to that of the alveoli) and the ambient air pressure P_{amb} at the buccal cavity, or

$$P = P_c \quad P_{amb} \tag{2}$$

The lung system, originally described by Jackson (1963), is easily simulated as shown in Figure 12.4.1(b). Readers may wish to investigate the system's response to a unit pulse and to a low frequency sinusoidal signal.

12.5   SOLVING THE LAMINAR BOUNDARY LAYER EQUATIONS

In fluid mechanics, boundary layer problems are usually solved on the digital computer. Analog computer techniques can also be used to provide fast and accurate results. Two important papers on this technique are by Dent and Mitchell (1967) who use an analog computer to solve various problems involving similarity variables and by Bartlett (1975) who employs repetitive operation techniques to solve the laminar boundary layer equations. The mostly ignored analog approach is revived here with a TUTSIM language adaptation.

The boundary layer formed by the steady flow of a viscous, incompressible fluid along a thin flat plate of infinite width at a $= 0°$ is considered here. Note that a is the *angle of attack* (U.S. notation) corresponding to the British term *incidence* found in most European writings. The equations of motion are

$$u\,\frac{\partial u}{\partial x} + v\,\frac{\partial u}{\partial y} = -\frac{1}{\rho}\frac{\partial p}{\partial x} + \nu\,\frac{\partial^2 u}{\partial y^2} \tag{1}$$

$$\frac{\partial u}{\partial x} + \frac{\partial v}{\partial y} = 0 \tag{2}$$

under the boundary conditions

$$
\begin{array}{llll}
u = v = 0 & \text{at} & y = 0 \\
u = U_\infty & \text{at} & y \rightarrow \infty \\
u = U_\infty & \text{at} & x = 0
\end{array}
$$

where

x,y	are space coordinates along and perpendicular to the plate
u,v	are the x- and y-direction velocity components
U_∞	is the freestream velocity (fluid velocity outside the boundary layer)
p	is the static pressure
ρ	is the fluid density
ν	is the kinematic viscosity of the fluid

The reader may recognize that Equations (1) and (2) are simplified forms of the Navier-Stokes equations due to Prandtl (1928) who shows that Equation (1) is a valid approximation assuming that viscous effects are confined to a thin layer over the surface. A variant of this equation where ν does not appear directly is discussed by Abbot and Von Doenhoff (1959).

In reality, the flow outside the boundary layer is potential governed by the Bernoulli equation

$$
\frac{dp}{dx} = - \rho \, U_\infty \, \frac{dU_\infty}{dx} \tag{3}
$$

We assume that the fluid is infinite in extent, so that $[dp/dx] = 0$. Then the system of Equations (1) and (2) simplify:

$$
u \, \frac{\partial u}{\partial x} + v \, \frac{\partial u}{\partial y} = \nu \, \frac{\partial^2 u}{\partial y^2} \tag{4}
$$

$$
\frac{\partial u}{\partial x} + \frac{\partial v}{\partial y} = 0 \tag{2R}
$$

In order to map the velocity distribution of the two-dimensional boundary layer of Figure 12.5.1 described by Equations (4) and (2), Bartlett (1975) uses the Blasius technique (Blasius, 1908) by adopting a boundary layer coordinate and a stream function. First, the similarity variable η is introduced

$$
\eta = \frac{y}{\delta} \tag{5}
$$

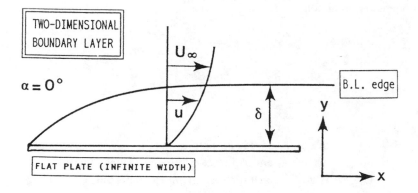

Figure 12.5.1   The two-dimensional boundary layer.

where δ is the boundary layer thickness ($\delta << x$). If $\mathrm{Re_x}$ is the Reynold's number based on x, so that

$$\mathrm{Re_x} \; - \; \frac{U_\infty x}{\nu} \tag{6}$$

then

$$\frac{\delta}{x} \; \sim \; \mathrm{Re_x}^{-\frac{1}{2}} \tag{7}$$

and

$$\delta \; \sim \; \left(\frac{\nu x}{U_\infty}\right)^{\frac{1}{2}} \tag{8}$$

Substitution in Equation (5) gives

$$\eta \; = \; y \sqrt{\frac{U_\infty}{\nu x}} \tag{9}$$

Secondly, a stream function ψ is introduced so that

$$u \; = \; \frac{\partial \psi}{\partial y} \tag{10}$$

$$v \; = \; - \frac{\partial \psi}{\partial x} \tag{11}$$

along with another dimensionless stream function f so that

$$\dot{f} = \frac{\partial f}{\partial \eta} = \frac{u}{U_\infty} \tag{12}$$

The Blasius equation is then obtained by computing the differentials of u and v and substituting into Equations (4) and (2) Dent and Mitchell, 1967; Bartlett, 1975). The symbol η denotes the nondimensional transverse displacement. It is

$$2 \frac{d^3 f}{d t^3} (\eta) + \frac{d^2 f}{d t^2} (\eta) \, f(\eta) = 0 \tag{13}$$

subjected to the following boundary conditions:

$$f(\eta) = \dot{f}(\eta) = 0 \quad \text{at} \quad \eta = 0 \qquad \left(f_0 = \dot{f}_0 = 0 \right)$$

$$\dot{f}(\eta) = 1 \qquad \text{for} \quad \eta = \infty \qquad \left(\dot{f}(\infty) = 1 \right)$$

Equation (13) is simulated in Figure 12.5.2. The output curve of Figure 12.5.3 (η vs [df/dt] and $\eta = t$) offers a very precise solution of the laminar boundary layer equations. It is of interest that Blasius solved Equation (13) by a approximate integration in a Taylor series (Bairstow, 1925). A numerical solution table of the Blasius results appears in Abbot and Von Doenhoff (1959).

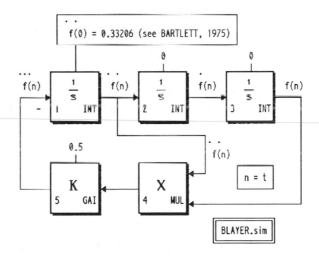

Figure 12.5.2 Implementing the Blasius technique (Equation 13).

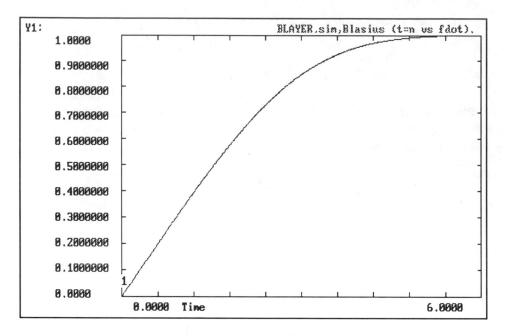

Figure 12.5.3 The solution curve of the Blasius equation (BLAYER.sim).

The discussion on boundary layer is incomplete without mentioning the Falkner-Skan equation

$$\frac{d^3 f}{dt^3}(\eta) + \frac{d^2 f}{dt^2}(\eta)\, f(\eta) + \beta \left[1 - \left(\frac{df}{dt}\right)^2 (\eta) \right] = 0 \qquad (14)$$

which is a sophisticated version of the Blasius equation (Schlichting, 1968; Cebeci and Keller, 1971; Marshall, 1973). Surprisingly enough, in their classic book *Theory of Wing Sections* first published in 1949 and subsequently reprinted with corrections in 1959, Abbot and Von Doenhoff (1959) do not mention the Falkner-Skan equation or reference the early works by Falkner and Skan (1931), Hatree (1937), Stewartson (1954) or the NACA report by Cohen and Reshotko (1956).

Equation (14) is important because, depending on boundary conditions and the pressure gradient parameter, it addresses important flow phenomena (Marshall, 1973) to include the wall boundary layer (Falkner and Skan, 1931; Hatree, 1937; Schlichting, 1968), reverse flow (Stewartson, 1954), separation (Falkner and Skan, 1931; Hatree, 1937; Schlichting, 1968), wakes (Stewartson, 1954; Kennedy, 1964; Steiger and Chen, 1965) and jets (Steiger and Chen, 1965). In his excellent review paper, Marshall (1973) uses CSMP (an IBM System/360 continuous system modelling language) to solve the Falkner-Skan equation.

12.6   THE QUANTUM-MECHANICAL OSCILLATOR

Quantum mechanics is an area where people tread lightly as they must deal with substantial amounts of combined mathematical and philosophical material. As Shirer points out in an early ACEUG Applications paper (Analog/Hybrid Computer Educational Users Group, now Computers in Education Group or CoED of the American Society for Engineering Education), analytic solutions to typical problems are often accompanied by formidable mathematical difficulties, often resulting in the student's loosing sight of the original problem. Shirer also states that all the advantages of the numerical approach are maintained when using an analog computer and, furthermore, the experimenter is not limited to the few cases which can be approached analytically. TUTSIM's tactical advantages over the analog/hybrid computer (e.g., no time or amplitude scaling and no static checks) make it a very impressive tool in the study and exposition of quantum mechanics.

The concept of quanta as introduced by Max Planck (1858-1947) is that of energy bundles exchanged by oscillations in the walls of a cavity filled with electromagnetic radiation. The interested reader is first referred to the excellent introductory article by Strnad (1981) which also offers a good historical background. Planck's constant, h, is of importance here, with action as a dimension (the product of energy multiplied by time). It is defined as the elementary quantum of action with a value (mks system) of 6.6260755E-34 joule-second. A modified form of h, the h-bar or Dirac h, $\hbar$, appears in most modern formulations of quantum mechanics, where $\hbar = h/\epsilon\pi$. The quantum-mechanical wave equation

$$\frac{\hbar^2}{2m} \frac{d^2\psi}{dx^2} = (U_{(x)} - E)\ \psi \tag{1}$$

where ψ is the wave function and $U_{(x)}$ is the potential energy function can be easily simulated. Obviously, when $U_{(x)} < E$ the system performs as a harmonic oscillator (Section 3.2) and when $U_{(x)} > E$ the solution switches to an exponential response (similar to the hyperbolic function generator of Section 6.2.2.).

TUTSIM can accommodate any analog/hybrid computer simulation model in this area, including Shirer's advanced experiments on quantum-mechanical eigenfunctions and those by Summers (1975, 1976, and 1978). The Summers papers are extremely valuable and most interesting, as the well-documented operational amplifier-based analog simulation circuits can be easily breadboarded or simulated with circuit analysis software or with a CDSS language (see also Hinson, 1976). Stewart (1976) presents an excellent and well-detailed paper on the simulation of the Schrödinger equation with a homemade analog computer (SHAC). Simulations for both the quantum-mechanical harmonic oscillator and the quantum-mechanical particle in a box are shown by Wylen and Schwarz (1973). In their paper the quantum-mechanical one-dimensional harmonic oscillator is described by the differential equation

$$\frac{d^2 \psi}{d\rho^2} = -2 \left(n + \frac{1}{2} \right) \psi + \rho^2 \psi \qquad (2)$$

where

$$\rho = r \left[\frac{mw}{\hbar} \right]^{\frac{1}{2}} \qquad (3)$$

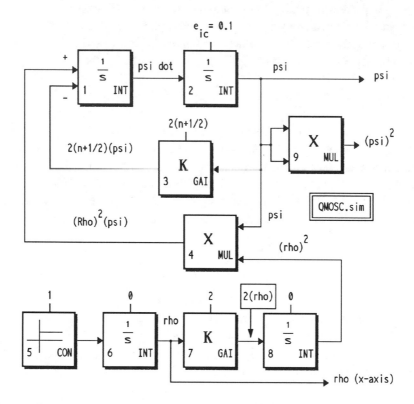

Figure 12.6.1   The simulator of the quantum-mechanical wave equation (Equation 1).

Equation (1) is implemented by using integrators to generate the integral power of ρ (see Section 6.3.1), the independent variable. The system exhibits sensitivity to the value of n, so that an oscillating solution diverges up to positive infinity or down to negative infinity rapidly after a few oscillations along the ρ (horizontal) axis. Figure 12.6.1 is the block simulator of Equation (1) (QMOSC.sim). Interesting initial experiments involve the values n = 5 → #3 GAI = 11 (downward departure) and n = 4.5 → #3 GAI = 10 (upward departure). Figure 12.6.2 shows the ψ and ψ^2 traces along the ρ-axis for n = 10 (#3 GAI = 22).

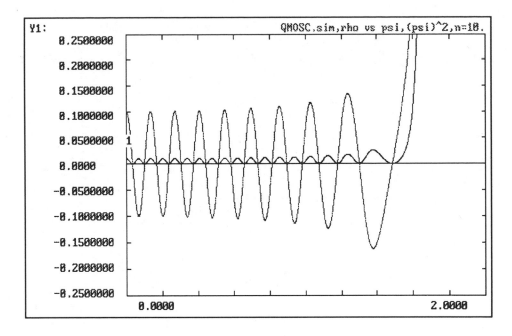

Figure 12.6.2   The results of QMOSC.sim.

12.7   THE ELOVICH EQUATION

A useful tool in correlating the kinetic data of chemisorption rates is the Elovich equation

$$\dot{q}(t) \ = \ a\,e^{-\alpha\,q(t)} \qquad q(0) \ = \ q_0 \tag{1}$$

where a, α and q_0 are constants to be selected when matching empirical data. As Sommerfeld (1968) points out, the integrated form of Equation (1) depends on initial conditions denoting the presence or absence of adsorbed gas at $t = 0$. Also if some initial amount of gas is absorbed at zero time, then $q(t = 0) = q_0$ and two variations exist depending whether the initial amount of gas was adsorbed according to the exponential law of Equation (1) or not. Sommerfeld proposes a complicated analog computer implementation of the Elovich equation requiring many side calculations. A subsequent paper by Krol (1969) employs the transformation

$$q(t) \ \triangleq \ \frac{1}{\alpha} \, \ell n \, \frac{a}{w} \tag{2}$$

to change the variables on both sides of Equation (1), yielding the quadratic, exponential-free relation

$$w(t) = -\alpha w^2(t) \qquad w(t) = \dot{q}(t) \qquad (3)$$

Initial conditions for the above equation are found by evaluating Equation (2) at $t = 0$, as in

$$w(0) = a \exp^{-\alpha q_0} = \dot{q}(0) \qquad (4)$$

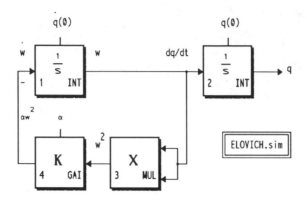

Figure 12.7.1   Simulating the Elovich equation.

Figure 12.7.1 (ELOVICH.sim) shows the simulation of Equations (2) and (3), where

$$a = \dot{q}(0) \, e^{\alpha q_0} \qquad (5)$$

Krol suggests that the model is used by estimating q_0 and dq_0/dt from visually inspecting a data plot and introducing first trial values, then adjusting α. The cycle may be repeated until the results are satisfactory. Essentially, an increase in q_0 increases the initial amount of adsorption, an increase in $[dq/dt](0)$ increases the initial adsorption rate, and α controls plot curvature. Readers may wish to investigate the effect of α on the plot's curvature under scaling conditions used in kinetic data correlation. For example, $\alpha = 7, 8, 9$ and 10 could be used.

12.8   RADIOACTIVE ISOTOPE DECAY

The natural decay of a radioactive isotope is described by the equation

$$A = A_0 \, e^{-\lambda t} \qquad (1)$$

where A is the amount (number of atoms) of the isotope at any time t, A_0 is the amount at $t = 0$ and λ is the decay constant ($\lambda = 0.693/$half life). The decaying isotope problem serves to demonstrate the automatic scaling features of TUTSIM.

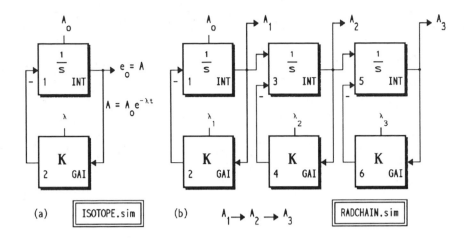

Figure 12.8.1 *The simulator of a radioactive isotope natural decay process (a) and a 3-stage decay series (b).*

The U^{238} isotope considered here has a half-life of 4.5E9 years or a decay constant of $\lambda = 1.54E-10$. If $A_0 = 10$mg, Equation (1) is written as

$$A = 10\, e^{-1.54E-10\,t} \qquad (2)$$

The block diagram of Figure 12.8.1(a) (ISOTOPE.sim) has the parameters $\lambda = 1.54$ and $A_0 = 10$ mg, so when scaling the graphic display we set Y1 as 0 - 10 mg U ^{238} and X (the zero block time axis) as 0-3E10 years (Figure 12.8.2). Excellent discussions of this problem in the analog computer context are presented by Zulauf and Burnett (1966), Evans (1974) and Wunderlich and Peastrel (1978). Berridge (1975) uses a FORTRAN-based digital method. The simple simulator of Figure 12.8.1(a) can be cascaded with others to simulate an n-stage radioactive decay process. If $A_1, A_2, ..., A_n$ are the amounts of the respective components of a decay series $A_1 \rightarrow A_2 \rightarrow ... \rightarrow A_n$ at any time t, the series is described by the following system of simultaneous differential equations:

$$\frac{dA_1}{dt} = A_{0_1}\lambda_1 \qquad (3)$$

$$\frac{dA_2}{dt} = A_{0_1}\lambda_1 - A_{0_2}\lambda_2 \qquad (4)$$

$$. . .$$

$$\frac{dA_n}{dt} = A_{0_{n-1}}\lambda_{n-1} - A_{0_n}\lambda_n \qquad (5)$$

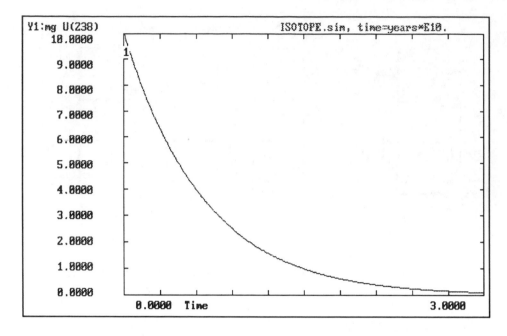

Figure 12.8.2　Results of ISOTOPE.sim.

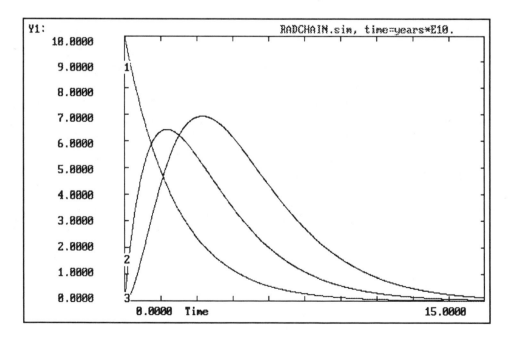

Figure 12.8.3　Results of RADCHAIN.sim.

A simulation example of a 3-stage process $(A_1 \rightarrow A_2 \rightarrow A_3)$ where $A_0 = 10$ mg, $\lambda_1 = 0.48$, $\lambda_2 = 0.67$ and $\lambda_3 = 0.74$ is shown in Figures 12.8.1(b) (RADCHAIN.sim) and Figure 12.8.3 (see also Wylen and Schwartz, 1973). Both of these examples are applications of the exponential function discussed in detail in Section 6.2.3.

In calculus courses the expression

$$y = C e^{\pm kt} \tag{1R}$$

is called the law of exponential growth and decay, where C is the *initial value* and k is the *constant of proportionality*. Exponential *growth* occurs when $k > 0$ and exponential *decay* is indicated when $k < 0$. In the case of radioactive decay, we consider the *half-life* of the isotope, i.e, the number of years required for the decay of half the atoms in a sample. The following table shows the half lives of some common radioactive isotopes:

Uranium (U^{238})	4.5×10^9 years
Plutonium (Pu^{230})	24,360 years
Carbon (C^{14})	5,730 years
Radium (Ra^{226})	1,620 years
Einstanium (Es^{254})	276 days
Nobelium (No^{257})	23 seconds

It is obvious that the very existence of radioactive materials, not to mention their poor management, has generated many problems for mankind.

12.9   TEMPERATURE TRANSDUCERS

The performance of feedback control systems in which transducers are used to provide feedback signals is closely tied to transducer performance. Temperature control is a case in point, where the slow response of an inexpensive transducer may be inhibiting. It is wise to consider transducer dynamics in control system simulation, rather than in closing perfect theoretical loops. The point is illustrated here by considering the thermocouple (TC) equation

$$\dot{T} = -\frac{1}{\tau} (T - T_m) \tag{1}$$

where τ is the TC time constant, T is the temperature indicated by the TC and T_m is the temperature of the ambient medium. The TC response involves different time constants for heating and cooling. In an early COED Note (Computers in Education of ASEE), Groves (1973) discusses an iron-constantan TC having a $1/\tau_{COOL} = 3.70$ s^{-1} and $1/\tau_{HEAT} = 2.85$ s^{-1}. The paper includes experimental data, analog and SMIMIC simulation

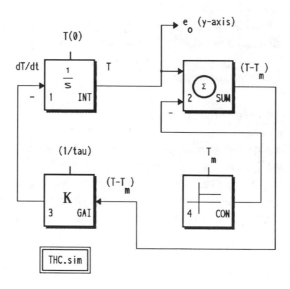

Figure 12.9.1   Simulation of a TC response.

results (SMIMIC is a variant of the early continuous dynamic system simulation language MIMIC, see Stechmann, 1972 and Stephenson, 1971).

Readers should plot the simulator of Figure 12.9.1 (THC.sim) outputs for $T(0) = 50°C$, $T_m = 200°C$ and $1/\tau_{HEAT} = 2.85$ s^{-1} ($\to \tau_{HEAT} = 0.350877$ s) and for $1/\tau_{COOL} = 3.70$ s^{-1} ($\to \tau_{COOL} = 0.27027...$ s). A modern alternative to the thermocouple is typified by the Analog Devices AD590 integrated circuit (IC) temperature transducer, having a $\tau = 13.5$ s ($\to 1/\tau = 0.074074 ...$ s^{-1}). Hutchings (1991) models the ic with the equation

$$\tau \, \frac{dV}{dt} + V = k \, (T_m + n) \tag{2}$$

where k is a steady-state gain ($= 0.1$), n is random white noise and V the voltage output (equivalent to T, the temperature indicated by the transducer as per Equation (1)). If $n = 0$, Equation (2) takes the form

$$\dot{V} = \frac{1}{\tau} \, (0.1 \, T_m - V) \tag{3}$$

Equations (2) and (3) can be easily simulated with TUTSIM. For further information on temperature transducers see Doebelin (1990).

12.10   PLOTTING TWO TEMPERATURE CONVERSION FORMULAE (INVERSE FUNCTIONS)

The well-known Centigrade-Fahrenheit conversion formulae are

$$f(F) \; = \; C \; = \; \frac{5}{9} \, (F \, - \, 32) \tag{1}$$

$$f(C) \; = \; F \; = \; C \, \frac{9}{5} \, + \, 32 \tag{2}$$

Mathematically, the two functions above are *inverse* with respect to each other.

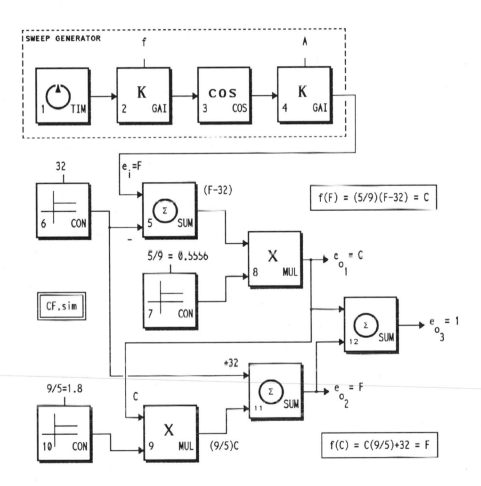

*Figure 12.10.1   This simulator allows the plotting of the two
Centigrade-Fahrenheit temperature conversion formulae.*

The simulator of Figure 12.10.1 (CF.sim) is useful in the instruction of inverse functions, intercepts, and the like. It mechanizes both Equations (1) and (2) simultaneously, thus allowing their plotting by superimposing the C-F and the F-C plots that intercept each other at about (-40, -40). Summing $e_0(1)$ and $e_0(2)$ produces a unity slope through quadrants I and III, thus verifying that $f(x)$ and $f^{-1}(x) = 1$.

12.11   MODELLING BACTERIA GROWTH

In the laboratory bacteria may be grown as batches or as continuous cultures. The rate of bacterial concentration (growth) for the batch culture is

$$\dot{x} = \mu \frac{s}{s + K_s} x \tag{1}$$

where x is the concentration of bacteria, μ is a growth constant, K_s is the saturation constant and s is the concentration of the substrate. It is

$$\dot{s} = - \frac{\mu}{Y} \frac{s}{s + K_s} x \tag{2}$$

where Y is the yield constant. The system of Equations (1) and (2) describe the batch culture mechanism.

In the case of the continuous culture—we also consider μ, K_s and Y as constants, an assumption that holds true for low flow rates of the culture medium. Given the volume of the culture vessel, v, and the flow rate of the medium, f, the dilution rate is $D = f/v$. The dilution rate is a significant control variable in the bacteria growth process. If s_R is the concentration of the limiting substrate of the inflowing medium, Equations (1) and (2) become

$$\dot{x} = \mu \frac{s}{s + K_s} x - Dx \tag{3}$$

$$\dot{s} = - \frac{\mu}{Y} \frac{s}{s + K_s} x + D \left(s_R - s \right) \tag{4}$$

In both cases (batch and continuous culture), when $f = 0$ (no flow rate), it is $D = 0$ and then Equations (3) and (4) reduce to Equations (1) and (2).

The generalized bacteria growth problem is described and simulated by Jamshidi (1971) on the EAI-680 hybrid computer. Jamshidi's report shows the complete solution trajectories for both batch and continuous processes, so the author decided to compare these results to those of TUTSIM. Having worked on the very same (expensive) machine situated at the Hybrid Computer Lab at the University of Illinois at Urbana-Champaign, the author

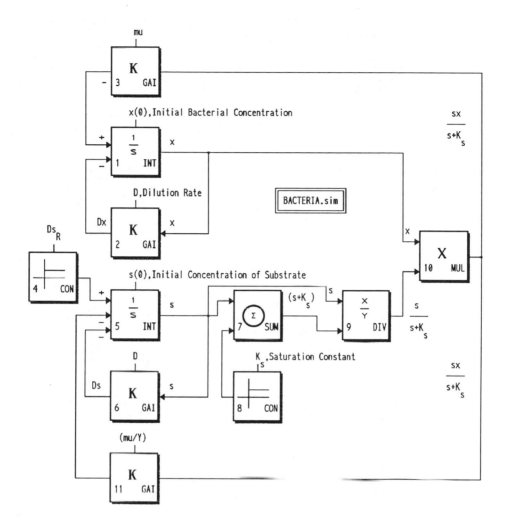

Figure 12.11.1   Block modelling of the bacteria growth process.

produced identical results with the TUTSIM simulator of Figure 12.11.1. The batch culture trajectories of Figure 12.11.2 are made with D = 0 (affecting blocks #2, 4 and 6) and K_s = 0.1. Figure 12.11.3 shows the continuous process trajectories where D = 1.5, s_R = 1.0 and K_s = 0.1. In both cases, trajectories are drawn by letting μ = 1 and Y − 1 and manipulating the initial conditions x(0) and s(0) as follows. For Figure 12.11.2, set s(0) = 1 and step x(0) via the MR command (case 1). Then set x(0) = 0.001 ($\approx$ 0) and step s(0) (case 2). For Figure 12.11.3, set s(0) = 0 and step x(0) (case 3) and then set s(0) = 1 and step x(0) (case 4).

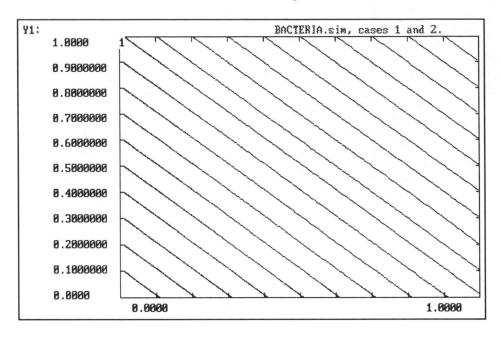

Figure 12.11.2   Batch culture trajectories for D = 0 and K_s = 0.1 (BACTERIA.sim)

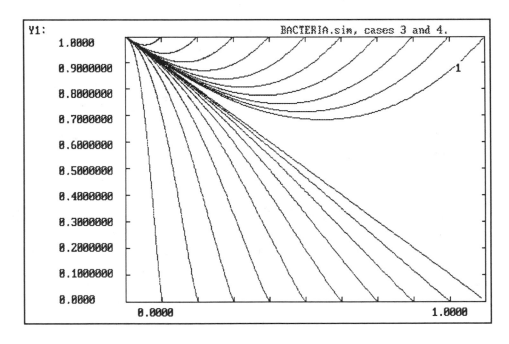

Figure 12.11.3   Continuous culture process trajectories (BACTERIA.sim).

12.12   THE LOTKA-VOLTERRA PROBLEM

The classical prey-predator problem of the Lotka-Volterra equation serves to demonstrate the utility of block diagram languages in solving nonlinear differential equations having a near-impossible analytic solution. The mathematical formulation of the problem is due to Lotka (1925, reprinted 1956) and Volterra (1928, reprinted 1931). It involves the phase plane investigation of the generalized autonomous system

$$\dot{x} \; = \; x \; (x, y) \tag{1}$$

$$\dot{y} \; = \; y \; (x, y) \tag{2}$$

This system describes various biological processes that occur as periodic functions of time under the synchronization of some biological clock. Typical processes may involve predator-prey relationships like that of the shark-food fish system of Volterra (1928), the limpet-seaweed system of Garfinkel (1967), and the wolf-caribou system of Spiegel (1981), to name a few. Problems examining relationships between hosts and parasites, inducible enzymes, insecticide and pesticide applications, and related events, are also cases of the Lotka-Volterra system.

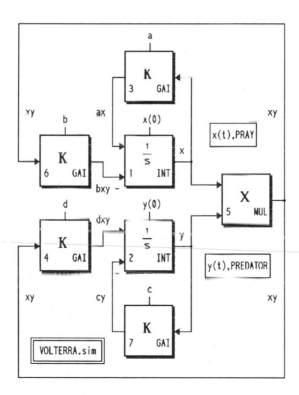

Figure 12.12.1   Simulation of the generalized autonomous Lotka-Volterra equation system.

In the original problem, Volterra considers two species of fish. There is a prey population of sharks x(t) that shows a net increase

$$\dot{x} = ax - bxy \qquad (3)$$

where the 'positive' increase (ax) accounts for births and natural deaths and a 'negative' increase (-bxy) is proportional to the number of encounters with predators. The prey population of food fish y(t) shows a net increase

$$\dot{y} = -cy + dxy \qquad (4)$$

where the term (-cy) denotes death due to starvation and (dxy) is the compensating growth rate proportional to the number of encounters with prey. The system of Equations (3) and (4) is simulated as shown in Figure 12.12.1. The results of Figure 12.12.2 are for y(0) = 10, x(0) = 40, 60, and 80.

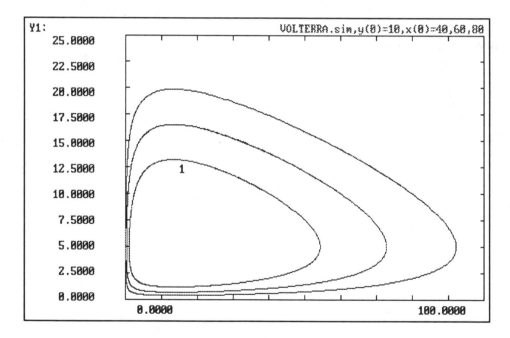

Figure 12.12.2   Results of VOLTERRA.sim (y(0) = 0, x(0) = 40, 60, and 80).

Mathematical investigation of the Lotka-Volterra problem appear in Jordan and Smith (1988), Spiegel (1981), Mohler (1991) and Davis (1962). The growth and regulation of biological populations are discussed by Goel et al. (1971), Slobodkin (1961), Brauer et al. (1976), Garfinkel (1967), Pielou (1969), Brennan et al. (1970), Rosen (1973), Murray (1979), Strebel (1979) and Peterson et al. (1984). The reader is also referred to the outstanding book on mathematical models in biology by Leah Edelstein-Keshet (1988) for a complete and lucid coverage of the topic.

12.13   THE GENERATION OF DISTRIBUTION FUNCTIONS

One extraordinary feature of block diagram languages is the ability not only to simulate the mathematical model in hand, but also some or all of the supporting signal processing functions. This important feature becomes apparent when the experimenter demands not just the output of a process but some statistical indicator of system performance. CDSS languages allow the building of virtual signal processing units on the basis of their mathematical model. These computational macros are equivalent to the analog/hybrid computer circuits found in the literature, most of which can be easily implemented with block diagram languages. In this section we show a few statistical signal processing devices and discuss the mechanics of their implementation. These devices can also be useful in real I/O situations, where a computer serves a specialized data processing unit.

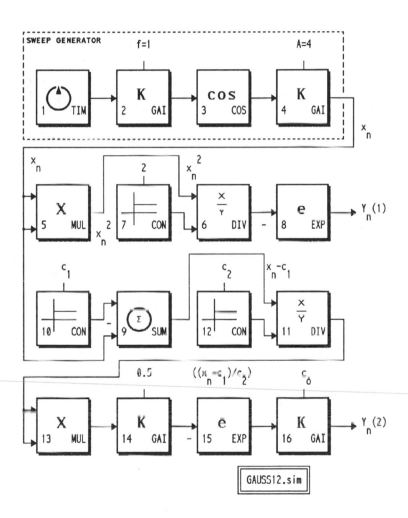

Figure 12.13.1   A generalized Gaussian function simulator.

The generalized two-dimensional bell-shaped function curve is important in signal processing. Bell-shaped functions are necessary in the statistical analysis of signals. They are used in statistical weighting, noise filtering, spectral analysis and many other specialized tasks. Statistical bell-shaped functions are also found in areas like chromatography, spectroscopy, pharmacology and chemistry, to name a few.

Bell-shaped transfer characteristics can be generated with multifunction converter integrated circuits (Graeme, 1977b), by polynomial synthesis (Dimitrov, 1990) or various other analog, digital or hybrid techniques. Here, our goal is to simulate the generalized bell-shaped transfer characteristic with simple analog blocks. The normalized Gaussian function described by the equation

$$Y_n = \exp\left[-\frac{X_n^2}{2}\right] \tag{1}$$

is simulated by Figure 12.13.1 (GAUSS12.sim) by blocks #5 through #8. A more versatile Gaussian peak characteristic with a center parameter c_1, a width parameter c_2 and an amplitude term c_0 is

$$Y_n = c_0 \exp\left[-0.5\left(\frac{X_n - c_1}{c_2}\right)^2\right] \tag{2}$$

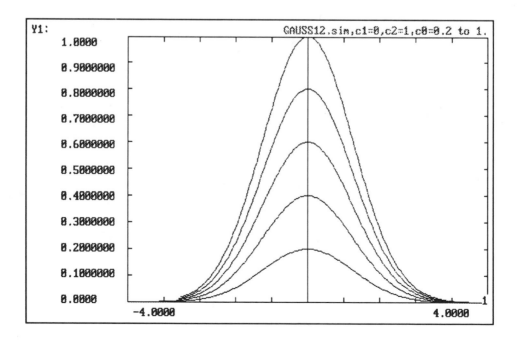

Figure 12.13.2   Results of GAUSS12.sim ($c_0 = 1$, $c_1 = 0$ and $c_2 = 1$).

Note that Equation (1) is derived from Equation (2) by letting $c_0 = 1$, $c_1 = 0$ and $c_2 = 1$. Figure 12.13.2 shows the curve for $c_1 = 0$, $c_2 = 1$ and $c_0 = 0.2, 0.4, 0.6, 0.8$, and 1. The reader may want to investigate the effects of c_1 and c_2 upon the transfer plot. An excellent paper by Brown (1991) discusses this and many other 'peak equations'—like the Lorentzian, the logistic, the log-normal function and others. Also, analog and hybrid computation techniques are described by Cameron (1965) and Bargh (1970).

12.14   THE EXPONENTIALLY-MAPPED PAST ESTIMATE OF THE MEAN

Generally speaking, exponentially-mapped past statistical variables, or EMP variables, are quantities relating to a set of observations computed so that the contribution of recent observation values is more powerful than that of the values observed in the more distant past. EMP variables are functions of time and they are useful in forecasting, control and detection problems. The EMP estimate of the mean (or exponentially-weighted average), is a sophisticated averaging technique. There are many different averages, but the most apparent definition of the average value of a continuously observable variable $f(t)$, observed over the interval $t_1 \leq t \leq t_2$ is

$$ f(\bar{t}) \; = \; \frac{1}{t_2 - t_1} \int_{t_1}^{t_2} f(t) \; dt \tag{1}$$

or, in more general terms

$$ f(\bar{t}) \; = \; \lim_{t \to \infty} \frac{1}{t} \int_{-t/2}^{t/2} f(t) \; dt \tag{2}$$

The equation above can be physically realized with a single integrator. However, integrators are subject to saturation and reset. The circuit will output a moving average involving the abrupt and total rejection of past information. Given that $f(t)$ is a continuous variable, it is desirable that past information is rejected *gradually*. This implies that $f(\bar{t})$ must be expressed in terms of *both recent* and *past* values where the recent values weight *more heavily* than the earlier ones. We are therefore seeking a weighted average. Mathematically, the weighted average $f(\bar{t})$ of a continuous function $f(t)$ over the observation interval $t_1 \leq t \leq t_2$ with a weight function $\phi(t)$ is defined by the equation

$$f(\bar{t}) = \left[\int_{t_1}^{t_2} f(t)\, \phi(t)\, dt \right] \left[\int_{t_1}^{t_2} \phi(t)\, dt \right]^{-1} \tag{3}$$

where $\phi(t) \geq 0$ over the interval $t_1 \leq t \leq t$ (Davenport and Root, 1958). The above equation has been normalized by the denominator integral. We must now decide on the weights to be assigned to each part of the time integral from t_1 to t_2. The continuous time-varying average must have a time constant and an increasing weighting function $\phi(t)$ must be chosen so that

$$\lim \phi(t) = 0 \quad\quad t = -\infty \tag{4}$$

An obvious solution is the implementation of an *exponentially decaying memory*. This becomes apparent if we'd consider the generalized differential equation describing the averaging process of a continuously observable variable $f(t)$.

$$\frac{df(\bar{t})}{dt} = a\left[f(t) - f(\bar{t}) \right] \tag{5}$$

where a is the reciprocal of the time constant (time constant $\tau = 1/a$). By choosing

$$\psi(t) = e^{at} \tag{6}$$

where $a > 0$, equation (3) can be written

$$f(\bar{t})_a = \left[\int_{t_1}^{t_2} e^{at} f(t)\, dt \right] \left[\int_{t_1}^{t_2} e^{at}\, dt \right]^{-1} \tag{7a}$$

or in the original Otterman (1960) form

$$f(\bar{t})_a = \int_{-\infty}^{T} \left[(f(t)\, e^{at}\, dt) \left(\int_{-\infty}^{T} e^{at}\, dt \right)^{-1} \right] \tag{7b}$$

or

$$f\left(\bar{t}\right)_a = \left[\int_{t_1}^{t_2} e^{at} f(t) \, dt\right] \left(e^{at_2} - e^{at_1}\right)^{-1} \tag{8}$$

Solving Equation (5) in integral form yields

$$f\left(\bar{t}\right)_a = a \int_{-\infty}^{t} f(\tau) \, e^{a(\tau-t)} \, dt \tag{9}$$

where τ is the integration constant and $0 > t > -\infty$ is the time interval. It is:

$$\int_{-\infty}^{0} e^{at} \, dt = \frac{1}{a} \tag{10}$$

where, again, $1/a$ is the time constant and the a coefficient used to normalize Equation (9) (see also Equation (7)). From Equation (9) we conceptualize $f(t)_a$ as the average of $f(\tau)$, determined from information available until time t. In the case of a negative t-value, i.e., an arbitrary instant t in the past, Equation (9) can be expressed as

$$f\left(\bar{t}\right)_a = a e^{-at} \int_{-\infty}^{t} f(\tau) \, e^{a\tau} \, d\tau \tag{11}$$

Note that the equation above may also be derived directly from Equation (8) by letting $t_1 = -\infty$ and performing the necessary manipulations. For a unit step function u(t) where $u(t) = 1$ for $t \geq 0$ and $u(t) = 0$ for $t < 0$, Equation (11) can be written as

$$f\left(\bar{t}\right)_a = a \int_{-\infty}^{\infty} f(\tau) \, e^{a(\tau-t)} \, u(\tau - t) \, d\tau \tag{12}$$

Equation (12) is the convolution integral of $f(\tau)$, describing the output of a filter having impulse response ae^{-at}, i.e., a first-order, low-pass filter with time constant $1/a$. Equation (12) can be physically realized by a 'leaky' integrator with a leakage time constant

RC = 1/a, (a simple integrator with a feedback loop) as shown in the analog computer diagram of Figure 12.14.1(a) and the TUTSIM simulator of Figure 12.14.1(b) (EMPEST.sim). Note that the exponential function and its mechanization are discussed in detail in Section 6.2.3.

It is important to understand the role of the a constant. Essentially, its value controls the *rate at which past information becomes obsolete*. An arbitrary constant with a value large enough to filter out meaningless random signals and yet small enough to ignore past trends is chosen. A useful value is that of 3/a, where a step f(t) results in an $\overline{f(t)}_a$ that makes 95% of the change in three time constants; the integrator 'forgets' 95% of the information it had prior to the step input. The output $\overline{f(t)}_a$ is, then, a running average for the time interval $\Delta t = 3/a$. Similarly, if a setting of 5/a is used, the integrator will 'forget' approximately 99% of the past information. This implies that the weighted average $\overline{f(t)}_a$ will not be influenced by occurances prior to time (t - 5/a).

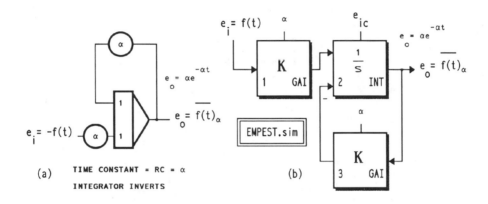

*Figure 12.14.1 Analog computer notation of a 'leaky' integrator (a)
and its block diagram simulator (b).*

Estimates of $\overline{f(t)}_a$ can be introduced as initial conditions to the integrator (Figure 12.14.1(b)). For the purpose of improving the initial computation and reducing solution time, a good guess of the expected $\overline{f(t)}_a$ value may be introduced (e_{ic}). A wrong guess will only affect the output for a few time constants, as per the a setting. The circuit does not show instability when t = 0. There is, however, a drawback: a linear trend will *lag* by an amount [(1 - a)/a] times the rate of change of the trend, something undesirable in forecasting (Lewis, 1966).

APPENDIX:
USEFUL DEVICES AND EXPERIMENTS

A.1 INTRODUCTION

The appendix is a collection of 'devices' used by the author in various projects over time. Many serve to demonstrate alternative thinking at the block level. Others show the versatility of some typical mathematical blocks. Years of exposure to CDSS languages have convinced the author that the user is the ultimate obstacle to a project's success. Examples in this appendix are offered as a somewhat metaphysical attempt to address the issue.

A.2 SYNTHESIZING WAVEFORMS FROM PULSES

It is possible to create a custom waveform $f(y,t)$ having a user-defined shape by synthesizing successive voltage ramps generated from driving an integrator by a succession of pulses having the appropriate amplitudes and durations. The process is analogous to producing a function curve $f(x,y)$ by a series of straight line segments as in diode function generators (Urbanek, 1975).

As a case in point we sum the signals

$$
\begin{aligned}
e_1(t) &= \text{PLS } (2,3,1) \\
e_2(t) &= \text{PLS } (3,4,0.5) \\
e_3(t) &= \text{PLS } (4,5,0.2) \\
e_4(t) &= \text{PLS } (5,6,-0.2) \\
e_5(t) &= \text{PLS } (6,7,-0.5) \\
e_6(t) &= \text{PLS } (7,8,-1)
\end{aligned}
$$

at the input of an integrator so that

$$
e_0 - (y,t) = k \int_0^t (e_1 + e_2 + e_3 + e_4 + e_5 + e_6)\, dt \tag{1}
$$

where k is the gain of the output as shown in Figure A.2.1. The resulting symmetrical function is shown in Figure A.2.2. This is a very versatile approach to the synthesis of

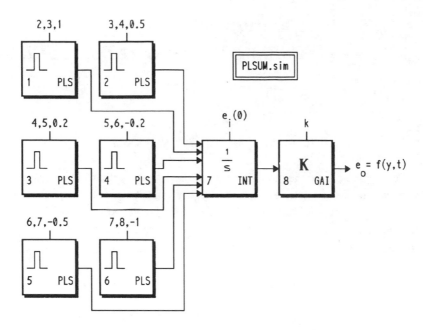

Figure A.2.1   Synthesizing a custom waveform form pulses.

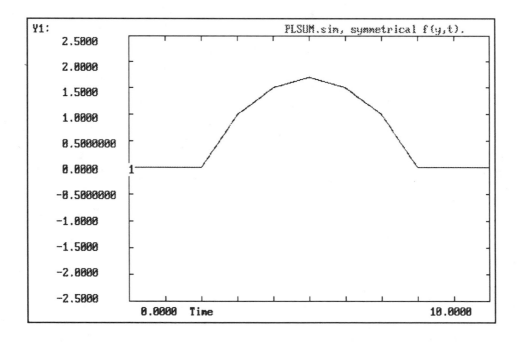

Figure A.2.2   The results of PLSUM.sim.

custom waveforms, often required in simulation and the testing of systems. The device described here may be modified in many ways; for instance, the constituent ramps may be generated from pulses of negative polarity and the output can be shifted by introducing initial conditions on the integrator. As in the case of any piecewise-linear approximation method, the higher the number of segments, the greater the smoothness and precision of the output.

A.3   A SIGNAL-CONTROLLED CHIRP FUNCTION

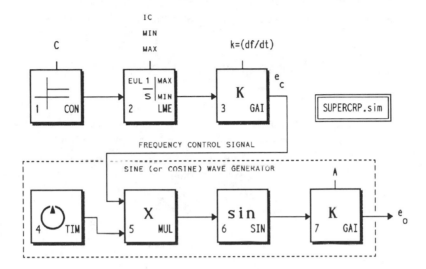

Figure A.3.1   A signal-controlled chirp generator.

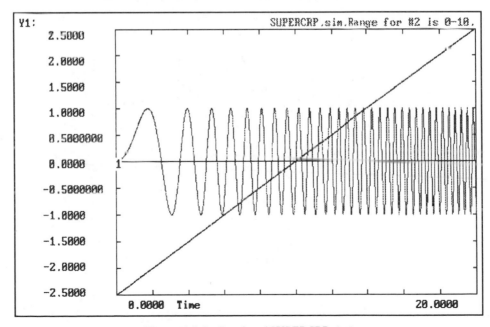

Figure A.3.2   Results of SUPERCRP.sim.

TUTSIM's frequency generation block (CRP) is very useful in system testing whenever a waveform of increasing frequency (chirp signal) is needed. Figure A.3.1 shows a device for the generation of a *signal controlled* chirp waveform that can be tailored to user needs. It consists of a modified sine/cosine wave generator (blocks #4 through 7) with the frequency controlling gain block replaced by a multiplier. The control signal $e_c = [df/dt]$ is supplied by integrating a constant C via an Euler limiting integrator block (LME). Figure A.3.2 shows the chirp output for $k = 0.5$, $A = 2$ and LME $= 0,0,20$. If a signal-controlled amplitude capability is required, the gain block (#7) is replaced by a multiplier. Of course, the same thing goes for block #3. Like the CRP block, this device requires a small delta time for accuracy.

A.4   SINEWAVE WITH LINEARLY INCREASING AMPLITUDE

A two-phase waveform generator capable of outputing sine and cosine signals with linearly increasing amplitude is shown in Figure A.4.1. It was used by the author to test a control system design. Two harmonic oscillators are combined; the initial conditions are applied on integrator #4. To maintain proper phase relationships throughout the system, all gain block settings (#1, #3, #5 and #7) must be equal.

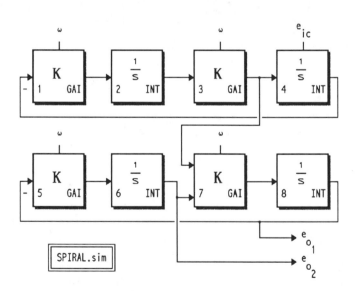

Figure A.4.1   Generating a cosinusoidal waveform with linearly increasing amplitude.

A.5   A VERSATILE WAVEFORM CONVERTER

The setup of Figure A.5.1 is another application of the versatile IFE block. A function generator (blocks #1, #2, #3 and #4) outputs the signal $f(t) = A \cos (2\pi ft)$ used as the control input e_c of the IFE block. When the waveform f(t) is positive, the IFE block takes

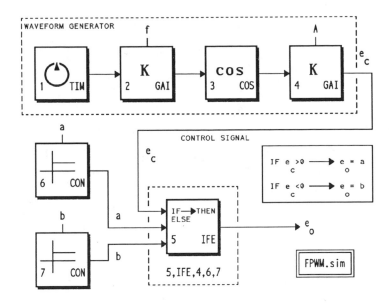

Figure A.5.1 A versatile waveform converter with many practical applications.

its input from block #6 ($e_i(1) = a$). When it is negative the IFE block takes its input from block #7 ($e_i(2) = b$). This general mechanism suggests many practical applications based on the arrangement of Figure A.5.1. A cosinusoidal to rectangular wave converter can be easily implemented. When $a > a$ and $b < 0$, the IFE block outputs a rectangular waveform symmetrical about zero if $|a| = |-b|$. Asymmetrical zero-crossing waveforms occur when $|a| = k|-b|$ or $k|a| = |-b|$ where k is an arbitrary positive constant. The reader may want to investigate the output of the IFE block for an f and 2f control input. This is a form of a frequency-to-pulse width conversion. If $a > 0$ and $b = 0$, the IFE block acts as a zero-crossing detector for positive peaks. If $a = 0$ and $b < 0$, we have a zero-crossing detector for negative peaks. Thus, the device can be adjusted to output positive or negative logic signals any time it detects a crossing waveform.

A.6   A SPECIAL MULTIFUNCTION GENERATOR

The versatile function generator of Figure A.6.1 (FUNGEN.sim) provides a square (or *trapezoidal*) waveform and a *triangle*, a *parabolic* and a *circular* waveform. The parabolic waveform can be seen in the context of a ball thrown with forward and upward velocities to a parabolic trajectory. Gravity reverses when the ball hits the ground and the ball follows a parabolic trajectory below ground level, and so on. The LIM block (#1) performs a comparator function and decides the sign of the acceleration. The triangular waveform output of the LMI block (#3) represents the ball's velocity. The output of the INT block (#5) is the displacement. The GAI block (#6) determine *how hard* the comparator (LIM) block is driven. Note that hard limiting produces a varying acceleration and soft limiting contributes to a lesser distortion. Finally, blocks #7 through #10 convert the

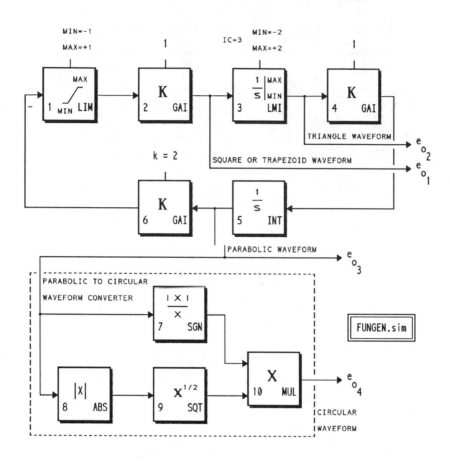

Figure A.6.1   A function generator for triangular, parabolic and circular waveforms.

parabolic waveform to a circular one. Figure A.6.2 shows the outputs of the generator. Both the parabolic and the circular waveforms are useful in system testing and should not be confused with the sine and cosine waveforms.

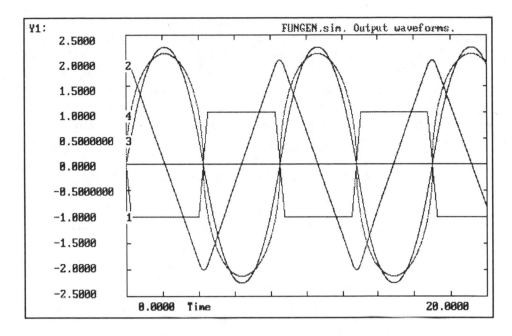

Figure A.6.2   Results of FUNGEN.sim.

A.7   STAIRCASE GENERATION

This is a unique application of the SOC (Strobe On Condition) block. The SOC block is an external command sample and hold block where the input value is sampled and stored each time the control input goes from FALSE (negative or zero) to TRUE (positive) state. Figure A.7.1 shows the block diagram for a staircase generator (STAIR.sim) that has two SOC blocks in a 'bucket brigade' configuration (this is hybrid computer talk for two cascaded

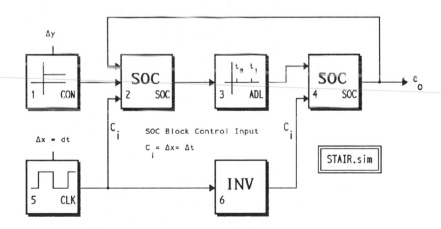

Figure A.7.1   A staircase generator.

track-and-store units). The SOC blocks are separated by an ADL block so that algebraic loops are avoided. Note the use of the logical invertor (INV) block, so that during a run the parameter c_i for SOC #2 is TRUE and c_i for SOC #4 is FALSE, making SOC #4 is holding a constant value of x. Meanwhile, as SOC #2 is sampling, its output is $(x + \Delta x)$ passes from SOC #2 to SOC #4. This sample is held during the next run while SOC #2 is incremented to $(x + 2\Delta x)$. Parameters Δy and $\Delta x = dt$ are determined by the CON (#1) and CLK (#5) blocks, respectively. This staircase generator is very useful in system testing and in achieving repetitive operation in problem solving.

A.8   A PERIODIC STAIRCASE GENERATOR

Figure A.8.1 shows an extension of the previous staircase generator. Its output is a fully adjustable periodic staircase. Here the REL (#7) block acts as a comparator having a

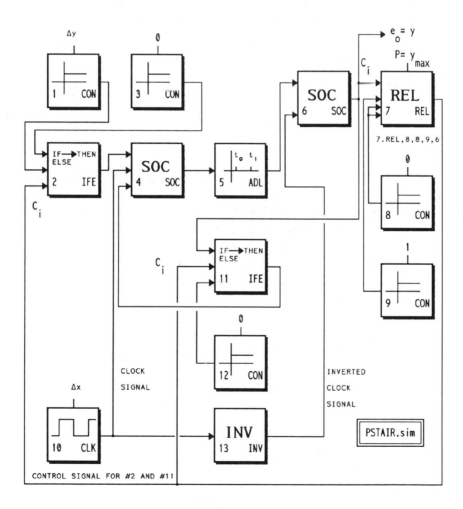

Figure A.8.1   A periodic staircase generator.

LOW output when $y < y_{max}$, controlling the IFE blocks (#2 and #11)that act as analog switches. Each staircase builds up until $y \geq y_{max}$, when the output of REL (#7) becomes HIGH and the IFE blocks (#2 and #11) switch to CON #3 and CON #12, respectively (both have $P = 0$), thus zeroing the staircase. Note that y_{max} is set by the REL (#7) parameter.

A.9 DRAWING GRIDS

When a solid line grid is required as in the case of a 10x10 grid, the single block program "1,CON" will do the trick. First, assign H:0,0,10 and Y1:1,0,10. Use the MR command as follows: Block number:1; Parameter Number:1; Parameter Starting Value:1; Parameter End Value:9; Parameter Step Size:1. Then assign H:1,0,10 and Y1:0,0,10 and use the MR command again. Any parameter step size can be specified and the screen can be divided by a *combination* of grids. Also, by limiting either H or Y1, only *part* of the screen can be divided.

A.10 CIRCULAR SWEEP

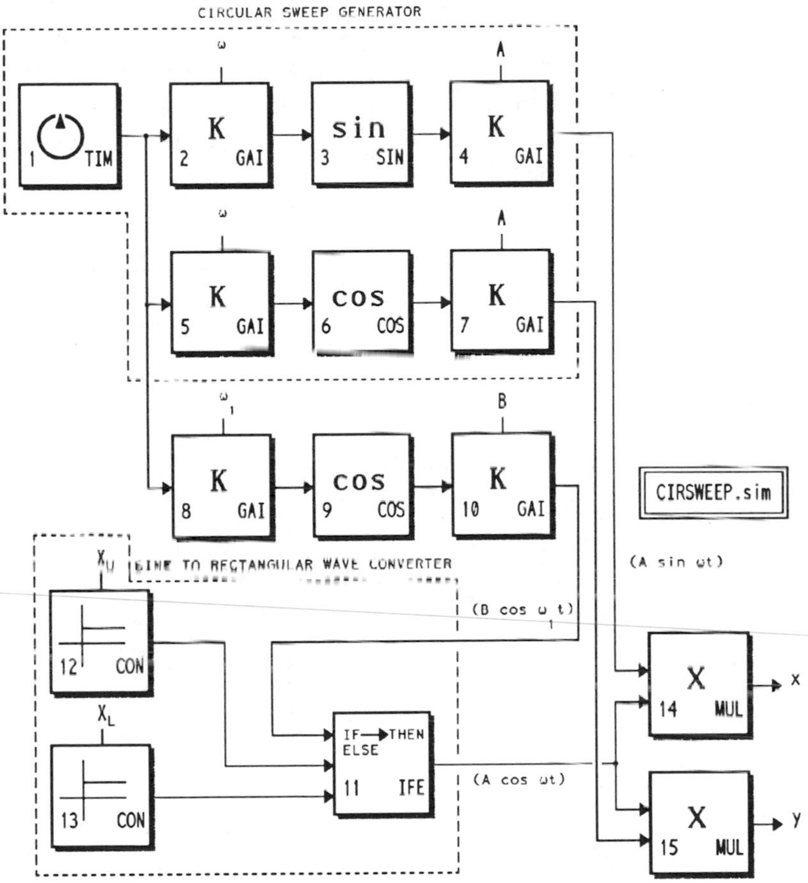

Figure A.10.1 A circular sweep generator.

Unlike the usual linear sweep where a signal is swept and displayed along a horizontal baseline of limited length, circular sweep offers some tactical advantages in the observation of signals. In the past, this technique has been used in conjunction with oscilloscopes and x-y plotters. It allows signal observation without retrace along a circular baseline. When necessary, a modified spiral sweep can be used in long-term observations. There, of course, practical considerations stemming from the inherent visual distortion of a circularly swept signal. The technique can be compared to Lissajous displays where interpretation skills are necessary. A modern circular sweep circuit is described by Kirchman (1978). It uses multiplier integrated circuits and works with any oscilloscope to produce some interesting visual displays. We recommend that readers seek this reference out. In his 1976 work on the solution of nonlinear vibration systems by means of analog computers, Fiala uses a circular scanning circuit. This little known technique is very powerful in assessing the dynamic properties of nonlinear systems. A circular sweep generator is shown in Figure A.10.1. Blocks #1 through #7 provide the sweep input A sin (ωt) and a 90° phase shifted signal A cos (ωt). By themselves, the two signals form a circular sweeping trace when fed into the x and y inputs of a display. Here they each inputed into multipliers #14 and #15 and the second input terminal of each multiplier connects to the common mode input. fluctuations of the input signal affect the amplitude of the circular sweeping trace. Figure A.10.1 shows a rectangular waveform generator used to provide input. Blocks #8, #9 and #10 provide the cosine waveform B cos (ω_1) subsequently processed by the sine-to-rectangular wave converter formed by blocks #11, #12 and #13. Note that the scheme has the advantage of a common time reference provided by the TIM block.

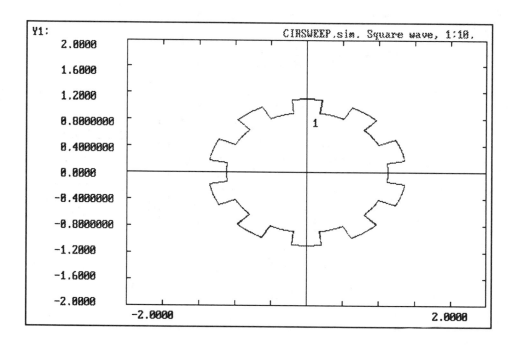

Figure A.10.2   Results of CIRSWEEP.sim.

Figure A.10.2 shows the circularly swept square wave. The constituent waveforms of Figure A.10.3 show how the generator works. We recommend that the reader experiment with sine- triangle-, sawtooth- and square-wave signals of different amplitudes and frequency ratios.

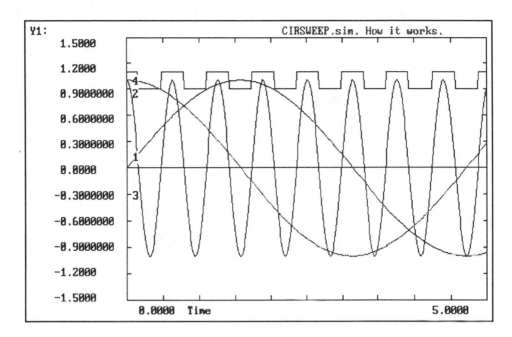

Figure A 10.3   The constituent waveforms of CIRSWEEP.sim.

A.11   A LOGIC-CONTROLLED SIGNAL SWITCH

A useful logic-controlled signal switch can be synthesized from both logic and linear elements. The switches discussed here are only basic examples of a category of hybrid networks TUTSIM prompts you to discover (a case of midnight engineering). Figure A.11.1 shows a normally closed (off in the absence of a positive logic pulse) switch and its truth table. The control input ec is supplied by a CLK block that provides a square wave, and the input e_i comes form a CON block with a unity parameter. Readers should print out and study the signals e_c, e_g (the output of the AND gate) and o_0 from the top down (LCSS1.sim).

The block diagram of Figure A.11.2 shows a variation on the theme, a normally open (on in the absence of a positive logic pulse) switch and its truth table. The operation is facilitated by adding a logical invertor in series with the AND gate (we could have simply chosen a NAN block, but this way we can see the switching operation better). The results are shown in Figure A.11.3 where the traces of e_c, e_g, e_2 (the INV block output) and e_0 are arranged from the top down (LCCS2.sim). At this point we should discuss the display arrangement method, as it can be somewhat confusing. In the first case (LCSS1.sim) we need to display three traces *without superimposition and with the same scale*. Given that TUTSIM's display (we use the /d=4 setting) has 10 vertical graduations, the following

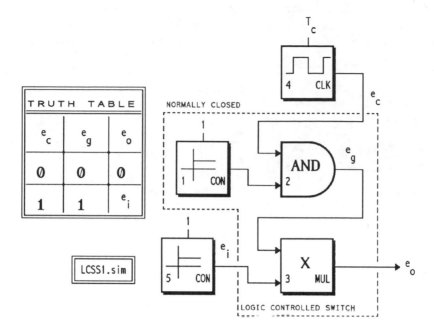

Figure A.11.1   A normally-closed logic-controlled switch.

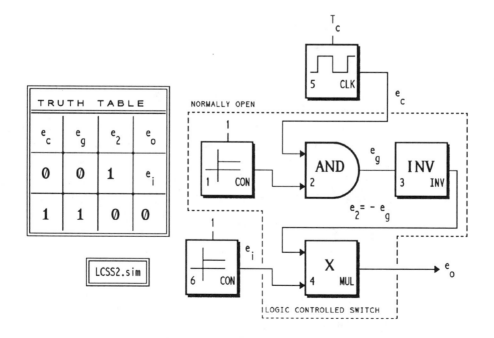

Figure A.11.2   A normally-open logic-controlled switch.

353

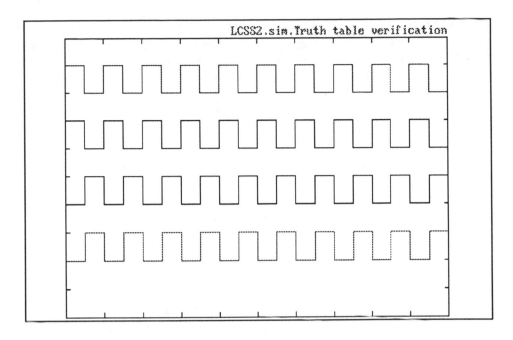

Figure A.11.3   Truth table verification for the LCSS2.sim logic-controlled switch.

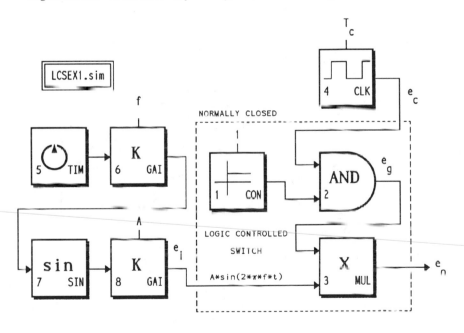

Figure A.11.4   Gating a selected portion of a signal.

arrangement allows clearance of two graduations between the traces: (-8,2), (-5,5), (-2,8). Similar thinking leads to the arrangement of the four traces as used in the second case (LCSS2.sim) as follows (-8,2), (-6,4), (-4,6), (-2,8). The example of Figure A.11.4 shows the gating of a selected portion of a sinusoidal waveform. The process is controlled by the period ratio (T_{signal}/T_{clock}). Readers should experiment with period ratios of 1/2 where $T_c = 1.570799$ and 2 where $T_c = 6.28318$, respectively. The last value provides, in fact, a *hybrid waveform rectifier*!

A.12   A LOGIC-CONTROLLED TWO-INPUT SELECTOR AND THE IFE BLOCK

Analog/hybrid computer enthusiasts know the device of Figure A.12.1 as an analog switch. It functions as a logic controlled two-input selector switch. It is indispensable in

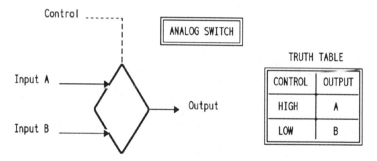

Figure A.12.1   The traditional analog switch (analog computer notation).

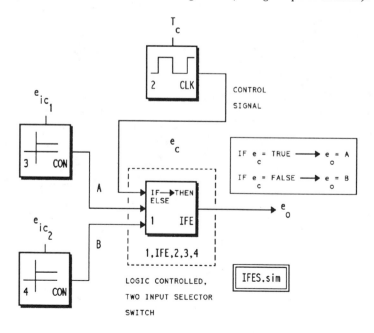

Figure A.12.2   A logic-controlled two-input selector design based on the IFE block.

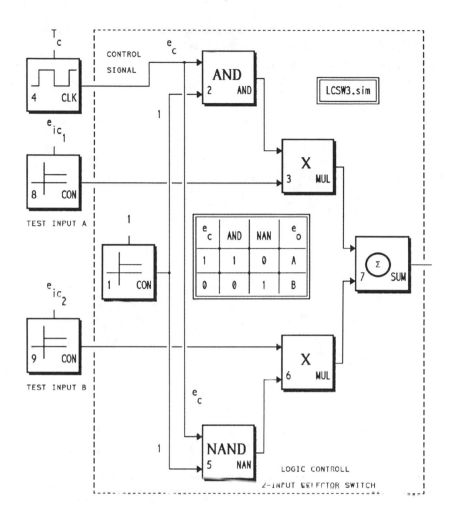

Figure A.12.3   Implementing the logic-controlled two-input selector.

hybrid simulation. In the case where such device is needed within a larger TUTSIM simulation, it can be represented by the IFE block as shown in Figure A.12.2. The diagram of Figure A.12.3 implements the same function as that of Figure A.12.1 It shows a combination of the two previously discussed logic-controlled signal switches and useful in real circuit design. This latter device demonstrates the combination of linear and digital blocks in creating a unique signal control unit.

A.13   APPLYING A DC BLOCKING FILTER

In this experiment we use a dc blocking filter to restore the level of a sinusoidal waveform. The input signal is $e_i(t) = A \sin 2\pi ft + C$, where C is the dc signal magnitude supplied by the CON block. The dc filter itself is the analog of a simple RC filter. Its integrator consists of blocks #9 and #10, where the GAI block is used to set the time constant T (note that the gain setting is $1/T$). The filter's transfer function is $[1/(Ts + 1)]$. Figure A.13.1 shows the simulator (DCBLOCK.sim). Readers should plot the signal $e_i(t)$, the original output of the function generator and the filter's output $e_0(t)$ for a setting of $1/T = 0.5 \rightarrow T = 2$.

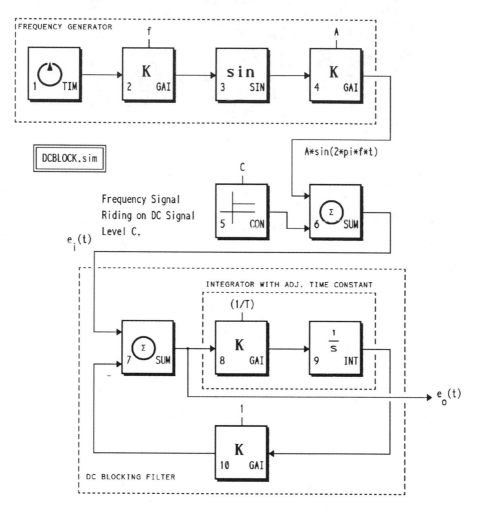

Figure A.13.1 Experimenting with a dc blocking filter.

A.14   A PEAK FOLLOWER

The sine oscillator of Figure A.14.1 (D.sim) outputs the waveform $f(t) = \sin(4\pi t)$ which is then rectified by block #5 to become $f(t) = |\sin(4\pi t)|/dt$. The rectified sinusoid and e_0 are shown in Figure A.14.2. This small exercise helps us visualize the properties of the DIF block. As it is expected, the derivative zeroes as the rectified waveform peaks and attains its maximum value at each half-period where the waveform zeroes. The simple peak

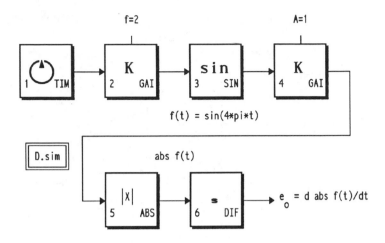

Figure A.14.1   Visualizing the properties of the DIF block (see text).

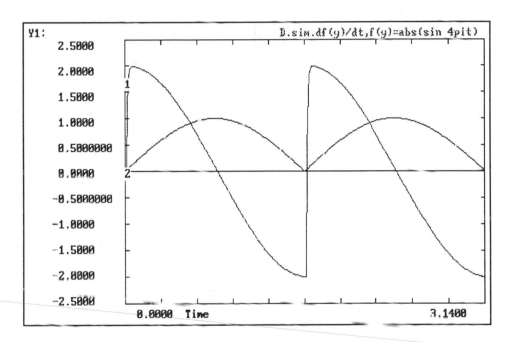

Figure A.14.2   The results of D.sim.

follower simulator of Figure A.14.3 (PF.sim) consists of a function generator (blocks #1,2,3,4,5,9,10,11) outputing a rectified sine wave having a continuously increasing amplitude. The rate of amplitude change is set by block #9 of the two block (#9 and 10) slope generator. A SOC (Strobe-On-Command) block samples and stores the function generator's signal (from block #5) each time the control input (from block #7) goes from false to true. Of course, the transition occurs when the waveform reaches its peak value and is held until the amplitude zeroes. The SOC block can be seen as an externally-commanded sample and

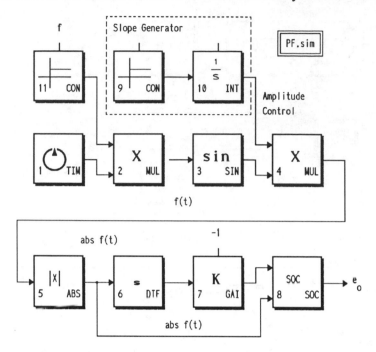

Figure A.14.3   A simple peak follower.

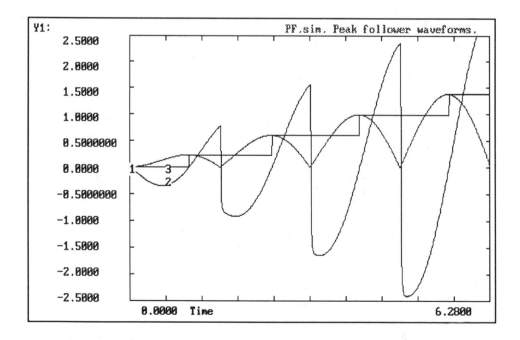

Figure A.14.4   The peak follower (PF.sim) waveforms.

hold (S/H) device. As Figure A.14.4 shows, the result is a peak follower that changes values only when the next maximum occurs.

A.15   THE FUNCTION $\omega^n \cos \omega t$ AND THE HARMONIC OSCILLATOR

In Section 3.2 we examined the harmonic oscillator. Here, we will point out some details useful in simulation. Figure A.15.1 (blocks #1 through #4) shows a four-block oscillator where ω is set as an (identical) parameter on blocks #2 and #4. Integrator #3 receives the initial condition U and outputs U cos (ωt). Gain #4 multiplies its input by ω and outputs U ω cos (ωt). Integrator #1 inputs -Uω cos (ωt) and outputs -U sin (ωt) because

$$\int_0^t - U\omega \cos (\omega t)\, dt = - U \int_0^t \cos (\omega t)\, d(\omega t) = - U \sin (\omega t) \quad (1)$$

Then, gain #2 inputs -U sin (ωt) and outputs U cos (ωt). Finally, integrator #3 inputs -U ω sin (ωt) and outputs U cos (ωt) because

$$\int_0^t - U\omega \sin (\omega t)\, dt = - U \int_0^t \sin (\omega t)\, d(\omega t)$$

$$= - U \left[- \cos (\omega t) \right]$$

$$= U \cos (\omega t)$$

$$(2)$$

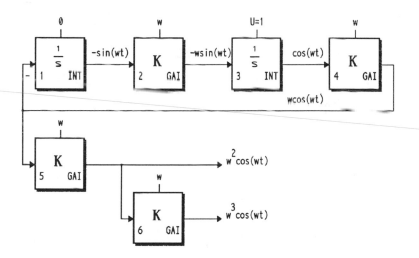

Figure A.15.1   Generating the function $\omega^n \cos \omega t$.

Note that we are using *noninverting integrators. In the case of an analog computer circuit where inverting operational integrators are used, the signs change and unity gain inverters may be used as necessary. Often, the function* $f(t) = U\omega^n \cos(\omega t)$ or $U\omega^n \sin(\omega t)$ is required as in the case of the Mathieu equation (Sections 7.2.4 and 7.2.5). Then gain blocks are used as shown in Figure A.15.1 (blocks #5 and #6). Note that (ω^n) may also be introduced as the initial condition $U = \omega^n$, rendering blocks #5 and #6 unnecessary, unless some of the other powers are required simultaneously.

B BIBLIOGRAPHY

Abbott, I. H., and A. E. Von Doenhoff. *Theory of Wing Sections*. New York: Dover, 1959.

Abramowitz, M., and I. A. Stegun, eds. *Handbook of Mathematical Functions*. National Bureau of Standards Applied Mathematics Series No. 55. Washington, DC: U. S. Government Printing Office, 1972.

Abramson, N. *An Introduction to the Dynamics of Airplanes*. New York: Dover, 1971.

Aburdene, M. F. *Computer Simulation of Dynamic Systems*. Dubuque, IA: Brown, 1988.

Achilles, D. "Apparative Signalanalyse und Signalsynthese mit Parabolischen Zylinderfunktionen." *NTZ* **12** (1968): 743-748.

Ackeroyd, J. "A Recent Bibliography of the Theory and Applications of Walsh Functions." In *Proc. Symposium of Walsh and Other Nonsinusoidal Functions*. Hatfield Polytechnic (UK), June 1973.

Ahmad, A. I. E. "Time Delay Generalized Integration." *Institute of Engineers (India) Journal* **57**, Section ET2 (December 1976): 65-68.

Acton, F. S. *Numerical Methods that Work*. New York: Harper and Row, 1970.

Aho, A. V., J. E. Hopcroft, and J. D. Ullman. *The Design and Analysis of Computer Algorithms*. Reading, MA: Addison-Wesley, 1976.

Alberth, O. *Precise Numerical Analysis*. Dubuque, IA: Brown, 1988.

Al-Charchafchi, S. H. "A Simple Current-controlled Negative Resistance Device." *Electronic Engineering* **47**, 568 (1975): 55-56.

Al-Charchafchi, S. H., and A. A. N. Abdulrahman. "Simulated Inductors Using Negative Resistance." *Electronic Engineering* **49**, 589 (1977): 43-45.

Al-Charchafchi, S. H., S. S. Al-Wakeel, and A. A. N. Abdulrahman. "A Voltage Controlled Negative Resistance Circuit." *Electronic Engineering* **49**, 596 (1977): 99-100.

Al-Charchafchi, S H., and F. A Dehlavi. "A Current-controlled Two-terminal Negative Resistance Network." *International Journal of Electronics* **38**, 2 (1975): 271-274.

Al-Khafaji, A. W., and J. R. Tooley. *Numerical Methods in Engineering Practice*. New York: Holt, Rinehart and Winston, 1986.

Amble, O. "On a Principle of Connection for Bush Integrators." *Journal of Scientific Instrumentation (London)* **27**, (December 1956): 284-290.

Ammon, W. "Zur Nachbildung von Totzeiten mit Elementen des Analogrechners." *Electron. Rechenanl.* **3**, 5 (1961): 217-224.

Anday, F. "Active Realization of nth-Order Allpass Transfer Functions." *Electronics Letters* **8**, 15 (27 July 1972): 399-400.

Anderson, N., and G. R. Walsh. "Phase-plane Methods for Central Orbits." *American Journal of Physics* **58**, 6 (June 1990): 548-551.

Andrew, H. R. S. "FET and Transistor Produce Negative Resistance." *Electronic Engineering* **49**, 547 (October 1977): 43, 45.

Andronov, A. A., A. A. Vitt and S. E. Khaĭkin. *Theory of Oscillations*. London: Pergamon Press, 1966.

Arden, B. W., and K. N. Astill. *Numerical Algorithms: Origins and Applications*. Reading, MA: Addison-Wesley, 1970.

Åström, K. J. "Computer-Aided Modeling, Analysis and Design of Control Systems: A Perspective." *IEEE Control Systems Magazine* 3, 2 (1983): 4-16.

Åström, K. J., and B. Wittenmark. *Computer-Controlled Systems: Theory and Design*. 2nd Englewood Cliffs, NJ: Prentice-Hall, 1990.

Aus, H. M., and G. A. Korn. "The Future of On-Line Continuous-System Simulation." *Proc. AFIPS/Fall Joint Computer Conference* 39 (1971).

Babloyantz, A. *Molecules, Dynamics and Life: An Introduction to Self-Organization of Matter*. New York: Wiley, 1986.

Bairstow, L. "Skin Friction." *Journal of the Royal Aeronautical Society* (1925): 3-23.

Balakrishnan, S. "Negative Resistance Using Positive Supply." *Electronic Engineering*, (February 1978): 24.

Ballico, M. J., and M. L. Sawley. "The Bipolar Motor: A Simple Demonstration of Deterministic Chaos." *American Journal of Physics* 58, 1 (January 1990): 58-61.

Bargh, J. K. "Measurement of First-Order Probability Density Functions Using a General Purpose Analogue Computer." *Proc. IRE (Australia)* (July 1970): 220-223.

Barker, R., and E. P. Reilly. "Odd-Order Frequency-Multiple Generation Technique." *Electronics Letters* 7 (1976): 159-160.

Baron, S., D. L. Kleinman, D. C. Miller, W. H. Levison, and J. I. Elkind. *Application of Optimal Control Theory to the Prediction of Human Performance in Complex Task*. Report AFFDL-TR-69-81. Wright-Patterson AFB, OH: Air Force Flight Dynamics Laboratory, March, 1970.

Barratt, C., and G. L. Strobel. "Sliding Friction and the Harmonic Oscillator." *American Journal of Physics* 49, 5 (May 1981): 500-501.

Bartlett, R. M. "An Analogue Computer Solution of the Laminar Boundary Layer Equations." *IJMEE* 3, 3 (1975): 271-275.

Beauchamp, K. G. *Walsh Functions and Their Applications*. New York: Academic Press, 1975.

Beer, T. "Walsh Transform." *American Journal of Physics* 49, 5 (May 1981): 466-472.

Bekey, G. A. "Generalized Integration on the Analog Computer." *IRE Transactions on Electronic Computers*, (June 1959): 210-217.

Bekey, G. A. and W. J. Karplus. *Hybrid Computation*. New York: Wiley, 1968.

Bellman, J. J., and R. Kalaba, eds. *Selected Papers on Mathematical Trends in Control Theory*. New York: Dover, 1964.

Bellman, R., and G. Straus. "Continued Fractions, Algebraic Functions, and the Padé Table." *Proc. National Academy of Science (USA)*, 35 (August 1949): 472-476.

Beltrami, E. *Mathematics for Dynamic Modeling*. New York: Academic Press, 1987.

Bendixson, I. "Sur les Courbes Défines par les Équations Différentielles." *Acta Mathematica* 24 (1901): 1-88.

Ben-Yaakov, S. "A Unified Approach to Teaching Feedback in Electronic Circuit Courses." *IEEE Transactions on Education* 34, 4 (November 1991): 310-316.

Berridge, H. J. J. "Radioactive Decay Chains: A Digital Model." *Physics Education (UK)* **10** (September 1975): 437-438.

Bierbauer, J. W., J. A. Eiseman, F. A. Fasal, and J. J. Kulikowski. "System simulation with MIDAS." *AT&T Technical Journal* **70**, 1 (January/February 1991): 36-51.

Blakelock, J. H. *Automatic Control of Aircraft and Missiles*. 2nd. New York: Wiley, 1991.

Blasius, H. "Grenzschichten in Flüssigkeiten mit kleiner Reibung." *Z. Math. Physik* **56** (1908): 1-37.

Bobillier, P. A., B. C. Kahan, and A. R. Probst. "Summary of Current Simulation Languages." In *Simulation with GPSS and GPSS V*, Appendix E, 465-482. Englewood Cliffs, NJ: Prentice-Hall, 1976.

Bogart, T. F. Jr. *Laplace Transforms and Control Systems Theory for Technology*. New York: Wiley, 1982.

Bohr, H. *Almost Periodic Functions*. New York: Chelsea, 1951.

Bramhall, J. N. *An Annotated Bibliography on, and Related to, Walsh Functions*. Technical Memorandum. Baltimore, MD: Applied Physics Laboratory, Johns Hopkins University, 1972.

Bramhall, J. N. "The First Fifty Years of Walsh Functions." *Proc. 1973 Symposium on Applications of Walsh Functions*. Washington, DC: Naval Research Laboratory, 1973.

Brauer, F., A. C. Soudack, and H. S. Jarosch. "Stabilization and De-stabilization of Predator-prey Systems under Harvesting and Nutrient Enrichment." *International Journal of Control* **23**, 4 (1976): 553-573.

Braun, M., C. Coleman, and D. Drew, eds. *Differential Equation Models*. New York: Springer-Verlag, 1983.

Brennan, R. D., C. T. deWit, W. A. Williams, and E. V. Quattrin. "The Utility of Digital Simulation Language for Ecological Modeling." *Oecologia (Berlin)* **4** (1970): 113-132.

Brennan, R. D., and R. N. Linebarger. "A Survey of Digital Simulation: Digital Analog Simulator Programs." *Simulation* **3**, 6 (December 1964): 22-36.

Brennan, R. D., and H. Sano. "Pactolus: A Digital Analog Simulator Program for IBM 1620." *Proc. AFIPS/Fall Joint Computer Conference* (1964): 299-312.

Brennan, R. D., and M. Y. Silberberg. "The System/360 Continuous System Modeling Program." *Simulation*, (December 1968): 301-308.

Briggs, K. "Simple Experiments in Chaotic Dynamics." *American Journal of Physics* **55**, 12 (December 1987): 1083-1089.

Brorson, S. D., D. Dewey, and P. S. Lindsay. "Self-replicating Attractor of a Driven Semiconductor Circuit." *Physics Review A* **28**, 2 (1983): 1201-1203.

Brown, G. *BEDSOCS: An Interactive Simulation Language*. Ph.D. dissertation. University of Bradford, 1975.

Brown, R. "All Peaks Aren't Gaussian." *Personal Engineering & Instrumentation News* **8**, 7 (July 1991): 51-54.

Burgin, G. H. "MIDAS III: A compiler Version of MIDAS." *Simulation*, (March 1966): 160-168.

Burr-Brown Research Corp. *Analog Shaping*. Application Note An-70. Tucson, AZ: Burr-Brown, 1975.

Bush, V. "The Differential Analyzer: A New Machine for Solving Differential Equations." *Journal of the Franklin Institute* **212** (1931): 447.

Buskirk, D. R. "Sources in Numerical Error." *Byte* **4**, 4 (April 1979): 46, 48-49.

Butcher, J. C., K. Burrage, and F. H. Chipman. *Stride: Stable Runge-Kutta Integrator for Differential Equations*. Report Series No. 150 (Computational Mathematics No. 20). Auckland, New Zealand: Department of Mathematics, University of Auckland, 1979.

Byers, T. J. "Understanding and Using Lissajous Figures." *Hands-On Electronics* **3**, 5 (Sept/Oct 1986): 41-44.

Cameron, W. D. *Hybrid Computer Techniques for Determining Probability Distributions*. Hybrid Computation Applications Reference Library. EAI Publication No. 2.4.2.h. West Long Branch, NJ: Electronics Associates, 1965.

Cannon, R. H. Jr. *Dynamics of Physical Systems*. New York: McGraw-Hill, 1967.

Carr, J. W. III. "Error Bounds for the Runge-Kutta Single Step Integration Process." *Journal of the Association for Computing Machinery* **5** (1958): 39-45.

Carrier, G. F., M. Krook, and C.E. Pearson. *Functions of a Complex Variable*. New York: McGraw-Hill, 1966.

Cartwright, M. L. "Forced Oscillations in Nearly Sinusoidal Systems." *Journal Institute Elect. Engineering* **95** (1948): 223.

Caswell, D. W. *Development of a Simulator for the Evaluation of Rigid and Movable Aircraft Controls. AD 703638*. M.S. Thesis. U. S. Naval Postgraduate School, 1969.

Cebeci, T., and H. B. Keller. "Shooting and Parallel Shooting Methods for Solving the Falkner-Skan Boundary Layer Equation." *Journal of Computational Physics* **7** (1971): 289-300.

Cellier, F. *Combined Continuous Discrete Simulation by Use of Digital Computers: Techniques and Tools*. Ph.D. dissertation. Zurich: Swiss Federal Institute of Technology, 1979.

Cellier, F. "Combined Continuous/Discrete System Simulation Languages: Usefulness, Experience and Future Development." In *Methodology in Systems Modelling and Simulation*, edited by B. P. Zeigler et al., 201-210. New York: North-Holland, 1979.

Cereijo, M. R. "Transport Delay—Neither Infinite nor Infinitesimal." *Instruments & Control Systems* **48**, 4 (April 1975): 41-43.

Chao, K. S., and D. L. Vines. "Computer Simulation in Nonlinear Circuit Analysis." *ACES Transactions* **III**, 5 (May 1971): 99-106.

Chapra, S. C., and R. P. Canale. *Numerical Methods for Engineers with Personal Computer Applications*. New York: McGraw-Hill, 1985.

Chapra, S. C. and R. P. Canale. *Numerical Methods for Engineers*. 2nd. New York: McGraw-Hill, 1988.

Chatterjee, B., and B. N. Chatterjee. "Amplitude Stabilized Transistorized Low Frequency Oscillator." *International Journal of Electronics* **22**, 5 (1967): 413-419.

Cheney, W., and D. Kincaid. *Numerical Mathematics and Computing*. Monterey, CA: Brooks/Cole, 1980.

Chien, K. L., J. B. Reswick, and J. A. Hrones. "On the Automatic Control of Generalized Passive Systems." *Trans. American Society of Mechanical Engineers* **74** (1952): 175-183.

Chu, Y. *Digital Simulation of Continuous Systems*. New York: McGraw-Hill, 1969.

Chua, L. O., and S. M. Kang. "Section-wise Piecewise-linear Functions: Canonical Representation, Properties and Applications." *Proc. IEEE* **65**, (June 1977): 915-929.

Chua, L. O., M. Komuro, and T. Matsumoto. "The Double Scroll Family." *IEEE Trans. Circuits Systems* **CAS-33**, 11 (November 1986): 1072-1118.

Chua, L. O., and R. N. Madan. "Sights and Sounds of Chaos." *IEEE Circuits and Devices Magazine* **4**, 1 (January 1988): 3-13.

Clancy, J. J., and M. S. Fineberg. "Digital Simulation Languages: A Critique and a Guide." *Proc. AFIPS/Fall Joint Computer Conference* **27-1** (1965): 23-26.

Cochin, I., and H. J. Plass, Jr. *Analysis and Design of Dynamic Systems*. 2nd. New York: Harper & Row, 1990.

Cohen, C. B., and E. Reshotko. *Similar Solutions for the Compressible Laminar Boundary Layer with Heat Transfer and Pressure Gradient*. NACA Report No. 1293. 1956.

Cole, J. D. *Perturbation Methods in Applied Mathematics*. Reading, MA: Blaisdell, 1968.

Collatz, L. *Numerische Behandlung von Differentialeichungen*. Berlin: Springer-Verlag, 1951.

Constantinides, A. *Applied Numerical Methods with Personal Computers*. New York: McGraw-Hill, 1987.

Conte, S. D., and C. DeBoor. *Elementary Numerical Analysis: An Algorithmic Approach*. 2nd. New York: McGraw-Hill, 1968.

Cook, G. E., and G. Willems. "z-Plane Damping Ratio Curves." *Instruments & Control Systems* **40** (December 1967): 67-68.

Corliss, L., R. K. Greif, and R. M. Gerdes. "Comparison of Ground-based and In flight Simulation of VTOL Hover Control Concepts." *Journal of Guidance and Control* **1**, 3 (May-June 1978): 217-221.

Corran, E. R., and P. Gaal. "Generation of Time-Dependant Functions Using Summed Exponentials." *Simulation* **13**, 6 (December 1969): 284.

Corrington, M. S. "Solution of Differential and Integral Equations with Walsh Functions." *IEEE Trans. on Circuit Theory* **CT-20**, 5 (September 1973).

Coughanowr, D. R. *Process Systems Analysis and Control*. 2nd. New York: McGraw-Hill, 1991.

Coughlin, R. F., and F. F. Driscoll. *Operational Amplifiers and Linear Integrated Circuits*. 3rd. Englewood Cliffs, NJ: Prentice-Hall, 1987.

Counts, L., and F. Pouliot. "Computational Module Stresses Applications Versatility." *Electronics* (17 July 1972): 93-94.

Cox, A. D. "Deadzone Simulation on an Electronic Analogue Computer." *Electronics Letters* **6**, 19 (September 1970): 632-633.

Crane, R. L., and R. W. Klopfenstein. "Optimum Weights in Delay Equalization." *IEEE Trans. on Circuits and Systems* **CAS-26**, 1 (January 1979): 46-51.

Crawford, F. S. Jr. *Waves*. In *Berkeley Physics Course*. Vol. 3. New York: McGraw-Hill, 1968.

Crisp, J. D. C. "On Vibration as a Dynamic Phenomenon." *Bull. Mechanical Engineering Educ.* **5** (1966): 361-373.

Crosbie, R. E., S. Javey, J. L. Hay, and J. G. Pearce. "ESL: A New Continuous System Simulation Language." *Simulation* **41**, (May 1985): 242-246.

Crossley, F. E. "Die Nachbildung Eines Mechanischen Kurbelgetriebes Mittels Eines Elektronischen Analogrechners." *Feinwerktechnik* **67**, 6 (1963): 218-222.

Crowder, H. K., and S. W. McCuskey. *Topics in Higher Analysis*. New York: Macmillan, 1964.

Crowell, A. D. "Motion of the Earth as Viewed from the Moon and the Y-Suspended Pendulum." *American Journal of Physics* **49**, 5 (May 1981): 452-454.

Crutchfield, J. P., J. D. Farmer, N. H. Packard, and R. S. Shaw. "Chaos." *Scientific American* **255**, 6 (December 1986): 46-57.

Cvitanovic, P., ed. *Universality in Chaos*. London: Hilger, 1984.

Dahl, O. J. *Discrete Event Simulation Languages*. In *Programming Languages*. Edited by F. Genuys, 349-395. New York: Academic Press, 1968.

Dahlquist, G., and A. Björck. *Numerical Methods*. Englewood Cliffs, NJ: Prentice-Hall, 1974.

Danby, J. M. A. *Computing Applications to Differential Equations*. Englewood Cliffs, NJ: Prentice-Hall, 1985.

Darbie, A. M. "Reduce Noise in Feedback Circuits." *Electronic Design* **25** (7 December 1972): 72-75.

Davenport, W. B. Jr., and W. L. Root. *An Introduction to the Theory of Random Signals and Noise*. New York: McGraw-Hill, 1958.

Davies, W. D. T. "On the Analog Simulation of a Pure Time Delay." *Simulation* **18**, 5 (May 1972): 161-170.

Davis, H. T. *Introduction to Nonlinear Differential and Integral Equations*. New York: Dover, 1962.

Davis, P. J., and P. Rabinowitz. *Methods of Numerical Integration*. New York: Academic Press, 1975.

D'Azzo, J. J., and C. H. Houpis. *Feedback Control System Analysis and Synthesis*. 2nd. New York: McGraw-Hill, 1966.

D'Azzo, J. J., and C. H. Houpis. *Linear Control System Analysis and Design*. 3rd. New York: McGraw-Hill, 1988.

deCastro, A. S. "Damped Harmonic Oscillator: A Correction in Some Standard Textbooks." *American Journal of Physics* **54**, 8 (August 1986): 741-742.

Degn, H., A. V. Holden, and L. F. Olsen. *Chaos in Biological Systems*. New York: Plenum Press, 1987.

Deliyannis, T. "Six New Delay Functions and Their Realization Using Active RC Networks." *The Radio and Electronic Engineer* **39**, 3 (March 1970): 139-144.

Demana, F., and B. K. Waits. "Pitfalls in Graphical Computation, or Why a Single Graph Isn't Enough." *The College Mathematics Journal* **19**, 2 (March 1988): 177-183.

Dent, J. C., and J. R. Mitchell. "The Electronic Analogue Computer for the Solution of Problems in Heat Transfer Involving Similarity Variables." *Bull. Mech. Engineering Educ.* **6**, 2 (1967): 155-163.

Deo, N. *System Simulation with Digital Computer*. Englewood Cliffs, NJ: Prentice-Hall, 1983.

Devaney, R. L. An Introduction to Chaotic Dynamical Systems. Reading, MA: Addison-Wesley, 1989.

Dhen, W. "Special Computer Units in the Darmstadt Repetitive Electronic Analog Computer." *Proc. I.A.C.M.* (Brussels) 1956:46-48.

DiFranco, D. *Flight Investigation of Longitudinal Short Period Frequency Requirements and PIO Tendencies*. AFFDL TR 66-163. Wright-Patterson AFB: Air Force Flight Dynamics Laboratory, 1967.

Dimitrov, J. D. "A Bell-Shape Pulse Generator." *IEEE Trans. on Instrumentation and Measurement* **39**, 4 (August 1990): 667-670.

DiStefano, J. J. III, A. R. Stubberud, and I. J. Williams. *Theory and Problems of Feedback and Control Systems*. Schaum's Outline Series. New York: McGraw-Hill, 1967.

Doebelin, E. O. "Measurement Systems, Application and Design." 4th. New York: McGraw-Hill, 1990.

Dommash, D. O., S. S. Sherby, and T. F. Connolly. *Airplane Aerodynamics*. 4th. New York: Pitman, 1967.

Dorf, R. C. *Modern Control Systems*. 5th. Reading, MA: Addison-Wesley, 1989.

Driver, H. S. T. "Demonstration of Transient Beats." *American Journal of Physics* **46**, 10 (October 1978): 1080-1082.

Duffing, G. *Erzwungene Schwingungen bei Veränderlicher Eigenfrequenz*. Braunschweig: F. Vieweg u. Sohn, 1918.

Duffy, D. G. *Solutions of Partial Differential Equations*. Blue Ridge Summit, PA: TAB Books, 1986.

Dvorak, V. "Optimum All-pole Approximation of exp(-sT)." *Electronics Letters* **12**, 1 (8 January 1976): 21-23.

Edelstein-Keshet, L. *Mathematical Models in Biology*. New York: McGraw-Hill, 1988.

Elkind, J. I., P. L. Falb, D. L. Kleinman, and W. H. Levison. *An Optimal Control Method for Predicting Control Characteristics and Display Requirements of Manned-Vehicle Systems*. AFFDL-TR-67-187. Wright-Patterson AFB, OH: Air Force Flight Dynamics Laboratory, 1968.

Elmqvist, H., K. J. Åström, T. Schönthal, and B. Wittenmark. *SIMNON User's Guide for MS-DOS Computers*. SSPA Systems, Göteborg, Sweden. Version 3.0. Palo Alto, CA: Engineering Software Concepts, Inc., 1990.

Enright, W. H., and T. E. Hull. "Comparing Numerical Methods for the Solution of Stiff Systems of ODE's Arising in Chemistry." In *Numerical Methods for Differential Equations*, edited by L. Lapidus and W. E. Schiesser, 45-66. New York: Academic Press, 1976.

Ernst, D. *Elektronische Analogrechner*. München: R. Oldenbourg, 1960.

Etkin, B. *Dynamics of Flight*. New York: Wiley, 1965.

Falco, C. M. "Phase-space of a Driven, Damped Pendulum (Josephson Weak Link)." *American Journal of Physics* **44**, 8 (August 1976): 733-740.

Falkner, V. M., and S. W. Skan. "Solutions of the Boundary Layer Equations." *Philosophical Magazine* **12** (1931): 865-869.

Fan, L. T., P. S. Shah, and L. E. Erickson. *Simulation of Biological Processes by Analog and Digital Computers*. Manhattan, KS: Institute for Systems Design and Optimization, Kansas State University, 1970.

Feather, N. *An Introduction to the Physics of Vibrations and Waves*. Edinburgh: Edinburgh University Press, 1961.

Fehlberg, E. *Classical Fifth-, Sixth-, Seventh-, and Eighth-order Runge-Kutta Formulas with Stepsize Control*. NASA Technical Report No. 287. 1968.

Feigenbaum, M. J. "The Onset Spectrum of Turbulence." *Physics Letters* **74A** (1979): 375-378.

Feigenbaum, M. J. "The Transition to Aperiodic Behaviour in Turbulent Systems." *Comm. Mathematical Physics* **77** (1980): 65-86.

Fiala, V. *Solution of Non-Linear Vibration Systems by Means of Analogue Computers*. Monographs and Memoranda No. 19. Praha: National Research Institute for Machine Design, Běchovice, 1976.

Filanovsky, I. M. "Sinusoidal VCO with Control of Frequency and Amplitude." *IEEE Proceedings of the 32nd Symposium on Circuits and Systems* **1** (1989):446-449.

Finkelstein, L., and E. R. Carson. *Mathematical Modeling of Dynamic Biological Systems*. Forest Grove, OR: Research Studies Press, 1979.

Fishman, G.S. *Concepts and Methods in Discrete Event Digital Simulation*. New York: Wiley, 1973.

Flanders, H. "Algorithm of the Month." *The College Mathematics Journal* **19**, 1 (January 1988): 72-78.

Forrest, J. "Simulating High-Order Algebraic Equations with Linear Analog Computer Elements." *Instruments & Control Systems* **38** (March 1965): 162-164.

Forrester, J. W. *Industrial Dynamics*. Cambridge, MA: MIT Press, 1961.

Forrester, J. W. *Principles of Systems*. Cambridge, MA: MIT Press, 1968.

Forrester, J. W. *Urban Dynamics*. Cambridge, MA: MIT Press, 1969.

Forrester, J. W. *World Dynamics*. Cambridge, MA: MIT Press, 1973.

Foresythe, G.E., M. A. Malcolm, and C. B. Moler. *Computer Methods for Mathematical Computations*. Englewood Cliffs, NJ: Prentice-Hall, 1977.

Franco, S. *Design with Operational Amplifiers and Analog Integrated Circuits*. New York: McGraw-Hill, 1988.

Franke, H. M., and G. Döpner. "Regeltechnische Untersuchungen Über Den Einfluss Des Stellgliedes in Schwebeflugsteuerungen." *Jahrbuch 1963 der WGLR* (1963): 67-75.

Freeman, E. A., and C. S. Cox. "Evaluation of Transient-gain Functions for Nonlinear Elements and Their Use in Step-function Analysis." *Proc. IEE* **114**, 11 (November 1967): 1772-1780.

French, A. P. *Vibrations and Waves*. London: Nelson, 1971.

Fritz, R., J. Sägebarth, and H. Wiederoder. "Analoge Funktionsgeneratoren mit Multiplizieren." *Internationale Elektronische Rundschau* 8 (1974): 161-163.

Frost, G. "Man-Machine Dynamics." In *Human Engineering Guide to Equipment Design*, revised, edited by H. P. Van Cott and R. G. Kinkade, 227-309. Washington, D. C.: U.S. Government Printing Office, 1972.

Fruhlinger, G. L., and M. F. Aburdene. "Computer-Aided Design of Control Systems: TOTAL, BUCOP, ACSL and NDTRAN." *Modeling and Simulation*, 16 (1986): 799-903. Instrument Society of America (ISA).

Fry, E. B., R. K. Greif, and R. M. Gerdes. *Use of a Six-Degrees-of-Freedom Motion Simulator for VTOL Hovering Tasks*. NASA TN D-5383. 1969.

Ganesan, S. "Smoothing a Processor's Analog Output." *Electronics* 56, 19 (22 September 1983): 170-173.

Garfinkel, D. "A Simulation Study of the Effect on Simple Ecological systems of Making Rate of Increase of Population Density-Dependent." *Simulation* 8 (1967): 111-122.

Garon, H. A. "Mechanical hysteresis with Inexpensive Equipment." *The Physics Teacher* 7, 2 (February 1969): 100-103.

Gaskil, R. A., J. W. Harris, and A. L. McKnight. "DAS: A Digital Analog Simulator." *Proc. AFIPS/Spring Joint Computer Conference* (1963): 83-90.

Gayakwad, R. A. *Op-Amps and Linear Integrated Circuits*. 2nd. Englewood Cliffs, NJ: Prentice-Hall, 1988.

Gear, C. W. *Numerical Initial-value Problems in Ordinary Differential Equations*. Englewood Cliffs, NJ: Prentice-Hall, 1971.

Geis, W. D. *Transform Analysis and Filters*. Englewood Cliffs, NJ: Prentice-Hall, 1989.

Genin, R., and P. Brezel. "The Generation of Negative Resistance by Three-pole Circuits." *International Journal of Electronics* 42, 6 (1977): 589-600.

Gill, S. "A Process for the Step by Step Integration of Differential Equations in an Automatic Digital Computing Machine." *Proc. Cambridge Phil. Society* 47 (1951): 96-108.

Gilliland, M. C. *Handbook of Analog Computation*. Concord, CA: Systron-Donner, 1967.

Gilliland, M. C., and E.M. Billinghurst. *Block Programming for Physical Systems*. Concord, CA: Systron-Donner, 1966.

Giloi, W. "Uber die Behandlung elektrischer und mechanischer Netzwerke auf dem Analogrechner." *Elektron. Rechenanl.* 4, 1 (1962): 27-35.

Glass, L, and M. C. Mackey. *From Clocks to Chaos*. Princeton, NJ: Princeton University Press, 1988.

Glauert, H. *A Generalized Type of Joukowski Aerofoil*. R&M No. 911. London: Aeronautical Research Council, 1924.

Gleick, J. *Chaos: Making a New Science*. New York: Viking, 1987.

Glushkov, V. M., V. V. Gusev, T. P. Marjanovitch, and M. Sachnjuk. "Programming Methods for Modeling Combined Continuous-Discrete Systems." *Kiev Scientific Proceedings*: 1975.

Goel, N. S., S. C. Maitra, and E. W. Montroll. *On the Volterra and Other Nonlinear Models of Interacting Populations*. New York: Academic Press, 1971.

Goldberger, S. *On the Relative Importance of the Low Speed Control Requirement for V/STOL Aircraft*. AEDC-TR-66-205. Arnold Air Force Station, TN: Arnold Engineering Development Center, December 1966.

Gonnet, G. H. *Handbook of Algorithms and Data Structures*. Reading , MA: Addison-Wesley, 1984.

Gottwald, B. A., and G. Wanner. "Comparison of Numerical Methods for Stiff Differential Equations in Biology and Chemistry." *Simulation* **38**, 2 (February 1982): 61-66.

Graeme, J. G. *Applications of Operational Amplifiers: Third Generation Techniques*. New York: McGraw-Hill, 1973.

Graeme, J. G. *Designing with Operational Amplifiers: Applications Alternatives*. New York: McGraw-Hill, 1977. (a)

Graeme, J. G. "Circuit Provides a Gaussian Response with a Multifunction Converter and Op Amp." *Electronic Design* **6** (15 March 1977): 104. (b)

Graeme, J. G. "Mold Nonlinear Circuit Response with a Multifunction Converter." *EDN* **27**, 12 (9 June 1982): 165-170.

Gray, P. "On the Equivalence of DYNAMO and a Financial Planning Language." *Simulation* **43**, 6 (1987): 293-297.

Greif, R. K., E. B. Fry, R. M. Gerdes, and T. D. Gosset. *Effect of Stabilization on VTOL Aircraft in Hovering Flight*. NASA TN D-6900. 1972.

Grossblatt, R. "Smoothing Out the Sinewave Generator Output." *Radio Electronics* **55**, 6 (June 1984): 88-89.

Groves, W. N. "Computer Simulation of a Temperature Transducer Response to a Step Change in Temperature." CoED Application Note No. 32. 1973.

Guckenheimer, J., and P. Holmes. *Nonlinear Oscillations, Dynamical Systems, and Bifurcations of Vector Fields*. New York: Springer-Verlag, 1983.

Gupta, D. K., and R. Nath. "A Negative Resistance Generator Using a Darlington Pair." *International Journal of Electronics* **34**, 1 (1973): 131-133.

Gurel, D., and O. Gurel. *Oscillation in Chemical Reactions*. New York: Springer-Verlag, 1983.

Guterman, M. N., and Z. H. Nitecki. *Differential Equations: A First Course*. 3rd. New York: Saunders, 1984.

Hale, J. K., and J. P. LaSalle. "Analyzing Nonlinearity." *International Science and Technology* **18** (June 1963): 46-53.

Hannauer, G. *Basics of Parallel Hybrid Computation*. EAI Publication No. 800.3039-0. West Long Branch, NJ: Electronic Associates, Inc., 1968.

Hansen, A. G. *Similarity Analyses of Boundary Value Problems in Engineering*. Englewood Cliffs, NJ: Prentice-Hall, 1964.

Harmuth, H. F. *Transmission of Information by Orthogonal Functions*. 2nd. Berlin: Springer-Verlag, 1972.

Harnett, R. T., F. J. Sansom, and L. M. Warshawsky. *MIDAS Programming Guide*. Report SEG-TRD-64-1. Wright-Patterson AFB, OH: Air Force Flight Dynamics Laboratory, 1964.

Hartmann, W. M. "The Dynamically Shifted Oscillator." *American Journal of Physics* **54**, 1 (January 1986): 28-32.

Hatree, D. R. "On an Equation Occurring in Falkner and Skan's Approximate Treatment of the Equations of the Boundary Layer." *Proc. Cambridge Philosophical Society* **33** (1937): 223-239.

Hausner, A., and C. M. Furlani. "Chebyshev All-pass Approximants for Time Delay Simulation." *IEEE Trans. on Electronic Computers* **EC-15**, 3 (June 1966): 314-321.

Hay, J. L. "Interactive Simulation on Minicomputers: Part 1—ISIS, A CSSL Language." *Simulation* **31**, 1 (1978): 1-7.

Hay, J. L., and R. E. Crosbie. "ISIM: A Simulation Language for Microprocessors." *Simulation* **43**, 3 (September 1984): 133-136.

Heinhold, J. "Konforme Abbildung mittels elektrischer Analogrechner." *MTW(Vienna)* **2** (1959): 44-48.

Heller, G. "Schieberegister für Gleichspannungen." *Regelungstechnik* **8** (January 1963): 348-353.

Helsgaun, K. "DISCO: A SIMULA-based Language for Continuous, Combined and Discrete Simulation." *Simulation* **36** (July 1980): 1-12.

Henrici, P. *Discrete Variable Methods in Ordinary Differential Equations*. New York: Wiley, 1962.

Hepner, C. F. "Improved Methods of Simulating Time Delays." *IEEE Trans. Electronic Computers* **EC-14** (1965): 239-243.

Hester, R. "Analog Chip Set Smooths Out Digital Signal Processing." *Electronic Design* **32**, 10 (17 May 1984): 243-246, 248-249.

Hinson, D. J. "Simplified Schrödinger." *Physics Education (GB)* **11**, 5 (July 1976): 347.

Hirsch, R. A. "Analog Simulation of a Single Degree of Freedom System with Nonlinear Damping." *ASEE Transactions* **VIII**, 6 (June 1976): 61-71.

Hohmann, R. "Totzeitmodelle nach der Padé-Approximation." *MSR* **15**, 12 (1972): 435-437.

Hojberg, K. S. "Transport Delay Simulation." *Instruments & Control Systems* **39**, 6 (June 1966): 165-167.

Holden, A. V., ed. *Chaos*. Princeton, NJ: Princeton University Press, 1986.

Holden, A. V., and M. A. Muhamad. "A Graphical Zoo of Strange and Peculiar Attractors." In *Chaos*, edited by A. V. Holden. Princeton, NJ: Princeton University Press, 1986.

Holmes, P. J., and D. C. Whitley. "On the Attracting Set for Duffing's Equation, I: Analytical Methods for Small Force and Damping." In *Partial Differential Equations and Dynamical Systems*, edited by W. E. Fitzgibbon III, 211-240. London: Pitman, 1984.

Holmes, P. J., and D. C. Whitley. "On the Attracting Set for Duffing's Equation, II: A Geometrical Model for Moderate Force Damping." *Physica* **7D** (1983): 111-123.

Holst, P. A. "Padé Approximations and Analog Computer Simulations of Time Delays." *Simulation* **12**, 6 (June 1969): 277-290.

Hostetter, G. H., M. S. Santina, and P. D'Carpio-Montalvo. *Analytical, Numerical, and Computational Methods for Science and Engineering*. Englewood Cliffs, NJ: Prentice-Hall, 1991.

Hostetter, G. H., C. J. Savant Jr., and R. T. Stefani. *Design of Feedback Control Systems*. 2nd. New York: Saunders, 1989.

Hundal, M. S. "Approximate Generation of Non-Integral Powers on Analog Computer." CoED Application Note No. 47. 1977.

Huntley, H. E. *The Divine Proportion: A Study in Mathematical Beauty*. New York: Dover, 1970.

Hurley, J. R. *DEPI 4 (Differential Equations Pseudo-Code Interpreter): An Analog Computer Simulator for the IBM 704*. Internal Memorandum, Allis Chalmers Mfg. Co. 1960.

Hurley, J. R., and J. J. Skiles. "DYSAC: A Digitally Simulated Analog Computer." *Proc. AFIPS/Spring Joint Computer Conference* (1963): 699-82.

Hutchings, H. "Interfacing with C, Part 13." *Electronics World & Wireless World* **97**, 1662 (April 1991): 320-328.

Hutton, D. V. *Applied Mechanical Vibrations*. New York: McGraw-Hill, 1981.

Imagine That, Inc. *Extend: Performance Modeling for Decision Support*. Version 1.1. San Jose, CA: Imagine That, Inc., 1990.

Irvine, R. G. *Operational Amplifier Characteristics and Applications*. 2nd. Englewood Cliffs, NJ: Prentice-Hall, 1981.

Iyer, T. S. K., and S. M. Sharma. "N-type Negative Resistance Circuit." *International Journal of Electronics* **33**, 2 (1972): 235-239.

Jackson, A. S. *Analog Computation*. New York: McGraw-Hill, 1960.

Jackson, J. S. *Passive and Active Analogs with Multidisciplinary Applications*. Engineering Experiment Station Bulletin No. 70. Lexington, KY: College of Engineering, University of Kentucky, 1963.

Jacoby, B. F. "Walsh Functions: A Digital Fourier Series." *Byte* **2**, 9 (September 1977): 190-198.

Jahnke, E., and F. Emde. *Tables of Functions with Formulae and Curves*. 4th. New York: Dover, 1945.

James, M. L., G. M. Smith, and J. C. Wolford. *Analog-Computer Simulation of Engineering Systems*. Scranton, PA: International Textbook, 1966.

James, M. L., G. M. Smith, and J. C. Wolford. *Applied Numerical Methods for Digital Computation with FORTRAN and CSMP*. 2nd. New York: Harper & Row, 1977.

Jamshidi, M. *Analog Simulation of Dynamic Processes with an Introduction to Hybrids Simulation*. Coordinated Science Laboratory. University of Illinois, 1971.

Kammler, D. W., and P. H. Lorrain. "Analog Generation of $1/t$ and $1/t^2$." *Simulation* **10** (February 1969): 95.

Kaplan, B. Z. "On the Simplified Implementation of Quadrature Oscillator Models and the Expected Quality of Their Operation as VCO's." *Proc. of the IEEE* **68**, 6 (June 1980): 745-746.

Kaplan, B. Z., and K. Radparvar. "A Self-Phase Modulated Oscillator and Some Implications." *Journal of the Franklin Institute* **314**, 4 (October 1982): 211-217.

Kaplan, B. Z., and I. Yaffe. "An 'Improved' van der Pol Equation and Some of Its Possible Applications." *International Journal of Electronics* **41**, 2 (1976): 189-198.

Karasz, J. "Hall Sensors and Flip-Flop Sustain Pendulum's Swing." *Electronics* **53**, 12 (22 May 1980): 139,141.

Karayanakis, N. M. "Analog Computer Generation of Mathematical Curves." *ASEE Transactions* **XII**, 9 (September 1980): 89-100.

Karayanakis, N. M. "Analog/Hybrid Computer Simulation of Hovering Experiments in Human Factors Research, Part 1: Generalized Mathematical Modelling." *ASEE Transactions* **X**, 3 (July-September 1990): 9-13.

Karayanakis, N. M. "An Analog Implementation of Fixed-Wing Lateral/Directional Dynamics and Guidelines on Aircraft Simulations in the Engineering Laboratory." *ASEE Transactions* **V**, 4 (October-December 1985): 4-20. (a)

Karayanakis, N. M. "An Analog Implementation of Fixed-Wing Longitudinal Dynamics." *ASEE Transactions* **XI**, 9 (September 1979): 91-102.

Karayanakis, N. M. "Electronic Generation of Higher Plane Curves and the Concept of Digital System Unloading." *Journal of Engineering Design Graphics* **50**, 3 (Autumn 1986): 37-40.

Karayanakis, N. M. "Graphical Solution of Mathematical Functions: The Analog Approach." *Journal of Engineering Design Graphics* **49**, 3 (Autumn 1985): 44-47. ((b)

Karayanakis, N. M. "Implementation Alternatives to Analog Graphic Function Generation: Some Examples." *Engineering Design Graphics Journal* **52**, 3 (Autumn 1988): 12-19.

Karayanakis, N. M. "The Streuding Rate of Change Limiter for Quantized Signals: A Simulation." *Computers in Education Journal* **1**, 4 (October-December 1991): 2-4.

Karayanakis, N. M., and R. W. Jones. *The Dual-Integrator Sin-Cos Oscillator Circuits: A Tutorial Point of View*. Applied Electronics Research Lab Monograph R1-M-187. Austin Peay State University, May 1987.

Karybakas, C. A. "A Second-order System with Time-varying Damping Factor." *Instruments & Control Systems* **39**, 8 (August 1966): 135-137.

Kay, I. M. "An Over-the-Shoulder Look at Discrete Digital Simulation Languages." *Proc. AFIPS/Summer Joint Computer Conference* **40** (1972): 791-798.

Keats, A. B. and D. W. Leggett. "A Transport Delay Simulator Using Digital Techniques." *The Radio and Electronic Engineer* **42**, 4 (April 1972): 179-184.

Kelley, J. L., C. Lochbaum, and V. A. Vyssotsky. "A Block Diagram Compiler." *Bell System Tech. Journal* (May 1961): 669-676.

Kennedy, E. J. *Operational Amplifier Circuits: Theory and Applications*. Fort Worth, TX: Holt, Rinehart, Winston, 1988.

Kennedy, M. P., and L. O. Chua. "Van der Pol and Chaos." *IEEE Trans. on Circuits and Systems* **CAS-33**, 10 (October 1986): 974-980.

Kennedy, R. D. "Wake-Like Solutions of the Laminar Boundary-Layer Equations." *AIAA Journal* **2** (1964): 225-231.

Kerr, C. N. "Rapid Production of System Phase-plane Portraits on the EAI 380 Hybrid/Analog Computer." *ASEE Transactions* **IX**, 1 (January 1977): 1-12.

Kiess, E. M. "Circuit for Displaying Hysteresis Loop of Two-Terminal Inductors." *American Journal of Physics* **58**, 8 (August 1990): 794-795.

Kindler, E. "Combined Simulation Languages: Some Results from Eastern Europe." *Simulation* **30**, 5 (May 1978): 170.

King, W. J. *A Study of Transport Delay Circuits for Analog Computers*. M. S. Thesis. University of Wisconsin, 1961.

King, W. J., and V.C. Rideout. "Improved Transport Delay Circuits for Analog Computer Use." *Proc. 3rd International Analogue Computation Meetings*. Bruxelles: Presses Academiques Europeennes, 1962: 560-568.

Kirschman, R. K. "Experimenting with Circular Sweep." *Popular Electronics*, March 1978, 41-46.

Kiviat, P. J. "Development of Discrete Digital Simulation Languages." *Simulation* 8 (February 1967): 65-70.

Kiviat, P. J. "Simulation Languages." In *Computer Simulation Experiments with Models of Economic Systems*, edited by T. H. Naylor, 406-489. New York: Wiley, 1971.

Knowles, J. B., and D. W. Leggett. "An Analysis of Transport Delay Simulation Methods." *The Radio and Electronic Engineer* 42, 4 (April 1972): 172-178.

Knuth, D. E. *Fundamental Algorithms*. Vol. 1 of *The Art of Computer Programming*. 2nd. Reading, MA: Addison-Wesley, 1973. 3 vols. (a)

Knuth, D. E. *Searching and Sorting*. Vol. 3 of *The Art of Computer Programming*. Reading, MA: Addison-Wesley, 1973. 3 vols. (b)

Knuth, D. E. *Seminumerical Algorithms*. Vol. 2 of *The Art of Computer Programming*. 2nd. Reading, MA: Addison-Wesley, 1981. 3 vols. (c)

Kogan, B. Y., and M. K. Chernyshev. "Simulation of Time Delays by Means of Operational Amplifiers." Original in *Avtom. i Telemekh.* 27 3 (March 1966): 164-177 (Russian). *Automation and Remote Control* 27, 3 (November 1966): 505-519.

Kolk, W. R. *Modern Flight Dynamics*. Englewood Cliffs, NJ, 1961.

Kolk, W. R. "The Describing Function." *Control Engineering* 20, 11 (November 1973): 62-63.

Kolomyjec, W. J. "Plot-a-Function." *Engineering Design Graphics Journal* 47, 3 (1983): 45-48.

Korn, G. A. "New Techniques for All-Digital and Hybrid Simulation." *Proc. 6th AICA Conference*, Munich, 1970. Brussels: Presses Academiques Europeennes, 1971.

Korn, G. A. "EARLY DESIRE: A Floating-point Equation Language Simulation System for Minicomputers and Microcomputers." *Simulation* 38, 5 (May 1982): 151-159.

Korn, G. A., and T. M. Korn. *Electronic Analog and Hybrid Computers*. New York: McGraw-Hill, 1972.

Korn, G. A., and J. V. Wait. *Digital Continuous-System Simulation*. Englewood Cliffs, NJ: Prentice-Hall, 1978.

Kovach, L. D. "The Advantages of Teaching Mathematics with Analog Computers." *Simulation* 4, 4 (April 1965): 219-221.

Krasnow, H. S. "Simulation Languages." In *The Design of Computer Simulation Experiments*, edited by T. H. Naylor, 320-346. Durham, NC: Duke University Press, 1969.

Kreutzer, W. *System Simulation Programming Styles and Languages*. Reading, MA: Addison-Wesley, 1986.

Krol, J. G. "Simplified Simulation of the Elovich Equation." *Instruments & Control Systems* 42, 8 (August 1969): 108.

Kuehnel, H. A. *Human Pilot's Dynamic-Response Characteristics Measured in Flight and on a Nonmoving Simulator*. NASA TND-1229. 1962.

Kulathinal, J. *Transform Analysis and Electronic Networks with Applications*. Columbus, OH: Merrill, 1988.

Janssen, H. J., R. Serneels, L. Beerden, and E. L. M. Flerackers. "Experimental Demonstration of the Resonance Effect of an Anharmonic Oscillator." *American Journal of Physics* **51**, 7 (July 1983): 655-658.

Jefferies, D. J., J. H. B. Deane, and G. C. Johnstone. "An Introduction to Chaos." *Electronics and Communication Engineering Journal* **1**, 3 (May/June 1989): 115-123.

Jensen, R. V. "Classical Chaos." *American Scientist* **75** (March-April 1987): 168-181.

Jess, J. "Zum Entwurf Einer Neuen Klasse Interpolierender Filter." *NTZ* **2** (1968): 75-81.

Jex, H. R., and C. H. Cromwell III. *Theoretical and Experimental Investigation of Some New Longitudinal Handling Qualities Parameters*. Report No. ASD-TR-61-26. Wright-Patterson AFB, OH: Air Force Flight Control Lab, June 1962.

Johnson, C. L. *Analog Computer Techniques*. 2nd. New York: McGraw-Hill, 1963.

Johnson, D. E., and V. Jayakumar. *Operational Amplifier Circuits: Design and Application*. Englewood Cliffs, NJ: Prentice-Hall, 1982.

Johnson, L. W., and R. D. Riess. *Numerical Analysis*. 2nd. Reading, MA: Addison-Wesley, 1982.

Jordan, D. W., and P. Smith. *Nonlinear Ordinary Differential Equations*. 2nd. Oxford: Oxford University Press, 1988.

Lackey, R. B. "The Wonderful World of Walsh Functions." *Proc. 1972 Symp. on Applications of Walsh Functions*. Washington, D.C.: The Catholic University of America, 1972: 2-7.

Lackey, R. B., and D. Meltzer. "A Simplified Definition of Walsh Functions." *IEEE Trans. on Computers* **C-20** (February 1971): 211-213.

Lalli, V. R. "Measurement of Frequency Response Characteristics of Transfer Device Analogs." *IEEE Trans. on Industrial Electronics and Control Instrumentation* **IECI-23**, 1 (February 1976): 108-109.

Langton, C. H. "Orthogonal Functions—An Introduction to Walsh Functions." *Electronics & Wireless World* **93**, 1613 (March 1987): 283-285.

Lapidus, L., and F. P. George. *Numerical Solution of Partial Differential Equations in Science and Engineering*. New York: Wiley, 1982.

Lapidus, L., and W. E. Schlesser, eds. *Numerical Methods for Differential Equations*. New York: Academic Press, 1976.

Larrowe, V. L. "Direct Simulation Bypasses Mathematics, Simplifies Analysis." *Control Engineering* **1**, 3 (November 1954): 25-31.

Lawrence, J. D. *A Catalog of Special Plane Curves*. New York: Dover, 1972.

Lee, A. H. "Flight Simulator Mathematical Models in Aircraft Design." In *Simulation*. AGARD Report CP-79-70. Neuilly-sur-Seine: NATO Advisory Group for Aerospace Research and Development, 1970.

Lees, L. H. "Optimization of a Third Order System." *Trans. of the Institute of Measurement and Control* **4** (February 1971): T19-T20.

Leighton, W. *Ordinary Differential Equations*. 2nd. Belmont, CA: Wadsworth, 1966.

Lesh, H. F. "Methods of Simulating a Differential Analyzer on a Digital Computer." *Journal of the ACM* (July 1958): 281-288.

Lether, F. G. "Curves Made Simple." *PC Tech Journal* **4**, 1 (January 1986): 159-60, 163, 165-66, 169-170.

Levy, B. N. "A MathCAD Exploration: Hunting for Hidden Roots." *Mathematics Teacher* **83**, 9 (December 1990): 704-708.

Lewis, C. D. "Generation of On-Line Analogue Statistical Parameters Using Operational Amplifiers Only." *Control* **10**, 99 (September 1966): 473-474.

Lewis, E. A. S. "Negative Resistor to Provide Self-Oscillation in RLC Circuits." *American Journal of Physics* **44**, 12 (December 1976): 1217-1218.

Lindsay, P. S. "Period Doubling and Chaotic Behaviour in a Driven Anharmonic Oscillator." *Physics Review Letters* **47**, 19 (1981): 1349-1352.

Lorenz, E. N. "Deterministic Nonperiodic Flow." *Journal of Atmospheric Science* **20** (1963): 130-141.

Lorenz, E. N. "Noisy Periodicity and Reverse Bifurcation." In *Nonlinear Dynamics*. Vol. 357 of *Annals of the New York Academy of Science*, edited by R. H. G. Helleman, 282-291. 1980.

Lotka, A. J. *Elements of Mathematical Biology*. New York: Dover, 1956.

Lotka, A. J. "Undamped Oscillations Derived from the Law of Mass Action." *Journal of the American Chemical Society* **42** (1920): 1595-1599.

Lucas, J. J., and J. V. Wait. "DARE P—A Portable CSSL-type Simulation Language." *Simulation* **24**, 1 (January 1975).

Luker, P. A. *Computer-Assisted Modelling of Continuous Systems*. Ph.D. dissertation. University of Bradford, 1982.

Luker, P. A. "MODELLER: Computer-Assisted Modelling of Continuous Systems." *Simulation* **40** (May 1984): 205-214.

Lyn, W. M., and R. N. Linebarger. "DSL/90: A Digital Simulation Program for Continuous System Modeling." *Proc. AFIPS/Spring Joint Computer Conference*. 1966: 165-167.

Lyn, W. M., and D. G. Wyman. *DSL/90 Digital Simulation Language Users Guide*. Report TR02.355. San Jose, CA: IBM Corp., 1965. (a)

Lyn, W. M. and D. G. Wyman. *DSL/90 Digital Simulation Language Systems Guide*. San Jose, CA: IBM Corp., 1965. (b)

Lynn, P. A. *An Introduction to the Analysis and Processing of Signals*. London: Macmillan, 1982. Reprinted by Howard W. Sams, Indianapolis, IN, 1983.

MacLeod, A. M. "Demonstration of Lissajous' Figures and Fourier Synthesis." *Physics Education (GB)* **15**, 5 (September 1980): 298-301.

Marienfeld, H. "Eine Variable Analogrechnerschaltung mit Einem Kardanisch Gelagerten, Servogesteuerten Flugzeugmodell zur Simulation Verschiedener Starrflügler." *Jahrbuch 1967 der WGLR* (1967): 306-314.

Marshall, R. S. "Solving the Falkner-Skan Equation Using CSMP." CoED Application Note No. 29. 1973.

Martens, H. R. "A Comparative Study of Digital Integration Methods." *Simulation* **12**, 2 (February 1969): 87-94.

Martinez, H. M. "Operational Electronic Analog Computers." *ISA Journal* **4**, 3 (March 1957): 82-88.

Mastascusa, E. J. *Computer-Assisted Network and System Analysis.* New York: Wiley, 1988.

Mathews, J. H. *Complex Variables for Mathematics and Engineering.* 2nd. Dubuque, IA: Wm C. Brown, 1988.

Matsumoto, T. "A Chaotic Attractor from Chua's Circuit." *IEEE Trans. on Circuits and Systems* **CAS-31** (December 1984): 1055-1058.

Matsumoto, T. "Chaos in Electronic Circuits." *Proc. IEEE* **75** (1987): 1033-1057.

Matsumoto, T., L. O. Chua, and K. Tokumasu. "Double Scroll via a Two-Transistor Circuit." *IEEE Trans. on Circuits and Systems* **CAS-33**, 8 (August 1986): 828-835.

Matsumoto, T., L. O. Chua, and M. Komuro. "The Double Scroll." *IEEE Trans. on Circuits and Systems* **CAS-32**, 8 (August 1985): 798-818.

May, R. M. "Simple Mathematical Models with Very Complicated Dynamics." *Nature* **261**, 5560 (1976): 459-467.

Mazanov, A., and K. P. Tognetti. "Taylor Series Expansion of Delay Differential Equations: A Warning." *Journal of Theoretical Biology* **46** (1974): 271-282.

McAvoy, T. J. "Least-squares Dead-time Approximations." *IEEE Trans. on Computers* **C-17** (February 1968): 174-178.

McDonnell, J. A. "Simulation Using Perturbation Methods." *Instruments & Control Systems* **37**, 2 (February 1964): 127-128.

McLeod, R. H. "The Analog Computer as an Instructional Tool for Elementary Differential Equations." *ASEE Transactions* **X**, 2 (February 1978): 13-19.

Mees, A. "Chaos in Feedback Systems." In *Chaos*, edited by A. V. Holden, 99-110. Princeton, NJ: Princeton University Press, 1986.

Mello, T. M., and N. B. Tufillaro. "Strange Attractors of a Bouncing Ball." *American Journal of Physics* **55**, 4 (April 1987): 316-320.

Melsa, J. L., and D. G. Schultz. *Linear Control Systems.* New York: McGraw-Hill, 1969.

Mendelson, K. S., and F. G. Karioris. "Chaoticlike Motion of a Linear Dynamical System." *American Journal of Physics* **59**, 3 (March 1991): 221-224.

Merritt, M. J., and D. S. Miller. "MOBSSL: Augmented Block Structured Continuous System Simulation Language for Digital and Hybrid Computers." *Proc. AFIPS/Fall Joint Computer Conference* **35** (1969).

Mesch, F. "Nichtideale Laufzeitglieder für Korrelationsmessungen." *Regelungstechnik* **2** (January 1966): 70-74.

Minorsky, N. *Nonlinear Oscillations.* Princeton, NJ: Van Nostrand, 1962.

Miron, C. "New Simulation of a Delayor for Polynomial Inputs." *Proc. IEEE* **57**, 4 (April 1969): 689-691.

Mishina, T., T. Kohmoto, and T. Hashi. "Simple Electronic Circuit for the Demonstration of Chaotic Phenomena." *American Journal of Physics* **53**, 4 (April 1985): 332-334.

Mitchell, E. L., and J. S. Gauthier. *ACSL User Guide/Reference Manual.* Concord, MA: Mitchell & Gauthier Associates, 1981.

Mohler, R. R. *Dynamics and Control*. Vol. 1 of *Nonlinear Systems*. Englewood Cliffs, NJ: Prentice-Hall, 1991.

Moll, H., and H. Burkhardt. "On an Interactive Digital Simulation System for Hybrid Structured Block Diagrams." In *Computer Aided Design of Control Systems*. IFAC Symposium, Zurich, Switzerland, edited by M. A. Cuénod, 337-341. London: Pergamon, 1979.

Montaner, F. R. "Use of the Zoom in the Analysis of a Curve." *Mathematics Teacher* **80**, 1 (January 1987): 19-28.

Moon, F. C. *Chaotic Vibrations*. New York: Wiley, 1987.

Moon, F.C., and P. J. Holmes. "Addendum: A Magnetoelastic Strange Attractor." *Journal of Sound Vibrations* **69**, 2 (1980): 339.

Moon, F. C., and P. J. Holmes. "A Magnetoelastic Strange Attractor." *Journal of Sound Vibrations* **65**, 2 (1979): 285-296.

Muckler, F. A., R. W. Obermayer, W. H. Hanlon, and F. P. Serio. *Transfer of Training with Simulated Aircraft Dynamics, I: Variations in Period and Damping of the Phugoid Response*. WADD TR 60-615 (I). 1961. (a)

Muckler, F. A., R. W. Obermayer, W. H. Hanlon, and F. P. Serio. *Transfer of Training with Simulated Aircraft Dynamics, II: Variations in Control Gain and Phugoid Characteristics*. WADD TR 60-615 (II). 1961. (b)

Muckler, F. A., R. W. Obermayer, W. H. Hanlon, and F. P. Serio. *Transfer of Training with Simulated Aircraft Dynamics, III: Variations in Course Complexity and Amplitude*. WADD TR 60-615 (III). 1961. (c)

Murray, B. G. Jr. *Population Dynamics: Alternative Models*. New York: Academic Press, 1979.

Mutharasan, R. *Time Delay Simulation Using Analog Memory Units*. M. S. Thesis. Drexel University, 1971.

Mutharasan, R., and D. R. Coughanowr. "Time Delay Simulation Using Analog Memory Units." *Proc. 13th Joint Automatic Control Conference*, (August 1972): 632-636.

Na, T. Y. *Computational Methods in Engineering Boundary Value Problems*. New York: Academic Press, 1979.

Nakamura, S. *Applied Numerical Methods with Software*. Englewood Cliffs, NJ: Prentice-Hall, 1991.

Nelson, R. A., and M. G. Olsson. "The Pendulum: Rich Physics from a Simple System." *American Journal of Physics* **54**, 2 (February 1986): 112-21.

Netzer, Y. "Variable Damping Speeds Servo Response." *EDN* **26**, 15 (5 August 1981): 138-139.

Newcomb, R. W., and S. Sathyan. "An RC Op Amp Chaos Generator." *IEEE Trans. on Circuits and Systems* **CAS-30**, 1 (January 1983): 54-56.

Newell, F. D., and P. E. Pietrzak. "In-Flight Measurement of Human Response Characteristics." *Journal of Aircraft* **5**, 3 (May-June 1968): 277-284.

Nicklin, R. C., and J. B. Rafert. "The Digital Pendulum." *American Journal of Physics* **52**, 7 (July 1984): 632-639.

Nielsen, G. "Digital Processing of Analogue Signals, Part 3." *Electronic Engineering* **51**, 617 (January 1979): 35-36, 40.

Nigro, B. J. "An Investigation of Optimally Stable Numerical Integration Methods with Application to Real Time Simulation." *Simulation* **13**, 5 (November 1969): 253-264.

Nilsen, R. N., and W. J. Karplus. "Continuous System Simulation Languages: A State-of-the Art Survey." *Proc. International Assoc. for Analog Computation* **1** (January 1974): 17-25.

Nilsen, R., and L. Levine. "A General Method for Simulating Continuously Variable Transport Lag Phenomena." *Proc. 6th International Analogue Computation Meetings*. Bruxelles: Presses Academique Europeennes, 1970.

Nishikawa, S. "Negative-resistance Circuit Is Adjustable and Versatile." *Electronic Design* **4** (18 February 1971): 90.

Nordsieck, A. "On Numerical Integration of Ordinary Differential Equations." *Mathematics of Computation* **16**, 77 (January 1962): 22-49.

Norman, F.A. "Parameter-Generated Loci of Critical Points of Polynomials." *The College Mathematics Journal* **19**, 2 (May 1988): 223-229.

Ogata, K. *System Dynamics*. Englewood Cliffs, NJ: Prentice-Hall, 1978.

Olsen, L. F. "The Enzyme and the Strange Attractor: Comparisons of Experimental and Numerical Data for an Enzyme Reaction with Chaotic Motion." In *Stochastic Phenomena and Chaotic Behavior in Complex Systems*, edited by P. Schuster, 116-123. Berlin: Springer-Verlag, 1984.

Olver, F. W. J. "Bessel Functions of Integer Order." In *Handbook of Mathematical Functions*. National Bureau of Standards Applied Mathematics Series No. 55, edited by M. Abramowitz and I. A. Stegun. Washington, DC: U. S. Government Printing Office, 1972.

Ord-Smith, R. J., and J. Stephenson. *Computer Simulation of Continuous Systems*. Cambridge, UK: Cambridge University Press, 1975.

Oren, T. I. "Digital Simulation Languages for Combined Systems: An Overview." *Proc. of the SCS Summer Computer Simulation Conference*. 1973.

Oren, T. I. "Software for Simulation of Combined Continuous and Discrete Systems: A State of the Art Review." *Simulation* **28**, 2 (1977): 33-45.

Oren, T. I., and B. P. Zeigler. "Concepts for Advanced Simulation Methodologies." *Simulation* **30**, 3 (1979): 70-82.

Osburn, J. O. "Inverse Simulation." *Instruments & Control Systems* **40** (April 1967): 131-133.

Osowski, S. "Frequency-Multiple Generation Technique Using Chebyshev Polynomials." *Electronics Letters* **16**, 3 (31 January 1980): 91-92.

Otterman, J. "How to Avoid Extra Integrators When Simulating RLC Networks." *Control Engineering* **4** (November 1957): 111-114.

Otterman, J. "On the Loop- and Node-Analysis Approaches to the Simulation of Electrical Networks." *IRE Trans. on electronic Computers* **EC-7** (September 1958): 199-206.

Otterman, J. "The Properties and Methods for Computation of Exponentially Mapped Past Statistical Averages." *IRE Trans. on Automatic Control* **AC-5**, 1 (January 1960): 11-17.

Packer, T. J. "An Extended Version of the 1130 CSMP." *Simulation* **13**, 5 (November 1969): 231-232.

Padé, H. E. "Sur la Représentation Aprochée d'une Fonction par des Fractions Rationelles", *Ann. Sci. de École Normale Sup.* (1892) 9.

Pasupathy, S. "Amplitude of Oscillation in a Negative Resistance Oscillator." *International Journal of Electronics* **35**, 3 (1973): 425-428.

Paul, R. J. A., and A. I. S. Ahmad. "Numerical Solution of Second Order Hyperbolic Partial Differential Equations by the Method of Continuous Characteristics." *IEE Proceedings* **117**, 6 (June 1970): 1166-1174. (a)

Paul, R. J. A., and A. I. S. Ahmad. "Analogue Solution of Second Order Hyperbolic Partial Differential Equations by the Method of Continuous Characteristics." *IEE Proceedings* **117**, 6 (June 1970): 1175-1184. (b)

Paul, R. J. A., and A. I. S. Ahmad. "Analogue Solution of Elliptic Partial Differential Equations by Conformal Transformation." *IEE Proceedings* **117**, 7 (July 1970): 1393-1397. (c)

Paul, R. J. A., and H. B. Gatland. "Design and Some Application of a Generalized Integrator." *IEE Proceedings* **114**, 9 (September 1967): 1193-1205.

Pavlidis, T. *Biological Oscillators: Their Mathematical Analysis*. New York: Academic Press, 1973.

Pedoe, D. *Geometry and the Visual Arts*. New York: Dover, 1976.

Perez, J. "Mechanism for Global Features of Chaos in a Driven Nonlinear Oscillator." *Physics Review A* **32**, 4 (1985): 2513-2516.

Perkins, C. D., and R. E. Hage. *Airplane Performance, Stability and Control*. New York: Wiley, 1949.

Petersen, H. E., F. J. Sansom, and L. M. Warshawsky. "MIDAS: How It Works and How It's Worked." *Proc. AFIPS/Fall Joint Computer Conference* (1964): 313-324.

Peterson, G. R. *Basic Analog Computation*. New York: Macmillan, 1967.

Peterson, N. D. "MIMIC: An Alternative Programming Language for Industrial Dynamics." *Socio-Economic Plan. Sci.* **6** (1972).

Peterson, R. O., R. E. Page, and K. M. Dodge. "Wolves, Moose and the Allometry of Population Cycles." *Science* **224** (1984): 1350.

Petit Bois, G. *Tables of Indefinite Integrals*. New York: Dover, 1964. (Unabridged English trans. of *Tafeln der Unbestimmten Integrale*, first published by Butterworths, 1906.)

Phaor, J., J. Fettich, and M. Tavzes. "A Harmonic Oscillator with Low Harmonic Distortion and Stable Amplitude." *International Journal of Electronics* **37**, 6 (1974): 765-768.

Pickover, C. A. *Computers, Pattern, Chaos and Beauty*. New York: St. Martin's Press, 1990.

Pickover, C. A. "Pattern Formation and Chaos in Networks." *Communications of the ACM* **31**, 2 (February 1988): 136-151.

Pielou, E. C. *An Introduction to Mathematical Ecology*. Cambridge (UK): Cambridge University Press, 1969.

Pimentel, J. R. "Analysis and Synthesis of Waveform Generators in the Phase Plane." *IEEE Trans. on Industrial Electronics and Control Instrumentation* **IECI-25**, 3 (August 1978): 217-220.

Pippard, A. B. *Response and Stability: An Introduction to the Physical Theory*. New York: Cambridge University Press, 1985.

Poincaré, H. *Memoire sur les Courbes Définies par les Équations Differentielles*. Paris: Gauthier-Villas, 1881-1890. 4 vols.

Pradtl, L. *Motion of Fluids with Very Little Viscosity*. NACA TN No. 452. 1928. Originally presented to 3rd International Mathematical Congress, Heidelberg, 1904.

Priest, J. "Interfacing Pendulums to a Microcomputer." *American Journal of Physics* **54**, 10 (October 1986): 953-955.

Prigogine, I., and R. LeFever. "Symmetry-breaking Instabilities in Dissipative Systems." *Journal of Chemical Physics* **48** (1968): 1695-1700.

Prigogine, I., and G. Nicolis. "On Symmetry-breaking Instabilities in Dissipative Systems." *Journal of Chemical Physics* **46** (1967): 3542-3550.

Pritsker, A. A. B. *The GASP IV Simulation Language*. New York: Wiley, 1974.

Pritsker, A. A. B., and R. E. Young. *Simulation with GASP-PL/1: A PL/1-based Continuous/Discrete Simulation Language*. New York: Wiley, 1975.

Pritsker, A. A. B., and P. Pegden. *Introduction to Simulation and SLAM*. New York: Halsted Press, 1983.

Pugh, A. L. III. *DYNAMO II Users Manual*. Cambridge, MA: MIT Press, 1976.

Pugh-Roberts Associates, Inc. *User Guide and Reference Manual for Micro-DYNAMO*. Reading-MA: Addison-Wesley, 1982.

Purdom, P. W. Jr., and C.A. Brown. *The Analysis of Algorithms*. New York: Holt, Rinehart & Winston, 1985.

Rabiner, L. R., and C. M. Rader. *Digital Signal Processing*. New York: Wiley, 1972.

Rademacher, H. "Einige-Satze von allgemeinen Orthogonalfunktionen." *Math. Annalen*. **87** (1922): 112-138.

Rao, S. S. *Mechanical Vibrations*. 2nd. Reading, MA: Addison-Wesley, 1990.

Raven, F. H. *Automatic Control Engineering*. 4th. New York: McGraw-Hill, 1987.

Relton, F. E. *Applied Bessel Functions*. New York: Dover, 1965.

Reynolds, J. A. *Applied Transformed Circuit Theory for Technology*. New York: Wiley, 1985.

Ricchiuto, A., and A. Tozzi. "Motion of a Harmonic Oscillator with Sliding and Viscous Friction." *American Journal of Physics* **50**, 2 (February 1982): 176-179.

Ricci, F. J. *Analog/Logic Programming and Simulation*. New York: Spartan Books, 1972.

Richardson, G. P., and A. L. Pugh III. *Introduction to System Dynamics Modelling with DYNAMO*. Cambridge, MA: MIT Press, 1981.

Richmond, B. *A User's Guide to STELLA*. Lyme, NH: High Performance Systems, 1985.

Rideout, V. C., N. S. Nagaraja, S. Sampath, V. N. Chiplunkar, and L. S. Manavalan. "Design of a Timing Device and Nonlinear Units for an Electronic Differential Analyzer." *Journal of the Indian Institute of Science* **38**, Section A (1956): 66-79.

Rietman, E. *Exploring the Geometry of Nature: Computer Modelling of Chaos, Fractals, Cellular Automata and Neural Networks*. Blue Ridge Summit, PA: TAB Books, 1988.

Roberge, J. K. *Operational Amplifiers: Theory and Practice*. New York: Wiley, 1975.

Roberts, N., D. Andersen, R. Deal, M. Garet, and W. Shaffer. *Introduction to Computer Simulation*. Reading, MA: Addison-Wesley, 1983.

Roberts, E. B., ed. *Managerial Applications of System Dynamics*. Cambridge, MA: MIT Press, 1978.

Robinson, L. F. "How GASP, SIMULA and DYNAMO View a Problem." In *Progress in Simulation*, edited by I. M. Kay and J. McLeod, 167-214. New York: Gordon & Breach, 1972.

Rocard, Y. *General Dynamics of Vibrations*. 3rd. New York: Frederic Ungar, 1960. (English translation of *Dynamique Générale des Vibrations*, 3rd, Paris: Masson, 1960.

Rockard, Y. *Theorie des Oscillateurs*. Paris: Revue Scientifique, 1941.

Rogers, A. E. *Analog Computers and Mathematics*. Applications Reference Library Publ. No. 7.6.4a. West Long Branch, NJ: Electronic Associates, 1969.

Rogers, A. E. *Nonlinear Relaxation Oscillations* . EAI Educator's Demonstration Series Publ. No. 7.6.5a. West Long Branch, NJ: Electronic Associates, 1966.

Rogers, A. E., and T. W. Connolly. *Analog Computation in Engineering Design*. New York: McGraw-Hill, 1960.

Rollins, R. W., and E. R. Hunt. "Exactly Solvable Model of A Physical System Exhibiting Universal Chaotic Behaviour." *Physics Review Letters* **49**, 18 (1982): 1295-1298.

Rosen, R., ed. *Supercellular Systems*. Vol. 3 of *Foundations of Mathematical Biology*. New York: Academic Press, 1973.

Rosenberg, R. C., and D. C. Karnopp. *Introduction to Physical System Dynamics*. New York: McGraw-Hill, 1983.

Rössler, O. E. "An Equation for Continuous Chaos." *Physics Letters* **57A** (1976): 397.

Rössler, O. E. "An Equation for Hyperchaos." *Physics Letters* **71A** (1979): 155-157. (a)

Rössler, O. E. "Chaotic Oscillations: An Example of Hyperchaos." *AMS Lectures in Applied Mathematics* **17** (1979): 141-155. (b)

Rössler, O. E. "Continuous Chaos—Four Prototype Equations." *Ann. New York Academy of Science* **316** (1979): 376-392. (c)

Rössler, O. E. "The Chaotic Hierarchy." *Z. Naturforsch* **38a** (1983): 788-801.

Roth, D. "Special Filters Based on Walsh Functions." *Prof. 1970 Symposium and Workshop on Applications of Walsh Functions*. Washington, DC: Naval Research Laboratory, (1970) 12-17.

Roth, M., and D. Reschke. "Ein neues Totzeitmodell nach Padé-Approximation." *MSR* **17**, 2 (1974): 57-60.

Rowland, J. R. *Linear Control Systems: Modelling, Analysis, and Design*. New York: Wiley, 1986.

Ruelle, D., and F. Takens. "On the Nature of Turbulence." *Comm. Mathematical Physics* **20** (1971): 167-192.

Rust, H.-P. "Sinus-Kosinus-Generator für die hohlkegelförmige Objectbestrahlung im Elektronenmikroskop." *Internationale Elektronische Rundschan* **6** (1973): 121-122.

Sadoff, M., and C. B. Dolkas. *Acceleration Stress Effects on Pilot Performance and Dynamic Response*. MIT-NASA Working Conference on Manual Control. 1966.

Salzmann, B. "Finite Amplitude Free Correction as an Initial Value Problem." *Journal of Atmospheric Science* **19** (1962): 239-341.

Salvadori, M. G., and M. L. Baron. *Numerical Methods in Engineering*. Englewood Cliffs, NJ: Prentice-Hall, 1961.

Sansom, F. J. "MIMIC: Successor to MIDAS." Paper delivered at the Joint Meeting of Central Midwestern Simulation Councils. July 1965.

Sansom, F. J. *MIMIC Programming Manual*. Report No. SEG-TR-67-31. Wright-Patterson AFB, OH: Air Force Flight Dynamics Laboratory, 1967.

Saraswat, R. C., and S.K. Saha. "Quadrature Oscillators with Extended Time Period Using Grounded Capacitors." *International Journal of Electronics* **52**, 5 (1982): 419-427.

Schlichting, H. *Boundary Layer Theory*. Oxford: Pergamon Press, 1955.

Schnakenberg, J. "Simple Chemical Reaction Systems with Limit Cycle Behavior." *Journal of Theoretical Biology* **81** (1979): 389-400.

Schuster, P., ed. *Stochastic Phenomena and Chaotic Behavior in Complex Systems*. Berlin: Springer-Verlag, 1984.

Schwarze, G., A. Sydow, and H. Dittman. "Zur Güte von Totzeitapproximationen in Regelkreisen." *MSR* **6**, 8 (1963): 319-322.

SCi Simulation Software Committee. "The SCi Continuous System Simulation Language (CSSL)." *Simulation* **9**, 6 (December 1967): 281-303.

Scott, N. R. "On the Use of Redundant Integrators in Analog Computers." *IRE Trans. on Electronic Computers* **EC-6** (December 1957): 287-288.

Seddon, J. P. "The Simulation of Variable Delay." *IEEE Trans. on Computers* **C-17**, 1 (January 1967): 89-94.

Sedgewick, R. *Algorithms*. Reading, MA: Addison-Wesley, 1983.

Selfridge, R. G. "Coding a General Purpose Digital Computer to Operate as a Differential Analyzer." *Proc. AFIPS/Western Joint Computer Conference* (1955): 82-84.

Shafai, L.. "Analysis of a Current-controlled Negative Resistance." *International Journal of Electronics* **33**, 6 (1972): 703-706.

Shah, M. J. *Engineering Simulation Using Small Scientific Computers*. Englewood Cliffs, NJ: Prentice-Hall, 1976.

Shampine, L. F., and C. W. Gear. "A User's View of Solving Stiff Ordinary Differential Equations." *SIAM Review* **21** (1979).

Sharma, S. M. "Current-controlled (S-type) Negative Resistance Circuit." *International Journal of Electronics* **37**, 2 (1974): 209-218.

Sharpe, E. D. *Analog Computer Simulation....A Way of Thinking*. EAI Applications Reference Library, Educational 7.6.13a. West Long Branch, NJ: Electronic Analog Associates, 1969.

Sheingold, D. II., ed. *Nonlinear Circuits Handbook*. Norwood, MA: Analog Devices, Inc., 1976.

Shervatov, V. G. *Hyperbolic Functions*. Boston: D. C. Heath, 1963. (Survey of Recent Eastern European Mathematical Literature series.)

Shirer, D. L. "Quantum-Mechanical Eigenfunctions: An Advanced Physics Lab Experiment with the Analog Computer." *CoED Applications* **II**, 3 (1978).

Shoup, T. E. *A Practical Guide to Computer Methods for Engineers*. Englewood Cliffs, NJ: Prentice-Hall, 1979.

Skala, K. "Eine einfache und günstige Modellbildung von Regelstrecken mit echter Totzeit." *Regelungstechnik und Prozeb-Datenverarbeitung* 6 (January 1971): 251-255.

Slobodkin, L. B. *Growth and Regulation of Animal Population*. New York: Holt, Rinehart & Winston, 1961.

Smetana, F. O. *Computer Assisted Analysis of Aircraft Performance Stability and Control*. New York: McGraw-Hill, 1984.

Smith, B. A. "Lissajous' Figures." *Physics Education (GB)* 16, 1 (January 1981): 38-43, 46.

Smith, B. A., and E. M. Smith. "Lissajous' Figures Revisited." *Physics Education (GB)* 17, 1 (January 1982): 121-113, 18.

Smith, D. E. *Special Topics of Elementary Mathematics*. Vol. II of *History of Mathematics*. London: Ginn, 1925.

Smith, J. I. *Modern Operational Circuit Design*. New York: Wiley, 1971.

Smoak, R. A., and I. Jacobson. "Analog Simulation as an Aid in Teaching Flight Mechanics." *ACEUG Transactions (ASEE)* II, 8 (August 1970): 217-224.

Sommerfeld, J. T. "Solving the Elovich Equation by Analog Computer." *Instruments & Control Systems* 41, 4 (April 1968): 137-138.

Sparrow, C. T. "An Introduction to the Lorenz Equations." *IEEE Trans.* CAS-30, 8 (1983): 533-541.

Sparrow, C. T. "The Lorenz Equations ." In *Chaos*, edited by A. V. Holden, 111-134. Princeton, NJ: Princeton University Press, 1986.

Sparrow, C. T. *The Lorenz Equations: Bifurcations, Chaos and Strange Attractors*. Berlin: Springer-Verlag, 1982.

Spasov, A. Y., and A. I. Enikova. "Parametric Oscillations in an Oscillating Circuit Utilizing Negative Resistance." *International Journal of Electronics* 35, 4 (1973): 483-495.

Speckhart, H., and W. H. Green. *A Guide to Using CSMP*. Englewood Cliffs, NJ: Prentice-Hall, 1976.

Spiegel, M. R. *Applied Differential Equations*. 3rd. Englewood Cliffs, NJ: Prentice-Hall, 1981.

Squire, P. T. "Pendulum Damping." *American Journal of Physics* 54, 11 (November 1986): 984-991.

Stanley, I. W., and D. J. Ager. "Current Controlled Negative Resistance Circuit." *Electronic Letters* 6 (1970): 380.

Stanley, W. D. *Operational Amplifiers with Linear Integrated Circuits*. 2nd. Columbus, OH: Merrill, 1989. (a)

Stanley, W. D. *Transform Circuit Analysis for Engineering and Technology*. 2nd. Englewood Cliffs, NJ: Prentice-Hall, 1989. (b)

Stechman, E. *The Design and Development of a MIMIC-based Analog-Hybrid Simulator*. M. S. Thesis. South Dakota School of Mines and Technology, 1972.

Steiger, M. H., and K. Chen. "Further Similiarity Solutions of Two Dimensional Wakes and Jets." *AIAA Journal* 3 (1965): 528-530.

Stein, M. L., J. Rose, and D. B. Parker. "A Compiler with an Analog-Oriented Input Language." *Proc. AFIPS/Western Joint Computer Conference* (1959): 92-102.

Stein, M. L., and J. Rose. "Changing from Analog to Digital Programming by Digital Techniques." *Journal of the ACM* (1960): 10-23.

Stephenson, R. E. *Computer Simulation for Engineers*. New York: Harcourt, Brace & Jovanovich, 1971.

Stewart, A. "Simulation of the Schrödinger Equation on SHAC." *Physics Education (GB)* **11**, 2 (March 1976): 104-110.

Stewart, J. L. "Generalized Padé Approximation." *Proc. IRE* **48** (December 1960): 2003-2008.

Stewartson, K. "Further Solutions of the Falkner-Skan Equation." *Proc. Cambridge Phil. Society* **50** (1954): 454-465.

Stick, M. E., and M. J. Stick. "High Resolution Plots of Trigonometric Functions." *Mathematics Teacher* **78**, 8 (November 1985): 632-636.

Stocker, J. J. *Nonlinear Vibrations*. New York: Wiley, 1950.

Stojamovic, V. S., and M. D. Radmanovic. "Chebyshev Delay Approximation of Even Degree with Constraint at the Origin." *Electronic Letters* **14**, 6 (16 March 1978): 202-204.

Stoker, J. J. *Nonlinear Vibrations in Mechanical and Electrical Systems*. New York: Interscience, 1950.

Stone, R. S., and R. A. Dandl. "A Variable Function Delay for Analog Computers." *IRE Trans* **EC-6**, 3 (September 1957): 187-189.

Storch, L. "Synthesis of Constant-time Delay Ladder Networks Using Bessel Polynomials." *Proc. IRE* **42** (November 1954): 1666-1675.

Strebel, D. E. "Analog Computer Laboratory with Biological Examples." *American Journal of Physics* **47**, 7 (July 1979): 612-618.

Streuding, G. C. "Rate-of-Change Limiter for Quantized Signals." *NASA Technical Briefs* **2**, 4 (Winter 1977): 457.

Strnad, J. "Quantum Physics for Beginners." *Physics Education (GB)* **16**, 2 (March 1981): 88-92.

Strong, J. D., and G. Hannauer. *A Practical Approach to Analog Computers*. EAI Applications Reference Library, General Section No. 957052. West Long Branch, NJ: Electronic Associates, Inc., 1969.

Stubbs, G. S., and C. H. Single. *Transport Delay Simulation Circuit*. Report WABD-T-38. Pittsburgh, PA: Westinghouse Electric Corp., 1954.

Sullivan, J. "Padé Approximants via the Continued Fraction Approach." *American Journal of Physics* **46**, 5 (May 1978): 489-494.

Summers, M. K. "Solution of the Schrödinger Equation for the Hydrogen Atom Using a Modular Analogue Computing System." Physics Education (GB) **10** (September 1975): 424-429.

Summers, M. K. "The Analogue Computer as an Aid to Teaching Elementary Quantum Mechanics." *Physics Education (UK)* **11**, 4 (June 1976): 296-302.

Summers, M. K. "A Quantum Mechanics Experiment for the Undergraduate Laboratory." *Physics Education (UK)* **13**, 1 (January 1978): 22-27.

Tanaka, S., T. Matsumoto, and L. O. Chua. "Bifurcation Scenario in a Driven R-L Diode Circuit." *Physica D* **28** (1987): 317-344.

Teasdale, R. D. "Time Domain Approximation by Use of Padé Approximants." *IRE Convention Record* **Pt. V** (1953): 89-94.

Temel, Z. B., and D. A. Linkens. "Medical Data Analysis Using Microprocessor-based Walsh Transformations." *Medical, Biological Engineering Computing* **16** (March 1978): 188-194.

Teodorescu, D. "Beschreibungsfunktionen von Regelsystemen mit Nichtlinearitäten, dargestellt durch harmonische und hyperbolische Funktionen." *Regelungstechnik und Prozeb-Datenverarbeitung* **1** (17 January 1971): 15-19.

Testa, J., J. Perez, and C. Jeffries. "Evidence for Universal Behaviour in a Non-linear Oscillator." *Physics Review Letters* **48** (1982): 710-717.

Theodorsen, T., and Garrick I. E. *General Potential Theory of Arbitrary Wing Sections*. NACA Report No. 452. Washington, DC: National Advisory Committee of Aeronautics, 1933.

Thompson, B. "MODEL-IT!: Simulation Software for Macintosh." *Computer Shopper* **10**, 11 (November 1990): 578, 581.

Thompson, J. M. T., and H. B. Stewart. *Nonlinear Dynamics and Chaos: Geometrical Methods for Engineers and Scientists*. New York: Wiley, 1986.

Thomson, W. (Lord Kelvin) "Mechanical Integration of the Linear Differential Equations of the Second Order with Variable Coefficients." *Proc. of the Royal Society* **23** (1876): 269. (a)

Thomson, W. (Lord Kelvin) "Mechanical Integration of the General Linear Differential Equations of Any Order with Variable Coefficients." *Proc. of the Royal Society* **24** (1876): 271. (b)

Tocher, K. D. "A Review of Simulation Languages." *Operations Research Quarterly* **16**, 2 (1965): 189-218.

Tocher, K. D. "Simulation Languages." In *Progress in Operations Research*, edited by J. S. Aronofsky, 72-113. New York: Wiley, 1979.

Tominson, N. P., M. Horowitz, and C. H. Reynolds. "Analog Computer Construction of Conformal Maps in Fluid Dynamics." *Journal Applied Physics* **26** (1955): 229-232.

Tomita, K. "Periodically Forced Nonlinear Oscillators." In *Chaos*, edited by A. V. Holden, 211-236. 1986.

Tomita, K., and T. Kai. "Stroboscopic Phase Portrait and Strange Attractors." *Physics Letters* **66A** (1978): 91-93.

Tomlinson, G. H. "Synthesis of Delay Networks for an Analogue Computer." *Proc. Inst. Elect. Engineers* **112**, 9 (September 1965): 1806-1814.

Tomovic, R., and W. J. Karplus. *High-Speed Analog Computers*. New York: Dover, 1970.

Tondl, A., V. Fiala, and J. Škliba. *Domains of Attraction for Non-Linear Systems*. Monographs and Memoranda No. 8. Praha: National Research Institute for Machine Design, Běchovice, 1970.

Trahanas, S. *Ordinary Differential Equations*. Vol. 1 of *Differential Equations*. Iraklion, Crete: Crete University Press, 1989. (in Greek)

Traub, J. F. *Iterative Methods for the Solution of Equations*. Englewood Cliffs, NJ: Prentice-Hall, 1964.

Truxal, J. G. *Introductory System Engineering*. New York: McGraw-Hill, 1972.

Tufillaro, N. B., T. A. Abbott, and D. J. Griffiths. "Swinging Atwood's Machine." *American Journal of Physics* **52**, 10 (October 1984): 895-903.

Tuma, J. J. *Engineering Mathematics Handbook*. 2nd. New York: McGraw-Hill, 1979.

TUTSIM Products. *TUTSIM Block Diagram Simulation Language*. Palo Alto, CA: TUTSIM Products, 1991.

Tzafestas, S., G. Frangakis, and T. Pimenidis. "Global Walsh Function Generators." *Electronic Engineering* **48**, 585 (November 1976): 45-49.

Veda, Y. "Explosion of Strange Attractors Exhibited by Duffing's Equation." *Ann. New York Academy of Science* **357** (1980): 422-434.

Veda, Y. "Steady Motions Exhibited by Duffing's Equation: A Picture Book of Regular and Chaotic Motions." In *New Approaches to Nonlinear Problems in Dynamics*, edited by P. Holmes, 311-322. Philadelphia: SIAM, 1979.

Veda, Y., and N. Akamatsu. "Chaotically Transitional Phenomena in the Forced Negative Resistance Oscillator." *IEEE Trans.* **CS-28** (1981): 217-224.

Ung, M. T., and R. A. MacDonald. *Application of Desk Top Analog Computers as Aids in Teaching Mathematics*. Hybrid Computation Applications Reference Library, No. 7.4.12a. West Long Branch, NJ: Electronic Associates, Inc., 1966.

Urbanek, E. D. "Waveform Is Synthesized from Linear Segments." *Electronics* (3 April 1975): 100.

van der Pol, B. "Forced Oscillations in a Circuit with Nonlinear Resistance (Receptance with Reactive Triode)." *London, Edinburgh and Dublin Philosophical Magazine* **3** (1927): 65-80.

van der Pol, B., and J. van der Mark. "Frequency Demultiplication." *Nature* **120**, 3019 (10 September 1927): 363-364.

Van Valkenburg, M. E. *Analog Filter Design*. New York: Holt, Rinehart and Winston, 1982.

Vichnevetsky, R. "Analogue Computer Simulation of Time-Dependent Delay Using the Concept of Generalized Transfer Function." *Journal of the International Association for Analog Computation* **6**, 2 (1964): 106-109.

Vichnevetsky, R. *Elliptical Equations and the Finite Element Method*. Vol. I of *Computer Methods for Partial Differential Equations*. Englewood Cliffs, NJ: Prentice-Hall, 1981.

Vichnevetsky, R. *Initial Value Problems*. Vol. 2 of *Computer Methods for Partial Differential Equations*. Englewood Cliffs, NJ: Prentice-Hall, 1982.

Vojtášek, S. *Autonomous Oscillatory Systems with Piecewise Linear Characteristics (In Czech)*. D.Sc. dissertation. Czechoslovak Academy of Sciences, Prague, 1969.

Vojtášek, S., and K. Janáč. *Solution of Non-Linear Systems*. London: Iliffe, 1969.

Volterra, V. "Variations and Fluctuations of the Number of Individuals in Animal Species Living Together." In *Animal Ecology*, edited by R. N. Chapman. New York: McGraw-Hill, 1931.

Wagner, C. "Smoothing the Output from a DAC." *NASA Technical Briefs* **5**, 2 (Summer 1980).

Wait, J. V., L. P. Huelsman, and G. A. Korn. *Introduction to Operational Amplifier Theory and Applications*. New York: McGraw-Hill, 1975.

Waits, B. K., and F. Demana. "Computers and the Rational-Root Theorem—Another View." *Mathematics Teacher* **82**, 2 (February 1989): 124-125.

Walker, J. "Strange Things Happen When Two Pendulums Interact Through a Variety of Interconnections." *Scientific American* **253** (1985): 176-180.

Wall, H. S. "On the Padé Approximants Associated with a Positive Definite Power Series." *Trans. American Mathematical Society* **33** (1931): 511-532.

Wall, H. S. "General Theorems on the Convergence of Sequences of Padé Approximants." *Trans. American Mathematical Society* **34** (1932): 409-416.

Walmsley, W. M. "Walsh Functions, Transforms and Their Applications." *Electronic Engineering* **46**, 556 (June 1974): 63, 65, 67-68.

Walsh, J. L. "A Closed Set of Normal Orthogonal Functions." *American Journal of Mathematics* **45** (1923): 5-24.

Walters, L. G. "Hidden Regenerative Loops in Electronic Analog Computers." *IRE Trans. on Electronic Computers* **EC-2** (June 1953): 1-4.

Walton, K. D., and J. D. Walton. "Computer-Assisted Polar Graphing." *Mathematics Teacher* **80**, 3 (March 1987): 246-250.

Wanner, G. "On the Integration of Stiff Differential Equations." In *International Series in Numerical Mathematics No. 37*, edited by J. Descloux and J. Marti, 209-226. Stuttgart: Birkhäuser Verlag, 1977.

Wassel, G. "A Study of a Ballistic Pendulum." *CoED Applications (ASEE)* **I**, 2 (1978).

Watts, D. *A Catalog of Operational Transfer Functions*. New York: Garland, 1977.

Weiner, M. "Linearize Analog Signals Continuously." *Electronic Design* **24** (23 November 1972): 156-159.

Weldon, T. P. "An Inductorless Double Scroll Chaotic Circuit." *American Journal of Physics* **58**, 10 (October 1990): 936-941.

White, J. E. "Teaching with CAL: A Mathematics Teaching and Learning Environment." *The College Mathematics Journal* **19**, 5 (November 1988): 424-443.

Willamowski, K.-D., and O. E. Rössler. "Irregular Oscillations in a Realistic Abstract Quadratic Mass Action System." *Z. Naturforsch* **35a** (1980): 317-318.

Williams, A. B. "Squaring Circuit Generates Second Harmonic for Controlled-Distortion Test Signal." *Electronic Design* **8** (12 April 1975): 78.

Wilson, G., and M. Papamichael. "Phase Invariant Delay Approximations." *Electronic Letters* **17**, 8 (April 1981): 294-295.

Wilson, G., and M. Papamichael. "Group Delay Transfer Functions with Least Squares Error." *The Radio and Electronic Engineer* **53**, 5 (May 1983): 199-208.

Wong, Y. J. "Design a Low Cost, Low-Distortion, Precision Sine-Wave Oscillator." *EDN*, **20** (September 1978): 107-113.

Wong, Y. J., and W. E. Ott. *Function Circuits: Design and Applications*. New York: McGraw-Hill, 1976.

Wunderlich, F. J., and M. Peastrel. "Electronic Analog of Radioactive Decay." *American Journal of Physics* **46**, 2 (February 1978): 189-190.

Wylen, H. E. "Uses of the Analog Computer in the Upper Level Physics Laboratory." *ACES Transactions (ASEE)* **III**, 9 (1971): 193-196.

Wylen, H. E., and W. M. Schwarz. "The Analog Computer as a Teaching Tool in Physics." *American Journal of Physics* **41**, 5 (May 1973): 622-631.

Yates, B. H. "Analog Simulation of Passive Networks." *Instruments & Control Systems* **38**, 2 (February 1965): 161-162.

Yorke, E. D. "Square-wave Model for a Pendulum with Oscillating Suspension." *American Journal of Physics* **46**, 3 (March 1978): 285-288.

Yoshikawa, K., N. Oyama, M. Shoji, and S. Nakata. "Use of a Saline Oscillator as a Simple Nonlinear Dynamical System: Rhythms, Bifurcation, and Entrainment." *American Journal of Physics* **59**, 2 (February 1991): 137-141.

Young, L. R., and L. Stark. *Biological Control Systems—A Critical Review and Evaluation: Developments in Manual Control.* NASA CR-190. March 1965.

Zagajewski, T., and E. Moll. "Pulse Multiplication Using Walsh Functions." *Electronic Engineering* **50**, 607 (Mid-May 1978): 29, 31-32.

Zhong, G-Q., and F. Ayrom. "Experimental Confirmation of Chaos form Chua's Circuit." *International Journal of Circuit Theory Applications* **13** (January 1985): 93-98.

Ziegler, W. "Zur Abbildung von Frequenzgängen auf einem elektronischen Analogrechner." *Regelungstechnik* **11** (January 1964): 494-498.

Zilio, S. C. "Measurement and analysis of Large-Angle Pendulum Motion." *American Journal of Physics* **50**, 5 (May 1982): 450-452.

Zulauf, E. C., and J. R. Burnett. *Introductory Analog Computation with Graphic Solutions.* New York: McGraw-Hill, 1966.

390

398